THE FOUNDATION

Advance Praise for *The Foundation*

"Joel Fleishman's *The Foundation: A Great American Secret* is the first book written to help the general public grasp how foundations benefit virtually every American. It is a reader-friendly look at the impacts foundations have and how they have gone about achieving them." —Vernon E. Jordan, Jr., Senior Managing Director, Lazard Frères & Co. LLC

"Fresh, insightful, and comprehensive, *The Foundation* combines strategic wisdom with rigorous research to illuminate the opportunities and issues confronting America's foundations. Anyone committed to pursuing higher impact philanthropy would benefit enormously from this pragmatic work— as would those interested in enhancing foundation effectiveness within the nonprofit sector and society overall." —Tom Tierney, chairman and co-founder, The Bridgespan Group; former chief executive, Bain & Company

"Joel Fleishman has produced a marvelously comprehensive account of American foundations that is rich in both generalizations and specific examples. Readers who know Joel will not be surprised by his enthusiasm for the positive accomplishments of foundations. Equally important, however, is his recognition that there is room for considerable improvement—that more openness and accountability are in order." —William G. Bowen, President Emeritus, The Andrew W. Mellon Foundation

"Joel Fleishman really does care a great deal about this troubled world, and is fierce in his aspiration that foundations, as the most visible and strongest philanthropic vehicle for the resolution of social dilemmas, realize their manifest destiny. Fleishman's radical prescriptions for the way the field must change its process, attitude, and governance will not be easy, but with this book, the odds have just gone up!" —Peter Karoff, founder and chairman of The Philanthropic Initiative and author of *The World We Want–New Dimensions of Philanthropy and Social Change*

"From Carnegie and Rockefeller to Buffett and Gates, Joel Fleishman has captured the world of foundations in a way that should be must reading for every thoughtful person whose life is touched by foundations, which means almost everybody. Never have I seen a more comprehensive, objective, and understandable analysis of this sometimes controversial and, as Fleishman agrees, singularly brilliant philanthropic invention." —Frank A. Bennack, Jr., retired CEO, The Hearst Corporation

"In this book, Joel Fleishman explores the tensions inherent in foundations, from their benefit to society to their ethical obligation to build trust. Everyone working in foundations, preparing to work in foundations, or donors interested in establishing foundations can benefit from examining Joel's thought-provoking presentation." —Eugene R. Tempel, Ed.D., Executive Director, The Center on Philanthropy at Indiana University

"Joel Fleishman writes with an insider's knowledge and an outsider's perspective. *The Foundation* traces the history and purpose of American philanthropy through the twentieth century and offers practical wisdom for how to make foundations more effective and transparent in the twenty-first century. Fleishman offers sensible and concrete proposals for greater self-regulation of the charitable sector. His faith that foundations can improve their performance and accomplish even more for humanity uplifts our spirits and should galvanize action." —Jonathan F. Fanton, President of the John D. and Catherine T. MacArthur Foundation

"In this definitive book, Joel Fleishman details what American foundations are and what they could and should be."—Howard Gardner, Hobbs Professor of Cognition and Education, Harvard Graduate School of Education, and author of *Good Work: When Excellence and Ethics Meet*

"The author has provided a thoughtful primer on what's good and not so good about institutional philanthropy in the USA. His keen perspectives are informed by direct experience and a lifetime's immersion in organizations and activities that touch on just about every aspect of a foundation's business and raison d'etre. . . . For foundations and philanthropists wanting to increase their chances of creating social value—and especially for new donors who want to learn from a wise and seasoned professional—Fleishman's observations, insights, and invaluable suggestions are 'right on the money.'" — Michael Bailin, former CEO and President of The Edna McConnell Clark Foundation

"Joel provides an in-depth and insightful assessment of The Foundation in America, a little known and little understood, but essential, element in our society's ability to assess and solve our most difficult and complex social problems. It is a 'must read' for anyone contemplating establishing a foundation or anyone interested in improving the effectiveness of an already existing foundation. The rich narrative on the entrepreneurial linkage and the cultural connection between business success and foundation formation is of real value as one attempts to understand *The Foundation*'s contribution to the unique social dynamism of our society." —Steven A. Denning, Chairman, General Atlantic LLC

"Amidst the general talk about civil society, Joel Fleishman has written a superbly knowledgeable and even-handed description and appraisal of one key American institution: the privately endowed foundation. Much more than a survey, this book analyzes outstanding successes and lame failures among foundation programs, and offers thoughtful new ideas for improving the effectiveness and accountability of foundations without impairing their essential freedom and independence. If the private foundation has been a great American secret, Fleishman, as a long-time, observant insider and outsider, has let us all in on it." —Robert M. Solow, Institute Professor Emeritus, Massachusetts Institute of Technology

"It's tough to get an accurate fix on the contribution that particular institutions make to the overall well-being of a society. It's tougher still to develop thoughtful, empirically grounded ideas about how a particular class of highly varied institutions might improve. But that is what Fleishman has done. He has taught all of us who have stakes in what foundations do (a group that turns out to include virtually all of us!) to appreciate their contributions. And he has given useful advice to those who regulate, lead, and staff such organizations about what they should do to improve their performance. A remarkable accomplishment." —Mark H. Moore, Faculty Director of the Hauser Center on NonProfit Organizations, Harvard University

THE

FOUNDATION

A GREAT AMERICAN SECRET

How Private Wealth is Changing the World

JOEL L. FLEISHMAN

PublicAffairs
New York

BOOK DESIGN AND COMPOSITION BY JENNY DOSSIN. TEXT SET IN ADOBE GARAMOND.

Library of Congress Cataloging-in-Publication Data
Fleishman, Joel L.
The foundation : a great American secret : how private wealth is changing the world / Joel L. Fleishman.
p. cm.
Includes bibliographical references and index.
ISBN–13: 978–1–58648–411–8 (alk. paper)
ISBN–10: 1–58648–411–7 (alk. paper)
1. Charities—United States. 2. Endowments—United States. 3. Associations, institutions, etc.—United States. I. Title. II. Title: Private wealth changing the world.
HV97.A3F54 2007
361.7'6320973—dc22
2006027765

FIRST EDITION
10 9 8 7 6 5

TO

William G. Bowen, Harvey P. Dale, Arthur W. Fried,

the late John Gardner, the late Robert Kreidler, Thomas W. Lambeth,

Margaret E. Mahoney, Lloyd Morrisett, Arthur L. Singer Jr.,

the late Mike Sviridoff, and the late Paul Ylvisaker,

consummate foundation professionals all,

from whom I learned over many years most of what I know

about how foundations can operate at their very best.

And in loving memory of my parents,

A. M. and Ruth Zeighauser Fleishman.

CONTENTS

PREFACE

In June 2006, a century after the great industrialists Andrew Carnegie and John D. Rockefeller Sr. established foundations and other endowed institutions to be named for themselves, Warren Buffett—in a single stroke that instantly caught the attention of much of the world—announced that he would donate thirty-one billion dollars, over a period of years, to a foundation named not for himself but for two other major donors—Bill Gates, founder of Microsoft, and his wife, Melinda.

With that announcement, Buffett, widely revered as the world's greatest investor, earned the title of history's greatest and most admired *divestor*. He would be giving away, for the public good, the bulk of his lifetime accumulation of wealth—more than two times, in 2006 dollars, what John D. Rockefeller Sr. and Andrew Carnegie, America's most generous philanthropists before Bill Gates and Warren Buffett, gave away *combined*!

It was not only the magnitude of Buffett's gift that compelled the attention—and the curiosity—of the entire world. Even more breathtaking was Buffett's decision not to memorialize himself with his gift by placing his wealth in a foundation named for himself, as all but a handful of previous philanthropists had done before him. Self- or dynasty-promotion has always been understood, accepted, and even lauded as perhaps the primary driver of the creation of perpetual foundations, as well as other kinds of institution naming in perpetuity. So, in an age in which aggressive self-promotion is rampant (if widely deplored), it was stunning to witness an act of historic altruism transformed into one of sacrifice by its donor's renunciation of the attention of posterity. Had Buffett followed the example of virtually all of his predecessors in giving, the foundation he could have created would have instantly become the wealthiest in the entire world, ahead of even the Bill and Melinda Gates Foundation, thereby assuring himself of perpetual admiration and the gratitude of history for all time.

Instead of that guarantee of fame forever, the summum bonum for most human beings throughout history, he chose to veil his magnanimity in the cloak of another foundation, thereby assuring himself of anonymity in the future even if his gift has already won him worldwide celebrity in the memory of those alive today. If Maimonides was right in lauding secret giving as the second most praiseworthy form of charity, Buffett has earned incalculable virtue for saving or improving the lives of millions of human beings who will never know his name.

Andrew Carnegie, founder of the first great American foundation, took a very different tack. His name appears today on some 2,500 libraries in the United States and elsewhere, as well as on more than two dozen major American think tanks, foundations, and other institutions, all of which continue to confer great benefits on society.

While Buffett obviously shares the conviction Carnegie expressed 125 years ago in *The Gospel of Wealth* that "he who dies rich dies thus disgraced," and obeyed his injunction to the wealthy to give away their riches while they're still alive, his approach to philanthropy differs from Carnegie's in another way. Carnegie urged the rich to give away their wealth during their lifetimes so that they could apply to their philanthropy the same entrepreneurial skills and zeal for efficiency that they employed in its accumulation. By contrast, Buffett is turning over control of his giving to another organization, although one of which he has become a trustee.

Buffett explained his reasons in an interview with *Fortune* magazine:

> I came to realize that there was a terrific foundation already scaled-up—that I wouldn't have to go through the real grind of getting to a megasize like the Buffett Foundation would—and that I could productively use my money now. . . . [Bill and Melinda Gates] do a much better job than I could in running their operations. What can be more logical, in whatever you want done, than finding someone better equipped than you are to do it?[1]

In other words, in his usual self-effacing way, the "Sage of Omaha" confessed that he felt he would not be as good in giving away wealth as he had clearly been in making it. Perhaps the same humility explains why the admiration of history doesn't tempt him. From now on, perhaps he will be known as the "Saint of Omaha."

Buffett's gift has drawn more sustained and intense press and public attention to the world of foundations and charitable giving than any other donation in the past hundred years. That attention is long overdue. Moreover, Buffett's example has raised to public consciousness a hitherto unconsidered option for those who are blessed with wealth that they are inclined to give to charity. Now, in addition to thinking about creating a foundation themselves or naming an endowed program for themselves at an institution that will outlive them, wealthy would-be donors will perhaps think about giving it to already-established foundations to administer.

The Gates Foundation's biggest challenge may be responding appropriately to the increased scrutiny it can expect as the steward of such a massive sum. The public attention drawn to a foundation governed by only three trustees who will oversee its annual spending of around $3.5 billion has already sparked public concern over its scale and the lack of broader accountability, as well as curiosity about how and how well the Gates Foundation will manage to spend such large amounts of money wisely and effectively.

That gargantuan annual grantmaking budget imposes great responsibility on the Gates Foundation to take the lead in becoming a model of transparency for American foundations. The public knows very little about foundations—how they work, what they do, their role in society. As a result, whenever foundations come under attack by politicians, public officials, or the press for one or another misdeed or mishap, there is no existing reservoir of public support upon which they can draw. The only way for foundations to protect the freedom, creativity, and flexibility they now enjoy—and which they need if they are to serve society to their fullest potential—is to open their doors and windows to the world so that all can see what they are doing and how they are doing it. At this dramatic juncture in the history of the Bill and Melinda Gates Foundation, as well as of the entire world of philanthropy that has now come into sharper public focus perhaps for the first time, it is essential that the Gates Foundation lead the foundation sector by becoming a model of what a transparently run foundation can be.

This book will explore many of the questions raised by Warren Buffett's historic action. It examines why the rich establish foundations, the roles foundations play in powering the civic sector, how they discharge their stewardship responsibilities, and the extent to which they produce significant measurable benefits for society. Above all, this is a book about how charitable foundations have sometimes achieved high impact in their grantmaking initiatives. I believe that most institutions and individuals with charitable dollars to spend are eager to wring as much benefit for society as possible out of those dollars. Therefore, I have distilled in these pages some major lessons about how high-impact philanthropic initiatives may be conceived and brought to fruition.

The lessons are drawn from my study of a hundred significant foundation initiatives, many of which are referred to and described in these pages. The complete list of these cases is in the Appendix, and those interested in learning more can find them all in a companion volume, *Casebook for The Foundation: A Great American Secret*, ISBN 1-58648-488-5,which can be ordered on demand from 1-800-343-4499, or as a read-only document on the Web site www.pubpol.duke.edu/dfrp/cases/.

American Foundations: The Golden Paradoxes

As I explain in this book, the role of America's sixty-eight thousand foundations is replete with paradoxes. Foundations must be free and autonomous in order to fulfill their mission of challenging, reforming, and renewing society. At the same time, in part because of the tax benefits they enjoy, they must somehow be accountable to society.

There is the paradox of enormous wealth, originally generated by greed and energetic pursuit of self-interest, being donated to help the less fortunate through motives of pure altruism.

There is the paradox of great social and economic power concentrated in the hands of a few unelected and largely unregulated foundation leaders, who nonetheless feel insecure and threatened by the real or imagined suspicion and resentment of society at large.

There is the paradox of foundations' striving to add value to society by working to enhance, strengthen, and guide grant-receiving organizations, yet doing so in ways that do not intrude on those organizations' autonomy.

There is the paradox of organizations that devote their efforts to changing society, yet rarely seek to measure, or even comprehend, the extent of the changes they actually produce.

Finally, there is the paradox of a huge number of wealthy organizations spending their wealth to serve the public interest even as the public remains largely ignorant about what they do.

All of these and other paradoxes will be explored—and, I hope, explained—in the chapters that follow.

Two major themes run through this book. The first might be called the "effectiveness and efficiency" theme. I'll propose that there are specific decision-making processes and progress-checking systems that foundations need to employ if they wish to increase the impact of their charitable money. Specifically, I'll recommend that those who command philanthropic wealth be strategic in deploying their resources, focus on problems that are ripe for solution, but remain flexible to be able to respond to opportunities that arise unexpectedly.

The second is the public policy theme. Like all other institutions, foundations operate in a social context that significantly influences what they are able to do, what they choose to do, and how they can go about doing it. It's important that those external influences, whether in the form of governmental regulation, public scrutiny, or self-policing, be designed to create positive incentives that will encourage foundations to use their money wisely and effectively for the broadest social good. In the final chapter of this book, I'll recommend several ways of strengthening the social context within which foundations operate. In particular, I'll strongly urge foundations to abandon their long-standing resistance to greater transparency in regard to their decision-making processes.

Foundations have long been, for good and ill, the least accountable major institutions in America. The challenge with which this book grapples is how to ensure that foundations can raise the level of their performance by reducing their insulation from beneficial external influences while retaining the independence they need. The reader will judge whether or not I succeed in striking the right balance.

Here is an analogy. As a music lover, I have found that composers most often reach the heights of greatness in musical expression when their creativity is constrained within a clear yet flexible structural framework. The tension between insistent lyrical impetus and ordered, restraining structure—between the emotional energy and the confines of the rational—is at the heart of the greatest compositions of Bach, Haydn, Mozart, and Beethoven.[2]

In a similar way, foundations operate at their highest level when they make their program choices within a structure of constraining boundaries and prolonged, disciplined focus. No single foundation can do everything. Therefore, a foundation must be willing to make hard choices and to stick with programs and grantees over a long period of time if it is to achieve significant impact. Creativity within a restraining structure is one key to high achievement in both philanthropy and the arts.

THE CONTRIBUTION OF FOUNDATIONS— AND THEIR FAILURE

In these pages, I have resolutely avoided any scholarly jargon, with one exception—the word *polyarchy*. Derived from Greek, this word defines and underscores the unique role that philanthropic foundations play in American society. Whereas *anarchy* refers to the absence of any central governing power, and *monarchy* refers to the dominance of a single power center, *polyarchy* refers to the existence of many separate, independent power centers in society. In America's civic (not-for-profit) sector, it is the foundations that put the power of concentrated money behind individuals and the associations they form, thereby transforming American pluralism into a polyarchy with effective firepower.

The greatest contribution of America's private foundations, therefore, is in continually empowering widely diverse individuals and groups, holding a rainbow of views on every conceivable matter of social policy and civic concern, to organize themselves, to make their views heard, and to transform their ideas and dreams into reality.

This book provides compelling evidence of the impacts that foundations have often achieved in fulfilling their mission of empowering America's polyarchy and the strategies they've employed in doing so. I consider foundations a major force for good in American society. Yet they have many shortcomings as well. Without sufficient pressure from what I call "accountability-influencing forces," many of today's foundations underperform in their critical civic-sector functions. They operate within an insulated culture that tolerates an inappropriate level of secrecy and even arrogance in their treatment of grant-seekers, grant-receivers, the wider civic sector, and the public officials charged with oversight. This needs to change.

A METHODOLOGICAL NOTE

There is a heart-moving and mind-convincing story here that has not yet been told, backed up by factual evidence, and that has rather been more often shrouded in the nitpicking and naysaying of the cynical, envious, and petty-minded, as well as the fuming of right- and left-wing ideologues. This book, in part, is about what pioneering philanthropists, their successors and others who emulated them did, through the foundations they created, each in their own respective images, how, and why, so far as we can ascertain, as well as with what impacts a selection of their benefactions have had. In making my case, I have sought to avoid the anecdotal, the superficial, and the gossipy. Instead, I have, with the help of very talented and dedicated research assistants, Scott Kohler and Steven Schindler, assembled and published in a casebook parallel to this volume a representative, although by no means comprehensive, sample of the evidence of such impacts, mostly beneficial but some less so, not heretofore available. Based on the evidence offered there, I have sought to analyze the strategies that guided the initiatives that succeeded in achieving significant, beneficial social impacts, and also those which, for one reason or another, fell short of doing so. Then, based on the incidence and timing of impact success rates, I have attempted to understand and describe relevant characteristics of those foundations that enjoyed high rates of success, either consistently or during particular periods of their history, especially the size and structure of their organization, the kinds of staff and board leadership they had, and the extent to which their institutional culture embodied the vision and values of the donors who established them. That analysis, let me underscore, rests not on conjecture or hearsay, but rather on evidence of the impacts of the actions taken by the foundations themselves.

Behind this book, therefore, there are no ideological axes to grind. I strongly believe that a fair, unbiased weighing of the evidence makes a persuasive case that foundations have succeeded in conferring significant social benefit on the people of the United States over the past century. At the same time, however, I am convinced that the foundation sector as a whole, as great as its social contribution is now and has been for most of its history, seriously underperforms its potential with respect both to the social benefit it might otherwise have conferred if it were not underperforming and also to the mission that its freedom from substantial government and social control is designed to enable it to fulfill. The exploration of both of those themes—significant documented impact accompanied by significant underperformance—takes up the bulk of this book.

My intention in writing this book is certainly not to praise particular foundations whose work is highlighted herein, but instead to provide some evidence that foundations in the United States do make highly valuable contributions to society—the lack of which would significantly diminish the robustness and creativity of America's nonprofit sector and indeed our economy and society as a whole. Not only would society be diminished without foundations to make such contributions, but it would also be seriously harmed, I believe, if foundation creators were without the legal ability to shape their initiatives as freely as they have been in the past.

Nor is it at all my intention to single out for special praise over and above other foundations and their initiatives those documented in the casebook. They are examples, certainly a partial and to some degree a subjective selection, hardly the whole story. Rather I have sought to understand why the included initiatives did or did not work, in the hope that foundation trustees and program officers, as well as the public and the press, can learn how philanthropic capital might be administered so as to take advantage of successful strategies and avoid some common mistakes. I am convinced that those that are included fully merit being selected because of the exemplary strategies and extensive impacts they represent. In writing each case, my research assistants and I have presented the evidence of impact that convinces us of the persuasiveness of its inclusion, and I hope that the reader will find such evidence convincing, too.

The Foundations Chosen for Interview

No single book can do justice to all that America's foundations have done or are trying to do. There are a few excellent works on foundations, most of which are included in the Bibliography, although only a tiny handful attempt any assessment of impact.[3] My practice in writing this volume is to be selective and illustrative rather than fully representative or comprehensive. The initiatives documented and analyzed here represent my personal choices, informed by my professional and scholarly experience with foundations, stretching across some forty-five years of seeking support from foundations, preparing program strategy papers for foundations, evaluating foundation initiatives of a variety of kinds, assessing the effectiveness of foundation governance and evaluation mechanisms, chairing the board of a foundation, serving as head of the United States program staff for a large foundation,[4] serving as president of a small foundation, raising money for universities and other grant-receiving organizations, and teaching for some twenty years about foundations and the not-for-profit sector. This book is also informed by two years of concentrated research in the existing literature on foundations, and more than a hundred interviews with observers of and participants in America's foundation world, especially the systematically philanthropic, a list of whom can be found in the Appendix.

The selection of foundations represented here, however, is not entirely subjective. Virtually all of the longest-existing American foundations are dealt with in one way or another, and one or more of their senior officers or trustees have been interviewed. Most of the wealthiest American foundations, irrespective of their age, are also included within the scope of this study, but almost none of those established or preponderantly endowed after 1990 are included, primarily because they have had too little time since their founding to achieve measurable impact comparable to longer-existing foundations. In addition, a few mid-sized private foundations and a small sample of community foundations, which have earned the admiration of others in the foundation community, were also interviewed.

The Interviewees

Those interviewees, too, are a personal rather than random or representative selection. Most of them are widely known and admired, expert nonprofit practitioners or scholars whom I have had the good fortune to come to know over the years. Some of them I sought out without any prior relationship because the institutions with which they are involved seemed to me responsible for foundation initiatives that I had come to believe had resulted in significant social impact. Some lead, or are trustees of, foundations, while others are the chief executives of grant-receiving organizations that depend in part on foundation support. It seemed essential to me to be able to triangulate the impact assessments by comparing the views of foundation-related individuals with the views of those who are both expert in substantive fields and who also are usually in the position of petitioning foundations for support. All of them, in my view, are persons of integrity, have judgment of high quality, and are capable of making objective judgments about foundation successes and failures. None of them, in my view, pulled any punches or allowed their self-interest or involvement in initiatives to undermine their objectivity.

This study, therefore, is not what social scientists would regard as a scientifically valid one, although ethnographers, who employ the so-called snowball sample, might well find the results of my sampling persuasive. The choice of interviewees and foundations covered is a personal, subjective one, but the initiatives included are supported by such objective data as are available and have been carefully examined with as objective a lens as could be brought to bear.

This book might be considered one prolonged salvo in my lifelong "lover's quarrel" with America's foundations. I'm convinced that foundations can and should do even better than they are already doing. I've written these pages in an effort to help them do just that.

JOEL L. FLEISHMAN

Durham, North Carolina
September 2006

ACKNOWLEDGMENTS

I owe great debts of gratitude to so many people that it is impossible to thank them all with whole sentences and still have room left over for the text of the book. They will know why I am profoundly grateful to them, and it is far more important to me that they know than it is to them that others know.

Let me express my heartfelt gratitude, therefore, to Adam and Roz Abram, Suzanne Aisenberg, Grace Avery, Mike Bailin, Rob Baynard, Tom Bernstein, Bob Boisture, Jeff Bradach, Richard Brodhead, Bill Cassell, Jack Coleman, Angela Covert, Chris Devita, Ralph Eads, Eli Evans, Jonathan Fanton, Charles Feeney, Marion Fremont-Smith, Melynn Glusman, Peter Goldmark, Ray Handlan, Mitch Hart, John R. Healy, Sam and Ronnie Heyman, the late Roger Heyns, Barbara Horton, David Ingram, Robert Ketner, Ralph and Ricky Lauren, Elizabeth McCormack, Michael and Pat McGinnis, Janice Molnar, Pete and Ginny Nicholas, Brit and Lessie Nicholson, Susanne Peace, John J. Piva, Field Price, Rebecca Rimel, David Rubenstein, Ben Shute, John Simon, Ed Skloot, Jim Spencer, Bob Steel, Michael and Judy Steinhardt, Max Stier, Punch Sulzberger, Tom Tierney, Steve Toben, Joe Weilgus, and John Whitehead.

In conducting the research for this book, I often sought, and promptly received, advice and guidance from Darwin Stapleton and Ken Rose of the Rockefeller Archive Center; Alan Divack of the Ford Foundation Archives; Elizabeth Boris, Linda Lampkin, and Eugene Steuerle of the Urban Institute's Center on Nonprofits and Philanthropy; and Sara Engelhard of the Foundation Center. All of them are professionals of the highest quality and all are deeply devoted to helping scholars and the public acquire a deeper understanding of the data that explain the workings of America's civic sector.

I am especially indebted to Susan Bell and Paul Brest of the William and Flora Hewlett Foundation, Susan Berresford and Barry Gaberman of the Ford Foundation, Carol Larson and Richard Schlosberg of the David and Lucile Packard Foundation, and Steve Denning and his colleagues in General Atlantic Partners for their confidence in the promise of the Duke Philanthropic Foundation Research Program, and the generous financial support provided to it by their institutions. The Duke Philanthropic Foundation Research Program supported the writing of this book and will receive all royalties from it.

If President Terry Sanford had not twisted my arm into running Duke University's Capital Campaign for the Arts and Sciences in 1983, it is unlikely that I would have gained the knowledge I have about the challenges inherent in charitable fund-raising that contributed substantially to my understanding of the workings of the philanthropic marketplace. If President Nan Keohane had not enthusiastically supported and facilitated my wish to continue teaching part-time at Duke when I was confronted with an offer to be president of Atlantic Philanthropic Service Company (now Atlantic Philanthropies [US]), I would not have acquired the experience of running a sizable foundation's program staff and the many insights about the challenges, satisfactions, and difficulties inherent in grantmaking that significantly inform this book. I owe a great debt of gratitude to both of them, as I do to Duke University Provost Peter Lange and Professor Bruce Jentleson, director of the Terry Sanford Institute of Public Policy, who facilitated my full-time return to Duke and the beginning of my work on this book. Both of the latter provided continuing support not only for my work in philanthropy and nonprofits but also for the establishment and strengthening of the Duke Philanthropic Foundation Research Program, starting in 2003.

If Yale President Kingman Brewster had not recruited me to work with him at Yale in 1965 and given me wide latitude with his full backing to pursue foundation grants to start educational programs for disadvantaged high school and college students from across the country, I would have missed my early introduction to the mysteries of foundations. It was also that six-year-long Yale experience that led to my friendship with Mike Sviridoff and my first foundation experiences in conducting evaluations and developing program strategy papers.

Over the years, I have received wise counsel and generous support in my teaching and research on nonprofits and philanthropy from my Terry Sanford Institute colleagues—especially Charles Clotfelter, under whose leadership the Institute's Center on Philanthropy and Voluntarism was established during the late 1980s; Phil Cook, who succeeded me as director of the Terry Sanford Institute in 1983; Fritz Mayer, whose constant participation in the Duke Philanthropic Foundation Research Program enabled it to get off to a strong research start; Jay Hamilton, who has regularly provided intellectual guidance; and Bruce Kuniholm, who became, as of July, 2005, once again the director of the Terry Sanford Institute and who has been an enthusiastic supporter of my work for more than two decades.

I cannot close these acknowledgments without something more than a mere mention for several persons who have played a direct role in bringing this book to fruition.

Professor Harvey Dale, director of the National Center on Philanthropy and Law and CEO of Atlantic Philanthropies worldwide from its founding in 1982 until 2002, was responsible for recruiting me to lead Atlantic Philanthropic Service Company in 1993. His meticulous knowledge of nonprofit law and policy is legendary, and his skill and wisdom in running a large philanthropy are widely admired among those who know about the work of Atlantic, which, for most of its history, was all done under conditions of strict anonymity. During my ten years of working with him, I learned an enormous amount that has helped shape this book, and his detailed line-by-line comments on parts of the manuscript helped save me from at least some errors, and encouraged me, when appropriate, to moderate my sometimes excessive enthusiasm.

My Duke colleagues Charles Clotfelter and Kristin Goss, as well as Marion Fremont-Smith of Harvard's Hauser Center, Michael Bailin of the Edna McConnell Clark Foundation, and Margaret E. Mahoney of MEM Associates, generously read the manuscript from beginning to end, responding with comments that enabled me to clarify and tighten the text. Tom Tierney agreed to read the manuscript at its earliest stage. His understanding of foundations and his insights about strategy helped me enormously in reshaping the sequence of the book's flow, as well as in strengthening the text as a whole. Because of the great amount of time and thought that they all graciously agreed to put into helping me by reading and offering criticism of my work, their perceptive comments greatly improved its quality. It goes without saying that any mistakes that remain are solely attributable to my stubbornness, wrongheadedness, or carelessness.

Scott Kohler, Duke 2004 and Columbia Law 2008, was my full-time researcher and case writer for this book during 2004–2005. He wrote two-thirds of the cases on which this book is based and made perceptive comments on the entire manuscript periodically. His cases, separately available in the *Casebook for The Foundation: A Great American Secret* by Joel L. Fleishman, J. Scott Kohler, and Steven Schindler, manifest how gifted a writer he is. One can only hope that that talent will not be dulled by its exercise in unraveling the law, the turgidness of which is the bane of most lawyers' attempts at good writing.

Steven Schindler, Duke Law 2007 and MPP 2007, has been my part-time research and teaching assistant for three years. He researched and wrote one-third of the cases, while helping organize the materials for my courses on philanthropy and nonprofits. His careful scrutiny of the end-notes and appendices saved the book from countless errors. His love of, as well as fascination with, the civic sector is the abiding purpose of his professional aspirations.

Pam Ladd has been my principal assistant at Duke since 1983, and de-serves great credit—as well as profound gratitude—for helping me keep in the air at all times the too-many balls I obsessively insist on juggling. She had a large hand in this book, too. She scheduled all of the interview ap-pointments, and, despite an operation to relieve painful arthritis in her hand combined with her happier duties attendant on the birth of her first grandchild at about the same time, orchestrated the consolidation of the se-quence of manuscript revisions into the final text that went to PublicAffairs. As everyone knows who knows me, Pam's omnicompetence, unflappability, warmth, friendliness, and grace are legendary. She has been a constant, ever-ready source of support, strength, and assistance in all that I have done.

I cannot close these acknowledgments of my gratitude without thank-ing PublicAffairs for its critical role in transforming my manuscript into a book. Peter Osnos, who was CEO and publisher of PublicAffairs when this book was in its earliest stages, expressed hearty enthusiasm for publish-ing it from the very beginning of our discussions. Clive Priddle, Nancy Hechinger, and Karl Weber helped greatly to sharpen, focus, and tighten my text, enabling the essential points to emerge much more clearly and forcefully. All four of them added great value to this book. One could not wish for better editors and advisors in such an undertaking.

Finally, and most of all, I thank God for leading me through the succes-sive stages of my career that have informed this book, and for giving me the strength, health, and energy to bring it to fruition.

PART

I

FOUNDATIONS: WHAT THEY DO

AND HOW THEY DO IT

I believe that private philanthropy is the last frontier of unconstrained freedom for private action in the public good.

Arthur W. Fried, President, The Avi Chai Foundation[1]

Consider these basic, familiar aspects of contemporary life. What do
they all have in common?

- The first 911 emergency telephone system was set up in Alabama in
1968. By the 1970s, the simple, uniform system had spread throughout
the United States. Since then, millions of Americans faced with an
emergency have rushed to phone 911, and thousands of lives have been
saved as a result. Have you ever wondered how this national emergency
response system came into being?

- Most Americans have heard about India's newly dynamic, rapidly growing economy. But do you know the story of how India, plagued for centuries by famines, became not only self-sufficient in food production
but also a food-exporting nation—the essential platform on which the
subcontinent's newfound prosperity is being built?

- Millions of people depend on PBS's *NewsHour with Jim Lehrer* for their
daily supply of serious news. Millions more habitually tune in to National Public Radio to stay in touch with the world throughout the day.
When you watch or listen, have you ever asked yourself how the institution of public broadcasting in the United States came to be?

- Every year, billions of dollars' worth of financial assistance is provided to college students through the Pell Grant program. Millions of students and their families take this aid for granted. Do any think to inquire about the origin of a government program that has enriched so many lives?

- In three hundred run-down inner-city neighborhoods and impoverished small towns, local community-development corporations (CDCs) are working to create jobs, build housing, and incubate small businesses. Countless Americans have benefited from their efforts. Where did the notion of the CDC come from?

In each case, the explanation is the same—the central force promoting the creation of these valuable social institutions was a *foundation*.

There are thousands of foundations actively working for the betterment of society here in the United States and around the world. And behind each foundation stands a wealthy individual or family that chose to declare "enough is enough," and then gave away a significant portion of their wealth for the benefit of the wider community rather than hoard it, invest it, or spend even more of it on personal pleasures. Why did they do so? As we will see, for many different reasons. But perhaps the motivation of the founders of major foundations—from Carnegie and Rockefeller to Gates and Buffett—was poignantly stated most recently by Joseph Hirschhorn, the wealthy art collector for whom the Hirschhorn Collection on the Mall in Washington was named: "I tried eating more meals a day and got sick. There are only so many suits you can wear or houses you can live in. So I collected art [and then gave it away]."

It's a remarkable phenomenon, a testament to human generosity and creativity, and one whose story has never been adequately told. In these pages, some of the achievements and triumphs of America's foundations will be explained, but so, too, will be examples of their failures and mistakes. Foundations, after all, are among our most powerful, least accountable, and significantly tax-benefited institutions, so it is all the more unacceptable that they are also among our least understood institutions. I'll examine the challenges foundations are now facing and the changes in philosophy, management style, and focus that are essential to meet those challenges. I'll also explore some of the implications of the work of foundations for the lives of all Americans.

The bottom line of this book is that foundations, along with the organizations that they support, are the great secret of the dynamism of America's civic sector. The civic sector is not just about social change in the narrow sense but rather about all kinds of organizations that are created, supported, and staffed by Americans acting independently of government. Just as private investors and venture capitalists spark the creation of new products and services in the for-profit sector, foundations provide the capital that powers innovation and diverse experimentation in the civic sector.

Foundations enable the creation of countless civic-sector organizations—groups dealing with human rights, civil liberties, social policy experimentation, public advocacy, environmental protection, knowledge generation, human capital building, and service delivery, among other causes—and assist them in building national, regional, and local constituencies that move into the forefront of continuing social change. Those organizations, together with the foundations that support them, play an influential role in the constant reinvention of American society, including the redistribution of power and wealth.

THREE ROLES THAT FOUNDATIONS PLAY

At the most basic level, what foundations do is very simple. The leaders of a foundation—usually a staff of professionals guided by a board of trustees—provide funds from the foundation's income or endowment to support not-for-profit organizations, charities, or other programs and organizations in accordance with the mission designated by the founder. But within this broad framework, many variations are possible. One way to analyze the work of foundations is by describing three different roles that foundations can choose to play. Of course, the lines dividing these roles are often blurred. But this three-part breakdown is a useful jumping-off point for a deeper exploration of what foundations do and how they do it.

The first role is that of *Driver*. When a particular social, economic, or cultural goal can be visualized clearly and a practical strategy can be developed to attain it, a foundation may choose to play the role of Driver. In this case, the foundation itself maps out and directs the change effort, making grants to organizations that will simply carry out the strategy devised by the foundation.

The second role is that of *Partner*. Here, the foundation shares the power to shape a strategy and makes crucial decisions together with other partner organizations, making grants to support those organizations as well as others that simply implement the strategy.

The third role is that of *Catalyst*. When tackling a problem for which a strategy is either inconceivable, inappropriate, or premature, a foundation may make grants to organizations that generally deal with the problem, without specifying or expecting particular outcomes. Here, the foundation acts as a kind of "Johnny Appleseed," broadcasting resources in many directions, knowing that most of the grants are unlikely to produce lasting change, but hoping that a few at least will take root and grow.

These roles do not have crisp, clean boundaries, however. The differences among them depend on the character, specificity, and ripeness of the problems in which the foundations are interested, and the nature of those institutions whose behavior they are seeking to change.

Let's take a closer look at these roles and consider some examples of each.

The Foundation as Driver

All of the examples listed at the start of this chapter illustrate what foundations can accomplish when they act as Drivers, pursuing specific objectives according to a strategy they develop and whose implementation they guide.

The so-called Green Revolution, which was launched in 1945 and came to full fruition during the 1950s, '60s, and '70s, was driven by the work of the Rockefeller Foundation. The goal was to develop new varieties of wheat, corn, and rice adapted to particular climates that would significantly increase crop yields and thereby help to alleviate the lack of adequate food, which was costing the lives of millions of people in the developing nations of Asia, Africa, and Latin America. The research agenda was formulated by Rockefeller Foundation staff scientists, and the research itself was carried out by scientists working full-time on the foundation's payroll in laboratories in Mexico. Rockefeller Foundation control was key to maintaining a focused pursuit of the objective of increased grain yields and to implementing the strategy as rapidly as possible.

As a result of the Green Revolution, the world increase in per capita production of agricultural commodities outstripped population growth in every year after 1950. So successful was the Mexican program, led by Rockefeller scientist Dr. Norman Borlaug, that Mexico, which had formerly imported half its wheat, attained self-sufficiency by 1956 and was exporting half a million tons of wheat by 1964. The program was expanded to India and Pakistan, where it is credited with saving over one *billion* people from starvation.

The Rockefeller Foundation had earlier played the same Driver role in its successful battles against yellow fever in the developing world and against hookworm in the southern United States. The foundation's role in the yellow fever victory and the Green Revolution led to two Nobel Prizes, one in Medicine awarded to Dr. Max Theiler in 1951 for his work on a yellow fever vaccine, the other a Peace Prize to Norman Borlaug in 1970.

When the national 911 emergency-response system was created, the Robert Wood Johnson Foundation took the Driver role. It catalyzed and financed 911 organizations across the United States, brought together emergency responders who hadn't previously cooperated, and created a national confederation that could easily work with the U.S. government on the details of implementation.

The Public Broadcasting System and Pell Grants were both driven by blue-ribbon commissions envisioned, organized, financed, and run by the Carnegie Corporation of New York.

Finally, community-development corporations were similarly driven by the Ford Foundation, which was later joined by many other foundations.

When a foundation can define and limit a problem, and believes that it can map a strategy for solving the problem, then the Driver role may be appropriate, especially when no other institution can play that role as well or as faithfully as the foundation. If you're familiar with the workings of venture capital, you might think of the Driver role as similar to that of the general partner, who invests a large—often the largest—share of the money required to start a new venture, occupies one or more seats on the venture's board, and plays a decisive role in hiring the CEO and making other critical decisions.

Note that a particular foundation may choose to play a Driver role in one or two initiatives while playing a less-central role in other projects. Driver projects must be chosen with great care. One important caution should not be overlooked. The fact that the program staff in a foundation exercises good judgment in filtering and recommending grants for approval by senior management and the trustees does not at all mean that the same staff is capable of doing a comparably good job as the Driver of grantmaking initiatives. Foundation senior managers should be very cautious in undertaking Driver roles in particular initiatives unless they have personnel with the entrepreneurial and operating skills necessary to make a success of such initiatives.

The Foundation as Partner

The second role, that of Partner, can be just as strategic as that of Driver, but it is both less hands-on and less controlling of the initiative. Typically, the Partner foundation shares control and accountability with the grant-receiving organization.

As examples, consider the academic field–building activities of the Rockefeller Foundation in molecular biology, the Ford Foundation and the Carnegie Corporation of New York in foreign area studies, the Alfred P. Sloan Foundation in computational neurobiology, the John M. Olin Foundation in law and economics, and the Hewlett Foundation in dispute resolution. In each case, the foundation had a specific goal to achieve and a strategy that involved making grants to universities to create centers, programs, or departments to conduct research, offer new courses, and finance student fellowships and postdoctoral study. In so doing, the foundations acted as Partners with the universities. By contrast, in the example of the Green Revolution, the Rockefeller Foundation placed researchers on its own payroll and created a new freestanding organization to conduct research in its chosen field.

The role of Partner is likely to be appropriate whenever a foundation has a strategic objective that can be accomplished by working with an existing, usually nonprofit, organization that shares with the foundation both the goal and the strategy for attaining it. The role of Partner is generally more cost-effective for the foundation than that of Driver, demanding less commitment of time and energy by the foundation's staff. The trade-off, of course, is a corresponding loss of control by the foundation. If things go wrong in the implementation of the strategy, the Partner foundation cannot set things right as quickly and easily as if it were the Driver.

And sometimes things do go wrong—occasionally very wrong. The most common problem is a poor choice of leadership by the nonprofit responsible for implementation or by the foundation itself. Other times, the foundation and the implementation organization are at odds about the goal, the strategy, or both. And still other times, the foundation's own practices may be faulty or its interference in implementation unwarranted. For all these reasons, some foundations are nervous about the risks involved in the Partner role and prefer to be Drivers whenever possible.

Nevertheless, most foundations choose to operate as Partners, and not just as a way of saving energy, time, and money. Most foundation initiatives are about promoting change, and the best way to achieve that goal is usually to engage and involve the organizations whose behaviors are to be changed. Thus, when a foundation wants to change academia by giving new vitality and prominence to a field of study that is currently neglected (as in the examples cited above), the fastest way to promote such change is by partnering with existing universities, which can then serve as role models for the rest of the academic universe.

In recent years, many foundations have sought a hands-on role in specific initiatives that is midway between the controlling role of the Driver and the less-powerful role of the Partner. Some are using the relatively new term *venture philanthropy* to describe this approach. Think of it as a philanthropic equivalent to the relationship between venture capitalists and the businesses they support. In this approach, the foundation provides financing in exchange for significant involvement in and some degree of control of the program being supported. For example, a foundation that is basically playing a Partner role might ask for the right to specify particular strategic implementation tasks to be performed by the grantees according to an agreed-upon timeline, with specified benchmarks and required performance reports. The result is that the foundation keeps the implementing organization on a short leash.

The Bill and Melinda Gates Foundation's $437 million Grand Challenges in Global Health is an excellent example of such a venture philanthropy role. The foundation works closely with grantee organizations to develop timelines and benchmarks for success. It also arranges detailed evaluations of the programs to monitor their effectiveness and to measure the impact on the health of target communities. Thus, the foundation is acting as something more than a Partner, though less than a full-fledged Driver.

The Foundation as Catalyst

The Driver role is difficult for foundations to assume. It is time- and labor-intensive, and committing one's foundation to the achievement of a specific objective is risky and anxiety-producing. It requires a high degree of resolve to commit the organization to a particular strategic focus and much deeper knowledge of the field of focus than the other roles. And, of course, when a foundation commits to a particular strategy and fails to achieve the goals it sets, the public failure is psychologically and organizationally painful.

For all these reasons, it's easy, even tempting, for foundations to deliver most of their resources through projects at the other end of the spectrum—lower-commitment grants in which the foundation restricts itself to the role of Catalyst, scattering resources like Johnny Appleseed in hopes that some of the initiatives supported will bear fruit.

There are also good reasons to emphasize the Catalyst role in dealing with particular types of social problems. Some problems are simply not ripe enough to lend themselves to a clear-cut strategic solution. They may be too big, too complex, or too unwieldy; they may be relatively new and little-understood; or they may require intervention by government agencies or the for-profit sector. In such cases, rather than undertake a high-risk strategic effort that is likely to fail, a foundation is wise to take a Catalyst approach, donating to a number of initiatives in the spirit of experimentation.

The Catalyst role may seem less impressive than the grandly strategic roles of Driver or Partner. The Catalyst is unlikely ever to receive a Nobel Prize for its efforts. Yet the role of Catalyst is important for foundations to fill. The fact is that, at any given time, relatively few significant problems are ripe for solution. Moreover, very few foundations have the resources to mount a strategy of sufficient scale to solve any really large problems in the first place. Thus, the ground is always in need of preparation so that ripeness can be hastened. Organizations need to be established and supported to research new solutions, to raise awareness, and to educate the public. For this reason, most foundations do most of their grantmaking in the hands-off role of Catalyst, scattering seeds for the future by supporting the existing efforts of grant-receiving organizations.

Despite the metaphor of the seed, you shouldn't assume that the Catalyst role inevitably involves either seed money for launching new organizations or grants that are tiny in size. Many of the grants in this category are actually large. What makes these Catalyst projects is not the size of the grant but the role of the foundation, which involves little active control and little specific accountability for results on the part of the grantee. The foundations sow seeds and move on, sometimes assessing the consequences of their grants and sometimes not. The results, if any, will often be evaluated and enjoyed by others.

In this book, I won't focus on Catalyst grantmaking but rather on high-impact initiatives launched by foundations themselves. I chose the roles of *Driver* and *Partner* as the focus of this book because the level and quality of the benefits conferred on society by such initiatives, if well-chosen and well-executed, usually reach a coherent critical mass whose causation one can trace. Moreover, they are discrete and therefore more easily visible than the more diffuse efforts in the Catalyst role in which most foundations do most of their work.

Such initiatives generally come about when an alert foundation officer—a founder, chief executive, or program officer—seizes on an inspired idea, refuses to let go of it, and tailors a precise strategy, either explicit or implicit, to implement it. In such cases, the foundation acts as either Driver or Partner, making the problem its own and then inventing and captaining the strategy, either alone, through a new purposely designed organization, or through existing organizations with similar goals. Though such Driver- or Partner-run undertakings represent only a small number of the total grants made by the foundation sector as a whole, they represent a large share of grantmaking dollars deployed by those foundations that strive to achieve significant impact.

THE LIMITS OF FOUNDATION POWER

The examples I've mentioned so far indicate the remarkable scope and influence that foundations can have when they tackle major social problems well and with intelligence. But there are clear limits to what foundations are capable of doing. When a social problem is *not* discrete and well-bounded, when it permeates large segments of society, or when it is created in part by dug-in interest groups, a foundation can usually do little to solve the problem beyond ameliorating some of its symptoms and suggesting, through research or pilot programs, some directions in which ultimate solutions may be found.

Consider, for example, the problems of elementary and secondary education in the United States. For years, foundations have struggled to improve the quality of American schools, and they have made a positive difference in some areas of education. One good example is the foundation-launched and -supported National Board for Professional Teaching Standards, which credentials teachers in subject-matter fields and has created the first national market for teachers in the nation's history.[2] But attempts to create more comprehensive solutions have been thwarted by a combination of factors, including the massive social and psychological burdens created by poverty and the opposition of teachers' and administrators' unions to fundamental changes in incentives.

The same is true of the U.S. health-care system. While many Americans enjoy better health care than that available anywhere else in the world, income and class differences prevent millions of their fellow citizens from receiving a decent level of care. The basic problem—majority self-interest combined with vigorous opposition by the health-care, pharmaceutical, and insurance industries to fundamental structural change—does not lend itself to solution by foundations. Here again, foundations have brought about some important incremental improvements that give the promise of ultimately contributing to an overall solution. And several foundations, including the Kaiser Family Foundation, the Commonwealth Fund, the Robert Wood Johnson Foundation, and the Pew Charitable Trusts, are working diligently to educate the public about the need to change how American health care is financed and distributed.

A third example of the kind of complex, intractable problem that illustrates the limits of foundation power—and perhaps the most daunting of all—is the problem of poverty. With Hurricane Katrina having dramatically returned the persistence of poverty in America—especially among African Americans—to the front burner of national consciousness, one might well ask, "What, if anything, can foundations do about poverty?" History's answer is that foundations can do something meaningful about poverty—but not by working alone.

Several factors make poverty—especially African American poverty—an overwhelmingly difficult challenge. First, the problem is extremely complex, involving every aspect of social, community, and individual life, from housing, health care, drug abuse, and family stability to education, employment, and racial discrimination. This kind of mega-problem is far too large for any foundation to get its arms completely around. Poverty is a problem that, ultimately, only government itself can completely remedy. After all, by definition the fundamental solution to poverty is somehow to put more money in the pockets of poor people—but only government has the resources necessary to do so at a meaningful level, and it can do so only if the American citizenry is willing to engage in large-scale redistribution of wealth. By comparison, foundations can only tinker at the margins.

That is not at all to say that foundations can do nothing about poverty. Foundations have already done and are continuing to do a great deal by focusing public attention on the severity of the problem, by generating empirical research about better ways of tackling it, and by pioneering solutions that governments could implement.

Consider these three examples of foundation-led initiatives for tackling the problem of poverty. First, the Earned Income Tax Credit (EITC) is today's largest public assistance program for the working poor. While the national EITC program was not developed by foundations, it was a foundation-created and -supported organization, the Center on Budget and Policy Priorities, a nonprofit think tank, that led the way in extending the EITC to the states.[3]

Second, the major focus of national welfare reform since the first Bush administration has been on making public support contingent on preparing for and taking a job, a policy often called "welfare to work." This policy became law under President Clinton in 1996, largely thanks to the efforts of the Manpower Demonstration Research Corporation (now called MDRC), foundation-launched and -supported for more than twenty-five years, which designed, conducted, and rigorously evaluated the welfare demonstration programs that showed how welfare to work could be effective.[4]

Third, a partial solution to one of the most serious problems in America—the lack of adequate health services for poor children—was pioneered by a foundation. The Child Health Insurance Program (CHIP), which was enacted by Congress in 1997, was shaped by preceding initiatives supported by foundations, and its state-by-state implementation has been facilitated by many foundations, including the Robert Wood Johnson and Annie E. Casey foundations. That federal program permits states to expand health coverage to children whose family incomes exceed the requirements for Medicaid but are insufficient to afford private insurance coverage.

Neither the EITC, welfare to work, or CHIP represents anything close to a full-scale solution to our nation's poverty problem. Such a solution waits on government action, which in turn is dependent on the public will to act as expressed through the political process. When the people are ready to take the steps needed to eradicate poverty—including steps that will inconvenience the majority and cost money—then and only then will those steps be taken. It would be naïve to expect foundations (or any other array of nonprofit organizations)somehow to wave a magic wand and solve so massive a problem.

While we wait for the public to come around to the tipping point at which the government can act, it's clear that there is much that foundations *can* do to improve life for those in need, to help meet pressing social, economic, and cultural challenges, and to educate both the citizenry and our political leadership about the problems we face and potential solutions to them. How do foundations fit into the network of civic, political, and economic institutions that shape contemporary American life? What role do they play—and what role *should* they play—in making that life better? We'll begin to examine those questions in the next chapter.

2

THE THIRD GREAT FORCE:

AMERICA'S CIVIC SECTOR

Americans of all ages, all stations in life, and all types of dispositions are forever forming associations. There are not only commercial and industrial associations in which all take part, but others of a thousand different types—religious, moral, serious, futile, very general and very limited, immensely large and very minute. Americans combine to give fêtes, found seminaries, build churches, distribute books, and send missionaries to the antipodes. Hospitals, prisons, and schools take shape in that way. Finally, if they want to proclaim a truth or propagate some feeling by the encouragement of a great example, they form an association. In every case, at the head of any new undertaking, where in France you would find the government or in England some territorial magnate, in the United States you are sure to find an association.

———

Alexis de Tocqueville, *Democracy in America* (1835)[5]

The American civic sector, of which our many foundations are an integral part, is a wonder of the world and an unprecedented social phenomenon—not unlike America itself, which, with all its shortcomings, is arguably the most dynamic, inclusive, and democratic society the world has ever seen. Created by Americans acting freely to meet their own needs and those of their fellow citizens, the civic sector is supported annually by nearly 70 percent of Americans of all colors, creeds, and socioeconomic conditions, to the tune of more than $260 billion.[6] Its expenditures constitute almost one tenth of the nation's gross domestic product, its employees represent more than one tenth of the labor force, and its volunteers constitute between 30 and 50 percent of the citizenry, depending on the age of volunteers we select and whose figures we use. Nowhere else in the world has there ever been so huge and broad-based a voluntary sector, or one so multifaceted, dynamic, and free—a powerful "third force," distinct from government and business, that balances and mediates social pressures through voluntary actions by millions of Americans.

The high value that the American people place on the civic sector is signified by the tax benefits it enjoys: tax exemption for civic organizations themselves and tax deductions for charitable contributions that support them. However, these benefits constitute tangible public support that is modest both in absolute terms and in comparison with the subsidies government provides for other purposes to businesses and individuals.

The civic sector goes by various names, including the nonprofit (or not-for-profit) sector, the third sector, the independent sector, the voluntary sector, the public interest sector, and the social sector. I prefer to call it the civic sector, because the word *civic* connotes what individuals do by virtue of their role as citizens acting voluntarily, whether to benefit themselves; their community; their city, state, or nation; or as members of some other community of interest.[7]

The uniqueness of America's civic sector is nothing new, as the epigraph from Alexis de Tocqueville suggests. Observing the richness of American civic life over a century and a half ago, Tocqueville insisted that, "The wealth of a democratic society may well be measured by the quality of functions performed by private citizens."[8] His perceptive observations are not only a revealing snapshot of the civic sector of his own time but also a prophetic template for the growth and evolution of that sector in the decades that followed.

THE SCOPE AND DIVERSITY OF AMERICA'S CIVIC SECTOR

Since the time of Tocqueville, America's civic sector has mushroomed. By 2006, the best estimates put its size at around 1.85 million formal organizations. This includes 1.5 million organizations that are certified by the Internal Revenue Service as satisfying the requirements for tax exemption under sections 501(c)(3) and 501(c)(4) of the federal tax code (which define charitable and mutual-benefit organizations, respectively), as well as another 353,000 religious organizations—churches, mosques, synagogues, and others—which are not required to seek IRS certification for tax-exempt status.[9]

Not included in these figures is the informal component of the civic sector, an impossible-to-measure array of groups that subsumes everything from neighborhood soccer leagues to book clubs to community-service groups that form, disband, and re-form on an ad hoc basis as needs and interests change.

The economic importance of the civic sector is also enormous. The most recent Internal Revenue Service estimates (for the year 2001, released in 2004) put the cash revenues of formally organized civic sector organizations at over $1.1 trillion in an overall American economy of some $12 trillion,[10] and that does not include revenues of religious organizations that are not required to file annual 990 forms with the IRS. Thus, the organized civic sector accounts for almost 10 percent of the U.S. gross domestic product.

And that's not the whole picture. The IRS figures do not include the value of time volunteered to formal and informal nonprofits. The Bureau of Labor Statistics estimates that some 65.4 million Americans have volunteered at least once a year in recent years.[11] Independent Sector estimates that the total number of hours volunteered annually in recent years is about 15.5 billion. Valuing each volunteered hour at $18.04, the amount chosen by Independent Sector, that organization estimates that one can therefore reasonably add another $280 billion to the total amount donated to U.S. not-for-profits.[12]

Perhaps most impressive is how the civic sector is supported. The overall revenues of America's civic sector come primarily from four sources—fees for services rendered; income from invested assets; grants or contracts from federal, state, or local governments; and charitable contributions.

Fees for services rendered include, for example, tuition income paid to private schools and colleges (which educate about a quarter of America's students), room charges paid to private hospitals (which contain half of America's hospital beds), ticket or admission income at arts organizations, and income from other commercial activities, such as services produced or products sold by nonprofit organizations. Some civic subsectors, such as arts organizations, are almost entirely supported by fees for services rendered, while other subsectors, especially social welfare, receive little from such fee revenues. These fees, together with income from invested assets, produce some 40 percent of civic-sector revenues in the aggregate. Government support adds another 35 percent.

The rest comes from voluntary contributions, which (in 2005) yielded some $260 billion, about one quarter of the civic sector's total revenues. Of that amount, 83.2 percent was given by individuals, 11.5 percent by foundations, and 5.3 percent by corporations.[13]

In comparison to other countries, the percentage of U.S. civic-sector support coming from voluntary contributions is unusually high. In fact, private giving by individuals, foundations, and corporations represents about 2.1 percent of America's gross domestic product, about three times as much as the next closest country, the United Kingdom.[14]

Sheer size is one thing. The diversity of views and interests in the civic sector is also staggering. It includes groups that advocate fighting terrorism by reducing Americans' traditional civil liberties and groups that would battle to protect civil liberties from any such encroachment; groups that passionately advocate affirmative action for minorities and groups that denounce affirmative action as unconstitutional and anti-American; groups that staunchly support the public school system and groups that call for subsidizing private schools through vouchers, charter schools, and other government programs. This diversity of competing views is perhaps the greatest strength of America's civic sector.

No one has better defined the importance of the diversity of America's not-for-profit sector than the late John Gardner, a president of the Carnegie Corporation of New York, a secretary of Health, Education, and Welfare, and founder of both Common Cause and the Independent Sector:

Every American knows some piece of the independent sector. Foundations generally know a great deal about it. But very few people have glimpsed its extraordinary sweep and its possibilities. Let me draw out first the possibilities and mention some stern realities. . . . At its best, it is a sector in which we are allowed to pursue truth, even if we are going in the wrong direction; allowed to experiment, even if we are bound to fail; to map unknown territory, even if we get lost. It is a sector in which we are committed to alleviate misery and redress grievances, to give reign to the mind's curiosity and the soul's longing, to seek beauty and defend truth where we must, to honor the worthy and smite the rascals with everyone free to define worthiness and rascality, to find cures and to console the incurable, to deal with the ancient impulse to hate and fear the tribe in the next valley, to prepare for tomorrow's crisis and preserve yesterday's wisdom, and to pursue the questions others won't pursue because they are too busy or too lazy or too fearful or too jaded. It is a sector for seed planting and path-finding, for lost causes and causes that yet may win, and—if I can borrow words from George Bernard Shaw—for the future and the past, for the posterity that has no vote and the tradition that never had any, for the great abstractions . . . for the eternal against the expedient, for the evolutionary appetite against the days of gluttony, for intellectual integrity, for humanity.

The words are eloquent, the rhetoric inspiring, the idealism palpable. But Gardner was nothing if not a realist. He went on to add these words of caution:

The nonprofit world does have its share of oafs and rascals. I have to say so. It has its share of unworthy institutions and, of course, it has its share of good people with whom you disagree fiercely. If you can't find a nonprofit institution that you genuinely dislike, then something has gone wrong with our pluralism.[15]

As Gardner's words suggest, America's civic sector is a true reflection of our nation: remarkably varied, contentious, cooperative, energetic, resourceful, and creative. The diversity of our civic sector is one of its greatest strengths. It is this uncontrolled cacophony of voices, sometimes harmonious, sometimes dissonant, that generates innovation and social progress. The friction thus generated helps to produce experimentation, change, and ultimately renewal of the whole.[16]

THE ORIGINS OF AMERICA'S CIVIC SECTOR

Why is America's nonprofit sector so large and diverse? History supplies some answers. In colonial times, new immigrants from Europe arrived on these shores *before* service-providing governments had been established. If the colonists' needs for education, social services, public safety, and other assistance were to be satisfied, it was up to the colonists themselves. Since many of the original colonists had fled religious oppression in Britain and France, the very first institutions they established in the New World were self-governing religious congregations, which quickly became the primary providers of schooling, health care, and other needed services. The pervasiveness and power of today's nonprofit sector stem from the strength and importance of those early, self-governing, private religious congregations.[17]

Moreover, America's civic sector is the world's largest and strongest because, from the beginning, it has been the freest. Jealous of their newfound religious freedoms, America's founders deliberately kept their churches free of control by either hierarchy or government. The independent congregational structures of the dissenting churches—mainly such denominations as Presbyterians, Lutherans, Methodists, Baptists, Puritans, and Quakers, which grew from the upheavals of the Protestant Reformation—decisively shaped the freedom and diversity of America's nonprofit sector. As Professor Max L. Stackhouse has put it:

> In the name of God, they claimed (1) the right to be, (2) the right to organize, (3) the right to care for their neighbors, and (4) the right to set forth their views publicly. This had a decisive impact on Western history.[18]

These historical factors help to explain why the American civic sector is larger than the comparable sectors in other industrialized countries. In Europe, for example, governmental provision of many social goods is a long-standing practice that has necessitated a heavier tax burden on the public. In the United States, many such goods are provided instead by nongovernmental, private, nonprofit enterprises.

And all of this is made possible because Americans are free to follow the dictates of their heart and spirit wherever they may lead, free to do so by undertaking specific initiatives in their pursuit. Tocqueville had this exactly right. He perceived clearly that at the heart of America's civic sector is a compulsion to act on a belief in the freedom—and responsibility— of individuals to support freely chosen endeavors larger than themselves about which they particularly and deeply care, and into which they are eager to throw themselves and pour some portion of their financial resources.

America's civic sector, then, is the natural product of a large nation made up of free people eager to pursue all kinds of interests. Some of those interests grow out of personal and group identity based on religion, race, gender, or ethnicity. Others grow out of beliefs, avocations, and aspirations and are related to political affiliations, educational programs, or passions for sports, the arts, or other activities. In short, the civic sector is a patchwork quilt of disparate activities that give meaning to the lives of the people who enjoy them. And as they do so, they are building social capital—the fabric of connections among people that strengthens communities, enhances mutual trust, and makes a shared life possible and rewarding.[19]

The Impact of the Civic Sector on Society as a Whole

Civic sector organizations produce a host of direct benefits to those who use their services. Nonprofit hospitals, schools, social-service agencies, arts organizations and advocacy groups contribute enormously to the richness and dynamism of America. Yet a persuasive case can be made that the civic sector has an even more significant impact through its influence on society's two other sectors—the public sector (government) and the profit sector (business).

Those who think, write, and teach about the American civic sector almost always conceive of its role as limited to what it does itself and tend to define and delimit it as "the social sector." The highly regarded historian of foundations, David C. Hammack, has described the role foundations have played more narrowly than I believe their history warrants:

> From their first appearance shortly after 1900 foundations
> have played their most important roles as reinventors of the
> nonprofit sector, as reshapers of nonprofit institutions, as
> organizers of new nonprofit institutions.[20]

Technically, Professor Hammack's view is correct. Foundations have done most of their giving to organizations that are nonprofit in form. But the organizations that foundations have created or reshaped do not exist for themselves, and, in fact, their reach is across society as a whole. The research data generated by the National Bureau of Economic Research and the National Research Council, for example, inform society's judgments about the entire range of America's problems and possibilities. The same is true of most other nonprofit institutions in society, so, when one reads Professor Hammack's words, one must keep in mind that the ultimate beneficiaries of foundation initiatives are the American people served by the nonprofit sector in countless ways and in all kinds of activities.

Some excellent examples of major government programs that grew out of civic-sector initiatives have been highlighted in two recent books by Professor Paul Light.[21] In *Government's Greatest Achievements: From Civil Rights to Homeland Security,* Light lists fifty successful government initiatives of the past half-century selected through a survey of 550 historians, political scientists, sociologists, and economists, and provides documentation of their impacts and their origins. More recently, in *Sustaining Nonprofit Performance: The Case for Capacity Building and the Evidence to Support It,* Light returns to the same list and observes:

> Nonprofit advocacy was essential to the success of the civil rights movement, for example, which produced three of the federal government's top five achievements: expanding the right to vote (number two), ending discrimination in public accommodations (number three), and reducing workplace discrimination (number five). Nonprofit research was central to the battle against life-threatening diseases such as polio and tuberculosis (number four), the campaigns to improve food safety and protect water (number six) and to restore clean air and water (numbers eleven and fifteen), and the battle to balance the federal budget (number nine). Its voice was essential to improving health care and financial security for older Americans (numbers eight and ten), and its intellectual energy helped to create support for rebuilding Europe after World War II (number one).[22]

Examples of nonprofit initiatives that spawned powerful government programs could be multiplied. The Pell Grants, for instance, originated when a Carnegie-financed commission chaired by former University of California official Clark Kerr recommended the creation and funding by the federal government of a program of grants for higher education. Now the Pell program provides over ten billion dollars to some five million students in educational assistance annually.

In other cases, changes advocated by nonprofit groups have transformed the way industries are overseen by government, as when the American Enterprise Institute led public policy thinking toward the deregulation of communications and air transportation. Today, ideas and information generated by civic-sector organizations continue to have a profound impact on both government and business thinking. For example, the research data generated by the National Bureau of Economic Research and the National Research Council inform our understanding of the entire range of America's problems and possibilities.

These are but a few examples of the universe of civic-sector spillovers in the profit and public sectors. When measuring the benefits provided by the civic sector, it's not enough to consider only the direct impacts; the indirect effects on government and business practices must also be calculated.

Social Support for the Civic Sector

The civic sector embraces two main kinds of organizations: charitable groups, which exist primarily to benefit others, and mutual-benefit groups, which serve mainly their own donors and members. Examples of the former are the United Way, the American Red Cross, CARE, and the American Civil Liberties Union; examples of the latter are labor unions, trade associations, the NAACP (National Association for the Advancement of Colored People), the American Medical Association, and the American Bar Association.

As nonprofits, both charitable groups and mutual-benefit groups are tax-exempt. Furthermore, all charitable groups as well as some of the mutual-benefit groups (such as religious organizations) are also eligible to receive tax-deductible contributions.

The fact that *both* types of civic-sector organizations enjoy tax benefits strongly suggests that society recognizes the intrinsic value of the civic sector. That value doesn't reside only in charitable activities that spread wealth to the less-fortunate members of our society; it also resides in mutual-benefit activities whose primary contribution to the community is the creation of social capital. Thus, there is an implicit recognition in our legal system and our tax code that civic engagement by groups of citizens is beneficial in and of itself—a form of activity to be embraced and encouraged.

Financial support encouraged by tax benefits provides the civic sector with its strong structural bedrock. Civic sector organizations know that they can count on this support year after year, which enables them to plan their operations in an orderly fashion and grow steadily. Furthermore, providing social support in the form of tax breaks rather than direct government subsidies offers an additional benefit. It directs the support through charitable choices by individuals rather than through the haggling and logrolling of politically elected legislative bodies or the choices of a particular governmental administration, Congress, or agency, thereby fostering polyarchy and encouraging the existence of the widest possible array of civic organizations. Both the deduction and the exemption, therefore, are brilliant mechanisms for providing societal support to the civic sector while keeping government's and politicians' hands off.

The problems that arise when social support comes more directly, in the form of explicit government subsidies, are illustrated by the 2005 contretemps over funding for the Corporation for Public Broadcasting (CPB). In support of demands from the politically appointed CPB chairman that the Public Broadcasting System be "less liberal" in its editorial choices, the House Appropriations Subcommittee voted to reduce the annual appropriation to CPB by one hundred million dollars (a decision later reversed by the full House).[23] Similar attempts at government censorship have involved organizations supported by the National Endowment for the Arts and the National Endowment for the Humanities.

Incidents like these demonstrate that, if nonprofits had to depend on government appropriations for most of their income, the civic sector would be much less dynamic and more fearful of the threat of political influence than it is. The freedom provided by public support for individual citizen's choices is unquestionably one of the greatest benefits of tax deductions and exemptions.

Some critics, however, contend that current policies extend tax benefits too broadly across the nonprofit sphere. They advocate dismantling or diminishing the tax benefits enjoyed by America's better-off individuals when they donate to what those critics regard as kinds of mutual-benefit organizations such as art museums, symphony orchestras, ballet companies, and elite universities. "These institutions," the critics contend, "serve primarily the upper-middle-class and wealthy. Thus, donations to them by the affluent produce benefits mainly to the donors themselves, both by perpetuating the survival of organizations that satisfy their aesthetic or intellectual tastes and by helping them gain privileged positions within those organizations, from special seating at opera performances to admissions preferences at Ivy League colleges. Why should the taxpayers subsidize such self-serving spending?"

I think the critics are missing the point. First of all, few people would disagree that the existence of cultural institutions such as great museums, orchestras, and universities contributes to the intellectual and aesthetic richness of society as a whole, and that our world would be a poorer place if such organizations were to disappear.

Second, most of those who donate to support these institutions are doing so not out of self-interested motives but to express their love for art, music, or learning and to ensure that future generations will be able to enjoy those cultural inheritances. Do motives such as self-interest or the quest for social prestige ever play a role? Sometimes they do. But what does that matter, if our shared culture benefits? And if those with the means who appreciate high culture do not support it, who will?

I agree with the conclusion reached by most scholars who study nonprofit organizations: The rationale for extending tax breaks to most civic-sector organizations lies not in any specific governmental policy objective but rather in the benefits to society created by the existence of the civic sector itself.

If, as some critics demand, the tax benefits now enjoyed by all kinds of nonprofit organizations were restricted only to those with a charitable purpose (that is, those engaged in activities centered on some kind of redistribution of wealth), the results, in the long run, would be negative both for the broader society and for the civic sector in particular.

Consider this analogy. Most government programs are designed to benefit the entire citizenry, not just the poor. National defense, public schools and libraries, parks and playgrounds, highways and water-supply systems—all serve rich and poor alike, and all are supported by taxes paid by members of every class and income group. What would happen if the benefits from these government programs were somehow restricted only to the poor? In short order, members of the middle and upper classes would withdraw their political support from the programs, and signal their representatives in Congress that they were unwilling to go on paying taxes to support spending whose benefits they would never see.

In the same way, if tax breaks for nonprofit organizations were restricted only to programs that benefited exclusively the poor, broad-based support for those tax breaks would soon dry up. And in a democratic society, that is a prescription for the eventual demise of those breaks—and with them the nonprofit organizations that rely on them.

Government, then, should not be in the business of separating "worthy" nonprofits that serve the poor from "unworthy" nonprofits that serve the middle and upper classes, and providing tax advantages only to the former. To do so would empower government to make invidious distinctions between some kinds of organizations that the public—by means of tax incentives—should encourage individuals to support, and other kinds of organizations that are to be left without such encouragement. For government to make that distinction would be to place a heavy official hand on the scale by which Americans have always made their own judgments about the kind of civic sector they wish to create. The current system in which the *entire* civic sector—including the foundations—receives indirect support via the tax code is justified by the broad social benefits that accrue from the existence of a vibrant civic sector, and should be retained.

THE CIVIC SECTOR AS MEDIATING FORCE

The civic sector has profoundly influenced the evolution of American society. It has offered a wide-open venue for citizen action without government sanction or control, producing an accumulation of social capital with one great benefit I haven't discussed yet. Perhaps the civic sector's greatest gift to America has been its role in peacefully mediating major, potentially disruptive changes in the workings of American society.

The social energies leading to most transformational changes in America—from the movements for women's suffrage and women's rights to those for civil rights for African Americans, fair labor practices, and environmental protection—have found powerful, peaceful expression through civic-sector organizations. The existence of this mediating sector has kept passionate demands for social change from being bottled up until they erupt in violence, channeling them into constructive and often successful organizational vehicles for social progress.

FOUNDATIONS: THE OPERATIONAL SECRET OF THE CIVIC SECTOR

The civic sector, then, has been a vital force for good in American society. And one of the most important contributors to the success of the civic sector has been the foundation.

As we've seen, the bulk of the money donated to the civic sector by Americans comes from individual giving. In 2005, for example, living individuals gave $199.07 billion of the $260 billion donated to not-for-profit organizations. This figure dwarfs foundation contributions, which are variously estimated in 2005 at from $30 billion to $33.6 billion.[24] Yet, in specific cases, foundation support may constitute the bulk of an organization's revenue stream, especially with young organizations, those promoting significant social change, and other organizations that are unlikely to attract widespread public support, at least in their infancy.

However, if the public tax benefits to civic-sector organizations are the structural secret behind billions of dollars in individual support to sustain America's civic sector, the operational secret is the priming role foundations play in starting new civic-sector organizations, in nurturing them into self-sustainability, and in providing a continuing supply of social venture capital to the civic sector. Without question, foundations are the primary source of start-up support for a whole spectrum of civic-sector organizations on the left, right, and center. As many of the cases documented for this book and available elsewhere make clear, foundations often continue to support for many years organizations they helped to start. Moreover, foundations provide civic-sector organizations with the wherewithal to launch the widest possible variety of major new initiatives. Some of the cases provide examples of them.

Money isn't the only form of support that foundations provide to their nonprofit grantees. Increasingly they provide advice on strategy, planning, information technology, human resources practices, and other operational imperatives. Foundations frequently use their influence to convene subject-matter experts to assist nonprofits in their work, to attract support from other foundations, and to leverage attention from the press and public officials.

TWO KINDS OF FOUNDATION GIVING

In his book *Strategic Giving: The Art and Science of Philanthropy*, Peter Frumkin draws a distinction between two types of charitable giving, including foundation grantmaking, which he characterizes as either *instrumental giving* or *expressive giving*.[25] Instrumental giving is "strategic" in the sense that it is focused on achieving a particular policy objective and intended to accomplish a significant impact on a specified social problem. By contrast, expressive giving reflects a donor's desire to show support for a cause or an organization without necessarily expecting to achieve a noticeable impact through his or her gift.

The notion of instrumental giving may have originated in Andrew Carnegie's book *The Gospel of Wealth* (1889), in which he described the goal of his philanthropy as systemic change through systematic philanthropy. Most of Carnegie's major benefactions, such as building libraries and founding universities, can be viewed through this lens. Today, instrumental giving tends to be characteristic of large foundations, whose resources are such that they can reasonably hope to achieve measurable impact through highly targeted grants in particular areas.

Expressive giving is more characteristic of smaller foundations, as well as individuals, who generally recognize that their more modest gifts are unlikely to have a significant impact in and of themselves and therefore are content with the feeling of satisfaction that arises from the symbolic value of their altruistic gesture—as well as the cumulative effect it may have in combination with many other gifts.

It would be easy to overstate the distinction between instrumental and expressive giving. There's a large gray area where the two kinds of motivations and goals overlap. Countless foundations do immense good for society simply by writing checks to assist charities that labor day in and day out to help the poor, protect the environment, improve education, defend human rights, and support other worthy goals. And this support often helps organizations that are working to bring about systemic social change. Thus, expressive giving may, in effect, be instrumental giving at second hand.

However, one aspect of the distinction between instrumental and expressive giving is important in considering the work of foundations. When individuals make charitable donations, they are giving their own money (even if we consider the donation as being partially defrayed by other taxpayers through the charitable contribution deduction). Therefore, it's enough for them that their gift expresses support for a goal or cause they admire; no further justification is required. However, a foundation is in a different situation, because the money distributed by its officers and trustees is usually not their own money at all but was accumulated and provided by someone else. They cannot, therefore, resort to merely expressive giving with an easy conscience. If the donor has established specific goals for the foundation (as is usually the case), the foundation's officers must think first about how to use their resources to make detectable progress toward those goals. They should fall back on expressive giving only when direct impact is impossible.

This logic doesn't apply only to the largest foundations. If smaller foundations so choose, they can be just as strategic about mission and goal selection, and can have just as great an impact through strategic guidance, business planning help, and crucial contacts. The dramatic growth over the past five years of the Grantmakers for Effective Organizations, which is another one of the cases, is composed of representatives of those foundations particularly interested in increasing the effectiveness of foundation grants through focusing on strategy, assessment, and measurement. This reveals the extent to which many foundations have come to understand the importance to nonprofits of such infrastructure strengthening and management assistance.[26]

Strategic impact, then, is predicated not on size but on intention and discipline. Many smaller foundations have proven remarkably adept at focusing their energies and resources on creating a significant beneficial impact on operating nonprofits and American society as a whole.

The Variety of American Foundations

In 2005, about 68,000 foundations of all kinds existed in the United States, controlling estimated assets of half a trillion dollars and making annual grants totaling $33.6 billion.[27] Most of these foundations are small and unstaffed, but a few are very large and powerful by national and global standards. As of December 31, 2003, forty-six foundations had assets of over one billion dollars, while another sixty-four had assets between five hundred million and one billion dollars. Fully 70 percent of all foundation assets were controlled by just 2 percent of foundations.[28]

In addition to the private foundations, there are about seven hundred community foundations holding approximately $39 billion in assets, of which a significant percentage is in donor-advised funds. There are also what are termed "supporting organizations," which are adjuncts to other 501(c)(3) public charities or educational institutions.[29] Both the donor-advised funds, whether in community foundations or financial institutions, and the three types of supporting organizations, function very much like private foundations.

But the differences among foundations involve much more than size. During my work with foundations in the United States and abroad over the past forty-five years, I can't recall encountering any two foundations that were exactly alike. Every foundation is sui generis, each reflecting the personalities, values, goals, and talents of the key people behind it, including the donor, significant trustees, and the major program officers. Over time, the decisions made by these individuals shape the distinctive culture of a foundation, just as the identity of a person is shaped by his or her decisions over a lifetime.

That culture shapes everything about a particular foundation, from the way it makes decisions to its relations with the external world. Even foundations with similar program focuses have important cultural differences that affect their behavior. For example, although several foundations share an historic commitment to medicine and health services, each approaches the field differently. The Kaiser Family Foundation, for example, has a narrow focus on health coverage for the uninsured, especially vulnerable populations, while the Commonwealth Fund has a broader reach toward improving the functioning of health financing for the entire population. The Robert Wood Johnson Foundation has a very wide range of interests that include major efforts to counter tobacco use and obesity. Ideological differences also shape foundation cultures. Some foundations are unabashedly liberal, others strongly conservative, still others resolutely centrist. Programming decisions and operational choices reflect these orientations.

Another variation among foundations involves risk tolerance. While few foundations undertake explicit risk analyses as a formal part of their strategy and grantmaking processes, all have implicit risk strategies that shape their daily decisions. Some foundations revel in their willingness to take risks, such as the Pew Charitable Trusts and the Bill and Melinda Gates Foundation, as reflected in their readiness to support projects with minimal chances of success as well as projects that are likely to arouse controversy. Others shun such risks.

Foundations also have widely varying decision-making processes. At most foundations, the trustees take action on individual grants, while at others, such as the Ford Foundation, the trustees simply approve overall program budgets and leave final decisions on individual grants to the senior managers. At some foundations, grants are always proposed by trustees, while at most foundations, program staff take the initiative. And at many foundations, grants proposed by the staff are routinely approved by trustees, while at others—especially family foundations—trustee decisions are unpredictable.

In short, foundations differ markedly from one another. Thus, they contribute distinctively to that characteristically American system of diverse polyarchy that we referred to in our introduction—encouraging and supporting the growth of thousands of alternative models of social change and progress. Under the circumstances, generalizing about so diverse an array of institutions is obviously dangerous.

Now begin the generalizations.

The overwhelming bulk of what foundations do has served the long-term good of American society. If some foundations' mission is pure and simple charity in feeding the hungry or housing the homeless—either of which is within the reach of any foundation, however small or large—that charity surely benefits society. Conversely, by striking at the root of hunger or homelessness, those foundations might have had a greater impact on the problems of hunger or homelessness. Such choices of mission should and indeed have to be made at the sole discretion of donors and trustees, or the very existence of a free, independent, not-for-profit sector that is unfettered by substantive government constraints cannot be assured. What is ultimately at stake in the decisions about what foundations should devote their resources to is the achievement and effective functioning of a polyarchical, independent, multi-power-center society.

Admittedly, there have been exceptions; foundations are not immune to intellectual and social fads, including pernicious ones. The sham science of eugenics is a case in point. Starting early in the twentieth century and continuing in Germany during the 1930s after Hitler came to power, such philanthropies as the Carnegie Institution of Washington and the Rockefeller Foundation were deeply involved in now-discredited eugenics programs, and even the widely admired Warren Weaver, director of the

Rockefeller Foundation's Natural Science Program, was swept along by the movement.[30]

Similarly harmful was the Rockefeller Foundation's support of unethical syphilis experimentation on prisoners without their informed consent in Alabama, a program that persisted from 1932 to 1972. That such episodes have been rare is persuasive testimony to the wise judgment with which most foundations are run. The vast majority of foundation initiatives appear benign in the eyes of history. The risks that many foundations have chosen to take may not always have paid off, but they have only rarely resulted in social harm.

On the whole, foundations have also been efficiently and ethically managed. This is not to say that foundations are always paragons of propriety, nor to deny that a handful—indeed barely a handful—of foundation trustees and managers have abused their fiduciary responsibilities for personal gain. But these abuses, too, are rare, and the positive social outputs of foundations tend to outweigh by far the abuses occasionally encountered.

IF FOUNDATIONS DIDN'T EXIST

What would the U.S. civic sector be like if foundations did not exist? Obviously, such speculation is fraught with uncertainty. But the role of the foundation in supporting the civic sector—and enabling the civic sector to bring about change in the profit and public sectors—has been so clear and pronounced that the following conclusions seem eminently reasonable.

- Without foundations, the civic sector would be significantly less dynamic, less innovative, and less responsive to the needs of society. If foundation funding were unavailable, it would be much harder to initiate, model, and promote substantive changes in public policy or in major social institutions such as universities, schools, and the health-care system.

- Many not-for-profit organizations that serve those in need would either be much further behind their for-profit analogues in terms of program and service quality or would not exist at all.

- Public discourse on government policy and social issues would be greatly impoverished, and many of the institutions—the broad array of think tanks, university-based scholars and policy analysts, and research and demonstration organizations—that inform our understanding of American society would be weakened or might not exist at all.

• Lacking the consistent, long-term funding that foundations and wealthy individuals have historically provided, and relying instead on one-time individual donations, the civic sector would be more idiosyncratic, more focused on short-term concerns, and probably much less diverse.

• Lacking the guidance provided by foundation boards and the skilled, thoughtful, and professional program staffs that serve at many foundations, civic-sector organizations would be less well advised, less efficient, and less strategically focused.

Without foundations, the American civic sector would hardly be a barren wasteland. But it would not be the powerful engine of American dynamism that it has been for so many years.

3

WHY THEY GIVE

We expect the rich to be generous with their wealth, and criticize them when they are not; but when they make benefactions, we question their motives, deplore the methods by which they obtained their abundance, and wonder whether their gifts will not do more harm than good.

———

Robert Bremner, *American Philanthropy*[31]

Almost everyone knows about the pioneering economist Adam Smith's masterpiece *The Wealth of Nations* (1776), in which he describes how what he calls the invisible hand of the marketplace leads individuals to make self-interested decisions that nonetheless benefit the public as a whole. Fewer know about the companion volume that Smith himself regarded as even more important, *The Theory of Moral Sentiments* (1759). In that work, Smith identifies the "impartial spectator" within each of us, which functions as our conscience and enables us to make choices divorced from self-interest. These two different but complementary influences on human behavior help to answer the question implied by our chapter title: Why do the wealthy create foundations?

POLYARCHY, DIVERSITY, AND MOTIVES FOR GIVING

As we've noted, the American political system is what some social scientists call polyarchical, characterized by many independent, freely acting centers of power. Polyarchy is at the opposite end of the spectrum from the sort of centralized, rigidly hierarchical system in which a single power center manipulates and dominates everyone and everything. In the former Soviet Union and China, the Communist Party constituted that single power center; in Iraq under Saddam Hussein, it was Hussein himself and the Baath Party. Today in North Korea, the regime of Kim Jong Il exercises a similar degree of control.

By contrast, the structure of the American federal system was designed by our founders, especially James Madison, to proliferate rather than narrowly concentrate the sources of initiatives and the power to translate them into action. In a society filled with independent actors, the government's role would be to weigh the claims and goals of all groups and, when they conflict, decide which should prevail in the public interest in a particular circumstance. Within the government, a similar polyarchical structure prevails. At the federal level, three coequal branches—executive, legislative, and judicial—provide independent sources of energy and power, while state and local governments serve as counterweights to the entire federal apparatus.

The same reliance on multiple power centers characterizes the U.S. economy. Individual and corporate initiative is the driving force of economic growth, with government stepping in only when crucial public needs go unmet by private enterprise or when coalitions of individuals and/or corporations conspire to thwart polyarchy by amassing monopoly or oligopoly power.

Yet perhaps the crucial role of polyarchy is seen most clearly in the civic sector, where individual initiative stands almost alone. In the civic sector, there is no government apparatus and there are no economic market forces to interfere with individuals acting, alone or in groups, on their own initiative to pursue goals they consider desirable, at least so long, of course, as the goals and means of pursuing them are legal.

Of course, the motives that catalyze action differ from sector to sector. In government, individuals are predominantly driven by the desire to be elected or appointed to positions of power and to retain those positions once they hold them. In the economic sector, financial self-interest is the driving force. But in the civic sector, a complex mixture of self-interested and altruistic motives prevails.

Consider, for example, the activities of what we described in Chapter 2 as mutual-benefit groups. Some of these, such as trade associations, labor unions, veterans organizations, and associations for the elderly, are moti-vated primarily by the well-being of their members. (Of course, they al-ways describe their programs as being in the public interest, too.) Other mutual-benefit groups, such as environmental, consumer protection, child advocacy, and public health groups, are motivated primarily by what they perceive as the public interest while also pursuing objectives that will ben-efit their members directly. For example, a member of an environmental club that advocates stricter controls on air pollution expects to benefit per-sonally from the cleaner air that will result. It is clear, therefore, that the leaders and members of mutual-benefit associations are motivated by some combination of altruistic and self-serving ends.

In the case of charitable organizations, the motivations might appear to be more clearly altruistic. But self-interest may also be involved, depend-ing on how we define it. For example, some individuals give time and money to particular organizations primarily because of the social status they confer. Others donate in hopes of acquiring wider fame, better repu-tations, more customers for their businesses, influence, or general ego-satisfaction. "Fame is the spur," in the oft-quoted words of philosopher David Hume.

What difference do these various motives make on our feelings about the actions involved? If the results are socially beneficial, should we care about the reasons? Someone seeking personal or spiritual improvement might want to strive to banish self-interest from his or her own heart, and we might agree that this is a worthy goal. But from a social perspective, it would be short-sighted to disparage social benefits that bear the taint of self-interest. If "impure altruism" were somehow to be forbidden, there wouldn't be much of a civic sector left.

In any case, banishing self-interest is probably impossible given the real-ities of human nature. Even the former Communist societies that claimed to be dedicated solely to social good weren't immune from self-interested behavior. In those countries, oligarchical control simply freed, sanctioned, and exacerbated the self-interested behavior of citizens, party *apparatchiks*, and bureaucrats at all levels, often producing outright criminal behavior. Better to provide socially beneficial outlets for our selfish drives, as Amer-ica's polyarchical system does.

The same issues and the same sorts of mixed motivations arise when we examine what drives wealthy donors to support the civic sector. There are two separate levels of decisions to consider: the more general and basic decision to give away large sums of money, and the more specific decision to do so through a foundation. We'll examine these in turn.

Why Give?

Reasons for making large donations to charitable or other civic organizations vary from the purely altruistic to the self-serving, and include a large gray area where the two blend.

The most frequently cited motivation for charitable giving is a desire "to give back." The recipients of "give-back" philanthropy may be either particular institutions that have benefited the donor, such as a school or college he attended or a hospital in which he was treated, or the community at large. Many successful businesspeople, for example, have attributed their charitable giving to gratitude: "America has been good to me," they say, "and made it possible for me to become successful and wealthy. Now I have an opportunity—and obligation—to repay the debt."

Other donors give out of a sense of religious obligation, especially when the recipients are religious congregations, divinity schools, or seminaries. Each of the three great Western religions—Judaism, Christianity, and Islam—requires regular donations to charity, and some denominations provide specific guidelines for giving, as in the custom of tithing (i.e., donating 10 percent of one's income) practiced by many Protestants. It is therefore not surprising to find that the largest fraction of all American charitable giving—over 35 percent of the total in 2005—is donated to religious organizations.[32]

Less altruistic (and to my mind less laudable) is the desire for ego satisfaction derived from the fame, admiration, and praise that often accompany large charitable gifts. Some kinds of donations, such as major gifts to the local opera house, symphony orchestra, or art museum, almost guarantee an *entrée* into elite society, fawning coverage in the newspapers, and invitations to stylish parties attended by artists and intellectuals who might otherwise shun the company of a "mere" businessman. These are heady rewards indeed.

It's easy to deprecate ego satisfaction as a motivation for giving, and the Christian Gospels specifically urge believers to give "in secret" rather than court prestige for their acts of charity (Matthew 6:1-4). But there are plenty of other ways for people to pursue fame, as the proliferation of buildings and businesses named for Donald Trump vividly illustrate, and surely giving to charity is more socially beneficial than most, as well as more desirable.

A variant on this motivation is the desire to redeem a negative reputation gained in the world of business competition, where aggressive tactics and self-serving strategies are common. Of course, donors themselves rarely acknowledge this motivation, although muckraking journalists and biographers often cite it.[33] John D. Rockefeller Sr. actually *refused* to make gifts when appealed to on the grounds that the donation would burnish his reputation. His biographer Ron Chernow reports one such attempt by Dr. Charles Strong, shortly before he became Rockefeller's son-in-law:

> You have the opportunity, [Strong urged Rockefeller], of turning the unfavorable judgments of the world at large into favorable judgments—and not only that—of going down to history as one of the world's greatest benefactors.

This argument miscarried on several counts: Rockefeller resented any references to his infamy, felt no need to cleanse his reputation, and rebelled against any insinuation that his charity was selfishly motivated.[34]

Understandably, other wealthy people are equally reluctant to acknowledge that a desire to burnish a negative public image is behind their charitable giving. In most cases, the world infers this motivation (rightly or wrongly) from circumstances and timing. For example, Bill Gates invited this interpretation when he created the Bill and Melinda Gates Foundation in the midst of the federal antitrust case against Microsoft.[35]

It's clear, however, that the desire to overcome a bad reputation is *not* the dominant force behind most charitable giving, even by the very wealthy. Otherwise, how could one explain the generosity of so many businesspeople whose reputations were never sullied to begin with? They include Alfred P. Sloan, James Buchanan Duke, Charles Feeney, Henry Ford II, Julius Rosenwald, DeWitt and Lila Wallace, Margaret Olivia Sage, Edward Harkness, George Peabody, Paul Mellon, W. K. Kellogg, Charles S. Mott, David Packard, William Hewlett, Eli Lilly, Pierre Omidyar, Jeff Skoll, Harry Weinberg, and many others. Clearly, large-scale charitable giving is not primarily the province of robber barons racked by personal guilt over their depredations, no matter what amateur psychologists or historians with an anticapitalist bent might assume.

Yet another variation on the theme of ego gratification—and another motivation much cited by cynics—is the desire for a kind of immortality. Certainly such desire seems to play a role in gifts that attach the donor's name in perpetuity to a particular building, institution, or project ("The John Smith Chair" in a university, for example). It may also figure in gifts that are designed to perpetuate a donor's influence over and interest in a certain charitable cause after his death. Some might fault this motivation as giving the dead an unfair influence over future generations. But in the vast majority of cases, such giving is highly beneficial, extending over time the positive effects of a donor's generosity and giving the recipient organization resources with which to help people whom the donor never knew.

It's hard to say exactly which of these varied motivations might predominate in any individual donor or even in a specific charitable gift. But, in the end, it doesn't matter very much. In every sphere of human activity, motivations are generally mixed. What does matter, however, is being able to place the results of foundation initiatives side-by-side with what foundations and/or their donors intended to accomplish through their benefactions. It matters not only in analyzing a foundation's fidelity to its donor's expressed intent, but also in understanding how donors' value commitments often shape the actions of the foundations that their wealth created.[36] Examining donors' motivations for establishing foundations and their intentions for the use of the philanthropic dollars their motivation created, therefore, is an indispensable component of measuring a foundation's impact.

Why a Foundation?

Just as there are many possible motivations for charitable giving, there are several reasons behind the decision to create a foundation. But here, the motivations are often more clear-cut and driven by practical considerations.

One reason for launching a foundation as a channel for charitable giving is simple uncertainty about how and where to give. Sometimes donors have trouble finding organizations that are large enough, focused enough, or effective enough to pursue the specific goals they favor. In other cases, tax or estate-planning considerations make it hard to match charitable objectives with potential donees. In still other cases, a donor may simply be unable to make a choice among several worthy recipients. When this happens, the donor may resort to creating a foundation that will provide a tax deduction when it's most needed, and leave specific allocation decisions to the future.

Another reason for choosing the foundation route is a desire to avoid giving excessive wealth to children or other heirs. Sometimes this arises when wealthy parents decide that their offspring are rebellious, errant, incompetent, or simply no good—in which case the children may be cut out of the parents' will altogether. In other cases, it grows out of a philosophical belief that inherited wealth can be debilitating, sapping the younger generation of ambition and energy. Andrew Carnegie clearly believed that this is so, and one can infer that Warren Buffett, Bill and Melinda Gates, and others who have given away the bulk of their assets rather than bequeath them to their children must agree. When this is the case, the parents usually leave a (modest) bequest for their children alongside a large endowment for the foundation. As Warren Buffett said, "You want to give your children enough money so that they can do what they want, but not so much that they don't do anything."[37]

Some foundations have been created from fortunes that were so large that their owners simply had no idea what to do with them. This problem of having too much money is, of course, very rare—but it does happen. Perhaps this was one reason that Bill and Melinda Gates decided to launch their foundation with a single vast donation of $23 billion. We know from the biographies of Andrew Carnegie and John D. Rockefeller that they felt they had more money than they knew what to do with.[38] Rockefeller articulated this sense of urgency when asking Frederick T. Gates to become his assistant in philanthropy:

> I am in trouble, Mr. Gates. The pressure of appeals for gifts has become too great for endurance. I haven't the time or strength, with all my heavy business responsibilities, to deal with these demands properly. I am so constituted as to be unable to give away money with any satisfaction until I have made the most careful inquiry as to the worthiness of the cause. These investigations are now taking more of my time and energy than the Standard Oil itself. Either I must shift part of the burden, or stop giving entirely. And I cannot do the latter.[39]

Frederick T. Gates, formerly a practicing Baptist preacher, became perhaps the first American *philanthropoid*, defined as someone who gives away someone else's money.[40] Fifteen years later, Gates explained even more forcefully the frightening extent of his necessity in a letter to Rockefeller:

> Your fortune is rolling up, rolling up like an avalanche! You must keep up with it! You must distribute it faster than it grows! If you do not, it will crush you and your children and your children's children.[41]

It was, at least in part, this plea that led Rockefeller to create the Rockefeller Foundation three years later, on June 29, 1909.[42] Necessity had won out.

Tax considerations involved in estate planning constitute yet another variety of motivation. Just as charitable gifts during the lifetime of a donor can diminish tax liability, gifts to establish a foundation upon death can significantly diminish or even eliminate estate tax liability.

Again, the importance of this motivation can be overstated. Some of the largest foundations were created with no tax incentives at all. Both the Rockefeller Foundation and the Carnegie Corporation of New York were established before the charitable contribution deduction was created. The Atlantic Philanthropies were established with zero tax benefit to the donor, and, in our own time, the Bill and Melinda Gates Foundation appears to have been created with little income tax deduction motivation.[43]

Another reason for creating a foundation has been to use it as a vehicle for retaining control of a closely held corporation. However, the Tax Reform Act of 1969 made it illegal, with very few exceptions, for private foundations to own more than 20 percent of the voting interest in any for-profit enterprise, making this strategy difficult to carry out. Later legislation also made it illegal for individuals involved in both a corporation and a related foundation—*disqualified persons* in the arcane jargon of the Tax Code—to engage in specified transactions, such as borrowing money from the foundation. The focus of regulators on such corporate/foundation relations has therefore virtually eliminated the usefulness of foundations in controlling related corporations.

A Vehicle for Social Change

Having considered all these practical reasons for creating a foundation, I conclude that one overarching motivation remains paramount for most donors: the desire to create a vehicle for promoting large-scale, lasting social change. And here the most deep-seated personal qualities of the founders come into play.

In reading the biographies of Carnegie and Rockefeller, one cannot help being struck by the relentlessness with which they pursued their objectives, sometimes with appalling consequences, as with Carnegie in the Homestead steel strike of 1891 or Rockefeller in the Ludlow Massacre of 1914.[44] But what truly distinguished Carnegie and Rockefeller from other businessmen was the extent to which the force of their personalities and their business visions utterly transformed their industries (steel and oil, respectively). They and the organizations they created embodied what Harvard Business School Professor Clay Christensen has called *disruptive technologies*.[45] They pushed the business envelope, occasionally across the boundaries of legality, and in so doing created corporate empires of unprecedented power and wealth, as well as gigantic personal fortunes amounting to the modern equivalent of one hundred billion dollars (Carnegie) and two hundred billion dollars (Rockefeller).[46]

Perhaps, then, after exhausting the universe of business opportunities, tackling the new arena of the civic sector was the only truly interesting and challenging thing left for them to do. Rockefeller hinted as much in his 1909 autobiography when he wrote:

> I am sure it is a mistake to assume that the possession of money in great abundance necessarily brings happiness. The very rich are just like the rest of us; and if they get pleasure from the possession of money, it comes from their ability to do things which give satisfaction to someone besides themselves. The mere expenditure of money for things . . . soon palls upon one. The novelty of being able to purchase anything one wants soon passes, because what people most seek cannot be bought with money. These rich men we read about in the newspapers cannot get personal returns beyond a well-defined limit for their expenditure. They cannot gratify the pleasures of the palate beyond very moderate bounds, since they cannot purchase a good digestion; they cannot lavish very much money on fine raiment for themselves or their families without suffering from public ridicule; and in their homes they cannot get much beyond the comforts of the less wealthy without involving them in more pain than pleasure. As I study wealthy men, I can see but one way in which they can secure a real equivalent for money

spent, and that is to cultivate a taste for giving where the money may produce an effect which will be a lasting gratification.[47]

Thus, men like Carnegie and Rockefeller found themselves drawn to do in the civic sector what they had done in the profit sector—pushing the envelope again, but this time in the arena of public problem-solving. To put it another way, having achieved unprecedented success in the world of laissez-faire capitalism defined by Adam Smith's *Wealth of Nations*, our greatest capitalists turned to the world of *Moral Sentiments*, there to pursue goals that Smith's "impartial spectator" might have approved.

Beginning in the 1880s, when the great age of American philanthropy was born, the biggest donors made explicit their desire to use their giving to influence society. Some foundation creators were more explicit than others in defining the problems they hoped to solve or ameliorate. A few even articulated not only what they intended to do but also the social rationale behind their priorities.

None did so more expansively than Andrew Carnegie in his 1889 articles, "Wealth" and "The Best Fields for Philanthropy," published in the *North American Review* and later revised and published as *The Gospel of Wealth*. Rockefeller enthusiastically admired and emulated Carnegie. After reading Carnegie's first article, Rockefeller wrote him: "I would that more men of wealth were doing as you are doing with your money; but, be assured, your example will bear fruits, and the time will come when men of wealth will more generally be willing to use it for the good of others."[48]

To both Carnegie and Rockefeller, it was self-evident that the advantage in using great wealth for the public benefit lay not in short-term amelioration of social ills but in changing the systems that produced those ills in the first place. Rather than simply making donations to the poor, Carnegie hoped to equip the poor with the skills needed to escape poverty. Thus, he built 2,509 libraries worldwide, including 1,681 in the United States alone, so that illiterate men and women could learn how to read. In a similar vein, both Carnegie and Rockefeller founded universities. Carnegie created the Carnegie Institute and Carnegie Library, which became Carnegie-Mellon University in Pittsburgh, while Rockefeller founded both the University of Chicago and Spelman College in Atlanta (named for his wife, Laura Spelman Rockefeller).

Again, both men saw their mission as not simply to heal the sick or repair the effects of conflict but to enhance society's ability to solve fundamental scientific and social problems. In support of this goal, both established great research institutions—the Carnegie Institution of Washington, the Carnegie Endowment for International Peace, the Carnegie Foundation for the Advancement of Teaching, and the Rockefeller Institute of Medical Research, which evolved into Rockefeller University.

Inevitably, this commitment to social change provoked controversy. And while Rockefeller's critics may have made him cautious about tackling controversial public issues, Carnegie was undaunted in pressing his proposals for promoting world peace. His last years were consumed with an ultimately futile effort to promote diplomacy in hopes of averting World War I, and one of his last great benefactions was the construction of the building that now houses the International Court of Justice in The Hague.

Other founders from the heroic age of philanthropy evinced the same passionate commitment to social reform. Margaret Olivia Sage, founder of the Russell Sage Foundation, was devoted to improving the social-welfare system. Edward S. Harkness, the founder of the Commonwealth Fund, and Robert Wood Johnson, the founder of the Robert Wood Johnson Foundation, were both determined to improve health and health services for Americans. Julius Rosenwald, founder of the Rosenwald Fund, spent almost his entire fortune in building schools for African American children across the South.

It's clear, therefore, that, from the beginning of American foundations, their creators have viewed their mission as involving advocacy for change, which included the shaping of public policy.[49] A useful context for this role can be found in the ideas of the "liberal society" and the politics of competing interest groups, developed in the 1960s by political scientist Robert A. Dahl. Applying Dahl's formulation, we can see foundations as another kind of interest group competing for the attention of the public, politicians, and the government and seeking to exercise its influence in pursuit of the public good. That is certainly the way the great founders used their foundations, even if they didn't explicitly describe them that way.

PHILANTHROPY, CLASS, AND POWER

It may seem curious that large-scale charitable giving including the creation of foundations—two activities reserved to the very rich—should be put in service of largely progressive social causes. Yet that is certainly true of the Ford Foundation, the Carnegie Corporation, the Rockefeller Foundation, and virtually all of the largest foundations in America. Why would America's wealthiest citizens give to support organizations that could be seen as undermining the bulwarks of privilege on which their own power was built?

Some critics, especially those of Marxist and Gramscian orientation, claim that the progressive image of philanthropy is a false façade—that both the donors' intentions and the effects of their philanthropies have been primarily to advance their own interests, those of their companies, or those of their socioeconomic class.[50] That contention, however, seems to be undermined by the actual nature of their giving, which objectively served not to strengthen but to weaken class differences and help rather than suppress the poor. Furthermore, one might note that both Carnegie and Rockefeller, like most of the foundation creators, were self-made men. Why would they be motivated to serve the interests of the class of the idle rich—a class into which they had not been born and which they evidently despised?

Whatever their motivation or intention, therefore, it's now clear that the early foundation creators and their successors over the past century have established institutions that have objectively transformed the landscape of civic-sector power, lessening the imbalance between the wielders of power for private interest and the wielders of power for the common good. Whereas moneyed interests, whether corporate or personal, once had a virtual monopoly on the influence of public policy, foundations have now made it possible for non-moneyed interests based on widespread popular participation, to mount effective legal, political, and advocacy efforts to protect themselves and advance their interests. Without foundations and the wide range of nonprofits they support, there would be today fewer institutions in America with the effective power to stand up to corporations and government where matters of the public interest are concerned.

Naturally, this public policy advocacy role has brought controversy. Individuals disagree on just what "the public interest" is as applied to most policy questions. Left, right, and center see the public interest through quite different lenses. It goes without saying, therefore, that increasing foundation activism on behalf of liberal causes was a major factor in energizing activism by donors to conservative foundations. Moreover, the controversy sparked by differences over what the public interest means has, in turn, focused the attention of critics on foundations' lack of any real accountability. Foundations have been criticized for wielding their unaccountable power in the public sphere irresponsibly and thereby influencing democratic processes unfairly.[51] This charge was brought as early as 1914, when a resolution was passed by the Normal Department of the National Education Association (the division charged with responsibility for teacher training):

> We view with alarm the activity of Carnegie and Rockefeller foundation [sic], agencies not in any way responsible to the people, in their effort to control the policies of our state educational institutions; to fashion after their own conceptions and to standardize after their own notion our courses of study; and to surround the institutions with conditions which menace true academic freedom and which defeat the primary purpose of democracy as heretofore preserved inviolate in our common schools, Normal schools, and Universities.[52]

Foundations are certainly not above criticism, and there is much to criticize in their decision-making styles and in their lack of openness to the public. And as I'll discuss in a later chapter, foundations are exempt from most of the mechanisms of accountability that affect other organizations. But foundations are hardly unconstrained in exercising their power. As tax-exempt institutions, they are, unlike corporations, prohibited from directly lobbying members of Congress and congressional staff, and from engaging in political campaigns for public office. Staff salaries are subject to IRS "excessiveness" tests, and the amount of their annual grantmaking is mandated by statute as a minimum percentage of their endowment assets.[53]

In any case, the foundations are hardly monolithic in their values and aims. It is true that, until the 1970s, foundations involved in public policy arenas overwhelmingly supported views and values that were liberal or centrist. But starting in the 1970s, some foundations began to develop program strategies to foster conservative policies in a wide range of fields from regulatory policy, education, and welfare to immigration and the environment. The conservative foundations' strategies and grantmaking practices, if not the specific policies they advocated, have been widely hailed for breaking new ground, and liberal and centrist foundations are now trying to emulate them. The world of public policy discourse is much richer in consequence.

Thus, neither the Marxist charge that foundations merely defend the interests of the rich, nor the conservative charge that foundations use their power irresponsibly to promote a liberal agenda stands up to scrutiny.

We've seen, then, the variety of motivations that spur charitable giving by the rich, and in particular the creation of foundations. Chief among these, we contend, is the desire to have a positive impact on society by advancing social change. How do foundations seek to promote this goal? And how fully have they succeeded? I'll begin to address those vital questions in the next chapter.

4

THE FOUNDATION'S MISSION:

THE HIGHEST USE OF

PHILANTHROPIC CAPITAL

Instead of giving alms to beggars, if anything can be done
to remove the causes which lead to the existence of beggars,
then something deeper and broader and more worthwhile
will have been accomplished.

———

John D. Rockefeller Sr.[54]

"You Always Have the Poor"

Giving as a religious duty has a long history. The three great monotheistic faiths of Judaism, Christianity, and Islam all enjoin acts of charity upon their believers. But the religious rationale for such giving is not always the same—nor is it always clear.

For some Christians, the primary purpose of giving is to achieve or sustain individual salvation, not the solution of a social problem. The Jesus of the New Testament does not command his followers to eradicate poverty; if anything, he implies that this is impossible: "For you always have the poor with you" (Matthew 26:11, RSV). Nonetheless, giving to alleviate suffering is strictly required and indeed is assumed to be one of the duties of every believer.

The prevailing attitude toward charity in Jewish tradition is somewhat different. The common Christian emphasis on "saving one's soul" is absent and even discouraged. In fact, for many Jews, any benefit, heavenly or otherwise, a donor might enjoy as a result of performing an act of charity should be an incidental byproduct, never its intended goal. Otherwise the motive would corrupt the act of charity and diminish any personal benefits that might otherwise flow from it. The stress, therefore, is on the beneficial impact that charity has on its recipients and indeed on the social capital of the community as a whole, rather than on the donor's "heavenly bank account" of spiritual credits. Still, no broader social goal is envisioned; neither the Prophets nor the Jewish teachers regarded the individual believer as obliged to strive for the elimination of poverty altogether. The Islamic approach to charitable giving appears to be similar to that of Judaism.

The subsequent evolution from individual-focused to socially focused charity occurred over many centuries.[55] The idea that philanthropy should properly be focused on social reform began to acquire its current preeminence with the establishment of the first great foundations, especially those of Rockefeller and Carnegie, early in the twentieth century. As Kenneth Prewitt, Andrew Carnegie Professor of Public Affairs at Columbia University, writes in summarizing Rockefeller's philanthropic vision, "The gift that matters is not to the individual beggar but to the situation represented by the beggar. To attend to the situation rather than the symptom was an idea that permanently and fundamentally altered the relationship between great private wealth and public purpose."[56]

From Expressive Giving to Instrumental Giving

I've already referred to the distinction between instrumental giving and expressive giving. Instrumental giving seeks to achieve particular social aims, while expressive giving reflects a donor's desire to show support for a cause or an organization without necessarily expecting to achieve a noticeable impact through the grant alone.

It would be wrong to disparage expressive giving. Most of what individuals and corporations do through their philanthropic giving has always been expressive rather than instrumental, and the same remains true of much foundation-based philanthropy as well. Moreover, such giving is the backbone of America's civic sector.

Indeed, for two reasons, the word *expressive* is exactly the right one to describe most American philanthropy. First, it's prompted by Americans' desire to express support for something larger than themselves. Second, it reflects our freedom of expression as guaranteed by the Bill of Rights. The First Amendment doesn't promise that we can have an impact on our society, but it gives us the right to express our support for organizations that try to do so. Thus, expressive giving is both crucial to our not-for-profit sector and an essentially American activity.

Moreover, it is not given to most human beings to place our own personal stamp on all or much that we do throughout our lives. The Talmud cautions us that, "You are not obligated to finish the task, but neither are you free to desist from it."[57] Yet we all yearn to associate ourselves in some meaningful way with the doing of what we regard as good for other people and for society as a whole. Besides the acts of kindness and generosity that we do for other individual human beings, acts of which only God properly takes notice, the only way most of us can place our stamp on society is through affiliating ourselves with other people in serving and supporting causes, institutions, and organizations that, because of the power of many, can achieve an impact on society over time that will outlive us. While the effects of our contributions will almost always be diffuse rather than discrete, we can take satisfaction from the fact that we put our shoulder to the wheel even if we can discern none of our fingerprints on it. And we can also reasonably know that, but for our commitment of time and money, the recipient movement or institution we support would not otherwise be as strong as we help make it, which is not an insignificant impact either.

Of course, if enough people provide expressive support for a particular cause, their collective impact may be enormous. As author Malcolm Gladwell shows in his best-selling book *The Tipping Point*, initiatives that transform society are often preceded by purely expressive actions that help to change minds and, in time, the behavior of millions. Thus, expressive giving may give rise to instrumental giving through sheer cumulative force.

Still, my intention in the remainder of this book is to focus mainly on instrumental giving—philanthropy that is intended and designed to have a measurable impact on society as a whole. The number of foundations seriously trying to transform their current programs of expressive giving into instrumental giving is steadily increasing. My hope is that, by analyzing initiatives that have succeeded in achieving social impact, I can help point the way for others who seek to do likewise.

Furthermore, I contend that, for most foundations, instrumental giving is the more appropriate and effective focus—much closer to the essence of the foundation's mission than the more widespread expressive giving. I will explain my reasons in the remainder of this chapter.

WHY FOCUS ON INSTRUMENTAL GIVING?

The social problems that our great foundations seek to solve are huge—global poverty, international conflict, inadequate systems of health care and education, ethnic and religious bigotry, and so on. By contrast, the resources they bring to bear may seem disproportionately small. This apparent mismatch has led some observers, such as Kenneth Prewitt, a widely admired expert on philanthropy, to describe foundations as "peripheral players" in the struggle for social change. The implication is that striving for meaningful impact through instrumental giving is quixotic at best.

Despite my great respect for Prewitt, I disagree with his view. Although I accept his point about the disproportion between the social problems we face and the foundation assets available to solve them, I believe this simply makes it all the more important that foundations focus on instrumental giving if they hope to achieve any meaningful social impact.

It may be true, in the biblical formulation, that we will always have the poor with us—that some of our greatest social problems may remain intractable for the foreseeable future. Under the circumstances, it's tempting to retreat to mere "checkbook charity"—expressive giving that eases individual suffering, salves the conscience of the donor, and earns (justified) praise from the rest of society. But I think foundations should strive for more. There are four reasons I do so:

The Scale of Foundation Giving

- The relatively large scale of foundations within the civic sector as well as in society as a whole demands that they strive for meaningful social impact.

What You Should Have to Produce for Getting a Tax Break

- The generous publicly granted tax benefits that enable foundations to be created and then to grow tax-free warrant a social demand for such impact.

Foundations Are Not, In Effect, Accountable to Anyone

- The relative freedom from accountability enjoyed by foundations demands that they undertake a significant level of social responsibility.

The Comparative Advantage Foundations Enjoy

- The enormous comparative advantage enjoyed by foundations requires holding them to the highest use of their resources.

Let's consider each of these reasons in turn.

The Scale of Foundation Giving

Measured by their assets, the current scale of America's foundations is unique among the nations of the world and unprecedented in history. I won't repeat the statistics provided in earlier chapters but simply note that, by any standards, our great foundations represent huge pools of money with few fixed claims on their use, collectively unequaled anywhere. Their sheer size warrants their being held to a high standard both of effectiveness and accountability in deploying their vast charitable assets.

Even more than other foundations, large perpetual foundations with no living donor call for ratcheting up the demand for the highest possible level of effectiveness. There is an assumption, not always correct but hardly unreasonable, that a living donor on the board of a foundation will be zealous in assuring that the great wealth he donates is used with great efficiency in pursuit of his philanthropic goals. But once the donor has died, and especially when there is no successor family member on the board, it is not unreasonable to assume that the foundation's zeal may tend to weaken. It is the rare foundation professional who has the same obsessiveness about spending philanthropic wealth as did the person who accumulated it. In such circumstances, doubts about the quality of the stewardship with which the trustees and staff are running the foundation may arise.

Thus, a rich foundation, with high aspirations for effecting social change, that is a generation or two removed from the founder's vision, must be especially careful about maintaining its fidelity to that vision—and that means redoubling its dedication to instrumental giving—giving aimed at achieving consequences of high social benefit—rather than merely expressive charity.

What You Should Have to Produce for Getting a Tax Break

Private individuals do and should enjoy absolute freedom from second-guessing of their (legal) charitable choices. After all, their right to make those choices is rooted in the First Amendment guarantees of free speech and free association that all Americans enjoy. They should be able to give to anything charitable to which their heart moves them.

By contrast, foundations, like for-profit corporations, are artificial creatures of the law, either incorporated or established as charitable trusts under state laws. Moreover, foundations receive the benefit of federal and state tax provisions that indirectly support both the donations they receive and the growth of donated funds when invested. Foundations pay no tax on their income or appreciation, and are required to pay only a modest annual federal foundation tax, amounting to 1 or 2 percent of their net investment income depending on certain characteristics.

The resulting loss of tax revenues to the U.S. Treasury and the states is very substantial. In 2003, for example, it is estimated that individuals gave $21.6 billion to foundations, all of which was likely deducted from either income or estate taxes.[58] Had the deduction not been available, the individuals or their estates would have paid income, capital gains, or estate tax on that amount. If these individuals had sold assets equivalent to the amount they donated, they would have had to pay at least a capital gains tax of 15 percent of the appreciated value. If there were no property to be sold but only income from which the donations were made, a federal income tax of between 30 and 40 percent or estate tax as high as 50 percent would have been payable.[59] So the loss to the U.S. Treasury from the tax deductibility of contributions to foundations in 2003 can be estimated at a minimum of $5.1 billion, although, had the contributions not been made, and the assets sold, the figure would be higher, depending on the marginal tax rate used. The tax loss can be estimated in other ways, all of which yield roughly similar conclusions.

In addition, if the annual income earned by foundations was not tax-exempt, another substantial sum—perhaps as much as fifteen billion dollars—would be owed to the U.S. Treasury (2004 estimate), depending on the marginal tax that, but for the tax exemption, would apply. Combining the two figures, we see about twenty billion dollars in taxes lost to the U.S. Treasury because of foundation tax benefits. And this doesn't take into account state and local taxes.

Society, then, is supporting the activities of foundations by foregoing more than twenty billion dollars per year. Are we getting our money's worth?

No one doubts that foundations confer some benefits on society, but whether the benefits measure up to the costs imposed is a matter of some dispute. A simple way of approaching the question is to compare the $32 billion given away by foundations in 2004 with the $20 billion in tax losses calculated above. By this crude calculus, society enjoys a net benefit of $12 billion.

Of course, this begs the question whether the nominal $32 billion in benefits are real or simply theoretical. And that leads us very directly to the question of social impact.

It's obvious that calculations like these won't suffice either to prove or disprove the proposition that society is being well repaid for its support of foundations. The point, however, is that society is making a substantial, if indirect, investment in foundations, and that any failure of foundations to live up to their responsibility for achieving significant social impact through their programs makes them vulnerable to attack.

A critic might say, for example, "If our goal is to encourage the wealthy to make donations that benefit society, why not eliminate the middlemen? Let's outlaw foundations and force the wealthy to make their charitable gifts directly to tax-exempt charities. Those charities will put the donations to work immediately, and the administrative costs of running the foundations will be saved."

I disagree with this logic, for reasons that I hope this entire book will make clear. But foundations and their supporters need a solid response to arguments like this one. And the best response is clear evidence that foundations are adding significant value to the money they handle and investing it to create the highest possible level of benefits for society. Otherwise, why should society continue to subsidize them?

The risk that foundations could lose their tax-exempt status is not merely theoretical. As foundation assets grow ever larger, Congress is already signaling its desire to take a closer look at whether foundations are fulfilling their social obligations. Unquestionably, that desire has been triggered by allegations of excessive salaries paid to foundation trustees and executives, as well as by a small number of instances of malfeasance, but whatever the trigger, the whole cloth of foundation regulation could easily be on the cutting table. The attempts in 2003 and 2004 to raise the annual foundation payout minimum are but one example of congressional unrest on the subject. Another is the focus on nonprofits and foundations in 2005 and 2006 by the Senate Finance Committee, the House Ways and Means Committee, and the Joint Committee on Taxation. If foundations hope to retain their current privileged tax status, they need to take very seriously the demands that they use their assets as effectively as possible and provide adequate evidence to the public that they are doing so.

Foundations Are Not, In Effect, Accountable to Anyone

In principle, every nonprofit—including foundations—above a minimum spending threshold is required to submit annual financial reports to the Internal Revenue Service and to a state officer or body (usually the attorney general or the secretary of state). That sounds like effective accountability, but in fact it isn't. The responsible agencies are woefully understaffed and have no real authority, except when illegality is suspected, to oversee the decisions made by the nonprofits. So the true accountability of nonprofits—again including foundations—to public agencies is, for all practical purposes, slight.

However, operating nonprofits are in a very different situation from foundations. Most have multiple constituencies that influence or constrain their decision-making in much the same way that paying customers influence the operations of profit-making organizations. The "customers" of universities, colleges, and private schools include the enrolled students and their parents, who pay tuition and fees. Other "customers" include alumni, who contribute to the school only when they feel inclined to do so; faculty members, who rarely hesitate to question or criticize school policies; and other employees, who may be organized to exert pressure in their own interests. Even more broadly, colleges and schools must answer to local government officials, who provide services such as police, fire protection, and the like; federal agencies, which provide grants, loans, and scholarships; and accrediting organizations, whose judgments about academic quality can make or break a school's reputation.

All of these groups observe, pass judgment on, and influence the actions of the school's leaders, creating a highly effective, if informal, system of accountability. A similar list of powerful constituent groups could be created for most other nonprofit organizations, including hospitals, museums, arts groups, and so on.

Foundations alone have no such accountability network. No one is really able to look over the shoulder of foundation trustees, executives, and program staff and evaluate their work. Except for the barebones financial reports required annually by government, foundations need not provide any account of themselves to anyone. For years, most foundations did not even issue annual reports to the public. (The first foundation to do so was the Commonwealth Fund in 1919.)[60]

Today, most large foundations do issue public reports, as well as offering information about their activities on their Internet sites. These sources of information lack objectivity, however. Only success stories are included, and generally with little of the factual data that would permit an independent evaluation of a project's effectiveness.

Most foundations also provide annual information to the Foundation Center, which publishes *The Foundation Directory* both in print and digitally and maintains a searchable database. But the information provided to the Foundation Center is very basic—little more than a listing of grant recipients' names and a brief description of their program focus.

Observers of foundations have long been troubled by this absence of public disclosure and the lack of accountability it implies. As long ago as 1925, Frederick P. Keppel was writing about the vulnerability of the foundations' tax-exempt status and linking it to the issue of public confidence:

> After all, the fundamental safeguard against the unsocial use of these [foundation] funds lies, in the long run, in public opinion and the possibility of public control. The apparent immunity of those who direct them lies in the freedom from taxation which the foundations enjoy,

but there is nothing irrevocable about the present exemption of such bodies, and the community, if at any time it felt so disposed, could tax an offending foundation, or all foundations, out of active existence. . . . The element of public confidence in the makeup of foundation boards is therefore of very practical importance. Even more important is as wide an understanding as possible of what they do and how they do it. . . . In my judgment, public confidence in foundations in general may depend to a greater degree than is at present realized upon public knowledge of their operations.[61]

In 1937, Keppel went further:

. . . it would carry the writer too far afield to reenter the discussion as to the proportion of American foundations which make no public record of their activities whatsoever—thereby failing to recognize their responsibility to the public. . . . The instances in which it seems impossible to obtain pertinent information is disquietingly large. The question is not whether the funds of these silent trusts are put to useful purposes . . . it is rather whether public confidence in the foundation as a social instrument, a confidence which is in no small degree based on the policy of complete publicity adopted by the better known foundations, may not be endangered.[62]

In 1963, Raymond B. Fosdick, president of the Rockefeller Foundation, weighed in on the same subject:

This doctrine [of public responsibility] is still valid today. Indeed with the proliferation of foundations, it has become an urgent aspect of policy. The public is entitled to know the facts—all the facts—about the operation of foundations. And most of them, I believe, have . . . nothing to hide, nothing to cover up. . . . They have a proud record, and that record should willingly be made accessible to public scrutiny. In no lesser way can the essentially public nature of the responsibilities of foundations be adequately demonstrated.[63]

Today, a full generation later, the situation is essentially unchanged. Foundation staffs are accountable only to their trustees, and their trustees are accountable to no one.

Note that I am not arguing here that foundations should be required to give an account of themselves to anyone. Instead I am arguing that the freedom from accountability that foundations enjoy is yet another reason that foundations should insist on holding themselves to performance standards that benefit the public to the greatest possible extent and to relentless, thoroughgoing transparency.

The Comparative Advantage Foundations Enjoy

"Comparative advantage" is usually used to mean being better able than others to serve a function or achieve an objective, primarily because of the nature of one's existing assets or demonstrated track record. In the realm of the civic sector, however, there really are no "others" against which to compare foundations and wealthy individuals in terms of their capacity to provide venture and nurturing capital. They are sui generis!

Because of their peculiar combination of attributes, foundations are able to deploy wealth in what they regard as the public interest in ways that are available to no other entities in society. Unlike for-profit businesses, they have only one mandate—to assist and improve the workings of the civic sector for the good of society. Unlike operating charities, they are not trammeled by the day-to-day demands of their many constituent groups. And unlike wealthy individuals, they have staffs that can research social issues, institutional memories that can inform strategies for effecting social change, and the staying power necessary for dealing with persistent problems.

In all these ways, foundations are unique. In the words of Paul Ylvisaker, one of the great foundation program officers of the twentieth century, "philanthropy is America's passing gear."[64] No other institutions in society are comparably equipped to play this role.

If foundations do not take full advantage of their unique resources, the loss to America will be incalculable—and probably irremediable. And because the role played by foundations is unique, America's polyarchy will also be damaged, measurably reducing the vibrancy and dynamism of our society.

Thus, foundations can't afford to settle for "doing good." They must "do the best," using the financial capital they control most effectively in pursuit of the highest possible goals. That requires regular strategic analysis; constant study of society's greatest and most urgent problems; the establishment of goals and performance benchmarks; and continual, thoroughgoing self-assessment to measure progress or the lack thereof.

At the very start of the foundation era, Andrew Carnegie wrote:

> It is not expected, neither is it desirable, that there should be general concurrence as to the best possible use of surplus wealth. For different men and different localities there are different uses. What commends itself most highly to the judgment of the administrator [i.e., donor] is the best use for him, for his heart should be in the work. It is as important in administering wealth as it is in any other branch of a man's work that he should be enthusiastically devoted to it and feel that in the field selected his work lies.[65]

This philosophy underlies the implicit bargain that American society has struck with the foundations: America will exempt your assets and income from taxation in exchange for your using them to produce the greatest possible benefit for society. That means pursuing large-scale and lasting *impact,* and this alone is the ultimate purpose and justification of foundations.

5

FOUNDATION STRATEGY

IN PRINCIPLE

The difference between success and failure is to do it right
at the beginning.

―――――

Ralph Gomory[66]

STRATEGY AND THE SCIENTIFIC METHOD

Over the last decade, *strategy* has become the favored word among nonprofit leaders in general and foundation leaders in particular. Tony Proscio,
a perceptive writer and observer of the foundation scene, has said it best in
his little book, *In Other Words: A Plea for Plain Speaking in Foundations*:

[M]any foundations . . . have taken up STRATEGY with the giddiness
of a soldier on leave. . . . At its worst, STRATEGY in foundation parl-
ance refers to transparently tactical decisions about particular grants, recipients, amounts, and points of intervention. . . . They concern how
to array and command forces more effectively according to an already-
determined battle plan, against an already-determined target. But the
main problem with STRATEGY is not that it is too often misapplied.
Rather, like many retired generals of recent years, it has developed an
aura of indispensability and universal relevance that grows wearisome
even if it is not really out-of-place. It is possible—and indeed, for cen-

turies it was normal—to discuss plans, goals, and resources without invoking STRATEGY at all. Because the word is becoming obligatory in many circles—such that no planning discussion is regarded as complete without it—the use of STRATEGY needs to be treated with the greatest distrust. It should, in fact, be treated the way the U.S. Constitution treats all generals—subject, ultimately, to a civilian review, answerable to ordinary people who are less at home with the argot of the war room and more likely to want their information in plain speech.[67]

Perhaps the giddiness with which foundations have rushed to embrace strategy is understandable. It represents an overreaction to the recognition by many foundation decision-makers that their work had lacked the well-ordered, data-driven, focused analytical framework that produced so many high-impact initiatives for the early foundations.

Rather than *strategy*, the early leaders of the Carnegie, Rockefeller, and Commonwealth foundations regarded themselves as applying the scientific method to grantmaking. For them, the scientific method involved: (1) getting the facts right by research and/or surveys; (2) identifying the problem clearly and precisely; (3) studying a number of potential options for action; (4) identifying those whose help would be needed or whose opposition must be neutralized in order to achieve the objective; and only then (5) developing a plan of action that included a clearly defined objective, benchmarks of progress, and methods of gathering data to evaluate accomplishment. This, in a nutshell, is strategic thinking.

Why did the habit of applying scientific thinking to foundation work become lost in the first place? I suspect it was caused by the passing from the scene of the older generation of foundation donors and leaders, many of whom came from the business world and had been trained in the philosophy of scientific management.[68] They were gradually replaced by non-business generalists, usually from liberal arts backgrounds, who lacked the scientific management mind-set and strategic skills of their predecessors.

As foundation staff, boards, and trustee leadership began to be drawn from the ranks of university presidents and faculty, the culture of scientific management gradually disappeared, except in those foundations that have continued to enjoy the influence of businessmen or their intellectual kin from academia, such as the Alfred P. Sloan Foundation and the Robert Wood Johnson Foundation.

The resulting period of nonstrategic foundation decision-making led to some vaguely defined and highly ineffective initiatives of a kind that hard-nosed business leaders like Andrew Carnegie and John D. Rockefeller Sr. would surely never have tolerated.

ENDS AND MEANS

Ellen Condliffe Lagemann, a perceptive historian of foundations, has defined strategy in the following simple yet elegant terms: "finding maximally effective means to achieve agreed-upon ends."[69]

Notice the implication here: Strategy comes second in time and logic, not first. What comes first is determining those "agreed-upon ends"—in other words, the objectives toward which a foundation or a specific set of programs shall be directed. Strategy enters only after the problem and the goal have been selected by careful research of all relevant facts, and by using human judgment, informed by experience, intellect, and intuition. This is exactly the process one finds in examining the history of high-impact foundation initiatives. In each case, the problem was selected for attention by a donor or program officer who had both prior experience with the general area involved and the good judgment required to identify and assess the ripeness of a particular target. Only after this did the scientific management approach—today's strategic thinking—kick in.

This sequence is important and, unfortunately, not intuitively obvious. Many foundations make the mistake of calling in strategic consultants to help them choose areas of grantmaking focus. That's not what strategic consultants are for. A skilled consultant can sometimes help trustees figure out what problems they care most passionately about, but it is the passions of the trustees that matter—not those of the consultant.

So foundation leaders must choose the ends of their efforts for themselves. The strategic consultant can then help find the most effective means for achieving those ends—or, when appropriate, deliver a warning that the means required for achieving a particular end are simply unavailable.

This distinction between ends and means helps explain why strategic thinking is harder for foundations than it is for grant-receiving nonprofits. The typical nonprofit has a reasonably specific organizational mission with easy-to-articulate, ready-made goals attached. The strategic challenge is to clarify and analyze those goals, and to chart a systematic course towards achieving them.

By contrast, the typical foundation has a very general mission—to do good for humankind, for example—and no inherent goals. For example, the very practical and tough-minded Andrew Carnegie left the Carnegie Corporation of New York with the most general of missions—"to support the advancement and diffusion of knowledge and understanding," a vague pronouncement described grandly in the foundation's underwriting announcements on National Public Radio as a "mandate from Andrew Carnegie." In the same way, Robert Wood Johnson wanted the foundation named after him to focus its resources on "improving the health and health care of all Americans," but he named no specific goals, such as reducing infant mortality, finding a cure for cancer, creating primary care clinics for the poor, or educating physicians.

Of course, it makes sense that a foundation designed to operate in perpetuity should be given a broad, open-ended mandate rather than a set of specific goals. As conditions change, specific goals inevitably become obsolete. If a foundation is to remain relevant to today's problems, its trustees and staff must be free to make informed choices about program goals. As a result, foundation leaders enjoy the broadest imaginable freedom, having large amounts of money to spend on unspecified social problems that they are free to define as they see fit. It's an enviable position to be in—but also a frustrating one, since it places the burden of choosing appropriate ends squarely on the shoulders of foundation leadership.

Their near-absolute freedom makes it hard for most foundations to focus on specific goals. Instead, most foundation trustees end up specifying "program areas" that delimit the fields within which they plan to do their grantmaking. But choosing a field for grantmaking is *not* the same thing as being strategic. It is merely a threshold requirement. There's a very long road between choosing a program area and zeroing in on specific goals as well as the routes to achieving them. Rather than travel that road, many foundations content themselves with leaving the goal-setting choices to external grant-seekers.

That is an understandable choice—but a regrettable one. A foundation that abdicates its goal-setting responsibility limits its potential impact on the problems it hopes to help solve. Passing the decision-making buck along to the nonprofit organizations that need dollars simply deprives the world of the possible benefits that might be derived from the broader insights and knowledge of foundation staff and leaders, transforming the foundation into a mere check-writing facility that contributes little to the problem-solving capabilities of society. Of course, the grant-seeking organizations have a crucial role to play in informing foundation decisions as they will play the major role in implementing them. But informing foundation decisions is hardly the same as making them in the first instance, and foundations can rarely achieve high impact by abdicating the decisive role of decision-making to grant-seekers.

THE BENEFITS AND COSTS OF STRATEGY

"Doing strategy," then, is difficult for most foundations. As a result, some resist investing the hard work required in strategy. Others, while paying lip service to the value of strategy, lack the skills and philosophical orientation needed to carry it out effectively. In the end, does it really matter? Why is strategy so important for foundations in the first place?

The most important benefit of thinking strategically is that it significantly increases the impact of a foundation's spending. When a foundation is consciously strategic in its choices, it selects the specific program areas it most cares about and restricts its activities to those areas, thereby focusing a larger stream of resources on a narrower target. This raises the odds of a major impact enormously.

Equally important, if not more so, the discipline of strategy also makes it easier for a foundation to assess the impact of its initiatives. When foundation staff concentrate their attention on one or a few program areas, they have a chance to become expert in those areas, and therefore competent to judge the effectiveness of particular initiatives. Moreover, without some formal strategic framework, it is virtually impossible for a foundation to know whether it is succeeding in achieving its goals. In other words, choosing a strategy forces the articulation of both the goal and the benchmarks by which the goal's achievement can be ascertained.

But being strategic isn't without cost. There's inevitably a trade-off between strategic focus and the lure of opportunistic grantmaking. Strategic focus can easily become a straitjacket that precludes support of promising but unforeseen ideas. To balance strategic focus with flexibility, foundations should take pains to reserve contingency funds for serendipitous opportunities that may arise *within* their target areas. (Somewhat paradoxically, discovery of such unpredictable opportunities is actually *more* likely when a foundation is strategically focused, since staff who are delving deeply into a particular problem area will often learn about promising small programs the nonexpert would never encounter.) Foundations may also choose to create a separate contingency fund for opportunistic grant-making outside of their target areas. However, this fund should probably be limited to a predetermined percentage of total grantmaking—say, 20 to 25 percent—to prevent the watering down of the overall program through unplanned, scattershot giving. (Smaller foundations might want to reduce this percentage—perhaps to the 12 to 15 percent range.)

There are trade-offs, too, between an exceedingly narrow, exclusive strategic focus and one that is more loosely defined. Lee Shulman, president of the Carnegie Foundation for the Advancement of Teaching, argues that a foundation must sow seeds as widely as possible because it cannot know in advance which, if any, will take root. Shulman points out that, whereas a tightly strategic approach might involve sowing only one seed after careful analysis and risk assessment, the standard venture capital approach would be to sow ten seeds in the expectation that one of them will be likely to succeed. Furthermore, he notes, even this decision doesn't exhaust the issues to be considered, since those ten seeds could either represent variations of the same strategy (ten experimental clinics in different regions of the country, for example) or ten different strategies (a clinic, a health educational center, a hospital unit, an endowed chair at a medical school, and so on).[70]

Yet another variation on the spectrum between tight focus and wide-open opportunism involves making an unrestricted grant to a particular group or individual for the express purpose of generating a range of innovative ideas. Frank Karel, a leader in foundation communication with many years of experience at the Commonwealth Fund, the Robert Wood Johnson Foundation, and the Rockefeller Foundation, reports that an opportunistic five-hundred-thousand-dollar Commonwealth Fund grant to the dean of the Johns Hopkins School of Medicine for unspecified new initiatives spawned several new, important initiatives—none of which could have been planned in advance based on a particular strategic focus.

Remaining open to such opportunistic grantmaking leaves room for the unexpected, the creative, and the surprising, as well as the spontaneous transfer of ideas and insights from one field to another, seemingly unrelated field (not unlike the cross-fertilization that underlies many major scientific advances, as described by historian and journalist Arthur Koestler in his book *The Sleepwalkers*). Unplanned grantmaking also gives meaning to the continual networking that the best foundation officers practice within their areas of expertise and interest. After all, representatives of the non-profit world would surely consider it a waste of energy to devote time to interacting with foundation staff if they knew in advance that no un-planned grantmaking could ever result.

Finally, a too-rigid approach to strategy can also make it difficult for a foundation to alter its approach to grantmaking based on what it learns from previous experience. A case in point is the contrast between liberal and conservative foundations in their approach to education reform in the 1980s and 1990s. The liberal foundations tended to select and fund spe-cific reform ideas all at once, which diminished the possibility of support for later-developing alternative concepts. On the other hand, the conserva-tive foundations first stuck their toes in the water by fertilizing a number of different approaches and only later supported the most promising ideas on a larger scale, as described by Stanford Professor William Damon:

> The conservative foundations went about education reform in the right way. They supported a number of people to write about the idea of vouchers and charter schools, and did not immediately try to imple-ment any of the ideas massively. Instead the various notions that were advanced were picked up by housewives and many others with a vari-ety of notions about how to configure the charter schools. The charter school movement is therefore highly variegated. How the people in the charter movement have spread the charter idea is very much like the many different, often conflicting, ways people have applied Howard Gardner's "multiple intelligence" insights.[71]

The narrower and more rigid the strategic focus, then, the less able the foundation will be to respond to unanticipated targets of opportunity.

THE FIRST CHOICE:
AN AREA OF PROGRAM FOCUS

The first step in strategy formulation is choosing one or more program areas that the foundation will focus on. There is no objective way to make this choice. Instead, it is usually guided by the interests, passions, or obsessions of the foundation's donor. During his lifetime, the donor may personally direct the foundation's activities, ensuring that the focus remains squarely on his area of interest. Once the donor has passed from the scene, his influence may be perpetuated through the foundation's trust indenture or other founding document. In the trust indenture by which James Buchanan Duke created the Duke Endowment, he required that the entire endowment document be read aloud annually at a trustees' meeting, just to ensure that his (almost literal) "voice from the grave" would continue to shape their deliberations and decisions.

Ultimately, however, after the death of the founder, the subjective preferences of the trustees will determine the focus of the foundation. Occasionally a board of trustees will choose to leave this most fundamental of decisions to the chief executive officer it recruits, as the Markle Foundation did in 1967 when it persuaded Lloyd Morrisett to leave his Carnegie Corporation vice presidency to become Markle's CEO. This is rare, however. More often, program continuity prevails, driven by prior commitments made by the donor or the trustees, and incoming CEOs have only modest latitude to make changes in the primary program focus.

Once the program focus has been determined, subjectivity should yield to meticulous objective analysis in identifying the problems within the field of focus that are most urgently in need of attention and seem ripest for solving within the foundation's time frame. Often a foundation will engage consultants to survey influential experts in the field to help guide these choices.

One of the most promising ways of surfacing possible problems for future foundation action is the "Appraisal List" used by President John Gardner at the Carnegie Corporation of New York. According to former Carnegie program officer Arthur Singer, Gardner defined "appraisals" as problems or situations within society that required new ideas or approaches. "Staff members," Singer says, "were encouraged to add items to the list as they thought of them from time to time."[72] The value of the appraisal system is that it makes the surfacing of potential foundation challenges into an ongoing process in which program staff members are continually engaged. This method increases the odds that no significant, relevant opportunity will be overlooked.

This, then, is an overview of the role of strategy in foundation leadership. Now we're ready to plunge into a more detailed analysis of the kinds of strategic choices foundations must make. That is the subject of our next chapter.

6

FOUNDATION STRATEGY

IN PRACTICE

God is in the details.

———

Ludwig Mies van der Rohe[73]

A Handful of Strategies and Many Tactics

Given how many foundations there are and how wide an array of projects they have successfully supported over the past century, it's remarkable how few and simple are the distinct strategies they've employed. At a more granular level, however, the number of tactics—specific steps taken in support of broader strategies—is quite large. In this chapter, we'll consider the basic strategies that foundations have pursued as well as some of the specific tactics most frequently used in support of each. In considering the strategies and tactics, I want to underscore again the fact that the line between tactics and strategy is not a bright one, and the assignment of a particular activity to one list or the other is an imprecise exercise. Moreover, the examples, of course, are illustrative only and far from exhaustive. The major examples described in this chapter can be found in the cases listed in the Appendix.

Strategy 1: Creating and Disseminating Knowledge

From seeking causes and cures for disease to plumbing the oceans to tracing the sources of social ills and devising remedies for them, knowledge creation has been a staple of foundation grantmaking initiatives. In some cases, foundations support knowledge creation for its own sake; in other cases, as part of a program to educate and enlighten the public about policy matters. In pursuit of this strategy, foundations have developed a number of specific tactics that have proven effective.

Founding an institution to support basic research. When a foundation detects a gap in the academic or research landscape, it may choose to found an institution designed to fill that gap by focusing on a particular area of knowledge. An early example in the field of basic biomedical research was the establishment in 1901 of the Rockefeller Institute of Medical Research (now Rockefeller University), which John D. Rockefeller Sr., and his philanthropic advisor Frederick T. Gates hoped would be a standard-setting scientific institution comparable to the Pasteur Institute in Paris.[74] Half a century later, the Howard Hughes Medical Institute was founded with a similar mission— world-class basic scientific research, focusing specifically on molecular genetics, structural biology, and bioinformatics. Both institutions have had major impact. Rockefeller University has more Nobel laureates on its faculty than any other university in the United States, while the Hughes Institute has had four Nobel Prize winners in the past five years alone.

Comparable institutions have been created by foundations in the social sciences. The Pew Trusts' Research Center on the People and the Press provides highly respected research on public attitudes toward politics, religion, the press, and other issues, while their Global Attitudes Project provides the only reliable worldwide opinion research on comparative public attitudes on the same questions—such as their views toward the United States. The Moscow Research Center of the Carnegie Endowment for International Peace has built the first objective, reliable community of researchers on Russian politics, economics, and international relations.

Founding an institution to promote public policy awareness. Institutions started by foundations with the goal of shaping public policy knowledge and attitudes include the Brookings Institution, the Urban Institute, the Center on Budget and Policy Priorities, Resources for the Future, Public/Private Ventures, the Manpower Demonstration Research Corporation, the National Bureau of Economic Research, and the National Research Council of the National Academy of Sciences.

Each specializes in a particular range of policy issues, generating a stream of relevant data and high-quality proposals for solutions.[75] Because they bring to bear on those problems accepted analytic and methodological skills of high quality, the products of their researchers have gained widespread credibility among other researchers, policy makers, the press, and the public, making them the authoritative providers of reliable, evidence-based policy solutions on their areas of focus.[76] For example, the Russell Sage Foundation has become a prime source for authoritative research on the problems of the poor in America. Half of its $12 million budget is spent on scholars in residence, half on grants to other institutions.

Some of the policy initiatives supported by such institutions have been highly influential. For instance, the Center on Budget and Policy Priorities has been primarily responsible for the adoption by most states of the Earned Income Tax Credit, the single most important government-financed lever for helping the working poor.

Founding an institution to promote specific reforms. The Police Foundation, originally created by the Ford Foundation, is widely credited with transforming the practices of local police departments. It has trained many police chiefs in neighborhood and community policing, crime mapping, improved methods for dealing with domestic violence, new technologies for criminal identification, risk analysis management systems, and quality of service indicators. As a result, the incidence of serious crime has fallen in many cities, which are also better equipped to deal with potential terrorist threats.

A similar example is the Ford Foundation's support of the VERA Institute, founded by the creative "social entrepreneur" Herbert Sturz. The Institute's Bail Project, which developed the Release on Recognizance method of assessing accused persons, has significantly reduced the need to rely on posting bail to ensure attendance at trial. The government of South Africa recently invited the VERA Institute to help improve the administration of criminal justice in that country.

A very different kind of knowledge-disseminating institution is J-Stor, founded by the Andrew Mellon Foundation. Its mission is to digitize major scholarly journals and make their archives available online, thereby easing the space crunch at hundreds of college and university libraries as well as making scholarly knowledge available to students worldwide whose libraries can't afford subscriptions to every major journal.

Founding an institution to research and solve a specific problem. In recent years, many foundations have targeted particular research problems for solution, usually with the goal of priming more extensive efforts by government and/or profit-sector organizations. Recent examples include the Aaron Diamond AIDS Research Center in New York City, which has attracted significant government support, and the Rockefeller and Sloan foundations' International AIDS Vaccine Initiative, supported by two $250 million grants in 2004 and 2005 from the Bill and Melinda Gates Foundation, which appears to have stimulated the $300-million commitment by the National Institutes of Health to a "Manhattan Project" aimed at finding an AIDS vaccine. The Gates Foundation has also announced a $437-million initiative to jumpstart a large number of targeted biomedical projects with specified deliverables and target dates, tagged "chutzpah science" by *Forbes* magazine.[77]

In the social sciences, a good example of research targeting is the National Violent Death Reporting System, supported by the Joyce Foundation and Atlantic Philanthropies, which tracks the use of handguns in violent deaths. Another is the Andrew Mellon Foundation's College and Beyond Research Project, which has created a unique longitudinal database about the experiences and attitudes of a large group of college and university students. These data have already made possible at least two influential studies, *The Shape of the River* by William Bowen and Derek Bok, which helped to shape recent court decisions on the constitutionality of affirmative action, and *The Game of Life* by Bowen and James L. Shulman, which examines collegiate athletics.[78]

Launching a new field of scholarly study or professional practice. A number of important scholarly fields owe their existence and spread to support from foundations, including molecular biology (originally seeded by the Rockefeller Foundation), computational neurobiology (the Sloan Foundation), area studies (the Ford Foundation), international security and arms control (the Rockefeller Foundation), and alternative dispute resolution (the Hewlett Foundation).

Among the efforts to create new fields of professional practice are the Commonwealth Fund's development, with the Robert Wood Johnson Foundation, of the professions of nurse practitioner and physician assistant/associate; the Commonwealth Fund's support for the creation of schools of social work and welfare, as well as the hospice care movement; and several foundation initiatives to develop medical geriatrics and gerontology. Those foundations that have stayed with such research have contributed mightily to beneficial social change.

There also have been highly successful strategies to reform fields of professional training, such as the Ford Foundation's support for quantification of business school curricula, the Carnegie and Rockefeller foundations' support for the Flexner reform of medical school curricula, and the Carnegie Corporation's reform of legal education and admission to law practice. Countless efforts have sought to reform the training of teachers and administrators in elementary and high schools. For example, the Carnegie Corporation and other foundations helped establish the National Board for Professional Teaching Standards, which has created the first widely recognized form of national teacher certification in substantive fields of learning, while the New Standards Project of the Pew Charitable Trusts has played a critical role in the development of tests and teaching materials for measuring student achievement.

Sustaining a traditional field of scholarly inquiry. Several foundations have helped to preserve fields that are suffering declines in student popularity and loss of faculty, especially in the humanities. The Andrew Mellon Foundation is the leader in this area. It has endowed numerous professorships, graduate instructorships, and postdoctoral fellowships; made grants to keep alive specific forms of humanistic scholarship, such as manuscript writing and archival training; and supported the application of information technology to humanistic research, especially in the fields of literature and history.

Strategy 2: Building Human Capital

Although it is impossible conclusively to demonstrate the impact of strategies aimed at building human capital, I'm convinced that such impacts exist. The logic on which such programs rest was summarized by L. K. Frank in *The Status of Social Science in the United States*, a 1923 report commissioned by Beardsley Ruml, president of the Laura Spelman Rockefeller Memorial, which became part of the Rockefeller Foundation in 1929. Frank wrote:

> [I]t should be remembered that these [doctoral] fellows will be the future teachers of social science, who would, by this training, be emancipated, in part at least, from the traditional conceptual thinking and

a priori generalizations of the present generation of teachers. Thus the processes of changing the formalized teaching of social science would be started with the young students of today and a way out of the speculative inertia of social science opened.[79]

As Frank suggested, the building and rebuilding of human capital is the only way society can refresh and renew itself. If we do not train young people (and retrain their elders) in new skills, new theory, new science, and new technology, society will stagnate. If a human-capital-building initiative is well-designed, its impact will be high because each person trained is transformed into an engine of social benefit.

Here are a few examples of the kinds of human capital programs that have been supported by foundations.

Undergraduate scholarships for leadership development. Foundations have endowed many undergraduate scholarships based on merit, need, or both, usually with leadership potential among the important qualifications. The merit-based John M. Morehead Foundation Scholarships to the University of North Carolina at Chapel Hill, described by the foundation as "the premier merit award for undergraduate study in the United States," are now over fifty years old and are open to any high school graduate in North Carolina, the United Kingdom and Canada, as well as to students recommended by selected secondary schools and cooperating programs and institutions.[80] The Duke Endowment has established similar scholarships at Duke University, including the Angier B. Duke and Benjamin N. Duke Scholarships.

Other undergraduate scholarships are targeted to particular fields or demographic groups. For example, the Clare Booth Luce undergraduate scholarships, sponsored by the Henry Luce Foundation, are available at thirteen designated four-year institutions to women interested in science, engineering, and mathematics.[81] The Freeman Foundation focuses on East Asian Studies, supporting appointments of faculty members and undergraduate scholarships. The foundation credits its strategy with a 20 percent increase in the number of U.S. students studying East Asian topics.

Fellowships for graduate study. A few graduate fellowships sponsored by foundations are unrestricted as to subject matter. The Rhodes Scholarships to Oxford University have long been among the most prestigious available for postgraduate study, while the similar Gates-Cambridge Scholarships are of more recent vintage. The Danforth Fellowships, created by the Danforth Foundation, fall into this category. Most graduate fellowships, however, target particular fields or student groups. For example, the Clare Booth Luce graduate fellowships for women have restrictions identical with those of the undergraduate scholarships.

The Ford Foundation targets minority group members; for instance, in 2000, Ford created the International Fellowship Program to give fellowships "to individuals from groups or communities that lack systematic access to higher education."[82] The program involves the largest fellowship grant in the foundation's history—now over half a billion dollars—and will provide 3,500 fellowships to experienced leaders who will later return to their developing-world communities.

Fellowships for post-graduate research or writing. Among the most prestigious fellowships for post-graduate work are the John Simon Guggenheim Memorial Foundation fellowships, which serve a wide variety of fields of academic scholarship and the nonperforming arts. Most other postgraduate fellowships target particular problems and specified social gaps. Among the most successful are the Robert Wood Johnson Foundation Clinical Scholars Program, which has created a new cadre of medically trained scholars proficient in clinical research on public health policy and epidemiology, and the Beeson Fellows for Geriatrics and Gerontology Program supported by the Hartford Foundation, the Commonwealth Fund, and Atlantic Philanthropies, which provides physicians with additional training in diseases of the aging and elderly.

From 1942 to 1967, the Markle Foundation made generous five-year unrestricted fellowship awards to promising young medical researchers. As with many such programs, the Markle Fellows gathered annually for networking and community-building. Many fellows later became prominent researchers and leaders in medical school administration. The Markle Fellows program was terminated only because of the flood of federal money that began to flow into medical research at the end of the 1960s. Since 1988, the David and Lucile Packard Foundation has been running a similar program that provides sixteen five-year fellowships to unusually creative scientists and engineers.

The oldest and largest foundation-backed fellowship program in the nation is the Alfred P. Sloan Research Fellowships. Launched in 1955, the program began with a focus on physics, chemistry, and mathematics, and has gradually expanded to encompass neuroscience, computer science, economics, and computational and evolutionary molecular biology. Today, 116 Sloan Research Fellowships are awarded each year. According to the foundation, "thirty-two Sloan Fellows have won Nobel Prizes later in their careers, and hundreds have received other honors."[83]

Fellowships for adult leadership and creative expression. Among the most famous of all fellowships are the MacArthur Foundation's so-called genius awards. Totally unrestricted as to field, these fellowships cannot be applied for but are awarded on the basis of confidential recommendations from a network of secret nominators around the nation. They require no specified duties other than to continue with one's life work.

Other adult leadership programs are typically targeted to particular fields of inquiry or personal background. For instance, the fellows program of the Wexner Heritage Foundation has become perhaps the most prestigious such program for rising Jewish leaders. The program selects, by nomination and screening, around twenty Jewish community leaders from across the United States, usually between the ages of thirty and forty-five, to participate in a year-long series of in-community seminars and out-of-town summer institutes, aiming to provide enrichment education about Judaism and current issues facing the Jewish people.

Strategy 3: Public Policy Advocacy

In all of the areas in which foundations do grantmaking, from environmental policy and medical research to civil rights, education, and the arts, foundations supply a large—perhaps even the largest—share of the advocacy dollars. One of the tactical approaches used here is to support existing groups that are already active in a particular area.

Supporting an existing advocacy organization. The advocacy organizations supported by foundations generally use a combination of approaches, including comprehensive research, membership building, and publication and dissemination of information. Some also lobby for changes in law or regulatory practice, although I'll reserve my discussion of such efforts for a separate section later in the chapter.

A popular category of advocacy activity is that of the disease-focused cause organization. Virtually every common illness—and many that are not so common—has its advocacy group, and most are buoyed by foundation support. For example, many foundations, including Atlantic Philanthropies, support what is now called the Christopher Reeve Paralysis Foundation, which performs advocacy as well as supporting researchers seeking methods whereby spinal nerves damaged in accidents can be regenerated. The Milken Family Foundation focuses its medical grantmaking on prostate cancer and epilepsy and has created a spin-off foundation, the Prostate Cancer Foundation, which raised more than two hundred million dollars between 1993 and 2003 to support advocacy efforts and research.[84]

Many nonmedical advocacy organizations are supported by foundations, including such well-known and influential groups as the Council on Foreign Relations, the American Civil Liberties Union, Amnesty International, and the United Nations Association.

Launching a new advocacy initiative. Some foundations choose to finance their own advocacy initiatives. A recent—and dramatically successful—example is the MacArthur Foundation's nuclear threat reduction program, which helped facilitate an agreement between the United States and Russia on the destruction of nuclear materials following the collapse of the Soviet Union.

Some foundations have created new institutions to spearhead advocacy of policies of interest to them. For example, the Population Council was established with foundation support to advocate policy change and practical programs for family planning and birth control. Human Rights Watch was established with significant early grants from the Ford Foundation and the MacArthur Foundations, and has received steady support from the Open Society Institute. Other newly established advocacy institutions include the Violence Policy Center, which the National Rifle Association labels "the most effective anti-gun . . . rabble-rouser in Washington,"[85] and the widely praised Center for Public Integrity, which has become a leading investigative research institution focusing on issues like arms trafficking, corporate crime, terrorism, and human rights.[86]

On the international front, Michael Posner, founder and CEO of Human Rights First (formerly the Lawyers Committee for Human Rights), credits the Ford Foundation for providing start-up money to indigenous human rights organizations in many countries around the world. "Ford went in," Posner says, "with the intention of funding change agents willing—perhaps eager—to take personal risks in bringing about change."[87] The effort has been enormously fruitful. According to Posner, prior to Ford's involvement, countries such as North Korea and Saudi Arabia were entirely without such organizations. Today, there are two to three *thousand* groups around the world working on behalf of human rights, many of which owe their existence to Ford's support.

A final example of effective advocacy. For more than fifty years the Albert and Mary Lasker Foundation has energetically, and with great success, waged a campaign to increase federal funding for medical research, and has done so both by making prestigious awards institutionally and indirectly by personal lobbying by Mary Lasker. According to the foundation, its mission is "to enlarge public awareness, appreciation and understanding of promising achievements in medical science in order to increase public support for medical research."[88] As the case prepared for this book documents, the Lasker Foundation is widely credited with bringing about the huge increase in federal research support for cancer and other diseases.

Strategy 4: Changing Public Attitudes

Subtly different from policy advocacy is the strategy of shifting public opinion on a particular issue. Here the focus is less on informing influential decision-makers such as political, business, and academic leaders and more on educating the general public.

One of the most dramatic and successful efforts at changing public attitudes has been the Ted Turner Foundation's initiative focused on the issue of UN dues owed by the U.S. government. The foundation orchestrated an effective campaign to crystallize public support for paying the back dues as well as discreet efforts to lobby Congress and the administration to the same end.[89]

Another initiative that succeeded in changing minds and laws was the Robert Wood Johnson Foundation's youth antismoking campaign, which is credited with reducing smoking by teenagers through public information programs and efforts to encourage tax increases on cigarettes. Other examples include the Pew Charitable Trusts' Sustainable Environment Program, which steadily played a significant role in changing attitudes about global warming; the MacArthur Foundation's Biodiversity Protection Program; the Surdna Foundation's Smart Growth Initiative; the Open Society Institute's program to legalize some forms of drug use; the Bradley Foundation's school choice program; and the Commonwealth Fund's hospice care program.

Strategy 5: Changing the Law

In the first half of the twentieth century, foundations were reluctant to engage actively in bringing about changes in the law. This reluctance began to weaken around mid-century, beginning with grants to civil rights organizations that lobbied for fair housing laws and brought lawsuits attacking segregation in education. Foundations soon embraced strategies focused on legislation and litigation in many other fields, including fair employment practices, voter registration for blacks and other minorities, women's rights, consumer protection, and environmentalism.

The Ford Foundation was particularly active in these areas, providing start-up and continuing grants for the Mexican-American Legal Defense Fund, La Raza, and the Puerto Rican Legal Defense Fund; the Natural Resources Defense Council and the Environmental Defense Fund (now simply Environmental Defense); and numerous general public-interest law centers. One especially successful program was the Women's Law Project of the American Civil Liberties Union, supported initially by the Ford Foundation and later by other philanthropies. Headed by Ruth Bader Ginsburg, who later became an associate justice of the U.S. Supreme Court, the project developed strategies for both legislation and litigation to expand the rights of women in employment and other fields.

TACTICS THAT CROSS STRATEGIC LINES

So far, we have looked at several core strategies that foundations have used over the years, together with specific kinds of tactical implementation for those strategies. In the rest of this chapter, I'll consider a number of tactics that may be used in conjunction with one or more broad strategies. Taken together, these tactics constitute a kind of tool kit that foundation managers can draw upon as needed to drive change in the directions they hope to move society.

Convening a conference, meeting, or strategy session. This tactic can serve several different purposes, all of which take advantage of a foundation's inherent convening power. Sometimes a foundation convenes a meeting of experts from a field of foundation interest as a means of informing staff or trustees about desirable areas of grantmaking. A foundation may bring together representatives of other foundations to introduce a new initiative in hopes that they will join in funding it. After a foundation has made a series of grants in a particular field, it may convene a meeting of grantees to encourage networking, spread mutual learning, and promote cooperation. (The Milken Family Foundation requires its prostate cancer research grantees to attend conferences with other grantees for just this purpose.)

Holding a conference is relatively easy for most foundations, since most nonprofit leaders are eager to respond favorably to an invitation from a foundation that may provide support in the future. When the Robert Wood Johnson Foundation was just getting started in 1972, its first national program was aimed at creating the National Emergency Response System we now associate with the 911 phone number. One of the first steps: a conference in San Bernardino County, California, attended by representatives of every county agency involved in emergency response—reportedly the first time they'd all been gathered in the same room. According to Warren Wood, the foundation's general counsel, similar meetings were later held in every state of the union, which illustrates the "power to convene" that many foundations enjoy.[90]

Creating a blue-ribbon commission. The idea is simple: Recruit a group of experts with recognizable names to study a problem and propose solutions to it. Then use the reputations of the experts to attract attention and generate momentum to implement those solutions.

Sometimes, the blue-ribbon-commission tactic works brilliantly. The Public Broadcasting System Commission (1966–67) and the Commission on Higher Education (1967–70), both funded by the Carnegie Corporation of New York, succeeded in catalyzing legislation to implement their respective recommendations. The fact that PBS and the Commission on Higher Education worked the way they were intended does not mean that all such commissions succeed. On the contrary, most such foundation-established commissions are convened, meet, publish reports that are promptly forgotten and are never heard of again. For example, Carnegie's follow-up commission on the Future of Public Broadcasting (1978) had no discernible impact.

What makes the difference? It depends on several factors: the magnitude of the problem, the reputations of the commissioners and their appropriateness to the problem, and, most of all, the strategies and tactics employed by the commission and the foundation for implementing their ideas.

The first Public Broadcasting Commission offers a case study in how to do a commission right. Arthur L. Singer Jr., the Carnegie program officer who conceived the idea, recruited as commission chair James R. Killian Jr., chairman of the Massachusetts Institute of Technology Corporation, who was a highly regarded scientist and public figure. Singer then persuaded Killian to hire Steven White, an acerbic but brilliant writer as his staff director. White, Killian, and Singer then personally handpicked and recruited each member of the commission, ensuring that a first-rate team of complementary talents would be assembled.

As the commission's work proceeded, its leaders met regularly with key stakeholders, including the heads of the three major television networks, the leaders of the Ford Foundation (prominent in supporting educational television), and significant political leaders, from members of Congress and relevant Hill committee chairs and staff, to S. Douglass Cater, assistant to President Lyndon Johnson. Finally, once the commission's ideas were fully formed, it hired the law firm of Wilmer Cutler and Pickering (now Wilmer Cutler Pickering Hale and Dorr) to draft a bill incorporating those ideas, arranged to have it sponsored by a number of congressmen, and then organized a lobby—Friends of Public Television—to promote the bill.

As Arthur Singer says, "The key to success was that we had neutralized all possible opposition. AND we had the right chairman, the right thinker/writer, and we carefully implemented the plan."[91] Other foundations that are considering using a blue-ribbon commission as a tactic for tackling a problem would do well to use this example as a blueprint.

Offering an award or prize. Sometimes giving an award to which a significant sum of money is attached can be an effective tactic for drawing attention to a specific policy goal or broader social value. When a large award and a high-profile recipient can be brought together, media coverage and a forum for the ideas being promoted are almost guaranteed.

Many observers of the nonprofit scene cite the Goldman Environmental Prize, an initiative of the Richard and Rhoda Goldman Foundation of San Francisco, as a powerful force in spreading public knowledge about critical environmental issues and fostering effective responses to the problems. The foundation describes the prize, which confers a total of $750,000 each year upon "environmental heroes from six continental regions," as "the world's largest prize program honoring grassroots environmentalists."[92]

For almost fifty years, the Lasker Awards Program for Basic and Clinical Medical Research and Public Service has focused attention on "an elite community of basic and clinical scientists whose work has been seminal to understanding disease and the human being's capacity to overcome it."[93] According to the Lasker Foundation, more than half of the recipients of the award have subsequently won Nobel Prizes in medicine.

Instead of awarding prizes to individuals, the Ford Foundation created an annual competition for the most innovative programs across state and local government, awarding $100,000 to each of fifteen winners and $20,000 to fifteen runners-up. Innovations in American Government is administered for the foundation by Harvard's Kennedy School of Government and helps spread new ways of solving programs more broadly across the national landscape.

Among other major foundation prizes that have surfaced recently, consider the Kavli Foundation's three-million-dollar prizes in astrophysics, nanoscience, and neuroscience—fields currently neglected by the Nobel Foundation. The Kavli prizes are to be awarded every two years starting in 2008 in a ceremony in Oslo, Norway, strikingly similar to the Nobel ceremony.[94]

While virtually all foundation prizes are used to recognize recipients for their achievements that occurred in the past, some foundations have recently begun to award prizes as an incentive to individuals to achieve desired results in the future. An example of such an incentivizing prize is the ten-million-dollar X Prize offered by Peter Diamandis's X Prize Foundation for the first private space flight. The distinction between recognition and incentivizing prizes was first pointed out to me by Matt Leerberg, an exceptional student in my Duke course on philanthropy in 2006.[95]

Building a model through a pilot program. One of the most common tactics used by foundations to bring about strategic change is to create a pilot or demonstration program in the hope that others will replicate it widely. An example is the Commonwealth Fund's Picker health-care program, the first foundation effort to focus on measuring the quality of medical care from the patient's perspective. It led directly to the establishment of the National Center for Quality Assurance, which now rates managed-care performance for the Department of Health and Human Services, as well as Medicare's Consumer Assessment of Health Plans Program. Both programs replicate the model pioneered by Picker.

Similar model building characterizes Fordham's and Walton's charter school reform program, Bradley's school voucher program, Surdna's Smart Growth program, MDRC's welfare-to-work demonstration programs, and many others.

The main problem with model building is that most foundations—unlike the Ford and Robert Wood Johnson Foundations, for example—usually do *not* stick with the task long enough to reap its full benefits. Most simply build the model, sustain it for a few years, and leave it to others to learn or not to learn from their work. Unfortunately, this isn't enough to drive meaningful social change. Model building works only when a foundation nurtures the model into self-sustainability and replicates it with enough copies to launch the network on a course of sustainable growth.

Financing litigation. Many foundations still shy away from supporting litigation, for obvious reasons: doing so is inherently controversial and likely to generate publicity, not all of it favorable. Among the large foundations, only Ford and, to a lesser degree, Carnegie, have been consistently open to supporting organizations that rely heavily on litigation, and Ford followed this route only after considerable internal debate under McGeorge Bundy. However, a number of small foundations, such as the J. Roderick MacArthur Foundation and the Taconic Foundation, regularly provide grants to organizations to bring specific lawsuits in the areas of human rights and civil liberties. A number of foundations are continuing to provide substantial support for educational equity cases now in the courts that challenge existing patterns of public school financing. The New York–based Campaign for Fiscal Equity, founded in 1993 by some twenty foundations, including Atlantic Philanthropies, Carnegie Corporation of New York, the Rockefeller Brothers Fund, and the Bill and Melinda Gates Foundation, is the best known. It has already won several court victories.[96]

Building institutions. As we've seen, foundations often pursue their strategic goals by building civic-sector institutions of all kinds, from knowledge-developing to policy-research to constituency-serving. Elizabeth Locke describes the work of the foundation she formerly headed this way: "The Duke Endowment is about building institutions, not about solving problems."[97] Her words could apply to many other foundations. For example, Ellen Condliffe Lagemann, who has written the two most authoritative foundation histories, has commented: "In the end, therefore, it was the Carnegie Corporation's capacity to build institutions that would serve as arenas for the politics of knowledge that was most enduringly significant."[98] She bases that conclusion on the impressive list of institutions that in part owe their existence to Carnegie support, including the National Research Council, the Carnegie Institution of Washington, the Carnegie Endowment for International Peace, the American Law Institute, and the National Bureau of Economic Research.

Building an effective institution to address a social problem is no simple task. It calls for accurate analysis of the problem, insightful understanding of the potential solution, and commitment to nurturing the fledgling institution.

Consider, for example, the Ford Foundation's effort to address the problems of insufficient decent housing and job opportunities in impoverished rural and urban areas, led by Mitchell (Mike) Sviridoff, Ford's vice president for national affairs during the late 1960s and 1970s. Sviridoff recognized that the problem was a classic market failure resulting from the lack of information—reliable assessments of borrowers' credit-worthiness—which is essential to opening the flow of dollars from for-profit financial institutions, corporations, and government. His solution was to create a new entity—the Local Initiatives Support Corporation (LISC)—to fill the knowledge-generating need. LISC would assess the creditworthiness of potential low-income borrowers and certify those who were likely to repay. This simple mechanism helped billions of dollars flow to build housing and create jobs. Sviridoff himself was so committed to LISC that he resigned his position at Ford to become its first president.

Building physical plant. Most foundations avoid making grants to help build buildings. They prefer to leave these kinds of projects to individuals, who are often attracted by the possibility of having a building named in their honor. But a few foundations do take on this role, including Kresge and Olin (building buildings on college campuses), MacArthur (particularly through its Chicago Public Housing Replacement initiative), the Andrew Mellon Foundation (which builds libraries in Central and Eastern Europe and built the East Wing of the National Gallery of Art in Washington), and the Getty Trust (which makes grants to restore historic buildings on college campuses). The Carnegie Corporation of New York made a grant to build Carnegie Hall, and Carnegie philanthropy should also be credited for the buildings built for the Pan American Union in Washington, the Central American Court of Justice in Costa Rica, and the International Court of Justice in The Hague, as well as the 2,509 Carnegie libraries. The Rosenwald Fund built nearly five thousand schoolhouses for African Americans in the South.

Catalyzing partnerships among foundations. Partnerships among foundations are relatively rare. Every foundation, of course, is happy to have its favorite initiatives supported by others, but few are eager to volunteer support to programs launched by others. Blame it on ego, politics, turf, or desire for control, basic factors of human motivation that make partnership-creation unusually difficult.

However, there have been exceptions. The National Community Development Initiative (now called Living Cities) brought a dozen or so foundations to the table for a joint effort in community development in urban and rural areas. The Energy Foundation, launched by the Pew Trusts, the Ford Foundation, and the MacArthur Foundation has lost its founding foundations but has gained two others as partners—Hewlett and Packard. And recently, under the leadership of the Bill and Melinda Gates Foundation, the Carnegie Corporation and the Rockefeller Foundation have joined in a funding collaborative to create small high-involvement schools out of large public schools.

Occasionally a group of foundations will form a partnership to nurture to self-sustainability a particular organization they all consider important. That was the case with Guidestar, the Internet-based provider of IRS Form 990 data on civic-sector organizations. Some eleven foundations worked together continuously for six years to get Guidestar on its feet, and most of them still continue to provide support.

In the partnerships described so far, one foundation generally took the lead and solicited support from others without relinquishing ultimate guidance of the program. True partnerships in which contributors collectively decide how all the money will be spent are rare. One of the few was an initiative by the Charles Revson Foundation, led for more than two decades by Eli Evans after a stint at the Carnegie Corporation of New

York. Evans created a partnership of foundations, corporations, and law schools whose goal was to increase the number of black civil rights lawyers in the late 1960s and early 1970s.

Evans reports:

> It was the partnership idea, a partnership that is based on trust that you had to earn and that worked because your partners would give you money to spend if they trusted you to do it well—and also trusted you not to take all the credit. I had to work hard at it, I had to keep everyone informed, and I had to involve them when they wanted to be involved. . . . Partnership—true partnership and not leverage—is the key. . . . The idea has to be good, you have to believe in it, you have to focus on it and you have to persist in it for a long time.[99]

I would add only that such partnerships as Evans describes are all too rare because so many obstacles—turf, ego, control, limelight, among others—operate to deter foundations from subordinating to others their respective final says about allocating their respective money. Evans's achievement is all the more noteworthy because of his success in overcoming those obstacles.

Catalyzing partnerships with the for-profit sector. These partnerships resemble the common partnerships between grant-receiving civic-sector organizations and corporations. Examples include the partnership between the Edna McConnell Clark Foundation and Pfizer, Inc., to tackle blindness-causing tropical diseases; the partnership between the Pew Charitable Trusts and Knight-Ridder Newspapers to further the trusts' Civic Journalism initiative in the 1990s; and the partnership between the Kaiser Family Foundation and various commercial media organizations, including the *Washington Post*, for priority distribution of its surveys and research reports on health issues.

More often, such foundation/corporation partnerships are catalyzed by grant-receiving organizations. For example, Environmental Defense created a partnership with FedEx and the Eaton Corporation for the development and use of hybrid vehicles, which was supported by the Richard and Rhoda Goldman Fund. A similar initiative was created when the Pew Charitable Trusts made a five-million-dollar grant to Environmental Defense to create the Alliance for Environmental Innovation to support projects with for-profit corporations.

It should become easier for civic-sector organizations to recruit corporate partners as corporations find themselves under increasing political and public-relations pressure to become more socially responsible and environmentally friendly.

Building organizational capacities for the long term. Foundations have often been criticized for keeping grant-receiving organizations on a short leash through two-to-three-year grants rather than longer-term support, and through narrowly defined support of specific projects rather than more flexible support for general operational needs.

Now this is changing, driven in part by the efforts of the Packard Foundation. Packard's "capacity-building grants" set a precedent for longer-term, more flexible foundation support. Packard then helped to establish Grantmakers for Effective Organization, currently the fastest-growing affinity group in the Council on Foundations, which is encouraging the trend.

In 2003, Paul Brest, president of the Hewlett Foundation, took up the cause. He convened a large group of foundations to consider how best to combine the effective use of a strategic framework for grantmaking with greater reliance on general operating support. His proposal for what he called "negotiated general support," which is contingent on agreed-upon performance benchmarks, has been widely praised. Both the Fidelity Foundation and the Edna McConnell Clark Foundation pioneered this approach even before Brest crystallized and named it for others to consider following.

Engaging various media. Thinking out of the box by using this tactic is all too rarely employed by foundations, but it heartens me greatly whenever I run across it. Sometimes it is highly controversial, as when Frank Karel, vice president for communications at the Robert Wood Johnson Foundation, bought prime-time television slots on NBC to air programs countering the pharmaceutical industry's attacks on the Clinton health-reform proposals. No foundation had ever purchased prime-time TV before, and none has since. The Markle Foundation undertook a variant of this approach when it contracted with CNN in the 1992 presidential election to create major program segments on the critical policy issues in that election.

Sometimes, however, programs to use various media engender universal admiration. This was the case when foundations financed the "designated driver" initiative created by the Center for Health Communication of the Harvard School of Public Health, which involved working with Hollywood sitcom producers to highlight the issue of drinking and driving in their shows. Similarly, the decision by the Alfred P. Sloan Foundation, which has a program devoted to improving the public understanding of science, to help produce theatrical plays dealing with scientific subjects has yielded enthusiastic approval. More than a dozen plays have been staged through Sloan's efforts, including the acclaimed dramas *Copenhagen* by Michael Frayn and *Proof* by David Auburn.[100]

.   .   .

Obviously, the list of foundation strategies and tactics provided in this chapter isn't exhaustive. In the years to come, new tools for the foundation leader's kit will continue to be developed by innovative managers, drawing inspiration from their own creativity as well as from initiatives pioneered elsewhere in the for-profit, not-for-profit, and government arenas. But the overview we've provided should help provide a context for the case studies we'll examine more closely in Part 2 of this book, as well as for the in-depth discussion of how foundations can improve their operations in Part 3.

PART

II

7

ACHIEVING IMPACT:

LEADERSHIP, FOCUS,

ALIGNMENT,

AND MEASUREMENT

Time is the test of quality.

———

Lloyd Morrisett, former president,
the John and Mary Markle Foundation[1]

As I hope the reader has noticed by now, one of the central focuses of this book is the *impact* of foundation initiatives. But what is impact? How do we recognize it? How can we measure it? And most important, how can foundations achieve it consistently?

Let me start my exploration of these vital topics by explaining what I think impact is *not*. Where a foundation initiative is concerned, impact is *not* about inputs—that is, the money, time, energy, and effort put into the initiative. Nor is impact measured by outputs—buildings built, scholarships awarded, studies financed, reports published, or even grants made. Rather, impact is the extent to which such inputs and outputs have actually changed society, creating viable new institutions, generating knowledge, creating opportunities, and improving human welfare generally. To measure the impact of a foundation initiative, one must find and record the ripples it creates in society—the broader and deeper the better.

PRACTICAL DIFFICULTIES
IN DETECTING IMPACT

For some classes of foundation initiatives, it is extraordinarily difficult to determine whether there has been any impact and, if so, how to measure that impact. Many of the world's problems are simply too big and too amorphous for foundation impact to be clearly discernible. Thus, when a number of wealthy individuals and small foundations focused on nuclear disarmament in the 1970s and 1980s, the problems proved to be beyond their capacity to accomplish.[2] Yet other foundations' initiatives in the international arena have proven more easily discernible, especially those that were highly focused on a limited, definable goal—developing new food grains, curing particular diseases, or creating a new problem-solving institution such as the International Criminal Court.

At the tactical level, too, the impact of a grant aimed at changing public attitudes by financing the production of documentary films or television programs on a particular subject is very difficult to measure. Any given film is seen by only a tiny fraction of the public, whose identity cannot be determined with any precision. Thus, only a small handful of such films, such as Edward R. Murrow's 1968 report *Hunger in America*, are believed to have had any measurable impact on public attitudes.

Achieving impact takes time, especially when the problem being tackled is large and complex. Time is required, in the early stages of the project, for thorough background research and methodical strategic thinking. Time is also required in the latter stages, when persistence, experimentation, adjustment, and refinement of tactics are required. Thus, recognizing and measuring impact are not tasks that can be done quickly, since impact usually becomes apparent only in the long run.

Impact is also clearly a function of geographical scope. For a large foundation with national or international reach, potential impact may need to be measured on a global stage. By contrast, a community foundation or any other foundation with geographic limitations will focus on a smaller region within which it is much easier to achieve—and detect—meaningful impact in a reasonable period of time.

Finally, any attempt to measure impact must begin by defining the object of change—the ultimate goal of the foundation initiative—and clearly distinguishing it from the means to be employed. Is the object of change an improvement in the environment? In that case, the passage of laws and regulations to control harmful emissions might be means to be employed, while the true measure of impact might be changes in levels of pollution in the air or water. Is the object of change improved economic opportunities for inner-city youth? In that case, creation of a work-training program that enrolls a specified number of young men and women might be the means, while the measure of impact might be the percentage of the participants who obtain and retain jobs, or even an improvement in the income levels, unemployment rates, and crime statistics in the relevant neighborhoods. Defining these parameters clearly and thoughtfully is essential if meaningful impact measurements are to be made.

Theoretical Differences in Detecting Impact

"Success has many fathers, but failure is an orphan."

As this book deals with social impact, and draws such persuasiveness as it has from examples of foundation initiatives that are thought to have produced social impact, a short discussion of causation and counterfactuality is certainly required. Two formidable intellectual problems are involved here. The first is both how to determine the existence and direction of causality—the proximate cause that produced the impact—and how to apportion causation among multiple actors or institutions. The second conundrum is the challenge of counterfactuality—how do we know whether what happened would not have happened anyway without the intervention that we are examining?

When the context in which complex foundation initiatives occur includes many other actors and forces at work, either simultaneously or sequentially, it is impossible to trace causality with absolute certainty. How can anyone identify the foundation initiative as *the* causal force, *the* proximate cause? And the causation analysis is made even more complicated by the fact that, while the foundation may have provided the wherewithal, the initiative was almost always carried out by others outside the foundation. A third factor still further complicates the analysis. Very often the idea for a foundation initiative originated with someone outside the foundation. So, scientifically speaking, it is unsound to attribute to foundations credit for being the cause of any impact that has been achieved.

With regard to counterfactuality in social policy demonstrations, however, there is a workable, if expensive, method of overcoming one's concerns. Some foundations and the research/demonstration organizations that they support have pioneered the use of scientifically constructed social experiments using control groups to eliminate, or at least diminish, any doubts about whether the outcome of the experimental initiative would have occurred anyway. Judith Gueron, for many years the president of Manpower Development Research Corporation and one of the leaders in the field of social experimentation, puts it as follows:

> Control groups are the only reliable way to deal with the counterfactual. Nominal outcomes tell one nothing solid about the impact of particular programs in the absence of the context of those outcomes, and the context of outcomes can best be demonstrated by control groups made up of populations of people similar to those in the experimental groups but who do not receive the experimental treatment. If the control groups show the same or similar outcomes as the experimental groups, then there really is no detectable impact, and one must conclude that the intervention really did not make any difference that wouldn't have occurred absent the intervention.[3]

In other words, impact is outcomes weighed in the scales of counterfactuality. *Impact* is outcomes in *context*.

Unfortunately, it is not practical for foundations to subject all or even most of their initiatives to scientifically rigorous randomized experiments. Most initiatives—such as scholarship and fellowship support, the creation of new institutions to serve a particular social need, efforts to popularize new ways of thinking about social problems, and innumerable other initiatives—simply do not lend themselves at all to randomized experiments. Of those initiatives that do lend themselves to such experiments, only a few are of sufficient potential social significance to warrant the enormous additional cost of subjecting them to experimental design. As we will see later in this book, however, some very consequential initiatives have been subjected to randomized experiments, and some foundations are increasingly employing sound experimental designs to attack counterfactuality.

The overwhelming number of foundation initiatives can never warrant the expense of true experimental designs, and I am convinced that an undue concern for unambiguously establishing causation could paralyze not only research but also action. If we assume that we can never know what would have happened had we not acted ourselves, and if such a thought deterred us from acting, nothing would ever get done.

The initiatives discussed in this book and attributed to particular foundations, therefore, cannot pass the strictest tests of causality determination or counterfactuality. Nonetheless, it is my view, which is shared by most of those I interviewed, that common sense must be the arbiter of an imperfect causality and counterfactuality.

Ways of Recognizing Impact

Here is a brief description of the kinds of major impacts that mark the most effective foundation initiatives.

Major benefits to the public. The foundation initiatives with the greatest impact—for example, the Green Revolution and the Population Council together with the related women's reproductive rights programs—have saved or enhanced billions of lives. If a foundation initiative prevents or cures a major disease, leads to legislation that benefits millions of Americans, or embodies a new and influential model of social change, these outcomes would be persuasive evidence of impact.[4]

Other grantmaking initiatives that may not have changed the world nonetheless have had extraordinary aggregate impacts by providing the civic sector with the resources that enabled it to modernize and to strengthen itself significantly.[5]

There are also many initiatives that have what might be called "high-intensity, low-extensiveness impacts," which focus on a restricted geographic or demographic area. For example, the Daniel and Joanna S. Rose Fund in New York City launched and continues to support the Harlem Educational Activities Fund, which seeks to raise the educational aspirations of Harlem youngsters by teaching them to play chess. The chess teams fielded by the organization have gone on to win New York City championships and place high in the national rankings. That is high-intensity impact for the chess players involved and their families.

Similarly, the high intensity, low extensiveness category would also include the often significant initiatives continuously undertaken by community foundations and those private foundations that are subject to regional or local geographical limitations.

Outputs and benefits created. Some foundations provide funds for building projects. But a building, in and of itself, is only an outcome, not an impact. The test of a building's impact is the extent of the benefits that accrue to the individuals or groups that make use of the building. The Kresge Foundation, which provides support for construction, renovation, and purchase of major equipment for buildings, focuses particularly on the construction of "green" (environmentally sound) buildings and buildings for historically black colleges and universities, both of which provide specific benefits to identifiable constituencies. Similarly, the 4,977 schools, along with 380 complementary homes and stores, that the Julius Rosenwald Fund built across the southern United States achieved significant impact on the lives of hundreds of thousands of black children who were educated in those buildings, just as the 2,509 libraries that Andrew Carnegie built around the world had an educational impact on hundreds of thousands of human beings who used the resources they provided.[6]

Expansion of knowledge. For the many foundations that support research, scholarship, and policy advocacy, books and reports published are an important part of their output. But books alone do not create impact. As Eric Wanner, president of the one-hundred-year-old Russell Sage Foundation, observes, "All social science can do is give democracy a more accurate picture of itself."[7] The impact of research lies in the social changes produced as a result.

Many books financed by foundations have had significant influence on society. Publishing initiatives focused on particular fields of knowledge or policy, such as the Alfred P. Sloan Foundation's Public Understanding of Science Program and the Russell Sage Foundation's research on improving social welfare for America's less-well-off population, have achieved significant impact. Two foundation-supported research initiatives that resulted in books deserve to be highlighted for their impact on society: Abraham Flexner's Report on Medical Education and Gunnar Myrdal's book on race relations, *An American Dilemma.*

There have also been major scientific discoveries that were made possible by foundation grants. At a recent conference, James D. Watson said that the discovery of the double helix structure of DNA made by himself and Francis Crick would have been delayed for twenty years without Rockefeller Foundation support through its molecular biology initiative.[8] Here, the impact is not social but scientific, helping to produce ancillary discoveries that depend on major breakthroughs like the one achieved by Watson and Crick.[9]

Some foundations create major basic knowledge–development initiatives. Among very significant ones in existence today are the Alfred P. Sloan Foundation's Digital Sky Survey, which is mapping all objects in the skies, and the Packard Foundation's Monterey Bay Aquarium and Research Institute.

Helping to launch a movement. Sometimes a foundation helps to start an organization that grows into a national movement. For example, the Ford Foundation provided start-up funds for the Mexican-American Legal Defense Fund and the Puerto Rican Legal Defense Fund, both of which went on to play change-causing roles in America's civic sector.[10]

Ford also played a crucial role in the founding of the Natural Resources Defense Council (NRDC). A group of law students, most of them from Yale, brought the novel idea of establishing an environmental public-interest law firm to Ford, which instantly recognized its potential social value. Ford then brokered a partnership between the Yale group and a small established group of practicing environmental lawyers, and provided support for the new organization over its first decade. Ford also orchestrated and won a battle of several months' duration with the Internal Revenue Service to gain 501(c)(3) status for NRDC. Together with the Environmental Defense Fund (now called Environmental Defense) and the Sierra Club Legal Defense Fund (also supported by Ford), NRDC helped create a national movement in environmental protection litigation.

Ford's success in this area seems to have triggered an opposite response. William Simon, former chairman of the conservative-leaning John M. Olin Foundation, admits to having "borrowed" the idea of socially active public-interest law centers from the more liberal Ford Foundation—an illustration of the fact that the impacts of a foundation initiative can't always be anticipated or controlled. The John M. Olin Foundation, the Scaife Foundations, the Bradley Foundation, and other conservative foundations founded and/or supported not only "conservative" public-interest law centers, but also university-based centers for research, teaching, and advocacy; think tanks such as the American Enterprise Institute, the Heritage Foundation, and the CATO Institute; and both demonstration models and academic research on charter schools and school vouchers.[11]

Helping an existing organization find a new path. The American Civil Liberties Union (ACLU) was founded as a membership organization in 1920, long before American foundations began engaging in significant work on civil liberties and human rights issues. Decades later, Ford Foundation support enabled the ACLU to mount its Women's Rights Program under the direction of Ruth Bader Ginsburg, who later became a justice of the United States Supreme Court.[12] The impact of this program on the rights of American women has been unmistakable.[13]

Catalyzing an urgent social change. When a foundation causes or accelerates a positive, radical change in an important social institution, that is an instance of significant impact. The Carnegie Foundation for the Advancement of Teaching had this kind of impact through its efforts to transform medical and legal education in the United States.[14]

Taking an initiative to scale. There are many effective organizations and movements that foundations didn't start but which they helped grow to the point at which they could have a major impact on the world. For example, the Grameen Bank in Bangladesh was not started with foundation money. However, it became a great success after the Ford Foundation's representative in Bangladesh recognized the potential of micro-credit and provided funds that helped take Grameen to scale, enabling the bank to provide seed money for hundreds of thousands of small entrepreneurial ventures.[15]

Do Foundations Really Want to Achieve Impact?

One might assume that every foundation officer is eager to achieve significant impact. But the actions of many trustees and staff members sometimes make me wonder. Foundations usually shy away from empirical measurements of the extent of their impact. They are wary about sharing information about their choice of goals and the strategies they employ to achieve them. And they avoid public—and often even private—analyses of their initiatives and the causes of failure or success.

How can we explain this behavior? I think the only conclusion we can reach is that many foundations are less interested in achieving real impact than in showing the world that their hearts are in the right place. This is expressive rather than instrumental giving, and hardly to be deprecated. But I hope that I've made it abundantly clear that more should be expected from foundations, which are not only among our nation's richest, freest, and most powerful institutions, but also often the only institutions in a position to introduce significant change in society.

Those foundations that are truly interested in using their resources in ways that will have the greatest positive impact on the world around them should study the stories of the most successful and effective foundation initiatives. They provide models for the future success stories that others in the foundation world should aspire to write.

8

HIGH-IMPACT INITIATIVES:

TWELVE CASE STUDIES

Philanthropy is America's passing gear.

———

Paul Ylvisaker[16]

This volume would be too long for any publisher, as well as perhaps too tedious for any reader, if it were to include all one hundred of the cases of extraordinary foundation impact written as part of the research for this study. On the advice of my publisher, I have chosen twelve of those cases to serve as examples to illustrate some of the strategies and tactics foundations use to try to achieve their objectives. As the cases differ in complexity, they are necessarily of different lengths.

All of the following cases are condensations of longer cases written either by Scott Kohler or Steven Schindler, under my supervision, and are offered here merely to give readers a taste of the detail available in the extended versions. Those cases are accessible both on a read-only Web site, www.pubpol.duke.edu/dfrp/cases, and in a separate volume, *Casebook for The Foundation: A Great American Secret,* ISBN 1-58648-488-5, by J. Scott Kohler, Steven Schindler, and Joel L. Fleishman, which is available via a print-on-demand service at 1-800-343-4499.

Lessons to Be Learned
from These Cases

As you read these cases, note the importance—and diversity of talent—of the critical actors, whether foundation founders themselves or the philanthropoids who administered their wealth. None of the outcomes described in these cases would have likely happened but for the fortuitous match between the nature of the problem to be tackled and the judgment, experience, and habits of mind brought to bear in solving it. If in *The Transformation of American Medical Education*, for example, Abraham Flexner had not been compulsively meticulous, thorough, and accurate in the research he did—interviewing every faculty member in every American medical school operating at the time and reporting back to them his findings about each of them—his report would neither have commanded the respect it instantly won nor would it have galvanized elite and public opinion to bring about the transformation Flexner believed necessary. This case is a notable example of both impeccable, inspired judgment in choosing the question to be pursued and also the power of superior evidence-based research in answering it in order to bring about desired change. If it weren't for Flexner's keen analytic skills and superior judgment in knowing what to look for and how to look for it, his report would likely have ended up on dusty shelves, leaving the major transformation of American medical education to occur sometime later.

The same quality and combination of intellectual skills that Flexner demonstrated characterize the research that gave Gunnar Myrdal's *An American Dilemma* its catalytic power. This case also well illustrates the creativity and resourcefulness with which a great foundation's chief executive—which Frederick Keppel certainly was—goes about nursing a simple idea into a significant initiative of great impact.

While the second case, *Building Schools for Rural African Americans*, illustrates how a foundation can pursue its mission by building physical structures, it also teaches a quite different lesson—the indispensability of overriding donor passion. Critical to the great outcome he achieved was not only Julius Rosenwald's determination to spend most of his wealth to try to improve the education available to African American children across the southern United States, but also the creativity, resourcefulness, and respect, not to mention the relentlessness, with which he orchestrated support and attracted informed cooperation from the five thousand communities in which his schools and stores were to be located.

The same lessons—donor passion, relentlessness of commitment, and extraordinary resourcefulness—can be learned from George Soros's role in *Support for Democratization and Civil Societies in Central and Eastern Europe,* albeit as brought to bear on building not physical structures but countless civil society organizations, and empowering them to function in bringing about regime change in a time of great political and social need. That case also teaches the great importance of adopting simple tactics—donating fax machines, for example—to achieve grand strategies.

A quite different model of public advocacy is embodied in *Conservative Legal Advocacy,* one that embodies the efforts of a foundation in stimulating conservative-oriented legal and economic scholarship, and in building a community of student and faculty scholars, as well as think tanks and action-oriented organizations dedicated to achieving public saliency for conservative thinking. This case details a bit of the brilliant strategy adopted for building the human resource and idea infrastructure that powered the "conservative revolution" in social policy, the success of which has been both the bane of liberals and moderates and a model they have rushed to emulate.

Founding a public policy research institution may be less compelling and dramatic than some other foundation initiatives, but, in the long run, it can be just as important. *Economic Policy Research of the Highest Quality: National Bureau of Economic Research* describes how foundations helped bring into being almost a century ago a freestanding research institution that now sustains the largest network of leading economists in the United States, who continuously contribute to the shaping—and improvement, most think—of public policies affecting a vast range of issues. That case illustrates how foundations can be of critical importance, even with comparatively small amounts of money, in launching new institutions.

Foundations are often criticized, with great justification, for their unwillingness to commit themselves to initiatives for more than a few years. *The Green Revolution,* which exemplifies foundations as basic knowledge-builders, should also serve as a clarion call that creating significant change in matters of great importance to society often requires a sustained commitment of talent and funds for many years—in this case more than twenty years. When the goal is to develop new scientific or technological knowledge, a narrow task-force approach may be indispensable. Another important lesson from this case is that foundations should be open-minded about how they go about solving some kinds of problems. It is very unusual for a grantmaking foundation to appoint to its own staff a large group of persons to be devoted to solving a single problem, but that is what the Rockefeller Foundation did in this case, and that may be the most important explanation of the success it achieved in developing the new food grains that have dramatically reduced world hunger and starvation. This case is a paradigm example of what I called "the foundation as driver" in Chapter 1.

Curbing Population Growth: Rockefeller's Population Council illustrates how developing new forms of applied knowledge differs from discovering new basic knowledge, and how that difference is relevant to the development of an effective strategy. To develop new methods of contraception was less a medical or scientific problem than it was a cultural problem—changing personal, indeed the most intimate personal behavior. That meant that, if the goal of actually reducing births was to be attained, the widest possible involvement of scholars, scientists, human and social development policy experts, and community organizations, among others, had to be engaged from the outset. Instead of the "in-house" method employed by the Rockefeller Foundation in the Green Revolution, an external grantmaking strategy was dictated by the need to reach out very widely in order to mobilize the various indispensable constituencies.

A very different kind of personal behavior change is the focus of *Tobacco Use Programs,* which underscores the indispensability of strategic thinking and concerted action in bringing about such change. The goal of the program described is to reduce teenage smoking. This, too, is an example of the need to reach out widely rather than to focus an effort internally, and teaches the importance both of engaging strategic partners who share the foundation's goals and of catalyzing the development of new activist organizations to orchestrate broad-based national change on a state-by-state basis.

Another of these cases, the *China Sustainable Energy Program,* illustrates another way foundations use partnerships—partnerships among several foundations—to orchestrate change in behavior.

Two of these cases—*Children's Television Workshop and Sesame Street* and *Grameen Bank*—are offered to exemplify some of the ways foundations go about helping build models to prime the changes they seek to bring about. Both of those cases teach how essential it is for foundations that aim to bring about significant change to be constantly alert to opportunities that serendipitously come knocking and to have program officers with the judgment and experience necessary to spot, and often deliberately to seek out, promising ideas for change. Clearly, the Ford Foundation program officer in Bangladesh who recognized the promise of Mohammed Yunus's micro-lending acorn, from which a worldwide tree of tiny loans has now sprouted, was alert and had such judgment. The same is true of Carnegie's Lloyd Morrisett, who had given so much prior thought to the urgency of figuring out how to use television to educate young children that, when he had a casual dinner-party conversation with Joan Ganz Cooney, he instantly recognized that they shared the same goal and that she might be the right partner to help achieve it. *CTW* is an example of a foundation's building a model, while *Grameen Bank* illustrates how a foundation can help recognize and take to scale a model developed by someone else.

LAUNCHING A NEW DISCIPLINE OR FIELD OF PROFESSIONAL PRACTICE

The Transformation of American Medical Education: The Flexner Report (1906)

Background. In 1905, Andrew Carnegie established the Carnegie Foundation for the Advancement of Teaching (CFAT) as a means through which he could develop a system to provide financial security and well-being for college faculty members and their families. Carnegie tapped Henry Pritchett, president of MIT and a recent acquaintance, to lead the new foundation.[17] Carnegie also gave the twenty-five individuals he appointed to serve as trustees of CFAT the flexibility to determine their own course to advance the teaching profession.

Carnegie's interest in medical education fluctuated. In "The Best Fields for Philanthropy," the sequel to the widely discussed "Wealth," both of which appeared in the *North American Review* in 1889, Carnegie listed "the founding or extension of hospitals, medical colleges, laboratories, and other institutions connected with the alleviation of human suffering" as third on his list of worthy philanthropic causes.[18] Consistent with the views he articulated in "Wealth," Carnegie gave priority to those causes aimed at the prevention of illness over those aimed at finding cures. He also praised Vanderbilt's gift to Columbia College for its chemistry laboratory. Laboratories, Carnegie thought, were an essential part of any medical college.[19]

Carnegie's early philanthropy, however, largely neglected the professional education of doctors, focusing instead on the support of college educators and public library construction. The proprietary character of medical education instilled in Carnegie a distaste for the field. His relationship with Henry Pritchett fifteen years after first articulating his philanthropic priorities was the real beginning of Carnegie's imprint on medical education.[20]

By the time CFAT undertook its study of medical education, philanthropy had already begun to play a role in it. Johns Hopkins, an institution established by the bequest of a Quaker merchant in Baltimore, quickly became a model of academic medical education. Its first president, D. C. Gilman, developed a medical school that rejected the prevalent model of education-by-practitioners in favor of a school that replicated typical university conditions: professors fully dedicated to academic pursuits and a centralized governing hierarchy.[21] Two of the school's first faculty members, William Welch and William Osler, would become profoundly influential in medical education reform. Osler's *Principles of Medicine*, picked up by Rockefeller's philanthropic advisor Frederick Gates in 1897, inspired Gates to promote medical education as an object of Rockefeller financial support.[22]

Strategy. Pritchett, sharing Carnegie's conviction about the great potential of higher education to benefit society, understood well the urgent need for standardization and reform in order to remedy outmoded practices in American colleges and universities.[23] Accordingly, he led CFAT to commission a series of studies of the then-current state of many individual components of higher education and the necessary course of action for reform in each.[24] Because some protested the use of CFAT funds for endeavors outside of pension provisions, one of the trustees of CFAT wrote a letter to the editor of the *New York Times* in which he explained the rationale for studying education:

> Mr. Carnegie intrusted [sic] the administration of the fund to men who were themselves necessarily students, as well as administrators, of education, and their habit of mind led them to look beneath the

surface and to face at once the problems on whose wise solution the proper administration of their trust must depend.[25]

The trustee went on to note the particular need for a study of medical education, given the central importance of adequately trained physicians to the nation.

Medical reform of the style championed by Flexner found its earliest prominent champion in the Council on Medical Education of the American Medical Association, a group of five academic physicians. This group strongly advocated high academic standards in medical education, and consequently more full-time medical faculty and fewer practitioner-professors. In 1906, the council conducted its own survey of the medical schools in the United States, and its findings anticipate those of Flexner in his later study. Fearing that the impact of its own study might be limited by bias accusations stemming from the fact that a medical organization produced it, the council chose not to publish its study and instead approached Pritchett and CFAT to propose that it engage in its own study.[26]

Abraham Flexner, having written while still in Europe a critique of American higher education in which he favorably quoted Pritchett, approached CFAT for employment upon his return to the United States in 1906. At Pritchett's second meeting with Flexner, he suggested, in accordance with the proposal by the Council on Medical Education, that Flexner undertake a comprehensive evaluation and prepare a report on the state of medical education in the United States and Canada, in which he was to identify the best practices of various institutions and to highlight the areas of greatest need and potential for reform. Flexner noted that he had no expertise in the field of medical education, but Pritchett insisted that both Flexner's educational expertise and his obvious objectivity with regard to medical education made him ideal for the project. Pritchett agreed to conduct the study, which involved visiting more than 150 medical schools and institutions throughout North America. Flexner enjoyed the cooperation of the Council on Medical Education of the AMA, particularly the advice of two of its members, throughout the study.[27]

Flexner's first report, *Bulletin Number 4: Medical Education in the United States and Canada*, set off an explosion of unprecedented controversy, protest, and change in the institutions of medical education.[28] In that report, Flexner first outlined the current state of medical education and identified the best characteristics of a medical-education institution, and then he provided an assessment (often harshly critical) of every medical school in the United States and Canada.[29]

Some institutions responded immediately and drastically. Washington University in St. Louis was the subject of some of Flexner's harshest criticisms. Robert Brookings, a wealthy merchant who had recently come to dominate the management of Washington University, requested an immediate audience with Flexner and Pritchett and a subsequent tour of the campus in St. Louis with Flexner. Brookings became convinced of the accuracy of Flexner's criticisms. Shortly after Brookings's second inspection of the medical school, the trustees adopted a plan of reconstruction that required the resignation of every member of the medical school faculty and replacement with faculty members with academic training.[30] Other medical schools also responded to Flexner's report favorably and with comparable action. The Yale Corporation, for example, approved changes exactly in line with Flexner's suggestions, although some schools reacted negatively and with forceful resistance to criticisms of their institutions.[31]

Flexner followed his initial study with a review of the systems of medical education in Germany, Austria, France, England, and Scotland. In *Bulletin Number 6: Medical Education in Europe*, he analyzed the effectiveness of the distinguishing aspects of those systems, and he promoted without reservation the English system of clinical education. He insisted on "a noncommercial relationship between medical school, hospital, laboratory, and university" in the American institutions.[32]

Ironically, Flexner's report had the effect of deterring Carnegie from focusing his own philanthropic resources on reform in medical education. Responding to Flexner, Carnegie said, "You have proved that medical education is a business. I will not endow any other man's business."[33] Until Carnegie's death, therefore, virtually no support for medical-education reform came from Carnegie philanthropies.[34]

Those leading the Rockefeller philanthropic endeavors, however, most notably Rockefeller advisor and chairman of the General Education Board (GEB) Frederick T. Gates, reacted in quite a different fashion to Flexner's *Medical Education in the United States and Canada*. In 1913, the GEB hired Flexner to deploy its resources to catalyze the changes he urged in his CFAT bulletins.[35] From his grantmaking post at the GEB and with its great financial power, Flexner set to work to raise the standards of medical education dramatically. More specifically, Flexner sought to replicate nationally the model of medical education developed at Johns Hopkins, where the medical faculty devoted themselves full time to clinical work at the university and its affiliated teaching hospital, rather than splitting their time between university work and their own private clinical practices.[36] To that end, the GEB systematically funded the reorganization of select medical schools, including, initially, the medical schools at Washington University in St. Louis, Yale, the University of Chicago, and Vanderbilt University.[37] In 1923, the GEB decided, over strong protest by Gates, to expand its mission of medical education reform to public universities in order to allow geographic expansion to the West and the South, including medical schools at the Universities of Iowa, Colorado, Oregon, Virginia, and Georgia.[38] The Rockefeller Foundation gave a $45 million grant to the General Education Board to reform medical education.[39] Other funding from private sources followed.[40]

Impact. CFAT's impact in the realm of medical education through the Flexner reports was at least two-fold. First, the bulletins collected and disseminated on a national basis the latest thinking on what modern medical education could be at its best. Changes at institutions such as Washington University and Yale attest to the immediate impact directly attributable to the study. At their least, the Flexner reports served as a catalyst for immediate change that would otherwise have come more slowly.[41] Second, by providing Flexner with early resources to establish his expertise that the GEB would later harness to bring about widespread reform, CFAT positioned Flexner as an individual with the empirical knowledge, organizational skills, and reputation required to lead a movement of radical change.[42] Without CFAT's original support of the Flexner reports, there may have been no Flexner—no central figure of leadership—to drive a national revolution in medical education. Flexner's signal achievement, first in highlighting the universally poor state of medical education and then in marshalling Rockefeller's philanthropic resources to focus on improving it, helped to elevate medical education as well as medical research in America to a position of dominant international leadership, from which it has not yet fallen.[43]

BUILDING PHYSICAL FACILITIES

Building Schools for Rural African Americans (1920)

Background. Julius Rosenwald amassed his fortune through the success of his clothing business and during his tenure as president of Sears, Roebuck & Co., and this fortune enabled him to do significant work in the philanthropic arena. Rosenwald's religious beliefs motivated his charitable activities.[44] Among the beneficiaries of his philanthropy were Hull House, Hebrew University in Jerusalem, and various entities aimed at the betterment of educational opportunities for African Americans. Rosenwald's interest in African American education was inspired by his reading *An American Citizen, the Life of William H. Baldwin* as well as writings of Dr. Booker T. Washington. Through his contributions to a number of YMCA and YWCA buildings dedicated to African Americans, Rosenwald developed a relationship with Dr. Booker T. Washington that further developed his interest in African American education.

On his fiftieth birthday in 1912, Rosenwald gave $650,000 in gifts to a number of charitable causes, including $25,000 to Washington to support the expansion of the Tuskegee Institute. Washington, after using less than the full $25,000 grant for offshoot campuses of Tuskegee, contemplated different uses for the remaining $2,100. After deciding on building six small rural schoolhouses for African Americans, Washington asked Rosenwald to approve this use of the money. Upon Rosenwald's agreement, Washington built the first six schools with the unused $2,100 of Rosenwald's Tuskegee gift.

Strategy. Washington prepared a glowing report of the dedication of the six new schools, particularly noting large numbers of both black and white attendees at dedication ceremonies. Rosenwald, pleased with Washington's report, contributed an additional thirty thousand dollars to Tuskegee to build one hundred similar schools throughout rural Alabama. State agents of African American education in other southern states, distressed with the condition of African American education in their own states, asked Rosenwald to expand the building program to other states in the South, but Rosenwald declined to expand the building program until the degree of success of the schools in Alabama could first be ascertained.

Tuskegee administered the building program with funding from Rosenwald for the construction of the first schools in 1913 until the Rosenwald Fund assumed control of the building program in 1920.[45] Throughout the duration of the program, Rosenwald annually reviewed the budget of the program, and he took great interest in the design and quality of the school buildings, even prompting an effort to modernize the designs of the school buildings midway through the program.

Rosenwald generally structured his philanthropic gifts in a way that attracted greater philanthropic and public financial support for his causes. He often offered less than 50 percent of the costs of various enterprises and challenged the recipients to raise the remaining funds from other sources.[46] His challenge formula was a variation on formulas first used by Andrew Carnegie and John D. Rockefeller.

In 1917, while Rosenwald was in Washington to advise President Woodrow Wilson on financial matters related to World War I, he made an appearance at a conference on education to report on the school-building program. State education agents and officials in other southern states urged Rosenwald to support similar building programs throughout the South, and Rosenwald agreed to do so. In October of 1917, Rosenwald incorporated his foundation, the Rosenwald Fund. Because the program had outgrown Tuskegee's administrative capacity, Rosenwald established a southern office of the Fund in Nashville in 1920 to take control of the rural school-building program, enlisting S. L. Smith, a former state agent of African American education in Tennessee, to serve the office as director. In the program's first year, 1920–21, the budget exceeded five hundred thousand dollars.

Impact. In *The Emergence of the New South*, George Brown Tindall calls the rural school-building program of the Rosenwald Fund "one of the most effective stratagems to outflank the prejudice and apathy that hobbled Negro education."[47] Julius Rosenwald embarked on a program to overhaul the educational infrastructure of African American education in the rural South. Rosenwald structured this gift as three hundred dollars to each school for building expenses and fifty dollars to Tuskegee for the promotion of and fundraising for the local school in its community. Rosenwald requested that each dollar be matched by community fundraising. Pleased with Washington's report of these first six schools, Rosenwald promised an additional thirty thousand dollars in 1914 for the construction of one hundred additional schools in Alabama with the same gift structure.

By the school-building program's termination in 1932 (the year of Rosenwald's death), the fund had facilitated the construction of 4,977 rural schools throughout the South with an additional 380 homes and shops to complement the schools. Many of the schools operated continuously until desegregation was ordered by *Brown v. Board of Education* in 1954. In 1928, Rosenwald schools accounted for one out of every five African American schools in the South, and these schools enrolled one of every three southern African American pupils.[48]

Rosenwald schools were noted for their modern architectural designs. In some communities, the Rosenwald schools surpassed the quality of the local white schools, prompting renovations or new building projects for white pupils. The Rosenwald school-building program served as a countervailing force in a public environment that often sought to undermine African American education in the South. At a time when Jim Crow laws and pervasive racism made large-scale public support of African American education highly unlikely, Rosenwald's program circumvented popular negative sentiment and sparked public financing for widely underfunded African American schools.

The final Rosenwald school was built in Warm Springs, Georgia, in 1937, after the termination of the program, at the special request of President Franklin Roosevelt. When Roosevelt was governor of New York, he sought funding from the Rosenwald Fund for an African American school in his summer-retreat town of Warm Springs, noting, "It must be a Rosenwald School because of the influence these schools have on the officials and communities." For five years, the Rosenwald Fund did not take up the Warm Springs school, in part because the building program's termination coincided approximately with Roosevelt's initial request. In 1937, however, President Roosevelt renewed his request that the Rosenwald Fund build a school in Warm Springs. The fund's board granted approval of special funding to build the school, and President Roosevelt personally dedicated the building.[49]

Tindall notes that the larger impact of the Rosenwald Fund's school-building program was the spark it ignited in providing public financial support for African American schools "while neutralizing the opposition of white taxpayers."[50] The fund's contribution to the cost of the program totaled only 15 percent of the overall building cost, but the program ignited local public funding of a majority of the building costs and almost all of the operating expenses of the rural schools.

FOUNDING AN INSTITUTION TO RESEARCH PUBLIC POLICY

Economic Policy Research of the Highest Quality: National Bureau of Economic Research (1921)

Background. The National Bureau of Economic Research, chartered in 1920, was the first economics institute to receive Carnegie Corporation funds.[51] For most of the previous decade, a debate had unfolded, particularly among Rockefeller Foundation officials and observers, about the direction of philanthropic support of economics. One side, led by Theodore Vail of AT&T and joined by John D. Rockefeller Jr. and foundation advisor Frederick T. Gates, argued that the public lacked a basic understanding of economics and that some provision of economic knowledge, coordinated by what Vail called a "publicity bureau," would best resolve the class dispute many capitalists and philanthropists sought to address.[52] Countering this sentiment, many, including economists Edwin F. Gay of Harvard and Wesley C. Mitchell of Columbia as well as Jerome Greene of the Rockefeller Institute for Medical Research, felt that this approach sidestepped the most significant national need—more and better basic economic research.[53]

Mitchell believed that economics research held the same promise for social policy that scientific research held for medicine. Gates, wholly committed to devoting the maximum possible proportion of Rockefeller philanthropy to the development of medicine, rejected this analogy.[54] The Rockefeller Foundation's interest in pursuing economics funding at all, however, was thwarted when the involvement of the foundation in managing the public perception of the "Ludlow massacre" turned the foundation against social-science research for more than a decade.[55]

Strategy. The Carnegie Corporation of New York first became interested in supporting economics research in 1916, when Henry Pritchett, a trustee of the Corporation and president of the Carnegie Foundation for the Advancement of Teaching, proposed support of an effort to spread a basic understanding of economics, a proposal more in tune with Vail and Gates than with the economists. The spark behind Pritchett's proposal was what he perceived as the promulgation of inaccurate information by newspapers and labor organizers for commercial and political gain. In particular,

Pritchett criticized the reports of the Committee on Industrial Relations, which to some degree shared the same interest in publishing its views regarding labor-related problems facing the nation's economy. Accordingly, the brunt of his proposal entailed the purchase and endowment of a newspaper with the mandate to print truthful information.[56] After it became clear that the costs of purchasing a newspaper were likely to be too great for the corporation, the discussion about economics funding was altogether dropped.[57]

Parallel to Pritchett's initiative, the economists initially involved in Rockefeller discussions were independently pursuing their interests in an economics research institute devoted to basic research. Gay and Mitchell became acquainted with Malcolm Rorty through the Committee on Industrial Relations. Rorty in particular sought a careful analysis and determination of the national income to inform possible policy decisions about income distribution. In their discussions, the three agreed that much disagreement about national economic policy was rooted less in differing economic interests than in disagreement about basic economic facts.[58] Gay's role as director of the Central Bureau of Planning and Statistics during World War I instilled in him a commitment to seek permanent coordination of federal statistics. Woodrow Wilson disagreed, however, with Gay's assessment of the value of peacetime statistics coordination, and so the Central Bureau was closed after the war.[59] In January 1920, Gay and Mitchell joined Rorty to charter the National Bureau of Economics Research (NBER).[60] In an effort to provide credibility and faithfulness to the mission of pursuing pure economic research, the NBER organizers placed control in the hands of a board of directors of a politically diverse group of economists, businessmen, and individuals linked to labor and economic associations.[61]

The Commonwealth Fund was one of the earliest supporters of the NBER, granting twenty thousand dollars to the bureau for its first year's operations, but, in accordance with the fund's decision to limit its focus to medicine, it ceased its support of the NBER with a second-year fifteen-thousand-dollar grant. The general director of the fund at the time, a Yale historian named Max Farrand, wrote to new Carnegie Corporation President James Angell in November 1920, to seek corporation support of the NBER.[62] The secretary of the NBER then wrote to the corporation in December requesting forty five thousand dollars in grant support, which the corporation granted a month later after attaching a matching requirement of twenty thousand dollars.[63]

Pritchett's likely disagreement with the objectives of the NBER, as they conflicted with his preference for widespread economics-education efforts over basic research, was likely overwhelmed by Pritchett's desire to support Angell in his efforts to centralize decision-making power and to wrest control away from the corporation's secretary and treasurer, James Bertram.[64] When Angell left the corporation after only one year as president, the NBER appealed to Pritchett in 1921 for further support. By this time, Secretary of Commerce Herbert Hoover was seeking a credible private research entity to conduct studies to propose actions to combat unemployment.[65] In support of NBER funding, Hoover contacted the Russell Sage Foundation, the Commonwealth Fund, and the Carnegie Corporation, writing to Pritchett on November 18, 1921. Although the first two declined to support the NBER to the degree Hoover sought, the corporation responded to Hoover's request in February 1922, with a fifty-thousand-dollar grant, which the corporation allowed the NBER to use to satisfy the corporation's own matching-grant requirement that it had attached to the first grant.[66]

The Carnegie Corporation also supported a number of other economics research entities in the early 1920s, but adopted a policy of distancing the corporation from the findings or positions of the economic research it funded.[67]

Impact. Little of the NBER's substantive work can be attributed directly to Carnegie Corporation support, but the corporation grants played a significant role in launching the NBER. Carnegie can therefore be credited, to some degree, with the NBER's existence. Among the NBER's earliest publications are studies determining national income and unemployment levels (the latter spurred by Secretary of Commerce Herbert Hoover and President Warren Harding). The bureau continues its work as a "private, nonprofit, nonpartisan research organization dedicated to promoting a greater understanding of how the economy works." The NBER is today the premier research organizational framework for some six hundred expert economists who together focus on public-policy work on a variety of projects while remaining based at their home academic institutions. While the only "official" action taken in the name of the NBER itself is the declaration of the beginning and ending of national recessions, the NBER is the nation's leading nonprofit economic research organization. Of the thirty-one American winners of the Nobel Prize in Economics, twelve of them have been researchers for the NBER.[68]

FINANCING RESEARCH ON PUBLIC POLICY

Transforming America's Perceptions of Relations Among Its Races: Gunnar Myrdal's An American Dilemma (1936)

Background. By the time the Carnegie Corporation approached Gunnar Myrdal to study race in America, it had already contributed $1.7 million to causes it categorized as "negro education" between its inception in 1911 and 1932. In the mid–1930s, the corporation caught up with its financial commitments to other Carnegie philanthropies, and then-President Frederick Keppel began to contemplate new strategies for the corporation's discretionary income.[69]

A member of the Carnegie Corporation's board of trustees, Newton D. Baker, first suggested at a board meeting in 1935 that the corporation consider "the general questions of *negro education and negro problems*."[70] Baker grew up in the South and was suffused with Confederate tradition. The intent behind his suggestion was clearly conditioned by his racist attitudes; Baker suspected that racism was based on biological distinctions, and he suggested that "an infant race like the black people in this country" would enjoy greater benefit from education if they were forced to work for it.[71]

Strategy. Keppel traveled to Cleveland in 1936 to visit with Baker about a possible corporation project embodying Baker's suggestion. In following Baker's advice and in light of the 1936 study on race published by the Rosenwald Fund (written by a Dutch scholar), Keppel sought a European, as a nod to the necessity for objectivity, to conduct the study.[72]

Keppel collected a list of nominations from a variety of advisors of potential European scholars to conduct the Carnegie study on race in America. Karl Gunnar Myrdal, a Swedish economist, was one of twenty-five nominees submitted by Beardsley Ruml, former Laura Spelman Rockefeller officer and assistant to a former corporation president. Myrdal had been a Rockefeller Foundation Fellow, along with his wife, in 1929–30, and his interaction with the Rockefeller philanthropies caused his path to cross Ruml's. In August 1937, Keppel asked Myrdal to lead the corporation's study. Myrdal first declined, but then accepted in an October telegram from Stockholm. Baker, when he learned of the decision, expressed to Keppel his satisfaction that the European professor was a better choice than any American. Baker died a month later, before the study commenced.[73]

Myrdal came to the United States in 1938 to deliver the Godkin Lectures at Harvard and to meet with Keppel about the proposed study. Myrdal then returned to Sweden until the fall while Keppel arranged a two-month tour through the South upon Myrdal's return, to be guided by Jackson Davis, associate director of the General Education Board.[74]

Beginning with his comments on Myrdal's initial report from the southern tour, Keppel demonstrated a desire for a focus more applicable to grantmaking criticism and guidance in the area of "Negro" education.[75] Aside from this concern for the matter addressed in the study, Keppel never directly ordered any particular approach nor wavered from steadfast support for Myrdal, despite growing criticism of Myrdal even before the study's conclusion. In assessing the relationship between Keppel and Myrdal, Ellen Condliffe Lagemann writes that Keppel's "willingness to help [Myrdal] by making suggestions, combined with his insistence upon regard for Myrdal's autonomy as a scholar, were vital to the inquiry from beginning to end."[76]

After submitting his initial plans to Keppel, fifty-one individuals reviewed Myrdal's plans for proceeding. In April, 1939, a group of scholars met at a weeklong conference to refine and finalize his plans. Myrdal then commissioned forty research memoranda from scholars from throughout the country on race-related issues.[77]

From the research memoranda and his own observations, Myrdal compiled and drafted the two-volume *An American Dilemma*, a vast study containing the commissioned studies of particular facets of the race problem as well as Myrdal's analysis stemming from his interpretation of these reports and his experiences on the southern tour. The Carnegie Corporation published *An American Dilemma* in 1944.[78]

Impact. Ellen Condliffe Lagemann, in her history of the Carnegie Corporation, wrote that *An American Dilemma* "had a lasting impact on public opinion and public policy."[79] In his assessment of the role of Myrdal's study in American public policy, David Southern compared the impact of *An American Dilemma* in the civil rights field to George Kennan's influence in the field of foreign policy through his famous "X" article in *Foreign Affairs*.[80] The Supreme Court decision in *Brown v. Board of Education* in 1954 rested its reasoning on Myrdal's conclusions and those of other social scientists in part because it found history "inconclusive."[81] Myrdal's study has been cited by the Supreme Court in five different opinions.[82] *An American Dilemma* served as supplemental proof to anecdotal evidence from the service of blacks in World War II that racial discrimination had no foundation in natural inferiority. It was a critical element of the persuasive case the early builders of the civil rights movement pieced together to combat institutional racism.[83]

John Stanfield, in *Philanthropy and Jim Crow in American Social Science*, takes a more skeptical view of *An American Dilemma*, at least of its intrinsic value. He declares that the Myrdal study "has been viewed as a seminal work because it is too big for most people to read and because at least through the early 1980s no other agency or foundation has successfully attempted such a comprehensive analysis about blacks."[84] In deriding the study for providing a paradigm that essentially distracted liberals with false hopes for racial integration in lieu of the more efficacious means of solving racial problems through power and pluralism, Stanfield notes that *An American Dilemma* stood as a formidable weapon for liberals in discourse on race on account of its origins and association with what he calls, with some sarcasm, "a great democratic organization." Despite Stanfield's reservations about popular and intellectual reverence accorded to the Carnegie Corporation, the credibility of Myrdal's study in social matters cannot be denied, and Stanfield's own critique demonstrates the value and forcefulness that the study gained, aside from financial support, from the study's association with a foundation such as the Carnegie Corporation.[85]

The corporation found little of practical use in *An American Dilemma*. No significant shift in its funding strategies can be detected. Only in the 1960s did the corporation first begin to celebrate its role in providing intellectual stimulus to the civil rights movement in Myrdal's study.[86]

BUILDING BASIC KNOWLEDGE

The Green Revolution (1943)

Background.

For the last five years, we've had more people starving and hungry. But something has happened. Pakistan is self-sufficient in wheat and rice, and India is moving towards it. It wasn't a red, bloody revolution as predicted. It was a green revolution.

Norman Borlaug recalls William Gaud speaking these words at a small meeting in 1968.[87] Gaud, who, at the time, administered the United States Agency for International Development (USAID), was describing an almost unbelievable surge in food output then being achieved by a number of Asian nations that had seemed, until very recently, to be on the brink of disaster. The two nations cited by Gaud were especially worrisome. Neither Pakistan, a country of 115 million people, nor India, whose population already exceeded half a billion, had been producing enough food to meet the growing needs of its rapidly expanding population. Famine, and its attendant turmoil, seemed inevitable. But Gaud was right. Something *had* happened. Within a few years, food production in India, Pakistan, and many of their neighbors, would outstrip population growth. The threat of mass starvation would loom less ominously over the land, and Borlaug, an agronomist working for the Rockefeller Foundation, would be a Nobel laureate credited with saving more lives than any person in human history.

Despite all appearances, this green revolution did not occur overnight. Its roots go back several decades earlier. In 1940, Vice President–elect Henry Wallace traveled to Mexico. He was appalled by the conditions there. Masses of people were eking out an existence on meager quantities of food. At the time, Mexico was forced to import over half its wheat, and a significant portion of its maize.[88] Wallace met with an official of the Rockefeller Foundation, and, soon after, with the foundation's president, Raymond Fosdick. He described the plight of the Mexican poor, emphasizing to Fosdick "that the all important thing was to expand the means of subsistence."[89] Fosdick and his colleagues at the Rockefeller Foundation were agreeable to the idea. The foundation had a long history of combating disease in poverty-stricken regions, and there was a feeling among its officers that hunger and malnutrition were closely related to many of the world's health-care problems. So, in 1943, when the Mexican government requested the foundation's assistance in an effort to improve that nation's agricultural productivity, its trustees agreed, seeing the new project "as a natural outgrowth of [the foundation's] interest in public health and the biological sciences. . . . "[90] With an initial outlay of twenty thousand dollars for a survey in 1943, followed, in 1944, by $192,800 for construction costs and equipment, the Rockefeller Foundation embarked, with the

Mexican Ministry of Agriculture, upon the Mexican Agricultural Project (MAP).

Strategy. From the start, the foundation was deeply involved in the programmatic aspects of the operation. A team of Rockefeller scientists was sent to Chapingo, outside Mexico City, where they established an office of special studies (OSS). Led by George Harrar (who, in 1961, would become the foundation's president), the group included Borlaug and four other agricultural specialists. For almost two decades, this team employed a three-part strategy to "improve the yields of the basic food crops" in Mexico.[91]

The first element of the strategy was to engage in ongoing research in an effort to produce ever-better varieties of corn, wheat, potatoes, and other crops, and to develop ever-better methods of growing these crops. As soon as a new variety or technique was developed, it was put to use. "Research from the outset was production-oriented and restricted to that which was relevant to increasing wheat production. Researches in pursuit of irrelevant academic butterflies were discouraged. . . . "[92] The second element of the strategy was a persistent outreach effort with two goals. First, the American scientists and their Mexican colleagues sought to teach Mexican farmers about their latest advances in agricultural science. And second, they worked to convince farmers to take advantage of these new breakthroughs, whether by planting a new type of seed or by fertilizing or irrigating their fields in new ways. The third element of the strategy adopted was to help train a corps of agronomists, plant protectionists, and other professionals, who would ultimately be able to assume primary responsibility for the well-being of agriculture in Mexico. This was accomplished by foundation-sponsored fellowships and scholarships enabling hundreds of Mexican students to study at American universities on the cutting edge of agricultural sciences. Moreover, an intern program was incorporated into the foundation's activities in Chapingo.

The goals of the Mexican Agricultural Project were simple. Gordon Conway, the former president of the Rockefeller Foundation, writes that the foundation wanted to "improve the yields of the basic food crops, maize, wheat, and beans."[93] Crop yields in Mexico were "low and static . . . soils were impoverished and chemical fertilizer virtually unknown."[94] But the foundation did not want Mexican agriculture to become dependent on its involvement. Rather, as Borlaug describes, "the philosophy of the Rockefeller Foundation was to 'help Mexico help itself' in solving its food production problems, and in the process work itself out of a job."[95] And the foundation was already thinking big. Conway writes that, "A conscious objective of the Green Revolution from the beginning was to produce varieties that could be grown in a wide range of conditions throughout the developing world."[96]

Outcomes. "Officials at the Mexican Ministry of Agriculture," writes Deborah Fitzgerald, professor of the history of technology at MIT, "were pleased to have not only a revitalization of agricultural science, but also the input of Rockefeller dollars."[97] But progress on maize started out slowly. Fitzgerald suggests that this was because of systemic differences between the primarily subsistence-oriented corn farming in Mexico and its more commercial counterpart in the United States. The farming techniques advocated by the Rockefeller team were not cheap, and few small farmers could afford the initial investment.[98]

Progress with wheat (which was Dr. Borlaug's division) was much faster. Mexican wheat farms were, in general, larger than local corn farms, and were more commercial than subsistence-oriented. In this way, they more closely resembled American farms. The scientists at Chapingo had developed wheat varieties resistant to stem rust, and these were distributed widely throughout the country. By 1956, Mexico was self-sufficient in its production of wheat, and it has remained so ever since. Furthermore, between 1954 and 1961, Borlaug had worked to produce a disease-resistant, high-yield, photo-insensitive[99] dwarf wheat. He succeeded at this by crossing indigenous Mexican varieties with a Japanese dwarf wheat that had been cultivated centuries ago.[100] When the first seeds of the new dwarf hybrid were distributed in 1961, yields per hectare became even more impressive. Between 1948 and 1970, Mexican wheat yields rose from 750 kilos per hectare to almost 3,000—a four-fold increase in productivity.

In 1943, there had not been a single trained plant protectionist in Mexico. Local agriculture was outdated. Twenty years later, the Rockefeller Foundation had contributed, by providing funding, hands-on experience, and often both, to the training of over seven hundred Mexican scientists in fields of agriculture.

The success of the foundation's efforts in Mexico led many of that country's neighbors to request similar assistance. To that end, the foundation set up a similar program in Colombia in 1950. Other countries soon followed, and the benefits of Rockefeller-sponsored research were spread throughout Latin America. The foundation's 1968 report proclaims that, "it had been clearly demonstrated . . . that, with organized assistance, a food-deficit nation could rapidly modernize its agriculture."

But Mexico had not been caught on a global wave of agricultural progress; the report continues: "Still, in most developing nations, efforts to increase production of major agricultural commodities were relatively ineffective [over the same period of time]." Several major factors had helped Mexico turn the corner. Certainly, the initiative of its government was one. But it was widely recognized that foundation-sponsored technological advances and the relentless labors of foundation scientists had been others.

Programs in Mexico, Colombia, and Chile had proven successful and had demonstrated the enormous potential for improvement in the food output of many developing nations. As the Rockefeller Foundation "worked itself out of a job," national governments began to assume primary responsibility for the existing programs, and the Rockefeller Foundation looked for the best way to apply the lessons of the past twenty years to other hunger-ravaged nations around the world.

And many nations were, indeed, being desolated by hunger. By the mid-1960s, India, already the world's second most populous nation, consumed fully a quarter of all U.S. food aid each year.[101] Explosive population growth in much of Asia was making it less and less plausible that nations like India, Pakistan, and the Philippines would ever be able to feed themselves. In *Famine—1975! America's Decision: Who Will Survive?* William and Paul Paddock argued that a Time of Famines would soon lay waste the developing world. "The famines are inevitable," they warned. And "riding alongside [them] will surely be riots and other civil tensions which the central government[s] will be too weak to control." The Paddocks derided the naïve hope that "something [would] turn up" to forestall this doom.[102] And the Paddocks were not alone in their assessment. Stanford biologist Paul Ehrlich, for example, argued that *Famine—1975!* "may be remembered as one of the most important books of our age."

The Rockefeller Foundation shared these men's sense of urgency. But, rather than advocate a triage system (as the Paddocks did), in which the worst-off nations would be denied assistance and left to their Darwinian fate, the foundation looked for new ways to attack the problem. The foundation had first extended its agriculture programs to India in 1956, at the request of the Indian national government. In the ensuing years, Rockefeller partnered with USAID and the U.S. Department of Agriculture (USDA). Together, they "helped establish five state agriculture universities in India."[103] These universities collaborated with their American counterparts on research and training. As it had in Mexico, the foundation thereby contributed to the development, in India, of a community of homegrown agriculturalists with access to the most advanced technologies in the world.

But their training would take time. And in India, as in many of its neighboring countries, time was of the essence, as Dr. Borlaug describes in his Nobel lecture:

> So great is the food shortage in many underdeveloped and emerging countries that there is not enough time to develop an adequate corps of scientists before attacking food production problems. A shortcut and organizational change had to be invented to meet the needs. And so was born the first truly international research and training institute, the International Rice Research Institute (IRRI) at Los Banos, the Philippines, in 1960, to work exclusively on the regionally all-important but too-long-neglected rice crop.[104]

In 1959, the Rockefeller Foundation was joined in its food production efforts by the Ford Foundation, which paid $7.15 million to build the International Rice Research Institute and contributed an additional $750,000 for research and training over the institute's first three years of operation. The land the institute was built on was provided by the Filipino government, and the Rockefeller Foundation assumed primary responsibility for staffing and operating IRRI, which proved to be the first of four major international centers for agricultural research and training on which Rockefeller and Ford collaborated.

International Rice Research Institute (IRRI)
Los Banos, Philippines
1961

International Center for Maize and Wheat Improvement (CIMMYT)
Chapingo, Mexico
1966

International Institute for Tropical Agriculture (IITA)
Lagos, Nigeria
1968

International Center for Tropical Agriculture (CIAT)
Bogotá, Colombia
1968

These international centers served as focal points for the global battle against hunger. No longer was the foundation restricted to tackling, one at a time, the problems of individual nations. Scientists from around the world brought home from these centers the most up-to-date agricultural advances, and new high-yield crop varieties could be exported from these institutes to a multitude of food-deprived nations.

Meanwhile, the Rockefeller and Ford foundations remained directly involved in India and Pakistan, respectively. From 1963–65, Dr. Borlaug worked in India and Pakistan to convince local farmers of the merits of Mexican dwarf wheat varieties and other recent advances. By 1965, food shortages on the subcontinent had gotten so bad that these nations' governments began to import large quantities of seed from CIMMYT and IRRI, especially after strong monsoons in 1966 and 1967 ravaged crop yields, leading to an increase in the global price of wheat and a greater acceptance, in those nations, that new techniques needed to be tried if widespread famine was to be averted.[105] In India, Rockefeller staff members "serve[d] as co-leaders of the national rice, wheat, and sorghum schemes. Leadership of the national coordinated maize program was provided by the Foundation for the first eight years," before it was assumed by an Indian scientist.[106]

Progress throughout Asia was dramatic. The first time Borlaug and his associates (mostly scientists he had trained in Mexico with Rockefeller Foundation funds) planted on the Indian subcontinent, they often worked "in sight of artillery flashes.[107] Sowed late, that [first wheat] crop germinated poorly, yet yields still rose 70 percent . . . the next harvest was . . . a 98 percent improvement."[108] At IRRI, researchers developed IR8, widely hailed as "miracle rice" for its high yields. By 1967, just five years after IRRI was completed, the Philippines achieved self-sufficiency in rice.[109] In the same year, the Turkish government imported dwarf wheat from CIMMYT for the first time. Yields on farms using the wheat soared to double, often triple, their previous averages. In 1968, Pakistan, which by then had imported tens of thousands of tons of high-yield seed from the international centers, became self-sufficient in wheat. And by 1974, India, which Paul Ehrlich had labeled "so far behind in the population-food game that there is no hope that our food aid will see them through to self-sufficiency," was self-sufficient in the production of all cereals. It has remained so ever since. By the time Norman Borlaug accepted the Nobel Peace Prize[110] in 1970, it was apparent that food production in the famine imperiled nations of Southeast Asia had, for a time at least, surpassed the rate of population growth, something that had seemed impossible to many observers.

Impact. The impact of the Green Revolution was enormous. High-yield agriculture is credited with saving at least a billion lives since the mid-1960s.[111] Global cereal production more than tripled between 1950 and 2000.[112] Absent an adequate supply of food, political stability and economic prosperity cannot be achieved. This is why, in 1970, the Nobel Committee recognized Dr. Borlaug with its prize for peace.

But Borlaug did not work alone. In his Nobel lecture, he explains, "I am but one member of a vast team made up of many organizations, officials, thousands of scientists, and millions of farmers—mostly small and humble—who for many years have been fighting a quiet, oftentimes losing war on the food production front." Certainly this is true. The Green Revolution could not have taken place without the collaboration of its many composite parts. And, as Borlaug, himself a Rockefeller scientist, makes clear, the Rockefeller Foundation was at the vanguard of the revolution.

Certainly other organizations deserve credit. The governments of Mexico, Chile, Colombia, Thailand, India, Pakistan, and a host of others sought help from foundations, the UN, and other governments. And they supported, within their own borders, the invigoration of agricultural sciences. But they were aware of the expertise that the Rockefeller staff had built up as one of the earliest coordinators of the modern attack on hunger, and they made the most of it. Foundation staffers were invited to direct national crop programs (as discussed earlier in the case of India) and, along with the international centers it helped to found, often administrated new efforts, as it did with Thailand's "network of 18 experimental [rice breeding] stations" in the mid–1960s.[113]

Other foundations deserve credit as well. From 1959 onward, the Ford Foundation was a major participant in the spread of high-yield technologies, and the Kellogg Foundation soon added its support.

The United Nations and the U.S. government were also deeply involved. But early on, they had little success transferring "production technology from the industrialized temperate zones to the tropics and subtropics." This is why, according to Borlaug, the cooperative Mexican government–Rockefeller Foundation model "ultimately proved to be superior" to "public sector foreign technical assistance programs. . . . "[114] By the time the Green Revolution really took off, these national and supranational bodies had recognized the success of the foundation-pioneered model and supported it, as demonstrated by USAID's commitment of funds to the international centers.[115]

The Green Revolution would not have been possible without earlier scientific breakthroughs. Dr. Borlaug estimates that fully 40 percent of the world's current population would not be alive today were it not for the Haber-Bosch ammonia-synthesizing process.[116] The spread of Mexican dwarf wheat and IR8 rice (and their continually improving offspring) would have been impossible without such breakthroughs in fertilizer technology. But that is the nature of progress. Scientific achievement is not diminished by its debt to the work of previous generations.

It has been argued that the Green Revolution produced negative side effects commensurate with its benefits. Critics point out that, in some parts of the world, the greatest benefits of new seed varieties and agricultural technologies have flowed more to well-off rather than poor farmers. They also claim that the irrigation needs of high-yield agriculture drain local water resources. And fertilizer use, essential if high-yield crops are to reach their full potential, can lead to runoff that pollutes streams and rivers. Observers have also worried that, by enabling the developing world to feed more and more of its people, the Green Revolution has been a disincentive for them to get serious about population control. But population growth historically levels out in developed nations, and it is impossible to make the leap from developing to developed without an adequate supply of food. Advocates of high-yield agriculture say that runoff and water table depletion are problems only when planting techniques are misapplied. More education is obviously needed.[117] Dr. Borlaug, yet again a convincing spokesman for the revolution he helped to lead, explains that, "Had we tried to use the technology of 1950 to produce the harvest of 2000 it would have taken an additional 2.75 billion acres of land."[118] Environmentalists would agree with Borlaug that deforestation on such a massive scale would have been disastrous. Even more disastrous would have been the mass starvations once predicted for much of the developing world.

This is not to say that famine is no longer a very real threat in many places, particularly in Africa. It is. But thanks to the Green Revolution, in which the Rockefeller Foundation was a widely acknowledged leader, food production has essentially kept up with population growth. If farmers, scientists, governments, and civil societies around the world continue to meet this challenge, and the associated challenges of environmental stewardship and the equitable distribution of food, then it may be possible to reach population equilibrium without anyone's worst fears coming to pass.

BUILDING APPLIED KNOWLEDGE

Curbing Global Population Growth: Rockefeller's Population Council (1952)

Background. Throughout the first half of the twentieth century, the Rockefeller Foundation had been a significant contributor to broad advances in medical research and efforts in worldwide disease eradication. In contemplating the work of the foundation his grandfather created, John D. Rockefeller III began to perceive that a reduction in mortality without a corresponding decline in fertility rates could contribute to population growth that may not be sustainable, particularly in developing countries. In the late 1940s, a Rockefeller Foundation-sponsored team returning from Asia noted that an imminent worldwide surge in population growth demanded immediate action.[119] Rapid worldwide population growth was known to be taking place, but scholarship on population and demography lacked organization and coherence in part because of the complexity of the problem of population growth and in part because of the cultural and religious sensitivities implicated in fertility issues. Rockefeller, however, felt that the complexities of rising population growth and the sensitivities of birth control should not inhibit the needed focus of science and public policy.[120]

Strategy. In the early 1950s, Rockefeller's interest in the problems related to population growth led him to provide the financial support for a two-day conference, held under the auspices of the National Academy of Sciences, the president of which was also the president of the Rockefeller Institute for Medical Research.[121] When the Rockefeller Foundation declined to take up population growth as an issue of concern, Rockefeller created the Population Council as an independent entity.[122] He provided a gift of one hundred thousand dollars to enable the council to begin functioning.

The council's charter members were Frank Notestein, demographer at

Princeton University who urged that attention be given to high fertility rates; Frederick Osborn, influential proponent of population research; Thomas Parran, dean of the Graduate School of Public Health at the University of Pittsburgh; and John D. Rockefeller III.[123] Shortly after its formation, Rockefeller provided an additional grant of $1.25 million to the council over five years. The Ford Foundation also made an early contribution to the council, a grant of $600,000.[124] Later financial backers included the Rockefeller, Mellon, Hewlett, and Packard foundations.[125]

Rather than develop and advocate a public policy position itself, the council made grants to individuals and research institutes in various countries and regions to improve research on population growth that promoted a wider understanding of population issues worldwide.[126] Also, understanding the diversity of sensitivities across cultures regarding population control, particularly birth control, the council sought to strengthen the capacity of indigenous researchers and governments in various countries throughout the world to address population issues in ways consistent with local culture. One of the council's earliest programs was the distribution of fellowship grants to students of population and demography.[127] In light of the dearth of scholarship in these fields, these fellows became the drivers of population-control policies and demographic scholarship throughout the world over the next few decades. When public attention began to focus on population issues in the 1960s and 1970s, alumni of the council's fellowship program were already placed and prepared to steer policy directions.[128] The United States, under the Kennedy administration, began to adopt foreign policy positions on global population reflecting Rockefeller's concerns articulated a decade earlier.[129]

At the same time, the council strengthened its own in-house expertise in population-related science and policy issues. Because of the council's early leadership on population issues, it became a source of crucial guidance to the United Nations as that organization began to take on responsibility for such issues around the world. After helping to fund the UN's first World Population Conference in 1954, the Council assisted the UN in establishing the first regional centers for demographic training and research in India, Chile, and Egypt.[130]

Impact. In the culturally sensitive field of birth-control development and research, the council played a significant role in the development, testing, establishment of local development, and distribution of the intrauterine device (IUD). Physicians had already begun developing IUDs thirty years before the Population Council became involved, but the council helped to coordinate international efforts to develop a safe and effective IUD.[131] In 1962, the council organized an international conference in New York for scientists to report on their usage of various forms of IUDs. Over the next two years, the council made research grants in excess of two million dollars to support IUD development. An innovation in the council's approach to IUD development was the large-scale statistical monitoring and analysis of data regarding the IUD's safety and effectiveness from different physicians using the IUD with council grants.[132]

In 1969, the U.S. Office of Economic Opportunity granted the council two-million dollars to support family planning for poor women in the United States.[133] The following year, in responding to a report issued by a panel chaired by John D. Rockefeller III, the United Nations transformed its capacity to respond to countries requesting assistance in reducing rapid population growth.[134]

Since its founding, the Council has pioneered research and enhanced understanding in numerous arenas of population growth, including demographic research and tracking, contraception use, family planning service delivery, and AIDS tracking and prevention.[135] During the time of the Population Council's operation, rates of population growth have begun to slow, and fertility rates are falling, particularly in the developing world. Total fertility rates in developing countries have declined from 6.0 per woman in 1965 to 3.2 in 2000.[136]

MODEL BUILDING

Children's Television Workshop and Sesame Street (1966)

Background. In the mid-1960s, children's programming was hard to find, with *Captain Kangaroo* as the only weekday show directed at the preschool audience. Ford, the primary financial supporter of National Educational Television, was interested solely in adult "liberal education."[137] A couple of studies in the late 1960s prompted new ideas in the potential for television to educate mass audiences of children. One reported that it could cost as much as $2.75 billion to educate, in a traditional classroom setting, the country's twelve million three-to-five-year-old children who at the time received no formal education.[138] Another, a Nielsen survey, noted that children under six watched an average of thirty hours of television a week.[139]

Strategy. The idea that led to the creation of Children's Television Workshop was sparked during a conversation in 1966 at the home of Joan Ganz Cooney. Cooney hosted a dinner party at her Gramercy Park apartment to celebrate her first Emmy, for a documentary entitled *Poverty, Anti-Poverty and the Poor,* to which she invited her boss, Lewis Freedman, and Carnegie Corporation Vice President Lloyd Morrisett.[140]

Morrisett, who had long worked on the corporation's efforts in childhood development, questioned Cooney whether television could be used effectively to educate young children.[141] Shortly thereafter the Carnegie Corporation agreed to fund a feasibility study that Cooney would conduct. She began the study in June, interviewing twenty-six cognitive psychologists, educators, and pediatricians.[142]

Cooney presented the study to the Carnegie Corporation in October 1966. In it, she suggested that a full scale evaluation be conducted in light of the widespread viewing habits of young children.[143] The corporation then sought to bring about the evaluation Cooney suggested, but it also noted that the high cost of the evaluation was beyond Carnegie's funding capacity. Morrisett, forecasting the cost to be about four million to five million dollars, began to seek foundation partners to join with Carnegie in funding the proposal.[144]

Morrisett's fundraising attempts with foundations and other organizations came up dry through June 1967. On June 30, however, at a meeting in Washington, U.S. Commissioner of Education Harold Howe II, a friend of Morrisett's, expressed great interest in the project and suggested that the U.S. Office of Education might provide substantial financial support.[145] The Carnegie Corporation board, understanding the necessity of demonstrating its faith in the project in order to attract other potential donors, approved a one-million-dollar commitment in January 1968, which the Ford Foundation followed with a commitment of $250,000 three weeks later, along with a promise of additional funds if the program got rolling. Ford later contributed an additional one million dollars. The Corporation for Public Broadcasting provided another one million dollars in one of its earliest major grants. The U.S. Office of Education contributed four million dollars.[146]

The Children's Television Workshop, the entity that would conduct the evaluation Cooney suggested, and *Sesame Street*, CTW's first program, were announced to the public in March 1968. Cooney was named CTW's executive director.[147] CTW was initially affiliated with National Educational Television for the legal and administrative services NET could provide, but it became independent a year later.[148]

David D. Connell, former executive producer of *Captain Kangaroo*, became the executive producer of *Sesame Street* on the recommendation of Michael Dann, programming chief of CBS-TV. Connell was initially deterred from taking the post by the large team of academicians affiliated with the project and the fear that their presence would force the entertainment value of the program to take a back seat to educational efforts. When Cooney assured Connell that the program would not sacrifice entertainment for educational value, Connell abandoned his resistance and agreed to join CTW.[149]

The comprehensive research effort that went into ensuring that the program would be both educational and able to sustain the attention of its young viewers was coordinated in large part by the Educational Testing Service. Former CTW President David Britt noted at the twentieth anniversary of *Sesame Street*'s debut that "research has been at the core of *Sesame Street*." Discussing the importance of research in ongoing series development, Britt said that, "Research is there during preliminary development of shows, and continues during production, helping us create programs that children both like and understand."[150]

Impact. Sesame Street premiered on November 10, 1969. Even taking into account the massive marketing campaign CTW undertook to promote a large audience for *Sesame Street*'s first few episodes, particularly among minority and underprivileged children, its ratings far surpassed the expectations of its creators and others at CTW.[151] Almost 1.5 million television homes tuned in to *Sesame Street* during its first week.[152] Research efforts monitoring the learning progress of *Sesame Street* viewers demonstrated significant advances; those children who watched the program benefited.[153]

CTW later drew some criticism for its "failure" to close the education gap between disadvantaged children and middle-class children. Early in the project, compensatory education was an objective—use television to reach those children who had no other access to early education. The problem with such an objective was that its premise required that middle-class children not watch *Sesame Street*. Disadvantaged children who watched the program did surpass middle-class children who did not watch, but in fact, middle-class children—and their parents—were drawn to the program, neutralizing the potential for any compensatory effect.[154] A Russell Sage Foundation analysis of the initial ETS study even found that, since whites watched *Sesame Street* more than blacks, the program increased rather than decreased the education gap. CTW responded that it had dropped compensatory education as an objective for *Sesame Street*, focusing instead on maximizing the educational potential of television programming, an objective on which it exceeded all expectation.[155]

Despite any criticism levied against it, *Sesame Street* is widely understood to be one of the most successful television ventures ever. Today, Sesame Street is seen in more than 120 countries.[156] As of 2005, *Sesame Street's* Emmy wins total 101, the most Emmy wins for any television series.[157]

BUILDING ADVOCACY ORGANIZATIONS

Conservative Legal Advocacy (1975)

Background. The Olin Foundation, beginning with its emergence in 1973 as a major contributor on the philanthropic scene, has remained committed to funding scholarship favoring "limited government, individual responsibility, and free society," consistent with the philosophies of its benefactor, John Olin, and its high-profile longtime president, William Simon. Among the concerns of the foundation's board was the direction of legal education and the fear that liberals controlled most law schools.[158]

Strategy. The Olin Foundation, along with one of its grantees, the Institute for Educational Affairs, an organization supported by the Olin Foundation to scout high-impact conservative projects, recognized the early promise of a group of conservative law students. Despite the increasing success of the law and economics movement in bringing about more conservative thought in legal scholarship, the students wanted to bring more conservative dialogue to their law schools. Early members of the group, which named itself the Federalist Society, included Spencer Abraham, later a senator and secretary of energy, and David McIntosh, later elected to the U.S. House of Representatives.[159] Olin and the IEA together sponsored the society's first major event, a conference that helped to jumpstart the organization's visibility and recruitment capabilities.[160]

Over the next two decades, the Olin Foundation contributed more than two million dollars in grants to the Federalist Society. The society now has local student chapters at 150 law schools and about sixty chapters for practicing attorneys.[161] The society's longtime executive director, Eugene B. Meyer, suggests that the Federalist Society might not exist had it not been for Olin's early, sustained support.[162]

In addition to supporting the intellectual foundation for conservative policy, Olin has also funded organizations litigating on behalf of conservative causes in the manner demonstrated by public-interest law organizations created earlier with the financial support of the Ford Foundation. The Olin Foundation has contributed over two million dollars to the Washington Legal Foundation, $1.3 million to the Center for Individual Rights (CIR), and one million dollars to support the Pacific Legal Foundation.[163]

Impact. The Federalist Society's impact has stretched beyond the imagination of its early donors. Some credit the society with effectively counterbalancing what the Federalist Society calls a shift to the left in the American Bar Association, particularly in enabling the Bush administration to cease the traditional practice of asking the ABA for evaluation of its judicial nominees. Many conservatives considered the ABA's recommendations to be detrimental to the judicial nomination process of conservative judges.[164] Furthermore, the society has enabled conservative law students to develop networks that are maintained as the students attain increasing public responsibilities in their careers. Three of President George W. Bush's first cabinet members, as well as Bush's solicitor general and staff members in the White House counsel's office, all belonged to the Federalist Society. In addition, members of the Federalist Society are said to have played central roles on President Bush's committee to suggest nominees for judicial appointments.[165]

On the conservative public interest litigation side, the foundation's grantees have also been successful. The Washington Legal Foundation has fought various government regulations, particularly regulations proposed by the FDA that the WLF considers to be outside the power of the FDA.[166] CIR has successfully litigated for professors accused of sexual harassment, for religious organizations seeking to participate in publicly funded activity, for constitutional limits on allowing Congress to criminalize gender violence, and against racial preferences in higher education.[167] The Pacific Legal Foundation has long advocated in favor of the California Civil Rights Initiative, or Proposition 209.[168]

Model Building

Grameen Bank (1976)

Background. When Bangladesh gained its independence from Pakistan in 1971, Secretary of State Henry Kissinger called it "an international basket case."[169] With a weak economy, overcrowded cities, and a high exposure to catastrophic weather, Bangladesh has remained one of the least developed countries (LDCs) in the world, and has received more than thirty billion dollars in international assistance over the past three decades.[170] However, Bangladesh is also the birthplace of the Grameen Bank, one of the great success stories in third world development.

Strategy. The Grameen Bank was created by Professor Muhammad Yunus, a Bangladeshi economics professor who, during the famine of 1974, felt compelled to reach out to the Bangladeshi poor in an effort to understand why they were unable to achieve economic success. Over the next two years, Professor Yunus studied the poor, landless underclass of Jobra, a village near his home in Chittagong. He concluded that the poor were poor not because they were inherently unable to support themselves, but rather because they lacked access to capital, a structural flaw that could be remedied. Yunus began by making small loans, of about twenty-five dollars each, to forty-three villagers in Jobra. His largesse soon grew into the world's first experiment in micro-finance. Using these small amounts of money, Yunus's borrowers were able to generate a steady stream of income, with which they not only paid off their debts but also improved the economic lot of their families.

Between 1976 and 1979, these micro-loans "successfully changed the lives of around 500 borrowers."[171] Working at first with only his graduate economics students, then later through the branch offices of several state-run banks, Yunus eventually decided to quit his academic post and incorporate the Grameen (meaning "rural" or "countryside") Bank in 1983. The bank makes small loans (averaging about $376[172]) to clients, who are required to be members of a five-person team of borrowers. Teams are responsible for encouraging, as well as helping, each other to repay loans. A loan is made first to one member of the group. If she successfully repays it, a loan is made to someone else in the group. So each borrower's access to credit is dependent upon her team's repayment of all loans made. This "peer group lending" uses a mixture of peer pressure and peer support to achieve a rate of repayment significantly higher than that enjoyed by even the most successful American banks.[173] Groups of five are organized into local centers, which are associations of eight to ten groups that act as a regional support net. Committed to transparency in a nation that has been plagued by corruption, the Grameen Bank makes all its loans publicly at the center meetings.[174] In addition, Grameen required its borrowers to pledge to maintain certain social principles, such as educating female children, not giving dowries, and helping to build schools in their communities. As a result, the bank achieves leverage beyond the scope of its financial benefits.

The loans must be used to generate income. Borrowers use the loans to become self-employed, whether by purchasing dairy cows, honeybees, or bamboo to make furniture that can be sold.[175]

To finance its early lending,[176] the Grameen Bank received grants and loans (market rate and concessionary) from banks (in Bangladesh and around the world), governments (such as those of Bangladesh and Canada), international aid agencies (like the International Fund for Agricultural Development), and foundations.[177] Most notable among the latter group has been the Ford Foundation, which supported Yunus from his earliest efforts, while he was still an economics professor studying the causes of poverty in rural Bangladesh. In the mid-1970s, the foundation gave Professor Yunus a twelve-thousand-dollar grant for his poverty research, which was then followed up by consistent support.[178] The foundation has contributed to the bank's resources for lending, and, according to Yunus, an early eight-hundred-thousand-dollar grant from Ford was the critical guarantee fund that enabled him to attract the support of skeptical commercial banks.[179]

Outcomes. The Grameen Bank has grown dramatically, and its results have been extraordinary. The Grameen Bank now turns a profit and has deposits worth $324 million.[180] Since its inception, the bank has made over $4.57 billion in loans. Its rate of recovery is 98.85 percent, despite the fact that the Grameen Bank refuses to make loans to anyone except the poorest members of Bangladeshi society. The bank now has over four million members (clients) in 48,000 villages serviced by over 1,300 Grameen branch offices.[181] The Bank also makes housing loans that have enabled the

Bangladeshi poor to construct over six hundred thousand new homes. The Grameen Bank has also empowered women in a society where they have traditionally been subservient to men. Ninety-five percent of all borrowers from the Grameen Bank are women. This is no accident. Professor Yunus realized early on that women are more likely to repay a first-time loan than men, and that women borrowers were far more likely than men to use the profits generated from a loan to support and uplift their families, rather than on personal consumption. So the bank has also been an engine of social change.[182]

Impact. Micro-finance was a true innovation. Its success flies in the face of traditional banking theory, which holds that destitute residents of third-world villages, often lacking any property of their own, do not make reliable borrowers. And the methods of the Grameen Bank have been emulated around the world. According to the United Nations, some 67 million people had access to micro-credit in 2003.[183] Institutions modeled after the Grameen Bank have sprung up in seventy countries; there are over five hundred such organizations in the United States alone![184] The Ford Foundation has supported the spread of the Grameen model. In the late 1980s, the foundation funded an exchange program between American development workers and the bank.[185] According to Anwarul K. Chowdhury, the United Nations Under-Secretary-General and High Representative for the Least Developed Countries, "Microcredit is an inducer, a catalyst for economic activity of the poor people" and "[leads] to the empowerment of women. . . . "[186]

Advocacy for Public Policy

Support of Democratization and Civil Societies in Central and Eastern Europe (1980)

Background. George Soros earned billions of dollars as a currency speculator, and has spent the last twenty-five years giving away his fortune at an astonishing rate. Preferring to underwrite his foundations' budgets each year, Soros has not endowed large philanthropies like Rockefeller and Carnegie. Last year, his Open Society Institute paid out slightly more than $110 million, ranking it twenty-sixth in giving among American foundations.[187] Yet even this high figure understates dramatically the extent of Soros's philanthropy. OSI serves today as the hub of the Soros network of foundations, which comprises thirty-three distinct private foundations, operating in more than sixty countries around the world.[188] In fact, George Soros's annual giving has for much of the last twenty years rivaled that of the Ford Foundation, which last year had assets worth $10 billion and made grants of $432 million.[189]

Soros, his network of foundations, and the grantees they have funded aided dissident movements behind the Iron Curtain in the 1980s, and later to help support throughout Central and Eastern Europe the transition to democracy and the rise of civil societies. Soros, who is Hungarian by birth, grew up in the shadow of occupation: first by the Nazis and later by the Soviets. So it is perhaps not surprising that, as his wealth grew, Soros in the late 1970s and early 1980s became increasingly active in supporting dissident causes around Europe. What is sure, however, is that Soros has acted on a scale larger than most governments. Some of his greatest success stories, such as the support of Russian science in the crucial period after Communism's collapse, and his creation of Central European University, are not told here, but are documented in separate cases available on the Web site and in the on-demand book. This case should stand on its own as an account of one philanthropist's part in weakening Communism's grip on Europe, and in promoting transformation and progress, both before and after the Berlin Wall fell.

There is no comprehensive record of Soros's philanthropy in Central and Eastern Europe. The Open Society Institute, which now monitors and oversees the vast network of Soros foundations, did not become fully operational until 1995. As a result, much of Soros's early philanthropy—that given out-of-pocket and that invested through one of his many private foundations—is difficult to trace, even for Soros himself. Furthermore, the Soros Foundations have not typically required, as a prerequisite for their grantmaking, extensive documentation or analysis of problems to be solved and the specific uses to which donations have been put.

This was particularly true in the early years, when a portion of Soros's philanthropy was targeted at groups and causes seeking to undermine their own repressive governments. For example, Michael Kaufman writes that, in the early 1980s, "Soros suppressed his curiosity and showed the tactful discretion of an experienced conspirator"[190] in not demanding to be told where all gifts had gone. It was enough for Soros to know that his gifts had been passed on discreetly to dissident movements bubbling just under the surface in Poland, Czechoslovakia, and other oppressed nations where Communist regimes were struggling to maintain their increasingly tenuous hold on power. The lack of a paper trail was not, however, a function solely of the clandestine nature of certain grantees. George Soros himself has said, "I don't believe in being able to calculate these things too closely, and we haven't made any profound needs assessment studies. We just recognize the need is there. We'll do the best we can."[191]

Whatever the cause, it is enough for our purposes to know that any description of the Soros network's support of democratization and the rise of civil societies in the former Soviet Union and elsewhere will be unavoidably incomplete. The limitations of time and space will make this case study particularly so, but we hope the reader will gain some sense of the breadth and depth of Soros's massive philanthropy in the region, will come to understand certain broad themes in his giving, and will appreciate that, while the impact of Soros's efforts may be impossible to quantify, it can be reasonably said that his philanthropy was—for many years—a crucial lifeline to a region profoundly challenged. It may be an exaggeration to say—as some have—that George Soros was "a one man Marshall Plan."[192] But just how much of an exaggeration will be up to the reader to decide.

Strategy. In the early 1980s, Soros began quietly and gradually to support dissident movements in Czechoslovakia, Poland, and Hungary. By 1987, he was pouring funds into these countries and, especially, the Soviet Union, where Gorbachev's reforms had convinced him it might be possible to crack the veneer of state control, enabling long-strangled values like openness, tolerance, and economic liberalization to grow. And in the late 1980s and early 1990s, as European Communism crumbled, Soros offered millions upon millions of dollars to put in place the building blocks of what his mentor Karl Popper termed "the open society." Characterized by freedom of speech and the press, freedom of association, and other democratic values, the opening of closed societies has been the guiding light of all of George Soros's philanthropic endeavors. As the *New York Times* editorial page explained in a piece honoring his achievements: "Mr. Soros recognized that a healthy democracy required more than just a plurality of political parties and an uncensored press. The institute also sponsored cultural activities and projects promoting financial accountability, more adequate health care and prisoner's rights."[193] At times, Soros foundations have supported innovative demonstration projects, as one of their American counterparts might do. Often, however, they have served a quasi-governmental role, providing critical social services and democratic infra-structure that states have been simply unable to offer. On into the 1990s, and even past the turn of the millennium, Soros has sought to repair the damage caused by years of Communist rule, whether by reforming primary education, retraining former military officers for civilian life, or seeking to limit the destruction caused by ethnic violence.

Outcomes. Here then, is a brief sample of the activities undertaken by George Soros and his network of foundations to introduce behind the Iron Curtain the elements of open society, and later to relieve suffering and to promote modernization and economic development in Central and Eastern Europe.

Poland. Soros began in 1981 to send money to the Polish opposition movement. Among his earliest philanthropic efforts was funding a network of unauthorized publishers in an attempt to make available some of Western literature and scholarship that had been banned by the Communist authorities. According to Kaufman, Soros understood that the Solidarity movement represented one of the most promising developments among the Warsaw Pact countries, and he supported it steadily and discreetly. Later, after the fall of the Berlin Wall, Soros helped Poland along the path to economic liberalization by sponsoring the renowned economist Jeffrey Sachs to help plan a set of rapid market reforms (the so-called "shock therapy" approach). Soros himself also consulted with the Polish economist who helped craft the highly successful economic conversion plan implemented by Polish Finance Minister Leszek Balcerowicz.

Hungary. In 1984, Soros—who was born in Budapest—created in Hungary the first of his philanthropic foundations. This very act was, in and of itself, a major challenge to the status quo in Soros's native country. Soros insisted on autonomy for the new foundation, and convinced the government not only to allow ostensibly forbidden dissidents to benefit from his largesse, but also to permit the foundation to publish freely the names of all its grantees. This was just the sort of openness the Hungarian regime had long been wary of. The negotiations to bring this freedom about were tense, and it took the personal involvement of Soros, including on several occasions the bare threat to cancel the enterprise outright, to convince the Hungarian government to concede to the Hungarian Academy of Science/George Soros Foundation the privileges it enjoyed.

The foundation's earliest donation was given to import some fifty thousand previously unavailable books to Hungarian libraries. Like Soros's support of publishers in Poland, this donation increased Hungarian citizens' access to democratic ideals they had long been denied. Both grants flowed from Soros's belief that Communist regimes could not withstand their citizens' knowing how deprived they were. The success of the book donation convinced Soros to purchase two hundred Xerox copiers for Hungarian universities and libraries. Prior to that gift, access to such machines was strictly controlled. Researchers were required to submit an application to photocopy anything, and then wait several weeks while the application was considered. For Soros, the rapid and free spread of information enabled by these two hundred copiers was analogous to the spread of openness, tolerance, and modernization he hoped to help enable throughout the region.[194] Soros's initial commitment to the Hungary foundation was for one million dollars per year. This was soon increased to three million dollars, and in the mid-1990s it would peak with donations from Soros of twenty-two million dollars in a single year.[195] The full range of the foundation's activities—as with the other philanthropies Soros went on to create—was larger, however, than just supporting the spread of information. Like a major American foundation, the Soros Foundation in Hungary supported an array of philanthropic endeavors. All of these, however, were unified by a commitment to help the country develop into a modern democracy with all the building blocks of a fully open society more firmly in place.

Czechoslovakia. In the early 1970s, George Soros began sending money to the dissident group Charta 77, which was led by the playwright and activist Václav Havel. As he became more interested in philanthropy, and also more committed to supporting reform in the Communist-controlled nations of Eastern and Central Europe, Soros became Charta 77's largest single backer.[196] In December 1989, as Charta became the Civic Forum, an embryonic political party, Soros flew to Prague and there set up a new foundation to support media outlets, cultural organizations, and other causes long neglected under Communist rule. While there, he also met with Marian Calfa, the acting Czechoslovakian president. In a discussion of the nation's future, Soros urged Calfa to support Havel for the presidency. Later, when Czechoslovakia split into two states, Soros opened another foundation in Bratislava to do in Slovakia what his Prague foundation would continue doing in the new Czech Republic.

The Soviet Union. By far the grandest of Soros's philanthropic efforts was in the Soviet Union, and, later, the republics that succeeded it. While his Moscow foundation remained much the largest, in the early 1990s, Soros created independent grantmaking foundations in the Ukraine, Belarus, Moldova, Georgia, Kazakhstan, Uzbekistan, Kyrgyzstan, and Tajikistan. Between 1987 and 2003, Soros spent over one billion dollars, first to pry open Soviet society, and then to help many of its millions of citizens to enjoy the fruits of democracy, or, more often, at least to survive the upheaval it brought. Soros spent one hundred million dollars on the Transformation of the Humanities Program, which published new works, and funded the translation and distribution of dozens of previously unavailable titles by scholars such as Hayek and Popper. The program also contributed greatly to the modernization of Russian scholarship by introducing the concept of peer review to such fields as history, political science, economics, and art analysis. In the mid-1990s, Soros also funded a project to link all thirty-three of Russia's regional universities to the Internet. His foundation promoted independent media outlets and helped retrain mid-level military officers for life as civilian entrepreneurs.[197] It also worked to reform nursery school education and to equip hospitals for more humane and more medically sound childbirth services. And in late 1997, Soros pledged a donation of five hundred million dollars to be made over three years.[198] With that gift, which was distributed among a range of causes, including one hundred million dollars for public-health projects, Soros for a time outspent the United States government, which was then giving about $95 million per year for reconstruction and democratization in Russia.

Yugoslavia. After the breakup of Yugoslavia, Soros created foundations in Croatia, Slovenia, Bosnia, and Macedonia. Without a doubt, the most notable grant made by any of these foundations was the fifty million dollars Soros gave in December 1992, to alleviate the suffering of the Bosnian people. Although Soros considers it a failure any time his foundations are forced to resort to such last-ditch efforts against a backdrop of violence, this grant funded a number of remarkable projects. In addition to supporting an independent newspaper, several radio networks, art exhibits, and academic journals, this grant funded the work of an American named Fred Cuny. A maverick by any standard, Cuny organized ambitious projects in Sarajevo, amid constant violence, that included a grassroots seed production campaign by which citizens could feed themselves, and an engineering project to restore power to much of the city, including the critical plasma unit serving all of Sarajevo's operating rooms. Cuny organized fifteen thousand Sarajevans for a project to tap safely into the city's damaged natural gas line, enabling the people to cook their food, and, most remarkably of all, he conceived and oversaw the construction of a water purification plant within the city limits. This last project was completely unprecedented; it spared residents the need to travel to the city's scarce drinking wells (a favorite target of snipers), and by August 1994, had restored running water to Sarajevo's 275,000 remaining residents.

Impact. The sheer scale of the Soros network's operations in central and eastern Russia is impressive. But it is important to remember that hundreds of millions, even billions, of dollars can be squandered without any noticeable result, particularly on problems of the magnitude that Soros and his associates faced down. Certainly, some of Soros's donations have suffered this fate. In Russia, for example, Soros was often forced to rely upon well-connected members of the old status quo, some of whom appear to have abused and even stolen the funds entrusted to them. Other times, the Soros foundations have simply fallen short of their goals. As Soros says of his giving: "When I got into this business of philanthropy it was definitely a process of trial and error. From '79 to '84 was a period of painful experimentation. I didn't know what the hell I was doing, and I made some wrong steps."[199]

At other times, however, he and his associates have succeeded brilliantly. The Xerox machines project, for example, leveraged a relatively small grant to change the landscape of Hungarian academia. According to Kaufman, "Quite suddenly, without any announcement, people in intellectual or university environments were able to copy whatever they wanted. . . . " This and other Soros initiatives made it far harder for the authorities to stem the flow of information. And in Sarajevo, the grants overseen by Fred Cuny achieved remarkable things under extremely difficult circumstances. While problems of counterfactuality are of course unavoidable in such instances as trying to assign one man credit for weakening global Communism, they are less so in the case of the Bosnian relief projects. Without OSI support, Fred Cuny would quite simply not have been in a position to restore power and running water to the people of Sarajevo. Soros says of Cuny: "Truly, I think that Fred probably did save Sarajevo. You know, water, gas, the seeds and gardening, running in the electric cable and the blood plasma unit. He really did it, and that, you know, is something."[200]

Some OSI projects in the region are still too young to be accurately judged. Step by Step, for example, is an early education program similar to

America's Head Start. Although it has been adopted by approximately thirty countries already, Aryeh Neier, the president of the Open Society Institute, feels that it will likely lead only to "a Rolls Royce early childhood for a relatively small number of children."[201] Others within the network, however, say that it is the best money Soros has ever spent.

Still, it is widely recognized that Soros has been a major player in the transformation of the entire region. Certainly, the various nations of Central and Eastern Europe still face a host of challenges, and they cannot be looked at as one bloc. As early as 1995, for example, OSI was fielding requests from the Poland foundation for public advocacy support for the rights of the disabled, while the Georgia foundation was buying generators to keep schools warm during the long winter.[202]

In aggregate, it is fair to say that Soros has probably made many grants that have had virtually no lasting impact. But he has also funded projects with enormous reach, and of major consequence. Many prominent Russians, including Mikhail Gorbachev, have nominated Soros for the Nobel Peace Prize. As the editorial page of the *New York Times* stated in 2003:

> Mr. Soros' bold ambition was to nurture a broader base for democratic transformation. To a remarkable extent, he succeeded. . . . For the most part, he has spent his money wisely and generously. Russia and the other Eastern and Central European countries he has helped toward democracy owe him their appreciation.[203]

CHANGING PUBLIC ATTITUDES AND BEHAVIORS

Tobacco Use Programs (1991)

Background. Tobacco use is the largest single cause of preventable deaths in the United States. Over four hundred thousand people each year die of tobacco-related health problems such as lung cancer and heart disease. And cigarettes are addictive. Over 65 percent of smokers say they want to quit. Over 50 percent, in any given year, make a serious effort to do so. Only 2.5 percent of them succeed.[204] The addictive nature and health risks of smoking are universally acknowledged.[205] But this was not always the case. As recently as 1994, the chief executives of the nation's seven largest tobacco companies each swore, in testimony before Congress, that he believed neither nicotine to be addictive, nor cigarettes to be harmful.[206] The estimated annual burden of tobacco-related health problems on the American health-care system is eighty billion dollars in direct expenditures and an additional fifty billion dollars in indirect costs.[207]

In 1990, the board of the Robert Wood Johnson Foundation selected Dr. Steven Schroeder to serve as the foundation's president, understanding clearly that Dr. Schroeder was interested "in taking the Foundation in the direction of working on substance abuse problems."[208] At the time, no American foundations were involved in the fields of tobacco policy or research.[209] In fact, the loudest voice in the public-health debate over tobacco was that of the Tobacco Institute, an organization created by the tobacco companies to communicate their message to the news media and the public.

There were many risks associated with entering the field, especially considering the enormous political heft of the tobacco industry, which has annual sales of over $45 billion.[210] However, the magnitude of the health risks associated with tobacco made it a tough issue to ignore.[211] The foundation's board was initially deadlocked on the issue, but, once the proposal was narrowed to focus the foundation's efforts on underage tobacco use, the board agreed, adopting as a primary goal, "[The reduction of] the harmful effects, and the irresponsible use, of tobacco, alcohol, and drugs."

Strategy. Between 1991 and 2003, the Robert Wood Johnson Foundation spent approximately $408 million on a wide range of tobacco-related programs. The foundation's primary aims have been to reduce the incidence of youth smoking, to publicize the negative health effects of tobacco use, and to help addicted smokers quit using tobacco. These goals have been pursued through a wide range of programs, including:[212]

- SMOKELESS STATES: Started in 1993, SmokeLess States is a state-level initiative designed to assist local groups in educating their communities about tobacco and about the policy options available to regulate it. SmokeLess States coalitions also offer prevention and treatment programs targeted primarily at teenagers. To date, the foundation has contributed approximately $92 million to the program, every dollar of which is matched by the local coalitions receiving support.[213]

- THE CENTER FOR TOBACCO-FREE KIDS: The center is the RWJF's largest national endeavor to curb smoking. The center was created by the foundation, in partnership with the American Cancer Society, and was intended to serve as a proactive counterweight to the Tobacco Institute. Since 1995, the foundation has provided over seventy million dollars to the center.

- THE TOBACCO AND SUBSTANCE ABUSE POLICY RESEARCH PROGRAMS: There is an enormous range of factors that influence a person's decision to smoke, and, likewise, a wide range of concerns in any tobacco policy discussion. Recognizing that no one field of inquiry can possibly encompass the multiplicity of angles from which tobacco can be viewed, the foundation has funded research exploring such issues as the biological and societal factors that can lead to nicotine addiction, the relationship between cigarette prices and consumption, and many others. Particularly important has been the RWJF-funded research into the elasticity of demand with respect to the price of cigarettes. The foundation has used its leverage as a funder and an acknowledged leader in tobacco policy discussion to convene experts from a range of fields to promote the sharing of insights and the undertaking of multidisciplinary research into tobacco issues.[214]

- THE SPORTS INITIATIVE: Through this endeavor, the foundation seeks to enlist professional athletes and sports leagues publicly to discourage young fans from using tobacco. Of particular note is the National Spit Tobacco Education Program (NSTEP), a partnership between the RWJF and Joe Garagiola, a former major-leaguer who for years has recruited fellow baseball stars to help break the stereotypical association between baseball players and spit tobacco.

- SMOKE-FREE FAMILIES: While the bulk of the foundation's resources have been dedicated to research and prevention, funds have also been allocated to tobacco-cessation programs. The flagship of these efforts is the Smoke-Free Families program, which targets pregnant women and single mothers, offering them information and cessation assistance in view of the serious health effects that smoking can have on their unborn children and infants.

Outcomes. Many of the programs supported by the Robert Wood Johnson Foundation have had a significant effect on the huge national debate over tobacco. SmokeLess States coalitions are active in thirty-one states and the District of Columbia. By publicizing such information as the public-health effects of second-hand smoke and the effect of excise taxes on tobacco consumption, the coalitions have contributed to the enactment of many local laws regulating the sale and consumption of tobacco products. Foundation-funded research showing that children's consumption of cigarettes declines as price increases has provided the impetus for passage of tobacco tax increases in states across the nation. The Center for Tobacco-Free Kids has received significant public attention. In the late 1990s, it was asked, by the attorneys general of several states, to participate, as a disinterested and trustworthy party, in the states' negotiations with the tobacco industry over pending litigation. The center received much criticism from its allies in the anti-tobacco movement when this was publicized, and a combination of interests from the far left (opposed to any deal with the tobacco companies) and the far right (opposed, for political reasons, to any regulation of cigarettes) narrowly defeated the agreed-upon settlement.[215] The National Spit Tobacco Education Campaign has been publicly supported by such all-stars as Alex Rodriguez, Lenny Dykstra, Hank Aaron, and the late Mickey Mantle. And a wide range of other outcomes has flowed from RWJF tobacco programs. Foundation-sponsored research, for example, was cited repeatedly by the FDA in its determination to seek jurisdiction over tobacco products, and RWJF-supported experts have advised members of Congress and testified before congressional committees.[216]

Impact. The Robert Wood Johnson Foundation was certainly not the first nonprofit organization to involve itself in tobacco research and advocacy. But the RWJF brought to bear the enormous resources of a major funder, and had the courage to tackle a problem that, for political reasons, the federal government had been hesitant to touch. The foundation was able to convene and support a wide spectrum of influential actors, and, in so doing, serve as a private center of power in the interest of the public—polyarchical in every way. The foundation, along with partners like the American Cancer Society, blazed a trail that many others have followed.[217]

Joe Garagiola, for example, had been working to spread awareness of the threat posed to young baseball players by spit tobacco for years before the RWJF sought him out. But with the foundation's help, he was able to take his message much more powerfully to scale. Garagiola himself recalls, "Until Robert Wood Johnson came along, I was working with a broken bat—now I had a Louisville Slugger."[218]

Despite the controversy surrounding its participation—and the eventual collapse of the settlement it negotiated—the Center for Tobacco-Free Kids has clearly been seen as a key fixture in discussions about tobacco control. This is demonstrated by the fact that its involvement was directly sought, first by the state attorneys general, but also by the FDA and the White House. And the center has succeeded as a counterweight to the Tobacco Institute. In fact, so discredited has the tobacco companies' message been that they shut down the institute several years ago.

Since 1995, smoking rates among adults have declined by 12.6 percent and among teens by 18 percent.[219] With a problem so enormously complicated, the foundation's influence cannot be called determinative. However, since 1991, the foundation has been at the forefront of tobacco research, education, advocacy, and treatment. As Sidney F. Wentz, former chairman of the foundation's board of trustees, wrote elegantly, in the Robert Wood Johnson Foundation's 1992 annual report, "There's no sword to cut through this Gordian knot, but we, as a Foundation, are obliged to keep picking at the strands of it with unremitting determination if we are ever to achieve our goal of improved health care for all Americans."

PARTNERSHIP AMONG FOUNDATIONS

China Sustainable Energy Program (1999)

Background. At the dawn of the twenty-first century, the Chinese economy is expanding at an incredible pace. Throughout most of the 1990s, China experienced 8 percent annual GDP growth. This rapid modernization has created enormous opportunity for millions of Chinese, but it also carries with it significant hazards. Curbing this economic boom is not a viable option; indeed, the Chinese government, hoping to keep up with the needs of its massive population, is committed to quadrupling its GDP over the next twenty years.[220] Among the risks posed by this ambitious goal is the very real possibility that China could destroy its natural environment for the sake of continued industrialization and economic growth. Such an environmental disaster could have environmental implications on a global scale—rapidly accelerated global warming, for instance. But it could also cause political and economic turmoil. As more and more nations demand ever larger shares of a limited pie of energy resources, geopolitical stability will inevitably be undermined.

Strategy. As part of its Conservation and Science Program, the David and Lucile Packard Foundation in 1999 convened "a series of meetings and consultations with scientists, policy-makers, business leaders, and analysts in China and the United States"[221] in an effort to understand the nature of this problem on the horizon. In March of that year, the Packard Foundation committed $22.2 million, over the next five years, for the China Sustainable Energy Program (CSEP). The program was to be managed by the Energy Foundation, and would aim, "To assist in China's transition to a sustainable energy future by promoting energy efficiency and renewable energy."[222]

Its strategy in seeking to do so is multipronged; it matches Chinese government officials, academic researchers, and NGOs to the best practices of international energy experts in an effort "to spot and pursue energy savings."[223] The CSEP makes direct grants to organizations in China; conducts workshops to tackle risks associated with China's continuing economic growth; and collaborates with local and national government officials, proposing policies and bringing to the fore problems of energy efficiency. Its six target areas are low-carbon development paths, appliance standards and buildings, industry, electric utilities, renewable energy, and transportation. In 2002, the William and Flora Hewlett Foundation joined the program with a grant of two million dollars for the program's transportation work.[224] Still, with a budget of approximately seven million dollars per year, the China Sustainable Energy Program is small, compared to other international efforts—those of the UN Development Program, World Bank, and European Union, for example. However, those organizations are not significantly involved in policy development. This has allowed the CSEP—through a combination of political connections, a sterling reputation (thanks both to the competence of its staff and the good names of the Packard and Hewlett Foundations), and an ability to harness international expertise—to carve out a niche that affords it great leverage in promoting energy sustainability.[225]

Outcomes. The CSEP has been highly effective in pursuing its mission.[226] Much of this is due to its excellent relations with many top Chinese government officials. Because of this working relationship, the CSEP has been able to propose new policy on such issues as Chinese auto emissions and the energy efficiency of appliances in a nation of 1.3 billion consumers of energy. Among the principal successes of the China Sustainable Energy

Program was its pivotal role in developing and winning support for the six mandatory energy efficiency standards adopted in China between 1999 and 2003. These standards will produce savings over the next fifteen years of three hundred million tons of coal and will prevent the emission, by China, of some 798 million tons of carbon dioxide (CO_2).[227] The CSEP also played a leading role in supporting the adoption of labeling laws and efficiency requirements for lighting, washing machines, TVs, and other appliances, "which by 2010 are expected to save [China] enough energy to avoid the need for at least 10 large new power plants."[228] And CSEP research and analysis helped shape the Chinese government's fuel economy standard—the first by a developing nation—which "could save 6 billion barrels of oil and reduce carbon emissions by over 800 million tons between now and 2030."[229]

Impact. Certainly, CSEP does not deserve all the credit for these and other promising developments. The Chinese government would, no matter what, be dealing with many—if not all—of the same issues that CSEP works on. No nation China's size could undergo anything like its degree of development and industrialization in this era of globalization and interdependence without being forced at least to consider the broad effects— environmental, economic, and political—of its policies. And the Chinese government has already managed, between 1980 and 2000, to quadruple its growth while only doubling its energy consumption.[230] But, according to an evaluation of CSEP carried out by Energy Resources International (ERI), the efforts of the Packard, Hewlett, and Energy foundations have definitely added value. In fact, the ERI evaluators were unanimous in their belief "that the CSEP has been exceptionally valuable to Chinese stakeholders," and "has both accelerated the development of policies and improved their substance."[231] As China continues to modernize, there will be a growing need for such acceleration of action and improvement of policy outcomes.

III

9

WHAT AILS THE FOUNDATIONS:

TRANSPARENCY AND

ACCOUNTABILITY

Foundations are dandy things, but the truth is few institutions are as complacent and potentially unaccountable to the real world as private foundations. When I was a public official, my dealings with philanthropy often left me with the question—who do they think they are?

Douglas W. Nelson, president,
The Annie E. Casey Foundation[1]

Everyone who has read the preceding chapters will recognize my strong conviction that foundations have been overwhelmingly beneficial for American society. Why, then, do we hear so much criticism of foundations? How much of it is justified?

Some criticism of foundations, of course, stems from the envy that wealth and power always attract. But some grows out of the foundation culture and the ways foundations relate to grantees. And some is triggered by foundation misbehavior, whether illegal, unethical, or simply inappropriate, much of it caused by insulation from external influences.

In this chapter, I'll examine the criticisms that foundations have received, fair and unfair. Like all generalizations, the observations I'll offer in this chapter are often inapplicable. Many foundations are very well run. But some are not, and in the next few pages we'll consider the kinds of mistakes to which foundations are particularly prone and the characteristics of today's foundation culture that help produce those mistakes.

THE BESETTING SINS OF FOUNDATIONS

Arrogance. Foundation staff are frequently criticized for being self-righteous, arrogant, and smug. Alan Pifer, the widely admired president of the Carnegie Corporation of New York (1967–82), put it this way:

> A particularly egregious fault evident among some officers is to begin to act as if the funds that have been assigned to them somehow belong to them personally. Thus, to applicants who are not part of an inner circle of favored grantees, they manage to convey a kind of thinly disguised hostility. "Who are *you*," they seem to suggest, "to have the nerve to come here and try to get some of my money?"[2]

A number of CEOs of grant-seeking charities interviewed for this book—all of them the recipients of many large foundation grants—cited instances in which foundation program officers and even CEOs treated them in a high-handed fashion, almost like subordinates to be ordered around. When a foundation behaves this way, it stops respecting the autonomy, intelligence, and judgment of the grant-seeker and begins imposing its own ideas on the grantee.

Discourtesy. Alan Pifer summarizes this problem well, too:

> The most common failing among foundation officers is just plain discourtesy—letting months go by before replying to an inquiry or request, or often not replying at all; delaying months before sending out checks—I would add even commitment letters *after* commitments have been firmly made orally—breaking appointments without explanation or apology; not returning phone calls; and so on.

Occasional delay in answering correspondence and in returning phone calls is, of course, inevitable because of the heavy time pressures under which some program officers labor. But there's no excuse for avoidable discourtesy, of which there is plenty; and, calculated or simply negligent, it is certain to infuriate grant-seekers.[3]

Inaccessibility. It's understandable that an organization whose purpose is to give away money will attract attention from many more grant-seekers than can be satisfied. And because most foundations are understaffed in relation to the ambitious goals they adopt, their officers have no choice but to turn down many requests for interviews and meetings. Furthermore, since most large foundations will not consider unsolicited grant proposals, their officers are reluctant to meet with people they don't know or who approach them without a recommendation from a previous contact. This problem is exacerbated among foundations with focused grantmaking strategies, whose program officers often believe they know everyone worth talking to in their field of interest.

For all these reasons, it's inevitable that many people who want to meet a foundation officer will be turned away. But it's inexcusable that many foundations fail either to acknowledge publicly their policy of refusing to consider unsolicited proposals or to explain forthrightly the reasons for their inability to spend time with everyone who seeks their attention.

Arbitrariness. Most foundations try to make their strategic choices and grantmaking decisions as rationally as possible. But in the end, all the decisions foundation officers make are based on individual human judgments and are therefore subjective. This makes it inevitable that disappointed would-be grantees will consider foundation decisions highhanded, unfair, and arbitrary.

Unfortunately, not all foundations do a good job of explaining the bases for their decisions, which only reinforces the impression of arbitrariness. Rather than try to explain the complicated set of factors they weigh when choosing grant recipients, they typically fall back on obfuscating rationalizations such as "outside of program priorities" or "sheer number of applicants." Such failure to provide the real reasons for rejection inevitably suggests that foundation officers have something to hide, and it deprives nonprofits of an opportunity to learn from the experience.

Failure to communicate. One of the most infuriating traits of some philanthropoids is their practice of dragging out grantmaking decisions beyond any reasonable time frame, while failing to offer any clear signals about the real likelihood of approval. When the proposal has been solicited by the foundation in the first place—which is usually the case nowadays—this behavior is even more reprehensible.

Consider the example described by Geri Mannion, of the Carnegie Corporation of New York, in an article several years ago:

> A well-respected scholar and head of an independent think tank spent almost twenty minutes with me angrily describing an experience with program officers at another foundation. The grant-seeker and other staff members had spent more than a year in dialogue with the foundation, responding to comments and questions and recasting the proposal to fit the foundation's requirements, only to be told that morning that funding would not be forthcoming because the "foundation's guidelines were changing." The organization's staff members had spent time and money working on the proposal in response to the foundation's demands, sending new drafts, incurring travel expenses to visit the foundation, not to mention the emotional investment of expectations. As the nonprofit executive explained, it would have been better if the foundation had just said "no" to begin with.[4]

Recognizing the inappropriateness of such behavior, some of the best program officers I have encountered over my forty years of seeking foundation support—Ford's Mike Sviridoff and Arthur Singer of both Carnegie and Sloan—made a point of giving very clear signals on first meeting and giving a firm answer within a few days.

"Foundation ADD." Virtually every observer I interviewed for this book complained that most foundations seem to be addicted to program change for its own sake, as if suffering from an extreme case of attention deficit disorder (ADD). Most foundations make grants only for three years or less—some only for one year. Some forbid grantees from requesting a follow-up grant for a specified number of years. They persist in this short-term behavior despite evidence that supporting an initiative over more than three years is usually necessary for lasting impact.

Another symptom of "Foundation ADD" is the tendency of foundations to flock to any new cause or institution that seems to be chic or trendy. I've heard of many cases in which foundations were reluctant to support any new initiative unless they could recruit other reputable foundations to give them cover. This herd mentality undermines the role that foundations should play in encouraging creativity, innovation, and diversity in the nonprofit sector.

LACK OF ACCOUNTABILITY

A major cause of the various sins committed by foundations—arrogance, discourtesy, inaccessibility, and the others—is their lack of accountability. Most other institutions in America, whether in the civic sector, the for-profit sector, or government, benefit from continuing challenges, criticism, and oversight provided by others to whom they are accountable. Officeholders must appeal to the voters periodically, or satisfy the demands of those who appointed them, who were themselves elected by the voters. CEOs of for-profit organizations must respond to the wishes of their board members and company shareholders, as well as an array of other accountability-influencing forces: attentive financial markets, the analysts who follow individual corporations, the institutional shareholders who read and follow the analysts, the bankers who lend to corporations, the independent agencies that rate the financial strength of corporations and their debt and equity instruments, and the financial press that watches eagle-eyed and reports every latest corporate happening twenty-four hours a day. In addition, corporations are accountable to a myriad of state and federal agencies. They have to file periodic reports and/or seek prior approval of proposed actions from federal agencies such as the Securities and Exchange Commission if they are publicly listed companies, the Federal Trade Commission and the U.S. Department of Justice Anti-Trust Division if they seek to acquire other companies, and the Food and Drug Administration if they produce regulated drugs or medical devices. Of course they are all subject to monitoring by such all-encompassing federal and state agencies such as those that protect the environment, labor-management practices, and occupational safety and health practices. And if all that were insufficient, the system of open competition among companies forces most of them to compete constantly with other companies for customers and to protect themselves from being acquired by their competitors or financial institutions that regard them as legitimate prey.

Operating nonprofit organizations, as distinguished from foundations, also have stakeholders to whom they are responsible—faculty and students in the case of a college or university, for example, or physicians and patients in the case of a hospital. All such charities gain insight and strength from the demands of their stakeholders. Moreover, operating nonprofits are subject to scrutiny by many external entities, Guidestar, created by a group of foundations, furnishes extensive online information about the finances and activities of individual nonprofits, while other organizations, such as the Better Business Bureau's Wise Giving Alliance and Charity Navigator, rate the performance of individual nonprofits. In addition, various national periodicals such as *Business Week* and *Forbes* have begun regularly ranking the efficiency of operating nonprofits based on the ratio between the amount of money they raise and the amount actually spent on the programs for which they raise it. Obviously, those organizations with the highest fund-raising and administrative costs suffer by the comparison. Another important accountability-providing publication is *The Chronicle of Philanthropy*, which focuses exclusively on civic-sector organizations. This publication, which has become the journal of record for the civic sector, has a staff of superb reporters and editors, and maintains an extensive Web site archive about all nonprofits covered in articles.

By contrast, foundations have no external stakeholders with effective influence on them, which means that the virtually unhampered freedom that foundations enjoy deprives them of such external feedback and constraints. Foundation staffs are accountable to their trustees, but the trustees are self-perpetuating and fundamentally unaccountable to anyone else. Having been funded by an individual or family at a particular point in time, most foundations need not solicit funds and therefore are not accountable to current or potential donors. (Community foundations, which continually raise money to build their endowments and to become home to donor-advised funds, are an exception. So are corporate foundations, most of which receive periodic infusions of capital from the companies that created and support them. However, in 2004 there were only some seven hundred community foundations in the United States and almost three thousand corporate foundations, so the overwhelming number of the approximately 68,000 American foundations are independent foundations that are effectively unaccountable to any outside force.)[5]

The competitive forces that affect other not-for-profit organizations have little impact on foundations. Among grant-seeking nonprofits, Darwinian survival of the fittest is the rule: When money dries up because donors lose faith in a particular nonprofit, it disappears. Yet foundations rarely go out of existence, no matter how effective or ineffective they are perceived to be. In other words, unlike in the public and profit sectors, and the grant-seeking civic sector, there is no functioning "market" in the grant-giving sector. The consequences of the lack of influencers of foundation accountability are so many that it is essential to consider how to strengthen foundation accountability—to someone—without undermining foundation freedom.

Operating without accountability and free from the competitive constraints of the marketplace may sound highly desirable, and it surely is— for those who run the foundations. But it creates an unhealthy cocoon-like insulation for foundations, one in which arrogance, arbitrariness, failure to communicate, and the rest of the besetting sins are all the more likely to flourish.

THE INVISIBILITY OF FOUNDATIONS

Lack of accountability leads directly to a second source of trouble for foundations, their relative invisibility. Being unaccountable, foundations are not obliged to provide anyone with meaningful information about their decisions or their decisions' consequences. As a result, few Americans know much about foundations—how they work, the roles they play, the goals they pursue, or the strategies they employ.

As far back as December, 1952, Charles Dollard, president of the Carnegie Corporation of New York, admitted in testimony before the Congress's Cox Committee, that, "All foundations, including the [Carnegie] Corporation, have done a relatively bad job of explaining their work to the public, including the Congress."[6] Since then, little has changed, as noted in a recent research report from the University of Southern California Center on Philanthropy and Public Policy: "In interviews, respondents described news coverage of the philanthropic sector as 'inconsistent,' 'spotty,' 'weak,' or 'virtually non-existent.' And, they noted that the coverage that existed was often uninformed."[7]

Eric Newton, Director of Journalism Initiatives at the John S. and James L. Knight Foundation, puts the current state even more forcefully: "The news media does a poor job of covering philanthropy, the philanthropic sector does a very poor job of communicating with the news media, and philanthropy is less effective because of it."[8]

Many factors contribute to the invisibility of foundations. Foundation activities are not regularly covered by the national or local press, and, among major journals or magazines, only *The Chronicle of Philanthropy* analyzes and reports on what they do. Barely a handful of watchdog organizations, including the populist, left-of-center National Committee for Responsive Philanthropy and the right-of-center Capital Research Center, scrutinize foundations from the outside and publish their criticisms.[9]

For their part, foundations have generally shared a "culture of diffidence" that discourages openness about their activities and agendas. This diffidence arises, perhaps, from the lack of confidence that many foundation officers may feel about the soundness of their strategies. Uncertain whether they are dispensing their funds in the best long-term interests of society as a whole, they shy away from public scrutiny and open debate. The diffidence also stems from a long-prevalent sense that it is unseemly for a charitable giver to "toot his own horn" by publicizing his gifts. For many tradition-minded philanthropoids, even issuing press releases about their grants feels uncomfortably like bragging.

Some foundations say they choose silence out of respect for the privacy of donors and grantees alike. When I sought to interview the president of the Lilly Endowment for this book, someone whom I know and respect, he responded that it, "generally does not participate in such efforts." The interview protocol that I sent specified a number of questions about impact. Staff members at another foundation simply failed to return my phone calls. Other foundations express reluctance to talk about the consequences of their grantmaking, explaining that it is the grantees who actually do what is done, not the foundations that merely facilitate the doing of it.

Finally, many foundations shun publicity about their failures for the same reason many other institutions do—to avoid embarrassment. With only a few exceptions that I know about, foundations do not discuss their failures in public.[10] And when foundations do release information about their successes, they rarely provide the underlying data that an impartial observer would need to form an independent judgment of the initiative. There are some notable exceptions to the latter, such as the Robert Wood Johnson Foundation, which now posts on its Web site all internal program evaluations, but these exceptions are few and far between.

Some of this closed-mouth behavior undoubtedly grows out of the foundations' lack of a firm knowledge about what their grants accomplish. They simply don't know for sure, and they don't know because they fail regularly to assess the consequences of their grants. Thoughtful foundation officers understand that this attitude is self-defeating. In 1973, Orville Brim, then-president of the Russell Sage Foundation, wrote that the most frustrating aspect of a foundation administrator's work comes from "the failure of a foundation to evaluate performance and measure what it does."[11] More recently, Richard Lyman, former president of the Rockefeller Foundation, commented:

> I found that every grant was called "evaluated" even before the books on them were closed. I found that young people were brought in and did routine once-overs. I instituted a serious, rigorous, non-routine evaluation system, which the program officers resisted mightily. Foundation program officers are sanguine and forward-looking. They don't like at all to look back.[12]

It's understandable, even if not excusable, that foundations don't want to examine the causes of their failures in public. No one likes to embarrass well-meaning and hard-working professionals whose programs haven't worked out, and frank criticism of a grantee organization might even leave a foundation open to a defamation lawsuit. But the fact is that foundations must do a much better job than they do at present in balancing the need for privacy with the need for openness and honest self-evaluation. Since foundations never publicly discuss their failures, observers understandably tend to discount whatever they write about their successes as self-serving hype.

A rare public criticism of foundation unwillingness to make public negative evaluations of the projects they support appeared in an opinion piece by Professor David C. Bloomfield, head of Brooklyn College's educational leadership program, printed in *Education Week*. He wrote as follows:

> It is time that the foundations take greater responsibility for their work than tweaking the program design. Privatizing research is simply unacceptable. Freedom-of-information laws do not reach privately funded evaluations undertaken on behalf of a not-for-profit organization, even when the investigation is about public schools and public school students. But foundations have an obligation to publicize these research findings, good or ill, and enter into public debate about their consequences....No one objects to grantmaking based on traditional models of proposal submission and acceptance. But when foundations enter into wholesale public-policy promotion using billions to lure tax-starved districts into scaling up untested models, they have a special obligation to act democratically. At this point in the small-schools movement, promoters have fallen short in civic responsibility.[13]

Contrast that closed-mouth attitude about shortcomings with a July 10, 2006, *Business Week* cover story on for-profit corporate mistakes entitled: "Eureka, We Failed! How Smart Companies Learn From Their Flops," which included "My Favorite Mistake" pieces by the CEOs of GE, Coca-Cola, iRobot, and USC. Wouldn't it be refreshing and reassuring to read similar headlines featuring the CEOs of such foundations as Ford, Rockefeller, and MacArthur?

Whatever the motivations for the diffidence of foundations, the invisibility that results is a serious problem. According to a recent Council on Foundations survey, 11 percent of those surveyed could name one foundation, and 12 percent, when asked to name a foundation, named an operating public charity instead.[14] That suggests that few have any idea of what foundations are or recognize the good that foundations do in addressing problems that almost everyone is concerned about. This isn't surprising; practically the only regular public acknowledgment that most foundations get by name are the cursory taglines heard by listeners to National Public Radio. If there were some philanthropic analogue to the "Intel Inside" seal displayed on many computers—a seal displayed by grant-receiving organizations in publicizing their initiatives and boasting, "X Foundation Funded"—more people might have a better idea of the difference foundations make.[15]

THE SCHOLARLY VOID

Another consequence—or perhaps cause—of the diffidence and invisibility of foundations is the sparseness of empirical literature and analysis on foundations in America. All the major works can be named and described in just a few paragraphs.

First, there are a few good histories of individual foundations, especially Ellen Condliffe Lagemann's two volumes on the Carnegie philanthropies, and several well-written biographies of foundation founders, especially John D. Rockefeller Sr., and Andrew Carnegie, as well as a recent one on Julius Rosenwald.[16] There have been a few books and articles describing particular initiatives by foundations, such as Stephen C. Wheatley's book on the reform of medical education, as well as several books on foundation initiatives in support of the Green Revolution and the biomedical sciences.[17]

Several widely-read volumes on foundations were written over some twenty years starting in the 1970s by Waldemar Nielsen. These focus mainly on the personalities of those who ran foundations, the ups and downs of particular foundations, and their style and culture, without delving into the impacts of their grantmaking and other initiatives.[18] There is also a good collection of essays on various foundation initiatives in Ellen Condliffe Lagemann's *Philanthropic Foundations*.[19]

There is an excellent synoptic volume published in 1967 by Warren Weaver, a much-admired executive of the Rockefeller Foundation, about the history and workings of American foundations through the mid-1960s. That book is informed by Weaver's keen mind and rich experience, supplemented by brief (and uneven) essays by other writers on achievements by foundations in eighteen fields. It says something sad about the sparseness of the field that so dense a book as the Weaver volume is still essential reading almost forty years after its publication.[20]

Finally, there is a small body of Marxist-oriented scholarship about foundations, much of it politically marginal and factually shaky. A recent example of work in this category is Joan Roelof's *Foundations and Public Policy*, which claims that foundations have been largely responsible for the worldwide triumph of capitalism through their shaping of academic life in Western Europe and the developing world.[21] And of course the foundations have done this because they were created by capitalists to advance and protect the interests of the "ruling class." When one finishes discounting for the conspiracy theories that underlie and explain such criticisms, there is little on which one feels comfortable relying.

This is a fairly scanty body of work analyzing one of the most important groups of institutions in modern society. What explains the relative lack of scholarly attention to foundations?

The first reason is that solid information about foundations is difficult to find. Most foundation archives are closed to the public, with a few exceptions, such as the Ford and Rockefeller archives, which are open to scholars under specific conditions.

Second, some scholars may avoid objective study of foundation activities out of fear that honest criticism will cost them or their institutions future foundation grants.

Third, and perhaps most important, foundations are not widely perceived among scholars as important actors in social change, and therefore are regarded as unworthy of scholarly attention.[22]

I hope that the general neglect of foundations as a subject of study may be changing. One sign of this change is the existence of an important new organization that seeks to gather and disseminate information on foundations: The Center for Effective Philanthropy, founded by Michael Porter and Mark Kramer of the Harvard Business School with support from several foundations. The center, now led by Phil Buchanan, surveys foundation grantees and ranks foundation performance on several different dimensions. Some foundations have posted the Center's Grantee Perception Reports on their Web sites, and many report that they have begun to change their practices in response to the center's assessments.[23] The work of the center is an important new force working to modify the long-standing insulation of foundations and to lay the groundwork for serious, objective, comparative study of foundations and the way they function in contemporary society.

Another hopeful sign is the several books on foundations published recently, all of which are excellent and have already been mentioned in the text—Marion Fremont-Smith's *Governing Nonprofit Organizations* in 2004, Peter Frumkin's *Strategic Giving: The Art and Science of Philanthropy* in 2006, and Kenneth Prewitt and associates, eds., *The Legitimacy of Philanthropic Foundations,* also in 2006.

THE POLITICAL VULNERABILITY OF FOUNDATIONS

All the qualities of foundations that we've discussed in this chapter— their perceived flaws of arrogance and arbitrariness, their lack of accountability, their invisibility, and the lack of scholarly work examining their role in society—have contributed to one of the most important trends affecting foundations today: their growing political vulnerability.

Public attitudes toward foundations have varied over time. In recent years, the tide of criticism of foundations has been rising again, focused on many alleged foundation shortcomings, from excessive staff compensation and benefit packages, inordinate honoraria for foundation trustees, and loans by foundations to executives and trustees, to overly modest annual payout requirements, foundation and nonprofit involvement in social issue advocacy at the border of legality, and other criticisms. The U.S. Senate Finance Committee released a white paper on foundations and nonprofits in March, 2004, citing these and other criticisms and proposed a number of legal and regulatory changes to correct them.[24] Partially because of the lack of scholarship and the general public ignorance about philanthropy, but also the result of foundations' failure to pay attention to assessing the impact of their work, the foundations are ill-prepared to defend themselves with substantial, factual arguments about the breadth and importance of the benefits they confer on society.

Are there real problems in the way some foundations are managed? Absolutely! Are malfeasance problems pervasive? Absolutely not! Of the 68,000 foundations listed by the IRS (2005), only a small percentage have been implicated in any documented instance of malfeasance.[25] But the lack of general public understanding of foundations—and the fact that critics among the press and politicians focus on their shortcomings and never on their achievements—makes foundations especially vulnerable to political attack.

Perhaps the most likely avenue for such an attack is the involvement of some foundations in public policy advocacy. Such advocacy is already legally limited. While corporations may freely lobby in support of their legislative agenda (though, since 1993, only with after-tax dollars), foundations may not do so, with narrowly specified exceptions. It would be only a short step for Congress to prohibit foundations from supporting activities by grant-receiving organizations that aim at changing public policy either through legislation or litigation. As recently as 1995, with the proposed Istook Amendment to the Lobby Disclosure Act, many members of Congress voted to impose such a restriction on all public charities that receive any public money.

Nor has it always been clearly legal for public charities to bring lawsuits in the public interest. For example, in 1966–67, when the Ford Foundation was considering grants to organizations such as the Natural Resources Defense Council (NRDC) that litigate environmental issues, the IRS initially balked at giving 501 (c)(3) status to the NRDC on the grounds that litigation was not an exempt purpose. So although congressional encroachments on the prerogatives of foundations are currently unlikely, this is subject to change at any time.

Foundations in Search of a Voice

The lack of accountability that foundations enjoy is a two-edged sword. It allows foundations to do whatever their trustees and staffs wish to do, but it also diminishes the force with which foundations can speak. After all, what *is* the answer when foundations are asked, "For whom do you speak?" Is it enough that the foundation simply speaks for itself? If the answer is "the sepulchral voice of Andrew Carnegie," is that enough? Wouldn't foundations be in a stronger position if they represented an identifiable constituency, even a small one?

A step in this direction—one is tempted to say an historic one—has been taken by the Independent Sector (IS), under the leadership of Diana Aviv. Its Panel on Nonprofits, which mobilized more than two hundred civic-sector professionals and scholars, and organized live and Web-based consultations that reached thousands all over the country, galvanized the nonprofit world in response to the 2004–2005 congressional scrutiny of nonprofits, including foundations. IS succeeded in shaping public and political discourse about the cited proposals under consideration. According to Senator Grassley, chairman of the Senate Finance Committee, and Dean Zerbe, his chief staff officer responsible for nonprofits, IS significantly—and positively—affected the discussion as well as the legislative and regulatory outcomes so far enacted.

Independent Sector is a newly reemergent and potentially powerful voice for America's civic sector, broadly speaking. But the foundations have yet to find a specific voice of their own. Partly, that is because foundations have a difficult time agreeing among themselves about anything, but the main reason, I believe, is that foundations still feel uncertain and insecure about themselves and their decisions.

I see that insecurity reflected in most foundations' unwillingness to measure their efforts by using rigorous data, their reluctance to benchmark progress toward predetermined goals, their resistance to exposing their decision-making processes, and their unwillingness to share their own self-assessment documents. I also see the insecurity in the excessive caution exhibited by many foundations in choosing initiatives, their faddishness, their herd mentality, and their susceptibility to ADD.

Thus, the arrogance foundations are accused of is, ironically, a disguised form of insecurity. Despite their immense wealth and power, many foundations seem to be afraid of their own shadows. It's a syndrome that derives, ultimately, from the fact that foundations have been so little exposed to forces demanding accountability that they have failed to develop the self-confidence that comes only from experiencing the back-and-forth with external accountability-influencing voices.

Despite their insulation from external scrutiny and challenge, foundations have made significant contributions to society. But they could have done much more if the demands of accountability had been present. As Justice Louis D. Brandeis wrote, "Sunlight is the best disinfectant." But sunlight is also a promising preventive measure for what ails foundations, as well as for what threatens to punish them.

It is all the more appropriate to quote Justice Brandeis because he instinctively understood the importance of the balance between openness and appropriate privacy. As Professor Harvey Dale points out, Brandeis not only coined the now-famous praise of "sunlight" but also coauthored with Samuel Warren one of the most famous, most frequently cited law review articles ever written on the right of privacy.[26] It is that kind of balance that foundations need to strike between the preservation of privacy and the provision of substantive information that is now available only to insiders.

The Culture of High Stewardship

How have the most successful foundations managed to rise above the absence of an external environment that challenged them and demanded accountability? The answer is by developing what I call a culture of high stewardship. They have recruited demanding trustees and high-performing program staff with a strong commitment to social benefit, a keen sense of self-discipline, and a deep awareness of the obligations of stewardship. More foundations must learn how to develop such internally generated norms.

Ask almost any observer of the foundation field and you will hear the names of one or two philanthropoids who continually conduct their business in a stewardly way. In my own experience, Jim Spencer, who led the Atlantic Philanthropies' Higher Education Program for about ten years, was one such leader. A retired professor and vice provost at Cornell, he was frugal to a fault. For example, when traveling on foundation business, he took a bus rather than a plane whenever possible (as between Ithaca and New York City). When he had to fly, he searched for rock-bottom fares, often taking advantage of his senior status to qualify for discounts, and he always took public transportation to the airport rather than a taxi or limousine. He rarely submitted an expense report for an official meal that exceeded ten dollars. Jim never forgot that the money he spent was not his, but other people's money. What an example he set for others in foundations!

An equally impressive example of the sense of stewardship appears in *The Saving Remnant*, a book about the work of the American Jewish Joint Distribution Committee in saving European refugees during and after World War II. The Pulitzer Prize-winning author, Herbert Agar, tells of a remarkable man who was a truly exemplary steward of other people's money:

> Saly Mayer was a retired manufacturer of lace who lived in Saint Gallen, Switzerland. He was about sixty years old when the Second War began. He was of modest means and had given all his time since 1937 to the protection of German refugees. He had become well known to the Swiss government as a stubborn negotiator, and to the [American Jewish] Joint [Distribution Committee] as a friend deserving of all possible support. He was an Orthodox Jew, deeply religious, president of the Jewish community of Switzerland. He was tall and robust, and tireless. . . .
>
> The Joint could never induce Saly Mayer to accept an expense account, although his expenses must have been cripplingly high for a man whose private fortune was on the scale of a hundred thousand dollars. . . . His view on this was absolute: if people gave money for charity, it must be spent on charity. If he was privileged to help spend it, he must pay for the privilege. . . . On the wall over his desk at Saint Gallen was a large sign, O.P.M., which meant "Other People's Money"—in English, presumably, because the "Other People" spoke English.[27]
>
> No one has ever been more meticulous with O.P.M. After the war, when accountants from the Joint visited Saint Gallen, hoping to get a general notion of how the money had been spent, they found an exact record of every transaction, above ground and underground, with every penny accounted for. Full reports had also been given to the

American legation at Bern on all the money spent, and on the sometimes devious methods of spending it. Since Saly Mayer was often disposing of a million dollars a month, during both hot and cold war dangers, such accuracy is as amazing as it is noteworthy.[28]

Of course, I wouldn't suggest that foundation executives should try to duplicate the saintly stewardship of Jim Spencer or Saly Mayer. But even approximating them would go a long way toward eliminating many of the criticisms that foundations receive.

Foundation managers need to keep the message of O.P.M. in mind in more than one way. Of course, the money they spend is other people's money because it came originally from one or more donors. But it is also other people's money to the extent that taxpayers shoulder part of the cost of the foregone revenue from the capital and income earned on that capital through the tax breaks that foundations enjoy. For this reason, the taxpayers, too, have an interest in how wisely and well foundation money is spent. Thus, the general public has a real, tangible, even proprietary interest in a foundation's deployment of its assets and in all of the ways it makes its decisions.

If foundation trustees, executive leadership, and program staff would remember and approximate the examples of Jim Spencer and Saly Mayer, they could become more admirable beacons of high philanthropic stewardship in America.

10

STEPS TO ACHIEVE

HIGH IMPACT: A COMMONSENSE

APPROACH TO STRATEGY

Strategy is no guarantee of impact. But without it you are
almost guaranteed to have no impact.

————

Paul Brest, president,
the William and Flora Hewlett Foundation.[29]

Having discussed the kinds of problems that dog many foundations today and suggested some of their root causes, in this chapter I examine the
most fundamental practices that characterize effective foundation initiatives. My analysis is based on a study of one hundred successful initiatives,
from which I've derived a series of operating rules that effective projects appear to share. Consider this chapter an overview of "best practices," or, as
Surdna Executive Director Ed Skloot calls them "pretty good behavior," or
reasonably achievable practices that every foundation ought to consider.

Of course, life is always messier than theory. Not all high-impact foundation initiatives were developed in accordance with the orderly pattern I'll
suggest in the next few pages. Many of the best-run foundations that employ
rigorous analytic processes infuse them with ideas that emerge from the in-
stincts, experience, and proven wisdom of their best staff members and consultants. They also know how to tap insights not just from a few gifted
individuals but from all those with whom they work, including grantees,

benefiting from the group knowledge somewhat like that described by author James Surowiecki in his book *The Wisdom of Crowds*.[30] Aggregating the views of a group of knowledgeable persons about the viability of an idea for tackling a problem is likely to generate a richer sense of the balance between the virtues and flaws of such an idea—in other words a wise decision—than one would be likely to obtain from any single individual member of the group, no matter how creatively or instinctively gifted.

Even foundations that have long prided themselves on their strategically focused programs leave wide scope in decision for the non-systematic. Ellen Condliffe Lagemann describes the Carnegie Corporation under one of its greatest presidents as

> dominated by a single individual, Frederick Paul Keppel, a genial and energetic man of unswerving integrity and character, of wide personal acquaintances and eclectic interests. Grantmaking during his long presidency was, at least technically, organized into programs, although it was actually directed more by hunch, coincidence, opportunity, friendship and a wish to help than by clear, specific, consistently applied "scientific" goals or principles.[31]

Some of today's largest foundations, however, usually subject ideas for new initiatives to strategic analysis before actually undertaking them or soon after. What follows is a brief description of how such an analytical process might ideally be designed.

STEP ONE: DEFINING, DOCUMENTING, AND DIAGNOSING THE PROBLEM

When a foundation initiative aims at solving a particular problem, the very first step toward achieving impact is to get the problem right—to define it clearly, quantify its scope, and define its causes accurately and objectively. As I reported in Chapter 5, that is exactly what the earliest foundations did, largely under the influence of their donors—successful businessmen who were strong believers in the "scientific" approach to problem-solving strategy.

Carnegie was, as usual, the most articulate among them. In his *Gospel of*

Wealth, he wrote, "[T]here is but one right mode of using enormous fortunes—namely, that the possessors from time to time during their own lives should so administer these as to promote the permanent good of the communities from which they were gathered." [32] By "permanent good," Carnegie meant systematically addressing the root causes of social problems over the long term, not merely ameliorating their symptoms. This requires, first and foremost, a clear diagnosis of the problem. "Communities from which they were gathered" clearly embraces not only the towns and cities in which manufacturing facilities are located but also the wider world across which products are consumed. Thus it is entirely in keeping with Carnegie's "right mode" that the Bill and Melinda Gates Foundation focuses its philanthropy on the problems of both Washington State and the wider world from which the profits on the Windows Operating System are generated.

The early foundations launched many such "scientific" approaches to major social problems. (I put the word in quotation marks because the "science" involved is really little more than common sense methodically applied.) Examples include Abraham Flexner's methodical survey of the state of medical education, on which he based his goal of a science-based medical curriculum;[33] the systematic approach by John D. Rockefeller Sr. and Frederick T. Gates to the global eradication of yellow fever and the elimination of hookworm across the rural American South;[34] Margaret Olivia Sage's adoption of applied sociology research as the basis for documenting social welfare problems in order to formulate solutions, and the Cleveland Foundation's systematic study of major social problems facing Cleveland in its early days.[35] In each case, the first step was a survey that gathered empirical data to document the problem before attempting to propose a solution.

Let's consider the Flexner Report as a paradigm of the process. While working at the Carnegie Foundation for the Advancement of Teaching, Flexner interviewed those knowledgeable about the current state of medical education, solicited advice from most of the leading medical experts of his day, and visited schools of medicine abroad (especially in Germany) to identify promising approaches. He also visited and interviewed faculty at every one of the 155 American medical schools then in operation, wrote a detailed report on each school, including observations on faculty and student qualifications, and then sent a copy of each report to the dean of that school.[36] Only after this intensive data-gathering process did he set about transforming American medical education during his thirty years as a program officer at the Rockefeller Foundation.[37]

Flexner's effort was greatly aided by the availability of pre-existing initiatives. The Johns Hopkins School of Medicine furnished a model for science-based medical education, and the American Medical Association's Council on Medical Education had already endorsed a plan for reforming the medical curriculum and establishing minimum admissions criteria. But the Flexner report played a crucial catalytic role, as described by Ellen Condliffe Lagemann: "The report quite literally excited public outrage and then interest on the part of the merchant Robert Brookings and other wealthy local businessmen, and, as a result, secured for medical reform the levels of financial assistance needed.[38] In fact, the outpouring of foundation support for the implementation of Flexner's recommendation was unprecedented, amounting to $154 million in grants between 1910 and the onset of the Great Depression.[39] Why was it able to generate such outrage? Because it was evidence-based objective data gathered through a careful survey of the facts!

The success of the Flexner report in galvanizing a new approach to medical education based on systematic analysis and study became the basis for reform in other fields. The Carnegie Foundation for the Advancement of Teaching commissioned the Charles R. Mann Report on reforming engineering education (1918) and a similar initiative to reform teacher education (1920).[40]

Soon thereafter, the Carnegie Corporation applied the same model to the reform of legal education, led by Elihu Root, who was not only chairman of the American Bar Association Section on Legal Education and Admission to the Bar but also chairman of Carnegie's board of trustees.[41] The Carnegie report, written by Alfred Z. Reed, indirectly stimulated the spread of more demanding standards for law school entrance and admission to the bar between 1921 and 1939—although, ironically, the relatively lax requirements advocated by Reed drew vigorous opposition from the ABA, which then spearheaded a drive in support of much more demanding standards.[42]

Carnegie also financed a 1919 study on justice and the poor authored by Reginald Heber Smith, after whom the so-called Reggie fellowships awarded by the Legal Services Corporation are named.[43]

Later, the Commonwealth Fund used analogous methods in tackling several other major problems: for example, in defining the need for child guidance by psychiatrically trained personnel in the schools, out of which grew the field of child psychiatry; in documenting and then addressing the lack of hospitals in rural areas, leading to the enactment of the Hill-Burton Act; and in publicizing maternal mortality rates in New York hospitals, which ultimately led to the reduction of those rates by two-thirds in just three years.[44]

As these examples illustrate, empirical research targeted to particular social problems is often a key component of high-impact grantmaking. But there have been notable exceptions, especially in the early days of modern philanthropy. Consider, for example, the creation of what has become TIAA-CREF, one of the largest pension funds in the world, which emerged almost full-blown from the fertile mind of Andrew Carnegie. His formula for building a pension fund using a multiyear stream of combined contributions from individuals and their employers continues to be employed not only by TIAA-CREF but also by most other pension funds.[45]

Today we can recognize the instinctive genius that lay behind Carnegie's scheme. At the time, it was not so obvious. Frederick T. Gates, the philanthropic advisor to John D. Rockefeller Sr. remarked, "Carnegie is putting his ten millions into a pension fund for teachers. I think this an extraordinary act of folly. Of all people, teachers should be examples of thrift."[46] Gates went on to offer a summary personal judgment of Carnegie as "a fit illustration of the millionaire as menace."[47]

The story illustrates one enduring truth of philanthropy: It is much easier to criticize an idea generated by a lone instinctive genius than one supported by a large amount of objective, well-documented research. For this reason among others, most foundations ought to devote the resources needed to do the research rather than relying on the genius that may or may not be residing among their leaders.

STEP TWO: IDENTIFYING KEY FACTORS THAT IMPEDE A SOLUTION

Before one can formulate strategies for solving a problem, it is essential to identify the factors that prevent the problem from solving itself. Sometimes the major obstacle is a lack of knowledge, as when there is no known cure for a particular disease. Sometimes the chief obstacle may be general ignorance or indifference, as when health dangers such as smoking, drunken driving, and obesity are perpetuated by an unwitting public. In still other cases, it may be the opposition of powerful institutions or individuals whose interests have helped to create the problem or stand in the way of a solution, in which case it will be essential to find ways to neutralize, convert, or at least win the acquiescence of those groups that are blocking the solution.

Some social problems that foundations undertake to solve are not so much "problems" as gaps to be filled—institutions, programs, or processes that do not exist, that will serve a useful public purpose once they have been created, and whose existence will not harm or challenge the prerogatives of any other person or organization. When this is the case, there may be no real "obstacle" to be overcome (other than, perhaps, a lack of money to fill the newly observed gap—which is always the easiest difficulty for a foundation to resolve). The Carnegie Corporation's support for the establishment of both the National Bureau of Economic Research and the National Research Council offers a clear example. In neither case was there any significant opposition to the creation of the institution—all that was needed to fill the gap was an awareness of the need, a bankroll sufficient to launch the program, and the willingness to spend it. All three were provided by the Carnegie Corporation.[48]

In other cases, however, a perceived gap may also involve the existence of a "problem" in the form of powerful individuals or groups who oppose the obvious solution. Such obstacles contributed to the lack of a high-quality, publicly supported broadcasting network, which the Carnegie Corporation moved to remedy when it created the Commission on Public Broadcasting. Various interested parties opposed, or at least questioned, the initiative, including President Lyndon Johnson, whose wife, Lady Bird Johnson, owned a number of commercial television stations; the heads of the preexisting commercial television networks; and the Ford Foundation, which fancied itself the foundation that "owned" the field of what was then called educational television. In that connection, it was no accident that Arthur Singer and Steve White chose James Killian to chair the commission. His successor as president of MIT was none other than Julius Stratton, who, in 1966, became chairman of the Ford Trustees! It was important for Carnegie and the commission to identify all potential obstacles so that a strategy for neutralizing them could be developed and implemented.[49]

STEP THREE: FORMULATING
A PROBLEM-SOLVING STRATEGY

A systemic process is the key to strategy. Strategy requires too many discrete steps, too many complicated processes for gathering and interpreting information, planning implementation, and evaluating outcomes, for any individual or group to manage in a casual, seat-of-the-pants fashion. The successful foundation leader must consciously launch a strategic planning process, articulate the steps for developing and implementing the plan, and make sure that all the members of the organization's leadership team understand both the constraints and the goals, so that no indispensable detail can fall through the cracks as a result of having been left to chance or memory.

Here is the sequence of key questions that the leadership of a foundation should address in order to be certain that the strategic planning process it is following is complete and methodical:

1. Have we identified and precisely defined the problem we intend to solve?

2. How ripe is the problem for being solved or significantly improved today or in the near future? If not, can an initiative hasten the ripening?

3. Have we developed a plausible strategy or mix of strategies appropriate to the size and complexity of the problem?

4. Is the problem of a size and character that make it appropriate for a foundation with our mission, culture, resources, and risk profile? How can we manage the risk? Can we afford what it will take to solve the problem? If not, can we attract sufficient supporting funds from other foundations or other sources?

5. How long will it take for the problem to be solved? Is our foundation prepared to commit itself to a consistent effort over that period of time?

6. What parts of the solution can we implement alone? What parts will require the efforts of other organizations, such as foundations or grant-receiving organizations?

7. How will we know if we are making appropriate progress all along the way?

These are not the only questions that a foundation needs to answer, but they are the most important.

Question four refers to the "risk profile" of a foundation. This deserves some elucidation.

Any attempt to solve or significantly ameliorate a major problem is fraught with risk, which must be understood, acknowledged, and managed. And it is essential that a foundation staff and trustees face the extent of the risk deliberately. The kinds of risk involved in launching a new social initiative include:

- The risk of *losing credibility and prestige* if the initiative becomes a public failure.

- The risk of *wasted financial resources* that might have been better spent on an initiative with greater prospects for success.

- The risk of *lost time* when a foundation devotes one, two, or more years to a major program with little to show for it.

- The risk of *damaged morale* among staff, trustees, and foundation leaders.

- The risk of *public cynicism and hopelessness* when a highly touted initiative proves inadequate.

- The risk of *worsening the problem* by encouraging the public and other organizations to assume that a problem is "all but solved" when in fact hopes turn out to be dashed.

- And, of course, the greatest risk of all is *the inadvertent violation of the physician's credo* "Do No Harm."

The magnitude of these risks differs from case to case, depending on the scope of the initiative; the existence of proven models that make success more likely, or the lack thereof; the amounts of money, time, and other resources involved; and the degree of public commitment required. Some foundation programs involve only modest risks; others may be so risky that leaders must virtually "bet the house" on their success or failure. Still others may require the foundation to wait until such time as the risks can, in fact, be managed.

Before embarking on any strategic initiative, the extent of the risk must be examined, quantified if possible—and then embraced. This means accepting risk as an inevitable concomitant of innovation, much as business entrepreneurs or venture capitalists accept financial risk in pursuit of gain. The difference between them and foundation leaders is that they *explicitly* face up to the risk while contemplating making the investment. Foundations require skilled leaders with an entrepreneurial mindset among their board members and program staff who are comfortable in calculating risk if they are to negotiate the shoals of risk successfully.

Question four also refers to the availability of adequate resources to solve the problem being targeted. Too often, foundation leaders focus on the urgency of solving a problem without accurately estimating the resources required. I recommend that a foundation back up its determination to solve a particular problem by being ready either to commit *all* the resources necessary, or, at the very least, fifty percent of the amount required, as "earnest money" to be supplemented by grants from other foundations.

These recommendations suggest a series of important corollaries for foundation program management.

First, most foundations ought to pursue only a few goals at any one time. Except for the very largest foundations, it's impossible to focus on more than a handful of goals, unless these are so small as to be essentially trivial.

Second, a foundation must strive to know everything about the landscape in each of its focus areas. Only a thorough knowledge of the problems being tackled, the obstacles to be overcome, and the resources required can enable a foundation to develop a mini-strategic plan for each problem tackled that will maximize the chances for success and minimize the risks involved.

Third, the tougher and larger the problem, the longer it will take to have a meaningful impact on it. Therefore, when deciding to grapple with a major social problem, foundation leaders must be prepared to make a serious long-term commitment to their strategy.

Fourth, financial, human, and organizational resources must be aligned with the strategy in order for the desired outcomes to be achieved. As a general rule, the larger the foundation bureaucracy and the more intense the internal competition for funds, the more difficult it will be to reach agreement on the strategy, as well as to reserve and protect the funds necessary to solve the biggest problems.

Fifth, avoid relying on outside resources. Collaboration among foundations is nice in theory, but difficult in practice. Collaborations should certainly be explored in advance and established if agreement can be reached. If an initiating foundation hopes to have a breakthrough impact on a social problem, however, it must be prepared, if it becomes necessary, to start on its own and hope that others will join in later.

STEP FOUR: SELECTING TACTICS

Strategy is the pattern for solving a problem; tactics are the specific means employed in carrying out the strategy. For example, suppose the chief obstacle to solving a problem is lack of knowledge. In this case, a knowledge-generating strategy would be called for, and appropriate tactics might include: (1) supporting the training of a new generation of experts dedicated to solving the problem; (2) mobilizing existing experts to devote their research time and energy to generating the knowledge needed; (3) encouraging the public and/or the government to support the generation of such knowledge; and (4) creating a new organization (such as a university department or a think tank) to help produce such knowledge.

To clarify further, let's look at an actual problem with which many foundations have struggled—environmental pollution. If the problem of pollution is defined as a market failure caused by the lack of adequate forces putting pressure for environmental protection on government agencies (such as the EPA) and for-profit organizations (such as polluting corporations), then a reasonable strategy for a foundation to pursue would involve rebalancing the market forces so as to increase the impetus and momentum toward environmental protection. Possible tactics for implementing this strategy might include: (1) creating new research institutions to provide solid empirical evidence about the problem and its solution; (2) supporting lawsuits against government agencies that fail to protect the environment and corporations that pollute it; (3) generating proposals for legislation to strengthen environmental safeguards; and (4) empowering new or existing membership organizations that engage in public education and advocacy on environmental issues.

As this example suggests, there may be many tactics available to support a particular strategy. How can foundation leaders choose among them? An important first step is *laying out the logic model*—that is, making explicit how any tactic under consideration is expected to contribute to the overall strategic goal. Without such a logic model, or theory of change, performance benchmarks that test whether the tactic is in fact supporting the strategy cannot be put in place. A very detailed logic model was developed and laid out by the Packard Foundation to guide its ten-year initiative to get every California three- and four-year-old into preschool. It is available for viewing on the sidebar at www.pubpol.duke.edu/dfrp/cases.

Next, when selecting the mix of tactics to implement a strategy, consider the following questions:

- What actions are necessary to bring about the solution to the problem, and in what sequence (for example, an act of Congress, a financial commitment by government, or a change in practices by a for-profit company)? Once the required actions are identified, tactics can be chosen on the basis of their ability to help generate those actions.

- Who are the principal actors whose cooperation will be necessary if the desired results are to occur? Tactics can be chosen that will maximize the chances that these key players will be influenced in the right direction.

- What outputs and outcomes can be specified for a particular tactic? Articulating these results in forms that are objective, clear, and easily verified will permit the formulation of benchmarks that will periodically measure the progress of the initiative. If no clear outputs and outcomes can be specified, the tactic may be merely a "feel-good" exercise, not one that actually contributes toward concrete progress.

A good example of benchmark specification can be found in the Hewlett Foundation's strategic plan for its Population program on the next page (reprinted from the Hewlett Web site).

Well-chosen tactics are often interdependent and mutually supportive. For example, many foundations identify institution-building as a preferred tactic, but it is virtually always used in support of some other tactic. For example, institutions have been built in support of such tactics as ongoing research (National Bureau of Economic Research, Manpower Development Research Corporation), public advocacy (Human Rights Watch), and litigation (Natural Resources Defense Council, Environmental Defense). Avoid developing a strategic plan that consists of a random collec-

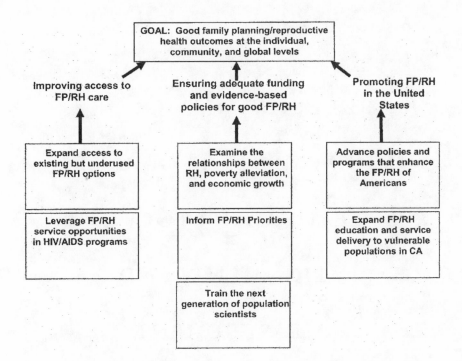

tion of tactics that have little or no coherent relationship. Such a plan forgoes the benefits of synergy and risks dissipating the foundation's energies in disparate activities that fail to achieve coherence enough to generate serious momentum.

STEP FIVE:
DRAFTING AN IMPLEMENTATION PLAN

Once the analyses specified in the prior steps have been carefully done, a plan that details the stages in which they will be implemented must be drafted, specifying the strategies and tactics to be employed, the performance benchmarks to be noted, and the schedule to be followed. Having such a plan will make it easier for managers to determine at any given moment whether the strategies and tactics are working as intended. Having discussed the crucial elements of strategy design for foundations, I'm ready to look a little deeper at the governance practices that characterize high-impact foundation programs.

11

CHARACTERISTICS OF

HIGH-IMPACT PROGRAMS:

LEADERSHIP, FOCUS,

ALIGNMENT, AND

MEASUREMENT

In responding to a letter from Albert Einstein requesting $500, John D. Rockefeller Sr. instructed Frederick T. Gates: "Let's give him $1,000. He may be on to something."[50]

Obviously, following a methodical strategy process like the one I described in the previous chapter is important for any foundation that seeks high impact. But equally important are the managerial style and spirit in which the program is conducted.

In this chapter, I look first at several systemic and managerial issues that well-run foundations consistently do a better job of addressing than others. These issues include:

• Focus

• Alignment

• Due diligence about the problem

- Due diligence about the solution

- Intelligent talent selection

- Due diligence about prospective grant-receiving organizations

Then I delve in detail into some of the characteristics of managerial style and spirit that mark the best-run foundations. These include:

- Entrepreneurial risk-taking

- Opportunistic thinking

- Independence

- Effective grantee selection and management

- Long-term thinking and commitment

- Maintaining focus and alignment

Taken together, these elements will sketch a portrait of the common characteristics found in the high-impact initiatives launched by effective foundations.

MAJOR ISSUES

Focus. By limiting the fields that a foundation officer must understand, focus maximizes available resources with which to tackle the problem and permits the acquisition of expertise. By contrast, lack of focus condemns foundation leaders to the status of perpetual amateurs. Fred Krupp, president and CEO of Environmental Defense, underscores the importance of focus this way: "I have seen many foundation program staff people. Some are doing great things even if they don't ever give us a grant. Other foundations are so unfocused and haphazard that one worries about whether they are accomplishing anything at all."[51]

Alignment. It is one thing to select a focus in principle and quite another thing to ensure that all foundation resources are aligned with it and with the strategies that are formulated within it. The trustees, the CEO, the senior management team, the program staff, as well as the financial and all other resources must be aligned within the focus and with the strategy if the foundation is to succeed in achieving its objectives.

Due diligence about the problem. High-impact foundations make due diligence a routine component of every decision-making process, starting with thorough study of the elements and dynamics of a problem, its causes and seriousness, its ripeness for solution, and the chief obstacles. Moreover, because the best program officers can be expected to be "expert" in the narrow areas in which they are charged with taking action, they are likelier to have or more easily acquire a good sense of whether, when, and how a problem proposed for solution is solvable.

Due diligence about the solution. Passionate concern about social issues characterizes most people in the nonprofit arena. But high-impact foundations are ruled by the head, not the heart. Before launching any program, they carefully and accurately analyze the practicality of the solution proposed, the resources required, and the risks involved.

Intelligent talent selection. High-impact foundations make a point of identifying, recruiting, and positioning the best talent available to solve the problems they tackle. They develop and maintain talent networks in their immediate areas of focus, as well as in adjacent areas from which skills might be transferable.

Due diligence about prospective grant-receiving organizations. Once the foundation has decided what it intends to do, it must figure out with whom to do it. That important identification and selection process requires the most careful due diligence as well. One cannot overemphasize the fact that foundations may indeed come up with the problem to be solved, but it is almost always the case that others—grant-receiving organizations—will necessarily be called upon to implement, sometimes even to devise, the solution.

ENTREPRENEURIAL RISK-TAKING

While the term *social entrepreneurship* has become fashionable only recently, the ideas involved in the concept are not new. The philanthropic successes of both Andrew Carnegie and John D. Rockefeller Sr. owe a great deal to this strategic approach. More recently, the foundations that launched the Children's Television Workshop, the Local Initiatives Support Corporation, the Kerr Commission, the 911 Emergency Response System, and the Clinical Scholars Program were all highly entrepreneurial in their styles. So are many of the most recently established foundations, including the Gates, Omidyar, and Skoll foundations.

In what way are high-impact foundations "entrepreneurial"? One answer is suggested by Professor J. Greg Dees, who defines "social entrepreneurship" as "the productive efforts of an individual, team, or organization that reform or revolutionize the patterns by which private resource relationships are mobilized and deployed to effect social change."[52] The key words here, of course, are *reform* and *revolutionize*. The entrepreneurial element lies in the introduction of *systematic change*. Whereas traditional charity treats the symptoms of social ills, social entrepreneurship seeks a long-term cure.

The methods of social entrepreneurs also differ from those of many "ordinary" nonprofits. In tackling the root causes of problems, social entrepreneurs often embrace strategies and tactics drawn from the for-profit sector. Foundations with an entrepreneurial bent also tend to operate in closer and more intense partnerships with grantees than other foundations. Abandoning the cautious arm's-length approach by which most foundations seek to skirt controversy, they work hand in glove with grantees, providing them continuing advice on management, strategy and organizational development. Foundations that practice social entrepreneurship pride themselves on getting their hands dirty.

Most important, foundations that follow the social entrepreneurship model explicitly—like venture capitalists in the for-profit sector—embrace risk, but only after considering whether they can succeed in managing it. They invest large sums of money in solutions they believe in, permit grantees significant flexibility in spending that money, and often commit to long-term funding—all subject, of course, to due diligence and the meeting of agreed-upon performance benchmarks. The caution and conservatism that mark most traditional foundations are not to be found among the ranks of the social entrepreneurs.

Finally, social entrepreneurship requires a clear focus—from the very beginning—on specifying outcomes, interim performance benchmarks, and periodic evaluations.

Perhaps the outlook of the social entrepreneurs is best captured in the words of the great city planner and architect Daniel Burnham: "Make no little plans; they have no magic to stir men's blood and probably will themselves not be realized. Make big plans; aim high in hope and work, remembering that a noble, logical diagram once recorded will not die."

OPPORTUNISTIC THINKING

Examining the practices of the most effective foundations shows that one key to success has been striking the right balance between strategic focus and opportunism. Not all of the problems that foundations ought to tackle are obvious, long-term issues with a well-established history. Some burst on the scene unexpectedly, as happened with the AIDS epidemic and the appearance of crack cocaine as a major drug problem in American cities. In other cases, promising ideas for solving existing problems may suddenly appear. And in still other cases, a confluence of circumstances or the arrival on the scene of the perfect individual to lead a change initiative may create an unpredictable opportunity for solving a previously intractable problem.

For all these reasons, it is important for foundations to treat their overall strategy as a guide, not a straitjacket, leaving room for creative improvisation within a broad, general focus. Foundations should include openness to serendipity among the grantmaking guidelines they publish. (As David Bergholz, former executive director of the George Gund Foundation, puts it, "We do list the things we do and don't do, but we also say explicitly that we make exceptions to both."[53]) And program officers should understand that their promotion and compensation will depend as much on the out-of-strategy ideas that they surface as on their success in developing and implementing successful strategies.

Foundations are magnets for individuals and institutions seeking financial support, but they are also magnets for people who wish, at least in part, to try out possibly innovative ideas on informed listeners. As I have noted, alas, all too frequently, foundation program staff are among the most insulated persons in America and need all the external contact and stimulation they can possibly get. If foundations close their doors, windows, and telephones to all who do not neatly fit into program areas and existing strategies, where will they get the independent perspectives, the wild ideas, the thoughtful viewpoints that just may turn on a lightbulb in their heads? My interviews for this book, as well as my personal experience in foundation work, leave me no doubt that some of the best ideas foundations discover are triggered in just such conversations, apparently but not really "unrelated" to the meat-and-potatoes strategies the foundation is pursuing. Louis Pasteur perceptively observed that "chance favors the prepared mind," and, when it comes to serious social innovation, there are few persons better prepared to be fertile ground to germinate serendipitous seeds of change than foundation officers who are skilled and experienced in strategic social problem solving. All they need do is keep their doors open, give strategy its due, but preserve some serious time for their minds to listen to, hear, and ruminate about those out-of-program, out-of-strategy wild ideas.

INDEPENDENCE

With few exceptions, foundations have more often achieved high impact by acting alone rather than by cooperating with other funders. This fact goes contrary to the current vogue for what is called *resource leveraging*. Let's examine this fashion to dissect its strengths and weaknesses.

There are two kinds of resource leveraging as foundations use the term: leveraging dollars already committed to grantee organizations through attracting matching foundation grants, and leveraging dollars in advance by persuading other foundations to join in supporting a particular initiative that is contemplated.

The matching-grant system has been around since the days of Carnegie, Rockefeller, and Rosenwald, each of whom developed it into a fine art as a way of measuring the seriousness of commitment that grant recipients brought to their projects. There is nothing wrong with matching requirements, so long as the undertakings being supported are of high priority for the grantee organizations. When they are not, the foundation that imposes a challenge/matching requirement is using its philanthropic dollars to push a grantee in a direction that may conflict with its own priorities. Besides, when a foundation requires a recipient institution to match a grant that is of high priority on the foundation's agenda but not at all a priority on the recipient organization's agenda, it is using its philanthropic dollars to force a recipient organization in need of funds to use highly flexible internal discretionary funds to subsidize a foundation priority at considerable harm to its own internal priorities. The result is usually a low-impact project, since organizations pursuing a goal they don't truly believe in generally perform poorly. It is worth noting, too, that a matching requirement is hardly the only way a foundation can divert a grantee from its priority missions. All foundation grants have the potential for doing so.

The second kind of resource leveraging is quite different. Resource leveraging by using a stipulated portion of grant funds to attract money from other foundations for the same purpose has become fashionable among some foundations in recent years. This approach can enable a foundation to tackle a problem that is too big for it to handle alone. "Thinking big" in this fashion is to be applauded and encouraged. A good example of such a shared commitment is the Energy Foundation, which was founded to improve energy policy in the United States and China, and is supported by several foundations, including Hewlett, MacArthur, McKnight, Mertz-Gilmore, Packard, and others.

But sometimes resource leveraging is used simply to spread the cost and risk of an initiative among several funders, thereby freeing up monies to be used on other projects and minimizing the potential loss of resources and prestige if the initiative fails. This kind of bet-hedging strikes me as a symptom of timidity and unwillingness to make a serious commitment, often arising not among trustees but among insecure staff members. The trend toward resource leveraging inevitably reduces the willingness of foundations to take risks in support of the causes they believe in.

The fondness for resource leveraging has other drawbacks. The only time it is realistic to expect other funders to join in supporting a project is *before* the project is publicly announced and launched. After the public announcement, other foundations will be much less likely to sign on, since they prefer to be perceived as leaders, not followers. This means that proposed initiatives for joint funding have to be designed to appeal to the broadest—and often lowest—common denominator, so that many foundations with various goals, strategies, and styles can be persuaded to join in support. If trustees increasingly make the leveraging of dollars from other foundations a criterion of effectiveness by which their foundation CEO's or program staff's performance is measured, they cramp the decision-making capacity of their CEOs to take significant risks with their own dollars. The net tendency, therefore, is to soften the edges or dumb down proposed initiatives, thereby diminishing their chances of success.

None of this is to suggest that foundations should shy away from joint efforts with other foundations. It is important, however, to urge foundations to go into joint efforts with eyes open to the stumbling blocks that surely lie ahead. If a proposed undertaking is so important to a foundation and has a scope that is much larger than that foundation can manage alone, the involvement of others will be essential. My advice then is to proceed cautiously with such initiatives.

It's not surprising, then, that the most effective initiatives have generally been launched by individual foundations acting independently. There are certainly exceptions to this claim, but not very many. In some cases, other foundations jumped on the bandwagon with support at some later date. But the initial impetus came from one source—a single foundation with the vision to see a need, the courage to try to do something about it, and the self-confidence to act on its own.

EFFECTIVE GRANTEE SELECTION AND MANAGEMENT

As the cases suggest, foundations have often, and properly, launched new institutions, which continues to be an important and laudable strategy for many foundations. Recently, however, a new model of grantmaking has been suggested—taking existing organizations to a higher level.

In an influential and controversial article in the *Harvard Business Review*, Harvard Business School Professor Michael Porter and Mark Kramer persuasively articulated their views about how foundations could modify their grantmaking procedures to create more value for society.[54] I find the Porter-Kramer formulation persuasive and, in fact, a fair description of the high-impact practices actually followed by our most effective foundations. In summary, Porter and Kramer urge that foundations follow these four steps: (1) select high-performing grantees; (2) help grantees develop stronger capabilities; (3) help them attract other funders; and (4) help them develop and disseminate knowledge about the fields in which they work. Let's consider the implications of this four-step system.

First and foremost, selecting high-performing grantees requires that a foundation focus on organizations that are already strong or that could be made strong with short- or medium-term foundation support. These are organizations that benefit clients of high priority to the foundation and carry out their programs in ways that are effective in achieving the desired outcomes. By nurturing such organizations with general operating funds and professional consulting assistance, the foundation can help them become more convincing role models for other civic-sector organizations. In return, the grantee should develop and agree to be measured by performance benchmarks and prespecified indicators of organizational strength. Paul Brest, president of the Hewlett Foundation, calls this kind of arrangement "negotiated general support."

In regard to Porter and Kramer's third step, let me distinguish the idea of helping grantees attract other funders from the resource leveraging I criticized earlier, which involves making foundations' grants conditional on donations from other foundations. The Porter-Kramer concept doesn't vitiate foundation independence as resource leveraging does, and I applaud it. Most well-managed foundations try to help their important grantees attract funds from other foundations, but do so *after* they have made grants to them. This practice is not at all like the large initiatives that *require* the participation of other foundations and that depend for their success on getting other foundation buy-in *before* announcing them.

About the same time the Porter-Kramer article was published, Michael Bailin was leading the Edna McConnell Clark Foundation in establishing its new Youth Development program, along very much the same lines. Bailin inherited five separate programs, eliminated all but one, and established an entirely new way of administering grants. Rather than scattering grants among organizations and hedging them within project-specific frameworks that limit grantee flexibility, the foundation now picks already high-performing organizations, gives them large amounts of multi-year funding and consulting support to enhance their performance, and works with them to generate and use data-based benchmarks to measure their performance.

Perhaps most important, the Clark Foundation, whenever possible, employs solid data obtained by reputable researchers in randomized, controlled experiments that prove what works in producing better lives for the individuals who constitute the foundation's selected client base. Guided by this research, the foundation supports youth-serving programs that wish to grow and produce three kinds of outcomes:

- Educational outcomes that strengthen academic abilities and skills intended to improve school performance and graduation rates.

- Employment and employability outcomes that enhance the likelihood of success in the labor market.

- Avoidance of high-risk behaviors that reduce the likelihood of achieving a successful transition to a productive adult life, such as too-early teen pregnancy or incarceration.

The Edna McConnell Clark Foundation focuses its grantmaking on organizations that can be further strengthened to achieve such outcomes for larger numbers of their young clients. In addition, it measures its own performance by tracking how well its grantees produce the desired outcomes in growing numbers of clients; build internal data-generating systems for self-evaluation; track participation patterns among subgroups such as males and females, Latinos and African Americans, and so on; and use participation patterns to drive program improvements. The foundation also measures growing organizational strength through such data as the amount of money raised from other sources and improvement in board member quality. The foundation staff reports quarterly to its trustees on the progress of portfolio organizations on each of these dimensions. And it is important to note that the outcomes by which the foundation holds itself accountable are *grantee* client outcomes—the ultimate beneficiaries of the initiatives![55]

In my judgment, the Youth Development program of the Edna McConnell Clark Foundation epitomizes the Porter-Kramer system in practice. It offers a model for other foundations that are eager to employ a proven, methodical program for managing their grantee relationships so as to produce desired outcomes effectively, and the Clark Foundation is always ready to welcome other philanthropies as investors in its growing portfolio of high-performing grantees.

LONG-TERM THINKING
AND LONG-TERM COMMITMENT

Any strategy focused on a significant social goal takes time to implement. Some high-impact initiatives, such as the Green Revolution, required commitments that lasted as long as thirty years, and virtually all involve sustained focus on the mechanics of implementation before launch and during many years of follow-through.

The Flexner report on medical education is a good example. The report itself was the impetus that dramatically catalyzed the desired change in the educational system, but the demand for change thereby created was satisfied only through more than two decades of patient effort supported by Rockefeller Foundation grants. The same was true of the Ford Foundation's continuing support for many advocacy organizations in the fields of human rights, civil liberties, and gender equality; for many evidence-based, knowledge-generating institutions such as MDRC, Public/Private Ventures, The Urban Institute, and the Center for Budget and Policy Priorities; and for many operating organizations that it founded, including LISC.

One form of effective long-term thinking by foundations involves giving to create an institutional endowment for a grantee organization, and many high-impact initiatives include endowment gifts. Indeed, virtually all high-impact programs focused on creating new institutions have an endowment component. Yet most leading foundations are firmly committed to a no-endowment-grants policy. Why is this so?

A couple of factors appear to be at work. First, foundation donors and trustees are usually determined to make their assets stretch as far as possible. They view a no-endowments rule as a barrier that will prevent them from disbursing their assets too quickly, in the huge lump sums necessary to create meaningful endowments.

Second, foundations often prefer to retain control of their own capital funds—sometimes for reasons of sheer pride. Some founders who have accumulated impressive fortunes have been heard to ask, "Why should I give some grantee endowment assets to invest, when I know I can invest them better and generate a bigger return?" And some trustees echo this logic—though perhaps with less justifiable pride.

Both arguments are understandable. But the effectiveness of endowment grants is demonstrated by history. (For example, every one of the knowledge-building institutions launched with operating support by the

Ford Foundation was also stabilized at some point with strategically timed endowment gifts.) By supporting and stabilizing programs that will serve the public for the long run, endowment grants to well-chosen institutions can have an enormous positive impact. Thus, a rigid no-endowment rule is tantamount to tying the foundation's hand behind its back.

Some of today's most effective foundations are making imaginative use of endowment grants. The Doris Duke Charitable Foundation offers endowment challenge gifts that require matching satisfied by raising operating funds. Thus, the endowment grant serves as a carrot to induce a fragile arts organization to build a strong development operation as a continuing source of general operating income. The Doris Duke program is enhanced by its partnership with Surdna, which has some of the same program interests but has a policy against making endowment gifts: Duke provides an endowment grant while Surdna provides general operating support, both requiring matches. The same formula has been used by other foundations, including Ford, Mellon, Rockefeller, Atlantic Philanthropies, and Hewlett.[56]

Finally, general operating support is another indispensable aspect of long-term foundation thinking. All the leaders of long-established grantee organizations I interviewed underscored the role of general operating support in their achievement of sustainability. An example is MDRC, launched in 1974 with support from the Ford Foundation as the Manpower Demonstration Research Corporation. Professor Robert Solow, a Nobel laureate in economics (and a long-time member of the MDRC board), has commented on Ford's role in the MDRC story as follows:

> MDRC has changed the way public policy-making is being made today. It has demonstrated the power of evidence-based public policy-making. That has been achieved by steady foundation support over twenty-five years. The record of Ford-MDRC support raises the question of how foundations can organize themselves to do such long-run, urgently needed tasks for society. Smaller foundations need to figure out how to aggregate assets to achieve such scale.

Judith Gueron, executive director of MDRC, agrees:

> Ford's seventeen years of general support to MDRC enabled it to stick to mission and follow its own lead in developing a strategy to deal with the next important research questions on its agenda, as well as provide

seed capital for new projects. If MDRC has any value to society, it could not have happened without a core amount of general support. Without the general support, organizations like MDRC would have had to become nothing more than contract research organizations.

Similar observations would surely be offered by the heads of countless organizations that owe their existence to years of operating support from foundations, including the Urban Institute, Resources for the Future, the Brookings Institution, the Center for Budget and Policy Priorities, and many others.[57]

MAINTAINING FOCUS AND ALIGNMENT

At the risk of over-emphasizing the obvious, let's underscore that focus has an inherent tendency to lose its sharpness under the insistent pressure of mission creep. Moreover, alignment of the many moving parts in a foundation and with its grantees is continually at risk of losing its coherence. Careful, persistent attention is required to preserve both intact.

.   .   .

These, then, are some of the crucial factors that appear to be common to most of the high-impact foundation initiatives I've studied. What about the *failed* initiatives? Do these have any common characteristics, from which cautionary lessons can be derived? Indeed they do, and I'll turn to these lessons in our next chapter.

12

HOW FOUNDATIONS FAIL

Foundations are one of the few institutions in society where there is no price to pay for failure.

_____

Robert Crane, The Jeht Foundation[58]

Venture capitalists learn from their failures, scientists almost always learn from their failures, society sometimes learns from its failures. Why not foundations?

_____

Warren Wood, Robert Wood Johnson Foundation[59]

The bulk of this book is about signal successes of foundations, of which some one hundred have been summarized in short descriptive cases, available in a companion casebook. This chapter constitutes a brief look at the other end of the scale—foundation initiatives that did not succeed quite as mightily. In considering these examples—and the low-performing grants mentioned here are nothing but a very few examples of the way the best-laid or not-so-well-laid plans of foundations can go awry—keep constantly in mind that, in my considered judgment, there are far more successes than there are outright failures. I selected these several instances of low performance from among several hundred that were suggested to me by the people I interviewed in writing this book.

With about 68,000 foundations in America making thousands of grants every year, it would be surprising if some of those grants didn't work out as well as their grant makers had hoped. Indeed, if a foundation doesn't experience some failures in its grantmaking, a persuasive case can be made that it is either not tackling sufficiently challenging problems or not undertaking high-risk solutions to solve them. From earlier chapters, I've made it clear that the comparative advantage of the foundation vehicle, the highest and best use of aggregations of philanthropic dollars, is the taking of risk to solve society's toughest problems, but it goes without saying that the taking of high risk is not the only way foundations can be effective in solving society's toughest problems.

Many foundations, especially the largest ones, do take risks, so of course there are bound to be many failures. Failures are nothing for foundations to be ashamed of, but rather badges of honor signaling that they are trying harder to serve the social mission that justifies their tax-favored treatment. But there *is* something to be ashamed of in failures—not so much the failures themselves but the unwillingness of responsible foundation officials both to own up to the fact that some initiatives, in fact, failed, and to provide the reason for such failures. So far as I can discover, only four foundations in America have given a public grade of failing to one of its initiatives. The John and Mary Markle Foundation was first, when President Morrisett wrote in his 1986–87 annual report of the failure of its grants to establish Television Audience Assessment. The Annie E. Casey Foundation was the next when it published a report describing one of its New Futures initiatives that failed. The Avi Chai Foundation, in its 2005 annual report, reported its conclusion that its JSkyway distance-learning, Internet-based, in-service training initiative had not worked as anticipated, and concluded its annual funding for the initiative.[60] And the John D. and Catherine T. MacArthur Foundation reported in 2006 that its middle school reform project in Minneapolis was not working as intended and that it would end funding for it.

Such public admissions of failure are rare to the point of near-nonexistence. But there is one major exception—the practice of the Robert Wood Johnson Foundation of posting, in the research center section of its Web site, reports on grants completed, as well as some grant clusters or national program evaluations, some of which report unsuccessful initiatives, usually providing only the facts of the grant without expressing a judgment that particular grants failed. Other than the foregoing, failures are never mentioned and receive no publicity: Press releases are not issued, ceremonial ribbon-cuttings don't take place, newspaper articles and TV news reports don't appear. Failures fade quietly into oblivion.

It's understandable that foundations should prefer to trumpet their successes and ignore their failures. That's what we all prefer to do in our personal and professional lives. Yet acknowledging, analyzing, and understanding foundation failures could go a long way toward strengthening foundation practices, improving their success rates, and enabling the entire nonprofit sector to learn what didn't work so that flawed approaches are not unwittingly repeated by others. Moreover, owning up to failures would be a sign of foundation maturity and self-confidence, both of which are undermined by covering up failures. In this chapter, I'll try to provide a short summary of the less-happy side of foundation history—not in order to embarrass or besmirch the reputation of hard-working, well-meaning foundation leaders but to draw out the lessons that failure can teach.

First, however—as always—a few caveats.

Recognizing and defining failure in the context of foundation work isn't always as easy as one might think. A "failed" grant may have achieved an underlying goal that was not explicitly stated at the time it was made. Here's an example recounted by Barry Gaberman, longtime senior vice president of the Ford Foundation:

> In the early 1960s when Sukarno was prime minister, Ford started out in Indonesia with a specified goal of building strong economics faculties in the best universities there. Acting on the guidance of distinguished Indonesian economists, Ford supported a number of Indonesians to attend Harvard and Stanford to get their PhDs.
>
> When Suharto succeeded Sukarno as Prime Minister in 1965, he hastened to show that he was different from his leftist predecessor by bringing those Harvard- and Stanford-trained economists into government to run the major ministries.
>
> If the goal of Ford's initiative was to build the Indonesian economics departments, Ford failed. If, however, the goal was to improve economic policy in Indonesia, which indeed was the ultimate but unstated goal, Ford succeeded even better than it had expressly hoped.[61]

One must also be wary of making judgments of failure too early in the history of an initiative. When dealing with a major social problem, the appropriate time frame may be long indeed. (As Chou En-Lai is supposed to have remarked when asked his opinion of the French Revolution, "It's too soon to tell.")

Consider, for example, the End of Life initiative started by the Robert Wood Johnson Foundation in 1989. As Molly McKaughan, a program officer at the foundation, points out, the initiative was judged a failure in the foundation's own evaluation in 1994, which concluded that little had changed in the management of care for the dying. But a longer time frame suggests a different perspective. The End of Life initiative prompted Bill Moyers to create a major series of television documentaries on end-of-life issues. The producers of the series organized citizen groups in twenty cities focused on strengthening end-of-life care, and those groups continue functioning today. What's more, by 2005, end-of-life care had gradually emerged as a recognized health-care discipline. For a "failure," the End of Life Initiative has produced some remarkably lively results.[62]

Something similar seems to have happened with respect to the same foundation's Teaching Home Nursing Program.[63] That program was considered a failure when it ended in 1987, but now, nineteen years later, many of the seeds that it planted have sprouted, and home nursing has now acquired a great deal of momentum.

Barry Gaberman offers a similar example from his experience at Ford:

> In the early 1960s, Ford started the Calcutta Metropolitan Development Project. The assumption was that if you could do metropolitan development in Calcutta, you can do it anywhere. If one looked at the project after it ended in the mid-sixties, which Ford did, one would have had to say that it was a failure. [But] thirty years later, in the 1990s, Louis Winnick, a long-time Ford senior program officer, did another assessment. Lo and behold Calcutta then had an impressively functioning metropolitan planning process. It simply took longer to get it going than we projected.[64]

The reverse is also true, alas. What has been long regarded as a huge success in mitigating starvation—the Green Revolution—has now come under attack by biodiversity advocates for causing environmental damage.[65] Most observers still regard the Green Revolution as a huge success in saving perhaps a billion lives, even if it had an unfortunate by-product in soil erosion and species loss. But the point is that the jury is *always* out in the long run.

Very often, a program may well not achieve the goal that was specified for it and that catalyzed its creation, but nonetheless yielded valuable knowledge that might provide guidance to others in their efforts to solve the problem in order to reach the same goal. It doesn't seem appropriate to brand such an outcome as a failure, any more than it would be to declare as failures scientific experiments that do not confirm the hypotheses that prompted the experiments. Indeed, the latter "failures" do help build scientific knowledge by teaching what doesn't work, thereby leading others to try to find yet different solutions. The same thing can happen in the social and policy sphere. Here's an example: In the 1980s, the Rockefeller Foundation launched its Minority Female Single Parent Program. Richard Lyman, then-president of Rockefeller, says that:

> After President Reagan took office, there was a feeling that Rockefeller should do something additional in civil rights, so we established a board committee, which held hearings that yielded the decision to concentrate on minority women in poverty. The goal of the program was to enable the women to move from welfare to work. The program design specified grants to 9 communities seeking proposals from community-based organizations within those communities to create initiatives that would train the minority single women parent participants and obtain employment for them. Most of the 9 came up with nothing. But we did learn that it is impossible to succeed in persuading an impoverished mother to take a job if there are no provisions for child care. We therefore learned 1) what didn't work, and 2) that child care is indispensable if one aims to move single women parents from welfare to work. We also learned that if you want to get scientifically valid evaluations, you have to get people in the 9 communities to do things the same way for comparison purposes. But if you insist on that, then you compromise the ability of the community organizations to do the things THEY want to do.[66]

For these reasons, I want to be careful in assigning a grade of F to any foundation initiative. Still, there's no doubt that true failures do occur, in foundation work as in every field of human endeavor. Our job is to make each failure into a learning opportunity.

THE WEAKEST LINK

Just as a chain is only as strong as its weakest link, foundation initiatives often fail because of a single significant flaw in design or implementation.

Sometimes the flaw is lack of preparatory research. If the definition of the problem to be solved or the cause to be advanced is vague, inaccurate, or incomplete, the program is likely to founder. If the theory of change underlying the strategy has not been clearly articulated and rigorously tested, success is unlikely. If there's no theory of change at all, and, of course, if the theory of change is flawed or just plain wrong, failure is inevitable, barring a miracle.

In other cases, neglecting important components of implementation destroys an initiative's chance of success. If the sponsoring foundation, for example, fails to consult with all the relevant parties whose cooperation is needed to solve a problem, their indifference or opposition may scuttle the program. If due diligence isn't carefully performed on the track record and reputation of program leaders, their behavioral flaws, lack of knowledge, or absence of commitment may doom the initiative. And if grantee organizations are allowed to operate without timetables, benchmarks, and systems for objective evaluation, drift and procrastination may waste time and money, ultimately causing the initiative to fail.

Unfortunately, it takes only *one* weak link to break a chain. Hence the importance of detail-oriented, persistent, focused leadership. "Ninety percent effectiveness" is not good enough to make most complex programs work; nothing short of 100 percent accuracy on indispensable details is likely to suffice.

Based on my study of the unsuccessful foundation initiatives that were nominated by my interviewees, what follows are thirteen of the most common problems that lead to failure.

LACK OF A GUIDING STRATEGY

Virtually all of the foundation professionals with whom I spoke cited the Annenberg Education Challenge as one of the major failures in foundation history. Launched in 1993, it was a half-billion-dollar initiative billed as "the largest public/private endeavor in U.S. history dedicated to improving public schools."[67] As described on the Annenberg Web site, the numbers were impressive:

Eighteen locally designed Challenge projects operated in thirty-five states, funding 2,400 public schools that served more than 1.5 million students and 80,000 teachers. Over 1,600 businesses, foundations, colleges, and universities, and individuals contributed $600 million in private matching funds. . . . Grants ranged from $1 million to $53 million.

Unfortunately, the results were less than impressive, largely because of a lack of coherent overall strategy. The national Challenge was essentially a set of disjointed and inconsistent programs, guided by no overarching strategy, that produced outcomes that were mixed at best. The Challenge program required that Annenberg funds be matched two-for-one by contributions from other foundations, and precluded grants directly to school districts. Annenberg support, therefore, could go only to outside groups with school-reform projects in mind. In New York, four different organizations received Annenberg grants. One of them, for the creation of the Center for Arts Education, has achieved continuing success. Another supported Deborah Meier in launching an initiative to break up larger schools into small schools, and that program is credited by some as the launchpad for the Gates Foundation/Carnegie Corporation/Open Society Institute Program to create small schools in many U.S. communities. In fact, my understanding is that the Gates Foundation, as well as others, has come to the conclusion that creating small schools from scratch is what works, not breaking up big ones into smaller units. The evidence, as far as knowledgeable observers can tell, is that small schools work very well in some cases, but they depend on getting the conditions right, and that's hard to do in the context of a dysfunctional larger school.

By contrast, Boston's story is regarded as one of success, thanks largely to the effective leadership of schools superintendent Tom Payzant. All of the Boston funds were channeled through a single organization, the Boston Plan for Excellence, which did work directly with school districts. As a result, the Boston initiative was one of only two in the nation that was deemed deserving of renewal by the Annenberg Foundation itself five years after launch (the other was in the San Francisco Bay area). The Bay Area program, however, was described to me by an official of one of its partner foundations as "clearly a significant failure" and by a Stanford education professor as "thrown-away money." The partner foundation officer called it a "Rube Goldberg effort with a theory of change beyond all reasonableness, with no results specified, and with no impact measures built in."

In the rest of the country, the Annenberg grants were spent on a hodgepodge of miscellaneous projects—many of them, according to another

professor at Stanford—on things the school districts would have done anyway. He said that, "the impact was negligible. This was a sad waste of potentially powerful foundation resources, all resulting from plunging ahead
in doing things before carefully thinking about what to do."

One can have only admiration both for Walter Annenberg's desire to improve public education and for his generosity in putting a then-unprece-
dented amount of money into fulfilling it. Very likely he would have been
better served by specifying how he wished his gift to be used, in other
words, by providing a framework within which the grant administrators
were to function in deploying it. One must weep all the more that the realization of his desire was frustrated by inadequate strategy and implementation on his own part, as well as by those who were tasked with realizing
his vision.

MISMATCH BETWEEN PROBLEM AND STRATEGY

Given the troubled state of American elementary and secondary education in the latter half of the twentieth century, and the complexity of the
social, economic, and political problems that are involved in education, it's
not surprising that this arena should be a source of other examples of ambitious but unsuccessful foundation initiatives. One of these is the at-least-
partial failure of the Coalition of Essential Schools (CES), a not-for-profit
organization devoted to school reform according to the principles enun-
ciated by founder Theodore R. Sizer in his book *Horace's Compromise*
(1984).

Stanford Professor William Damon describes what went wrong as being
similar to what often happens with school reform initiatives: "Foundations
simply fail to think through the issues and how best to go about dealing
with them. Instead, they get caught up in attractive rhetoric that makes solutions sound much easier than they really are."

Sizer's nine principles, which included such unobjectionable notions as,
"Teaching and learning should be personalized to the maximum feasible
extent," and, "The school should demonstrate non-discriminatory and inclusive policies, practices, and pedagogies," were made central to a full-
blown program for redesigning schools. Despite a lack of substantive

research testing and documenting the effectiveness of the Sizer principles, foundations rushed into wholesale implementation, seeking to involve as many schools as possible as quickly as they could.

In retrospect, it's clear that CES and its supporting foundations were looking for a magic bullet that offered an instant cure to the problems of American schools—something that simply doesn't exist when dealing with as massive and complicated a problem as is created when education is administered by fifty states and thousands of municipal, county, and district school systems. It's quite possible that a more deliberate, research-based approach might have identified (say) four of the nine Sizer principles as being truly effective, and then moved forward with implementing them on a limited basis in a handful of test schools. The result could have been the emergence of a much clearer and stronger approach to school reform, rather than the wasteful disappointment that actually occurred. As Damon comments, however, "some good things came out of the coalition, and one of them was the idea of small schools."[68]

A similar pattern of behavior occurred with a project to curb binge drinking among college students, sponsored by the Robert Wood Johnson Foundation. Professionals with strong backgrounds in preventing alcohol abuse set up shop on a number of campuses and organized serious training programs that appeared to have at least partial success. Nonetheless, the effort has not caught on. For one thing, the intractable, depressing reality is that college students *like* to get drunk. For another, it is very hard to change the behavior of adolescents who are living away from home for the first time. Thus, the intervention provided, though well-meaning and competently executed, was either incommensurate with the intractable demands of the task, or focused on the wrong problem. As a result, none of the campuses where the program was tested has shown any long-term, dramatic decline in the use of alcohol. That outcome does not mean that the problem cannot be solved but only that that the initiative failed to solve it. Other, more promising approaches, such as Outside the Classroom (www.outsidetheclassroom.com), appear now to be spreading across campuses.

Some years ago the Spencer Foundation, wishing to increase the number and background diversity of scholars who do research on education, asked eleven schools of education to submit proposals to receive funds to support research training grants for doctor of education or PhD candidates and to conduct seminars for them. The primary goal of the program was to redress the imbalance between the number of students with disciplinary backgrounds and those students with education school backgrounds. Grants were made to the eleven institutions, which then allocated the funds to their own students. The process did not yield candidates of the quality that had been hoped for. In retrospect, the foundation realized that the program should have been a nationally competitive selection process, similar to its long-running, successful dissertation fellowships program, most of which went to students at elite institutions, rather than grants to preselected education schools, which it chose primarily to get greater diversity among students. Clearly the strategy selected was a bad fit with the goal sought.

A now-legendary instance of a foundation's rushing in before giving careful thought is the Ford Foundation's 1967 School Decentralization experiment, which was an egregious mismatch. Its premise was that many of the problems depressing educational quality and effectiveness in New York were the result of the lack of control of the local schools by the communities that they served. One of the three district experiments in community school boards—that in Ocean Hill-Brownsville—blew up when the Ocean Hill-Brownsville community board decided to transfer several employees and teachers out of the local schools, as described as follows in an article, "School Boards," by Derek Alger in the November 13, 2000 issue of *Gotham Gazette*:

> A large fracas began when the Ocean Hill-Brownsville Governing Board, comprised of nine parents and three community leaders, announced its intention to transfer 19 school employees, including 13 teachers, out of the district for allegedly sabotaging efforts at decentralization. Supporters of the employees charged the ousters were ethnically based. Amid charges of racism and anti-Semitism, the United Federation of Teachers went on strike over the issue, and its president Albert Shanker went to jail. Eventually the teachers were reinstated, though all transferred to other districts. The State Education Department took over as the interim authority of the Ocean Hill-Brownsville district.

While the movement for community control of schools was torpedoed by this disaster, it was slowed down but did not immediately sink. Perhaps it was appropriate for the Ford Foundation to put resources into such an experiment, but, before doing so, it should have taken the time to find districts in which such an experiment had a decent chance of showing the positive differences that community control might have. Instead, by experimenting with the most fractious of districts, Ford ensured negative outcomes that could not possibly be helpful in advancing the principle on which the experiment was premised. Whether community control of schools would ever have prevailed is not likely to be known; the momentum in school governance in 2006 is in the opposite direction—control of schools by city mayors.

LACK OF A CREDIBLE LOGIC MODEL

One of the most common characteristics of foundation failures is the lack or inadequacy of the logic model that is intended to lead from the action taken to the result desired. An example of the failure was a Ford Foundation grant to achieve organizational reform of the United Nations and to promote United States global engagement. The program officer then responsible for making the grant, Anthony Romero, now president of the American Civil Liberties Union, was brutally frank in taking responsibility for its shortcoming:

> My program produced great reports on bringing about a more egalitarian Security Council, but the truth is that there is not much to show for what we were able to accomplish towards that end. I did not have a theory of implementing change when I recommended the grants. I knew what we wanted to change but I didn't think carefully about how to achieve it. I thought that if we supported all the different issues we wanted to address, it would have made a difference, but most times it didn't.[69]

Like some of the other characteristics of foundation failures discussed here, more often than not this failure results from the combination of a strong desire to do something about a problem and a lack of understanding about just what to do. The foundations that act in this fashion might be said to be operating on the imperative of, "Don't just stand there; do something, anything."

Another example of a flawed logic model, or the absence of any real strategy at all, was the Getty Trust's Discipline-Based Education in the Arts program, which was aimed at adding an arts component to individual academic disciplines in colleges by developing curricular materials. For many years, it had been the largest single grant program of the Getty Trust. When Barry Munitz took over the presidency of the Getty Trust, he terminated that program. It was never independently evaluated. According to Harvard Professor Howard Gardner, the program was not "intellectually honest." Gardner elaborates that conclusion: "The leaders at the Foundation did not care what you did under the label of DBAE so long as you wrapped yourself in the label. And so, from my point of view, DBAE was more about spin and about public relations, than it was about quality arts education. And once the money disappeared, so did the label and many of the programs." [70]

WEAK GRANTEE COMMITMENT

I've stressed the importance of strategic focus for the foundation—clearly defining goals and selecting grantees whose programs and activities will help in achieving those goals. At times, however, not-for-profit organizations that are desperate for funds will stretch or distort their self-definition in an effort to appear suitable for a foundation grant. The result can be a grant going to a recipient that is not *truly* committed to the same goals as the foundation. William Bowen, president of the Andrew Mellon Foundation, has witnessed this problem firsthand:

> When recipients of a grant are not fully committed to doing what the foundation intends, that can lead to serious failure. In a couple of cases, Mellon has asked for the return of the grant. Foundations should beware of "reluctant dragons," who are frequently the cause of major disappointments. They read a foundation's annual report and then come in for grants that seem to fit [the goals of the foundation], but really don't. They are being opportunistic and trying to fit what *they* want to do into the framework of what the foundation wants to do. And unfortunately, the foundation sometimes disregards the evidence that that is the case and nonetheless makes a grant to a grantee who really isn't committed to what the foundation intends to achieve. [71]

LACK OF RELEVANT GRANTEE EXPERIENCE

A frequent mistake of foundations that have a desire to get a particular program done is to pick a reputable organization to run it, whether or not that organization has any experience or special competence in carrying out that particular kind of program.

The RWJF Faith in Action program is a good example of this flawed approach. Support was given to faith-based organizations that were thought to be capable of helping solve health problems of poor people, but the recipient organizations were not supposed to use the program to proselytize for their religion. Many of them, however, were not sophisticated enough to know how to use the money properly. David Morse of RWJF comments that, "It was hard to understand what the objective of the grants was to be. If it was to get faith-based organizations to work together to improve health services, it was clearly not a success, but the jury is still out with respect to the overall effects."[72]

The American Council of Learned Societies sought and obtained support, from several foundations, to engage in a national program of school reform that brought college faculty members together with K–12 teachers. In the hindsight of the foundation officers, it was clear that this initiative had little congruence with the mission or track record of ACLS, which is a confederation of college faculty professional associations. The program never acquired any traction.

INCOMPATIBLE GRANTEE PARTNERS

Foundations sometimes choose to support a group of grantees in a joint project to tackle a single problem or a group of closely related problems. This can be an effective approach when the grantee organizations are highly compatible and have complementary skills. But when the individual leaders involved have strong and conflicting personalities, or the organizations have cultures that do not blend effectively, or the organizations do not share the same vision for dealing with the program, the result may be an initiative that founders.

The ATLAS Project, supported by several national foundations, is an example. Its general goal was to improve education for disadvantaged youngsters through "whole school" reform efforts. While the principal leaders of the several school reform efforts who were supposed to collaborate on the project—including such well-known figures as Howard Gardner, James Comer, Janet Whitla, and Ted Sizer (the founder of the Coalition for Essential Schools [CES])—turned out to be thoroughly compatible personally, their respective organizations had a harder time working together, which led to management confusion and mistakes.[73] Harvard Professor Howard Gardner puts it this way:

> The 4 PIs [project investigators]got along very well, perhaps too well. The problem was that each of our constituent organizations had taken on our personal coloration; they worked well under our leadership but they never were able to work with the other partner organizations. I blame myself for not working harder to get Project Zero to mesh with the organizational cultures of Sizer's Coalition of Essential Schools, Comer's School Development program, and Whitla's Educational Development Center. I should note, for the record, that ATLAS still exists, and is in over 100 schools, so it can't be labeled a failure in the long run. The failure was a leadership one, for which I take partial blame.

The Hewlett Foundation's Neighborhood Improvement Initiatives in three Bay Area communities, on which the foundation spent about twenty-five million dollars with little or no result, according to Hewlett's president Paul Brest, is another example of a lack of compatible grantee partners. Brest attributes the failure to a number of causes, including a lack of clarity about how the responsibility for strategic planning should be allocated between the Hewlett Foundation, the community foundations, and the community organizations.[74]

FAILURE TO INCLUDE
RELEVANT STAKEHOLDERS

Most complex social problems involve many stakeholders with varying goals, concerns, interests, needs, and points of view. The stakeholder list may include organizations representing differing subgroups among those who suffer from the effects of the problem, experts and professionals working to address the problem, businesses that profit either from exacerbating the problem or mitigating it, and government agencies charged with fixing the problem. It may be impossible to develop a strategy that will please all or even most of these stakeholders. But it's important for a foundation to try to involve them all in devising and implementing the strategy. Otherwise, they may prove to be indifferent or actively hostile to the initiative once it is launched, often with disastrous effects. Many a foundation program has collapsed because of the failure to involve one or more key stakeholder groups.

Consider, for example, the Youth and Families Initiative launched in some half a dozen inner-city neighborhoods in 1991 by the Chicago Community Trust. The idea was for local neighborhoods to bear some responsibility for developing community programs to support children and youth as well as for orchestrating support from all the relevant city departments. It was a reasonable concept, but it was handicapped by the failure of the program's leadership to recognize the legitimacy and value of participation by neighborhood citizens. Because the directors of the initiative refused to reach out to local people, the program quickly deteriorated into a series of power struggles with community groups, draining its effectiveness and reducing its impact.

Another example is the National News Council initiative, launched by The Twentieth Century Fund in 1971, and later joined by the John and Mary Markle Foundation as a joint undertaking. The Markle Foundation soon assumed full responsibility for supporting the initiative. The idea was to establish a council that could make objective judgments about accuracy and fairness in reporting in response to complaints of error or bias. However, according to Lloyd Morrisett, then-president of Markle, "It was doomed from the start because of the refusal of the *New York Times* to participate." This refusal, in turn, Morrisett added, "may have been occasioned by the involvement in the project of Murray Rossant, head of the Twentieth Century Fund and a colorful character with a controversial reputation who had once been at the *Times*."[75] This is a case where the failure to engage key stakeholders—the *New York Times* and the *Washington Post,* two of the nation's most prestigious and authoritative newspapers— almost certainly doomed an otherwise promising project. One would have thought that the Twentieth Century Fund would have resisted the impulse to create the National News Council until it had first obtained the consent of the *Times* to join, and that Markle, before deciding to pick up where the Twentieth Century Fund left off, would have verified, instead of assuming, the willingness of the *Times* to join.[76]

Failure to assure that key collaborators are ready to cooperate fully became a serious problem in the Andrew Mellon Foundation's Fostering a Community of Learners collaborative program, which was administered by the Russell Sage Foundation. The goal of the project, which originated at the University of California at Berkeley, was to take to scale a school re-form methodology called "fostering a community of learners" that seemed promising—indeed seductive—in both practice and theory. According to Lee Shulman, then a professor of education at Stanford who participated in the project, now president of the Carnegie Foundation for the Advance-ment of Teaching, the five-plus million dollar project successfully recruited some of the leading lights in American K–12 education reform to organize the scale-up. Shulman elaborates:

> It was quite frustrating. We soon discovered that the original reform, while theoretically elegant and with impressive empirical support from early experiments, was far less robust than we had thought. The few ex-isting "alpha sites" in Oakland turned out to be quite fragile. The orig-inal principal investigators worried that having many outside researchers descend on those sites would wreck the places where the reform was working. They therefore made those sites unavailable to their collaborating researchers, even though they were also the Project Investigators for the scale-up collaboration. Therefore, we had no acces-sible "existence proofs" on which to base teacher education and pro-fessional development initiatives. To make matters worse, we had no extensive high quality videotapes that could have provided concrete ex-amples of how these extraordinary teachers had implemented the re-form in the sites where they appeared to be working. So we were unable to provide the new recruits with a vision of the reform, much less with direct experience with the teachers and students who had al-ready pulled off the reform in their own contexts. Although everyone worked very hard, I felt the project failed because of those difficulties. It was one of the more painful experiences in my research career."[77]

FAILURE TO SPECIFY *DESIRED* OUTCOMES PRECISELY

Some years ago, the Hewlett Foundation made a series of grants to community environmental collaboratives to enable farmers, ranchers, en-vironmentalists, and other stakeholders to better understand one another's interests and goals. Paul Brest, who assumed the Hewlett presidency after the grants had been running, says that "the objectives specified were process objectives rather than impact measures. The stated goal was essentially for the parties to talk to and understand one another. There were no other clear goals, no attempts to measure outcomes other than the talks held." On attending one meeting of evaluators of these collaborative efforts, Brest said, "I kept on asking about outcomes but all they would talk about was meetings held."[78]

Another good example of failing to specify the correct success criterion is the Robert Wood Johnson Foundation's Fighting Back national program, which utilized local coalitions to fight substance abuse. The success criterion chosen for the program was a decline in drug selling and use in the particular communities. According to James Knickman, former RWJF vice president for research and evaluation, none of the data generated by the research showed any changes in substance use. He added that there is a federal program to form local coalitions, but that is only an easy way to enable people to feel that they have done something—form a coalition—even if the coalition doesn't accomplish the intended results. Federal officials responsible for that program worked with RWJF on the initiative, on which RWJF spent one hundred million dollars. "The flaw," Knickman says, "was in setting the effectiveness measure as a change in the addiction rate."[79]

RELYING ON INADEQUATE LEADERSHIP

As we've seen, developing a sound strategy and creating a solid management structure are both vital steps in launching a high-impact initiative. But the personal strengths, weaknesses, skills, and deficits of the individuals tapped for positions of leadership in the implementation are also highly important. Even a well-designed organization isn't likely to thrive for long under the guidance of a director who simply lacks the abilities or interests needed to run the program wisely and make intelligent decisions on a day-to-day basis.

The Chicago-based Joyce Foundation launched a project called the Center for the Great Lakes that foundered largely because of ill-considered leadership choices. Perhaps because of a failure to conduct due diligence, the foundation hired the wrong person for the top job at the center, a former governor of one of the Great Lakes states whose commitment to the project turned out to be minimal. His main interest, it seemed, was in the perks of the job and the public platform it provided for him to promote his personal interests and political agenda. He then compounded the problem by hiring a former staff member to fill the number-two job at the center. This was a position centered mainly on fund-raising—which turned out to be the kind of task the staff member hated. The foundation finally pulled the plug on the Center for the Great Lakes when it became clear that the poor personnel choices had doomed the project to ineffectuality.

In the mid-1990s, considerable excitement about "sustainable development" first appeared in the nonprofit sector. This was an approach to business and the environment that looked for compatible uses so that the former could earn money and the latter would be unharmed. Job development was a goal of such projects as well.

One such approach was taken by the Nature Conservancy, which launched a program at several sites to test various sustainable-development enterprises. A particularly prominent part of the effort was the establishment of the Virginia Eastern Shore Corporation (VESCOR). The Ford Foundation, the Surdna Foundation, and several others contributed to the project.

Based on the eastern shore of Virginia, VESCOR was to promote sustainable development in the region by encouraging the development of small-scale businesses such as bed-and-breakfast inns, artisans' co-ops, and the production of a new kind of potato chip using the Hayman potato, a sweet potato with white flesh native to the area that is highly prized by aficionados.

The VESCOR model might have worked, but designing and implementing a sustainable-development program calls for a high degree of complex business planning and management skills. Despite the enthusiasm for the project by the Nature Conservancy, the venture proved unsuccessful; it was far too risky and undercapitalized, and it was beset by many problems—from inadequate tourist traffic at bed-and-breakfasts to inadequate potato production capacity of local growers. The effort foundered for many months and an outside consultant was hired by Ford to review VESCOR's progress and its financial statements. Neither gave cause for optimism and the program ultimately folded.

Fragmented Leadership
and Uncertain Collaboration

Some foundation initiatives struggle not because of a single overwhelming failure but because of weaknesses in focus and implementation. Here is one illustrative case that is less a story of failure than of underperformance and drift. While much good has been, and still is being, done, greater clarity, sharper midcourse corrections, and stronger leadership might have made the venture—now fifteen years old—a home run.

The National Community Development Initiative (NCDI), launched in 1991 and now rechristened as Living Cities, was the creation of Peter Goldmark, then-president of the Rockefeller Foundation, and Mike Sviridoff, a deeply knowledgeable expert in community economic development.

The idea was to aggregate the funds of foundations, banks, and insurance companies—both grants and loans—to support the work of community development organizations (CDCs), primarily in housing. More than a dozen institutions and the Federal Housing and Urban Development Department, and later Health and Human Services, ultimately participated.

In its first decade $250 million was raised to mount and deliver this program. NCDI was designed as a "wholesaler" of the monies. It chose the two premier community development intermediaries in the country, the Local Initiatives Development Corporation (LISC) and the Enterprise Foundation, to select the participating cities and CDCs, and to manage the program. NCDI became the largest trisector collaboration ever mounted. Today, NCDI is five years into its second decade.

An unprecedented large consortium such as this could be expected to run into start-up and operational problems, but most were kept manageable by the simplicity of the financing arrangement and the focus of the responsibilities on the intermediaries. In fact, the initiative was seen as a way to educate the CEOs of major institutions in the complexities of urban revival.

Trouble began to appear late in the first decade when some existing players moved on, new ones joined, the informal rotating leadership changed, and the perspectives of the members became scattered. As the leadership changed, the consensus over supporting LISC, Enterprise, and the CDCs began to fray. New projects were added, like leadership development, which diminished the clarity and singularity of NCDI's purpose.

Furthermore, despite several efforts to define and report out the success of the initiative, an authoritative and conclusive document could not be produced. An overdesigned, constantly changing evaluation effort was unable to define and report out measures of success. In addition, a small but serious initiative to identify and train CDC professionals failed. And despite constant effort, NCDI was unable to build the case with the national media for larger investments in cities. (Alas, it is all-too-well known that good inner-city development stories are rarely carried in the press.)

Heading into its second decade, NCDI changed its name to Living Cities in an effort to sharpen its public profile. While twenty-three cities had initially been selected for funding, it was clear that funds were sliced too thin to make the difference NCDI intended. The number of cities was reduced to twelve. Four cities were chosen to develop special outsize projects to demonstrate what focused investment might accomplish, and to model the results for others—an initiative that has not yet proved out. In addition, NCDI/Living Cities decided further to expand its reach into policy research and advocacy, still uncertain what influence this relatively small collection of philanthropy and business leaders could do to influence the climate of policy change in Washington—one which was increasingly tilting against urban-development funding.

Thus, shifting approaches, uncertain results, and increasingly diffuse strategies seemed to act as a brake on this organization, whose unique, collaborative nature always seemed to be "in process." To this extent, Living Cities appears to have been unsuccessful in its own terms.

Nonetheless, the initiative continues, no doubt making serious headway in particular cities and with particular CDCs. New members have contributed additional dollars, and the organization continues to deliver funds in an efficient way. Perhaps the most that can be said is that this unique experiment has yet to reach the scale and achieve the impact its great resources would clearly seem to merit.

INADEQUATE MARKET RESEARCH

Failure to do good market research on whether there is a demand for what a foundation is considering is almost always fatal.

The Markle Foundation invested heavily in launching *Channels* magazine, which was at the time, according to Lloyd Morrisett, then-president of Markle, "the best magazine on the media." He stated that Markle's success criterion was the achievement of self-sustainability, and that Markle, given its comparatively small size, could not afford to sustain it alone indefinitely . He says now that, "apparently there is not a sufficient audience for a journal of criticism on the media, and, while Norman Lear kept it alive after the Foundation support ended, it appears in retrospect that it never really had a chance to achieve self-sustainability."[80]

Unanticipated Consequences

Before a foundation launches any initiative, the most important question to ask is: "What are the things that might possibly go wrong with it or as a consequence of it?" Simply put, this is risk analysis, and it's astonishing that so few foundations explicitly perform risk analysis on their initiatives in the process of shaping and deciding whether to implement them. Here is an emblematic example: Shortly after the assassination of Robert F. Kennedy in June 1968, the Ford Foundation, in a well-intentioned act motivated by a desire to help Kennedy's talented policy aides in their transition to other jobs, made a series of fellowship awards to some of them. Clearly, Ford misread the politics of the times, because those grants triggered a firestorm of criticism, and are now widely regarded as important causes of the Tax Reform Act of 1969, which levied the first tax ever on foundations and otherwise significantly increased the stringency of government regulation of foundations.

Failure and Its Lessons

The above accounts of these "failures" make clear both that virtually none of the failures was total but that all of them, as well as many other foundation initiatives like them, could, with a bit more care and common sense in their conception and implementation, likely have had outcomes that realized to a much greater degree the hopes that sparked the initiatives in the first place. What was it that prodded the foundations involved to go off, as it were, half-cocked and undertake ideas that were half-baked? I think it always is the triumph of hope over experience, as Samuel Johnson said of the motivation to undertake a second marriage. All of these failures can be explained as a rush to judgment without adequate thinking, giving in to an impulse to do something in response to a crying need, or giving way to expressive philanthropy, as Peter Frumkin describes it, with regard to a problem that requires careful instrumental philanthropy for its solution.

It bears repeating here that the almost surefire way for foundations to diminish the likelihood of mistakes in the first place is to require program officers and grantees to make explicit the logic model, the theory of change, that a prospective grant embodies, and to be certain that the fit between the foundation's goal in undertaking a program and the strategy proposed to achieve it is persuasive. By specifying in as much detail as possible what is supposed to cause what to happen, why the recipients are thought likely to be able to facilitate the causal chain, which eventualities might frustrate the causal flow, whose support must be gained and whose opposition must be overcome, how one will know at successive points in time whether the logic model is proving accurate or not, a foundation can significantly reduce its exposure to failure. The most important task of all is to make explicit the implicit assumptions of a proposed initiative so that each of them can be tested by all those engaged in approving the grant, including the trustees where applicable.

If foundations are doing what they are supposed to be doing—maximizing social value by solving hard social problems—they are bound to suffer failures. Instead of hiding them, they should be exulting about them alongside the successes, because it is the failures that prove that foundations are not simply picking the low-hanging fruit. Most of all, foundations should wear them like the badges of honor they are, so that other foundations and the entire nonprofit sector can learn from their failures. And if foundations will muster the courage to talk and write about their failures, everyone will give much greater credence to the far more numerous successes that foundations have achieved.

Alas, the great dishonor is that there are no officially published analyses of the failures discussed above, or of any other for that matter. It is heartening that the Bill and Melinda Gates Foundation has announced its determination to make public and write about its failures. Perhaps its example will persuade other foundations to honor their obligation to learn from their mistakes and to teach others, which they can easily do by commissioning and publishing independent analyses of why any of their significant initiatives failed.

13

THREE ESSENTIALS:

DISCIPLINE, BOUNDARIES,

AND PERSISTENCE

Less is more.

———

Ludwig Mies van der Rohe

If "less is more" in architecture, something analogous seems to be true of foundation initiatives: Fewer are better. With fewer program areas, a foundation can concentrate its attention and resources over a longer period of time, and acquire a greater depth of experience accompanied by a more extensive familiarity with the relevant context.

Unfortunately, thinking smaller and more targeted does not come easy to very wealthy, often self-made, men and women who have gotten accustomed to thinking expansively and who believe that mountains of philanthropic capital can indeed move the world. In an effort to convince them (as well as the people who work for them), let me now provide the evidence, based on my in-depth study of foundation initiatives and their relative success.

DISCIPLINE STARTS AT THE TOP

As I observed earlier, no two foundations are exactly alike. But what special characteristics do the most effective foundations share? Longevity is not indispensable. Some of our oldest foundations have compiled an impressive list of high-impact programs. But some of our youngest foundations have already established, or seem likely to establish, remarkable track records. The list includes the Annie E. Casey Foundation, George Soros's Open Society Institute, Atlantic Philanthropies, and, of course, the Bill and Melinda Gates Foundation, none of which has been fully active for more than fifteen years. Furthermore, two of the foundations with the highest-impact programs—the Robert Wood Johnson Foundation and the Ford Foundation—were only forty-four and fifty-five years old, respectively, when they began serious grantmaking, about half the age of such venerable counterparts as the Rockefeller, Carnegie, Commonwealth, and Russell Sage foundations. And some of the conservative foundations, which have had great impact in achieving significant change in public policy starting in the 1970s, are all quite young. The John M. Olin Foundation was founded in 1953, the Scaife Foundations in 1973, and the Lynde and Harry Bradley Foundation in 1985.

Longevity alone, then, is no prerequisite to program impact. Far more significant are the culture and history of a foundation, as shaped by the founder and the first generation of trustees, and as transmitted to later years by successor trustees and program staff.

The trustees play an especially critical role. It is the trustees who revisit, reaffirm, or reshape the foundation's original program focuses and their relative priority. It is the trustees who decide whether and how a foundation will be strategically focused and what risk profile it will assume. It is the trustees who instill an ethic of staff accountability and evidence-based decision-making into the governance dynamic of a foundation—or fail to do so. And it is the trustees who select the CEO, the chosen instrument through whom they project to the program staff, the wider civic sector, and the public as a whole the values that guide the foundation.

The trustees, then, are crucial to the success of the foundation. But trustees rarely have a completely free hand. Almost always there is another hand at work—the hand of the donor—reaching out, as it were, from the grave (hence the legal expression *mortmain*, literally "dead hand"). If the CEO is the instrument of the trustees, the trustees are in some sense the instruments of the donor. I'm convinced, therefore, that donor influence is the most powerful of all determinants of the impact of a foundation. Constraints and limitations on trustee actions imposed by the donor have both legal and moral authority—and, as I argue in this chapter, wisely chosen constraints have helped to shape the effectiveness of many of the best-run and highest-impact foundations. If donor influence is strong, persistent, and nondestructive, it can often be beneficial in helping to bring about high impact. If it is weak or nonexistent, it seems to conduce to a more erratic record of significant achievement.

But foundation founders do not always seek to project their influence over time. Not every donor has chosen to wield his or her legal and personal authority in shaping the work of the foundation. John D. Rockefeller Sr. symbolically distanced himself from the foundation he created. Rockefeller refused to serve on the board of trustees of the Rockefeller Foundation, yet clearly exerted very substantial influence in its early days through the friends and associates he named to its board. Henry Ford II inherited rather than created the Ford Foundation, and later resigned from the Ford Foundation's board over policy differences with staff and other trustees. Moreover, John D. MacArthur did not seek to put his personal stamp on the foundation that he named for himself and his wife, but, like many other foundation creators, appointed business associates as trustees, along with his son Roderick and Paul Harvey, the celebrated radio commentator. He gave no instructions to the board and died in 1978, just about the time the foundation was getting going. That five-person board contained great differences of opinion about the focus of the foundation, especially between Roderick and the other members. Ultimately, the board enlarged itself to fifteen in 1979 to include several distinguished scientists including Nobelist Murray Gell-Mann, Jonas Salk, and Jerome Wiesner, as well as other prominent, "big-think" persons, who succeeded wisely in guiding the future of MacArthur. Five years later, Roderick MacArthur brought suit against the other trustees, but died in the same year.[81]

However, most donors have indeed tried to influence the policies and programs of their foundations, and, in the next few pages, I will consider five examples, all of which rank as high performers in any analysis of foundation effectiveness.

FIVE FOUNDERS AND
THEIR SHAPING INFLUENCE

Five of America's highest-impact foundations—the Commonwealth Fund, the Alfred P. Sloan Foundation, the Andrew W. Mellon Foundation, the Robert Wood Johnson Foundation (RWJF), and the Carnegie Corporation of New York—have shown strong evidence of founder influence. In each case, however, that influence appears to have been created in a different way.

The two most straightforward cases are the Robert Wood Johnson and Alfred P. Sloan foundations. Both illustrate a donor's deliberate choice both of program focus and of specific characteristics in the trustees to whom they handed their legacies.

Robert Wood Johnson took the unusual step of drawing the majority of the members onto his foundation's board from among executives or former executives of the company he built, Johnson & Johnson, and the remainder of them from the wider business world. Moreover, he limited the foundation's focus to the field of health. The first board of the foundation, chaired by Johnson & Johnson executive Gus Lienhard, selected as CEO Dr. David Rogers, the brilliant dean, at age twenty-nine, of Johns Hopkins University School of Medicine. Rogers proved to be one of the greatest founding CEOs of any U.S. foundation. Before taking on RWJF's leadership, Rogers was already steeped in the field of health, cared passionately about its problems, and had an impressive track record in running perhaps America's greatest school of medicine. Consequently, he hit the ground running and never stopped until his own health failed fifteen years later. He recruited what turned out to be the best large foundation start-up staff perhaps ever, which enabled him to roll out imaginative programs one after the other in steady succession starting with the Emergency Medical Services Program.[82] With Johnson's death, RWJF became in 1972 the largest health foundation in the United States, and Rogers's personal stature enabled him to position himself instantly as the leader in U.S. health philanthropy.

As unusual as the choice of a young prodigy as CEO was the division of labor between the board and the foundation staff. It was understood that the board would reserve to itself decisions about financial, investment, management, and budget issues—collectively referred to as "the state"— while deferring to the CEO and staff about grantmaking, which they called "the church." The arrangement worked very well throughout Rogers's tenure, during which many high-impact initiatives were successfully launched. The interaction between the strong, business-minded discipline—especially the focus on impact measurement, assessment, and evaluation—imposed by the executives on the board and the substantive knowledge and creative brilliance of the program staff have helped make

RWJF one of the world's premier foundations. About half of the fifteen members of RWJF's present board are from the business world, four of whom are retired Johnson & Johnson executives.

Thus, Johnson put a permanent stamp on the foundation in two significant ways. He confined its program to health, and, by the board he chose, he assured that the foundation would take a hard-nosed, disciplined approach that placed great importance on evaluation and measurement.

When Alfred P. Sloan created his foundation in 1934, he, too, recruited to its board of trustees a number of executives or former executives of General Motors Corporation, which he headed from 1923–46 and helped lead to a new level of preeminence among automakers. He also set several clear priorities for the foundation's programs, including science, technology, economics, and business.

Almost seventy years after its founding, Sloan continues to show very strong donor influence. As of 2005, eight of the eleven Sloan trustees have business backgrounds, while the other three are distinguished scholars, including two economists—former Princeton President Harold Shapiro and Nobel laureate Robert Solow. And science, technology, economics, and business remain the chief areas of focus for Sloan-financed initiatives.

The Commonwealth Fund is yet another example of strong founder shaping. Its first president, Edward S. Harkness, was the son of founder Anna Harkness and placed his stamp on the fund in his twenty-two years of leadership. The fund has a remarkable, nearly one-hundred-year-long record of pioneering initiatives in health and health care, many with significant impacts, largely the result of the fund's scientific method of decision-making and deep focus on its field of concentration. Several of its greatest achievements are included among the cases prepared for this book, such as The Rural Hospitals Program, #13; Support for the Development of the Pap Smear, #18; The Rochester Regional Hospital Council, #21; and The Development of the Nurse Practitioner and Physician Assistant Professions, #31. Today, most of the board's members are distinguished individuals from the field of health, although some equally impressive generalists also serve.

The Andrew W. Mellon Foundation clearly reflects the interests and passions of Paul Mellon, who served as a founding board member for many years, although he resisted ever taking the role of chair. The foundation traces its history to two predecessor organizations, the Avalon Foundation, created by Ailsa Mellon Bruce in 1940, and the Old Dominion Foundation, created by Paul Mellon in 1941. After his sister Ailsa's tragic death in 1969, Mellon consolidated the two foundations and named the new entity after their father, the source of the family wealth.

Paul Mellon's passion for art, the humanities, universities, libraries, and the environment shaped major Mellon Foundation priorities during his lifetime and continued to do so after his death in 1999. Unlike Johnson and Sloan, Mellon imposed no explicit constraints on his foundation, but he influenced his fellow trustees by his moral authority and the passion of his convictions. Borrowing from Professor Joseph Nye's usage, we might aptly call Paul Mellon's influence over the Mellon Foundation "soft power," in contrast to the "hard power" with which Johnson and Sloan shaped their foundations and their boards.[83] The one occasion when Mellon wielded hard power was when he leaned on the other trustees to make a multimillion-dollar gift to build the east wing of the National Gallery of Art.

William Bowen, in his final report as president of the Mellon Foundation, described the organization's intensely focused programming this way:

> More generally, as resources have grown, Mellon has followed a deliberate policy of "sharpening and deepening" commitments. The idea has been to find new ways to work ever more effectively within established program areas, rather than to spread out into entirely new areas. This is somewhat unusual. The more typical pattern in the foundation world is for growth in total resources to be accompanied by a broadening of programmatic interests. But as the Mellon Foundation's Trustees weighed various strategies in September 2000, during the substantial run up in the equities market, they concluded that—for Mellon— strengthening and deepening activities in core areas of interest would take fullest advantage of our capacities and would be especially beneficial to fields such as the humanities that were of less interest to many other donors.[84]

Certainly the strategic focus of the Mellon trustees has been significantly shaped by the legacy of their founder.

In the early days of the Carnegie Corporation of New York, founder Andrew Carnegie seems to have enjoyed personally shaping its policies and programs. He knew his own mind clearly, and was always sure that he was right—a sense of self-confidence one might describe as arrogance were it not for the fact that events nearly always supported his judgment.

Carnegie also worked hard to institutionalize his philosophy of grant making. As Henry Pritchett, head of the Carnegie Foundation for the Advancement of Teaching, once remarked, "When Mr. Carnegie formed the Carnegie Corporation, he simply incorporated himself."[85] All of the original trustees were close friends of Carnegie, business associates, or both, and most were also trustees of other Carnegie institutions. Carnegie appointed his friend and lawyer Elihu Root to succeed him as president, but, under the pressure of other involvements, Root chose instead to serve as chair or trustee from 1911 until 1937, when he was succeeded by his son Elihu Root Jr., who served as trustee until 1960. The elder Root played the decisive role in the selection of Frederick P. Keppel, who served as one of Carnegie's greatest presidents from 1923–41.

Thus, if anyone ever dominated the culture and history of a foundation, Andrew Carnegie did, just as one might have expected from the author of *The Gospel of Wealth*. While he acknowledged that, "no wise man will bind trustees forever to certain paths, causes or institutions," he nonetheless instructed his trustees that they "best conform to my wishes by using their judgment."[86] He remains a powerful influence on the Carnegie Corporation today, although successor trustees are not legally bound by any instructions he left behind.

Of course, these five foundations are hardly the only ones to have benefited from the continuing influence of a founding donor. Other large foundations similarly influenced include the Annie E. Casey Foundation, the Kaiser Family Foundation, the William and Flora Hewlett Foundation, the David and Lucile Packard Foundation, the Surdna Foundation, the Robert Woodruff Foundation, the Duke Endowment, the McKnight Foundation, the John S. and James L. Knight Foundation, and of course the Bill and Melinda Gates Foundation.

THE BENEFITS OF FOUNDER-IMPOSED CONSTRAINTS

Among smaller foundations in particular, it has been a common practice for founders to confine giving to specified fields. Frequent choices include religious organizations or denominations to which the founder or his family belonged, educational scholarships, children's problems, medical research, health care for the poor, and the arts.

Less frequently, foundation founders have limited grantmaking to specific recipient institutions. Perhaps the most famous example is the Duke Endowment, which was restricted by James Buchanan Duke to five colleges, including Duke University, and to hospitals located in North and South Carolina. (The latter constraint represents a very common type of restriction: Fully ninety percent of all foundations in the United States are restricted by their donors to some degree to specific geographic regions, usually to the city, county, or state in which the donor spent his or her life. The many community foundations are also well-known examples.[87])

Those donors who choose to limit their foundations to specific geographical areas are very wise to do so, because such limits increase the possibility of greater impact. The same amount of money used strategically in a confined geographical area can do much more than if spread out widely. The impact of the McKnight Foundation in Minnesota, the Z. Smith Reynolds Foundation in North Carolina, and the Gund Foundation in Cleveland are excellent examples. Moreover, such community foundations as the St. Paul Foundation in Minnesota, the New Hampshire Charitable Foundation and the Cleveland Foundation illustrate how smaller foundations can achieve significant impact if they are strategic in a small region. Similarly, foundations whose donors target their support on specific institutions are yet other examples of how impact can rise as the number of recipients shrinks. Both the Duke Endowment, with its largest focus on Duke University, and the Robert Woodruff Foundation's focus on Emory University are excellent examples. Both universities have been transformed into world-class institutions in large part because of the focus of the foundations that continue to support them.

Are donor-imposed constraints a good thing? In general, I think they are, because they provide focus for the grantmaking. Moreover, in many cases—not all—foundation donors bring to their philanthropy the same passion, vision, and concentration on results that made them successful in business. When this is the case, their strategic choices are often highly astute, perhaps more so than the choices made by less intensely motivated trustees.

Other, more tangible, benefits flow from founder constraints. As I've already noted, the hardest task foundation trustees face is choosing specific program areas on which to focus. When a foundation creator has already made that choice, the trustees' job is greatly simplified. They can concentrate on how best to implement the founders' choice, a task of lesser complexity and subjectivity. Ironically, then, the more constrained the trustees, the better their performance is likely to be.

Donor constraint as to program focus also sharpens and simplifies the job of selecting a CEO and other staff members because it usually narrows the search to those who already know something about the field of programming. The narrower and more focused the pool of potential candidates, the easier it is for the trustees to conduct a targeted—and effective—executive search. And the staff members who are ultimately selected will have a better chance of mastering their field of operations when strategic limits reduce the universe of social problems with which they are expected to deal.

Of course, constraints by themselves do not make a foundation effective. Trustees and staff must be able to adapt their programs and policies to changing times while remaining true to the broad outlines of their founder's vision. When Alfred P. Sloan directed his foundation to focus on the public understanding of science, he surely didn't envision support for Broadway and off-Broadway plays as part of the program. Today, however, the Sloan Foundation contributes to public understanding of science not only by sponsoring the publication of books and articles but also by producing plays like *Hubbell* and *Copenhagen*, financing movies and television productions, and sponsoring Internet blogs.

Donor constraint does not—and should not—equate to rigidity. Within any donor-designated field of activity, problems change and solutions evolve. Although the Robert Wood Johnson Foundation is limited to health, Johnson's constraint leaves more than enough room for his successor trustees to adapt to changing problems in tune with the changing times. Finding ways to update the donor's dream by addressing the needs and problems of today and tomorrow is the essence of creativity in foundation management.

WHEN THE FOUNDER ESTABLISHES NO BOUNDARIES

What happens when the original donor does not establish any clear limits or focus on the activity of his or her foundation? History suggests that trustees and foundation leaders operating with a free hand tend to perform less effectively than those constrained by some donor choices. Often foundation donors think that they are doing the generous, gracious, and noble thing when they leave to successive generations of trustees all the decisions about the future use of their philanthropic wealth. Ironically, however, by deferring decision dilemmas to later generations, founders thereby make the burdens of their successors much heavier.

Among the largest philanthropies, the Rockefeller Foundation and the Ford Foundation offer histories that illustrate this point. At both of those venerable institutions, the impact track records appear to have been cyclical. At Rockefeller, the impact of early programs was stunningly high; it began to taper off about forty years ago. At Ford, the impact took a decade or so to reach a significant level, but then remained high for reasons that we shall soon see.

John D. Rockefeller Sr. chose to define his foundation's mission in the broadest possible terms—to promote "the well-being of mankind throughout the world"—rather than confine it to any particular fields of activity. In addition, not only did he refuse to serve on the board of trustees, but he placed no requirement in the governing instruments that any of his descendants serve (although at least three Rockefellers have served on the board at one time or another). Moreover, any direct influence by him on the foundation was deliberately played down in order to deflect populist criticism directed against Rockefeller personally. (The virulence of that criticism certainly contributed to the refusal of Congress to provide the foundation with a congressional charter after three attempts between 1911 and 1913. And the so-called Ludlow Massacre of 1914, when twenty people were killed during a strike against a Rockefeller-owned coal mine in Colorado, exacerbated public concern about the influence of Rockefeller and his foundation.)

Nonetheless, there's no doubt that Rockefeller's views on grantmaking policy, as revealed in his many interactions with advisor Frederick T. Gates, were reflected in the foundation's early programs. Its focus on preventing and curing disease, on alleviating hunger, and on basic science research reflected Rockefeller's personal interests.

By the late 1960s and early 1970s, however, most of the foundation's greatest achievements—the yellow fever vaccine, the Green Revolution, and the support for molecular biology—were in the past, and a period of drift had begun. The foundation employed a succession of short-term presidents and took on programs in which it lacked the expertise necessary for high impact.

Finally, the trustees acted. In 1999, they established a new focus for the work of the foundation—"the lives and livelihoods of poor and excluded people"—and, in 2005, they recruited a new president, Judith Rodin.

Rodin, a successful president of the University of Pennsylvania, had been credited, among other achievements, with turning around the university's medical center.

Will the new focus enable the Rockefeller Foundation to return to the same level of impact as in its earlier years? The jury is still out. I think a still tighter focus on specific ways in which the lives of the poor and excluded might be improved—for example, through health care or hunger relief— would provide more guidance to trustees and staff and build more directly on Rockefeller's history of successes.

What is already clear, however, is that Rodin and her senior management associates have brought a new level of rigor to the way Rockefeller is run. In what is the first public discussion of such matters I have ever heard, Nadya Shmavonian, one of the foundation's new vice presidents, reported the following findings, based on a careful examination of comparative data, to the fifth anniversary celebration of the Center for Effective Philanthropy, which was indeed a fitting venue for such a disclosure:

- The Rockefeller Foundation needed to focus more externally on achieving social impact

- We had a higher cost structure than many of our peers

- Our organization and processes were overly complex, and people were not effectively deployed in all instances

- Overall decision-making was cumbersome

- We did not link foundation-wide goals to department and individual goals

- The culture did not consistently expect and reward high performance

- Nor did we have a *shared* culture, but rather many distinct individual cultures that had emerged over the years in different departments and divisions

The announcement of those findings augurs well for the future course of the Rockefeller Foundation. Moreover, it sets an entirely new standard, not only for how foundations should monitor their organizational policies and their grantmaking effectiveness, but also for more candor in communicating to the outside world what they do and how they go about doing it.

Reviewing the long arc of that foundation's history, it seems clear that, after the founder and his close associates passed from the scene, the lack of any significant donor constraints made it easy for the Rockefeller Foundation to decline significantly from its heyday of Nobel Prize-worthy impacts. Could the Rockefeller Foundation trustees have self-corrected for the absence of donor guidance? Of course they could have, but that would have required them to compromise their own respective, strongly held individual program priorities in order to reach a consensus on a few rather than many things to undertake. And that is what seems to have been beyond their grasp. Perhaps there was insufficient strong leadership among the trustees to forge the consensus necessary to change.

By contrast, the Rockefeller Brothers Fund, which was established in 1950 by the grandchildren and great-grandchildren of John D. Rockefeller Sr., and which continues to be family-dominated to this day, has managed to maintain a substantial continuity of focus on its areas of interest, including promotion of democracy, global peace and security, and sustainable development. Family members who were committed to those program areas, which are all broad enough to afford room for adaptation to changing problems, were recruited to successor trusteeships, along with expert outsiders.

The Ford Foundation story is both similar and different. Like Rockefeller, Edsel Ford gave his newly launched foundation no specified focus, narrow or broad, but rather the broadest possible mission, virtually adopting the statutory language defining tax-exempt organizations in section 501(c)(3) of the federal tax code: to "receive and administer funds for scientific, educational, and charitable purposes, all for the public welfare."[88]

By 1949, a great deal of Ford Motor Company stock had been transferred to the foundation and soon greatly appreciated in value, making it obvious to the trustees that decisions had to be made about the kinds of programs on which the foundation would spend its vast and growing resources. Henry Ford and his son Edsel had died, and the leadership of the company and the foundation had passed to Henry Ford II, who assigned the task of mission definition to a board committee chaired by H. Rowan Gaither, a distinguished San Francisco lawyer.

The committee published its recommendations in what is known as the Gaither Report (1950). That report established five areas to which the foundation, already the world's wealthiest, would devote its income to:

- "World peace and the establishment of a world order of law and justice."

- "Basic principles of freedom and democracy in the solution of the insistent problems of an ever-changing society."

- "[Advancing] the well-being of people everywhere, and to improve economic institutions for the better realization of democratic goals."

- "Strengthen, expand and improve educational facilities and methods to enable individuals more fully to realize their intellectual, civic, and spiritual potential; to promote greater educational opportunity; and to conserve and increase knowledge and enrich our culture."

- "Increase knowledge of factors that influence or determine human conduct."[89]

While the Gaither Report contains much more verbiage than John D. Rockefeller's promise to promote the "well-being of mankind throughout the world," it boils down to pretty much the same unconstrained, generalized mission to do good. One has to struggle to think of a program that would *not* fit within its terms. This open-ended mission did little to help staff and trustees define specific areas in which to develop program initiatives. With Ford Company stock continuing to grow in value, the foundation's staff was under increasing pressure to make major financial payouts. In 1955, they responded by making a wholesale distribution of about half a billion dollars in higher education, nonprofit hospital, and medical school grants.

Warren Weaver, the highly regarded vice president of the Rockefeller Foundation, describes that Ford decision as follows:

The manner of distribution was surprisingly, and to many disappointingly, mechanical. Each of our country's 630 privately-supported liberal arts colleges received a sum equal to their 1954–1955 faculty payroll.

Each of 3,400 nonprofit private hospitals received a sum determined by the number of births and patient days on an average annual basis.[90]

Fred Hechinger, the respected *New York Times* education reporter and editor, commented on one possible benefit of the Ford decision:

> In fact, the foundation encountered its most severe criticism over its departure from past foundation practice: it failed to ask the institutions to match.
>
> Nevertheless, the publicity value of the giant gift, at a time when faculty salaries were still critically low and when few private donors were aware of this grave deficiency, was widely credited with a rapid and dramatic change in the situation. Subsequently, many colleges reported, it became far easier to solicit gifts specifically for the raising of faculty pay.[91]

Was Hechinger right about this positive impact of the Ford grants? It's difficult to say. What's clear is that Ford's decisions to distribute so much money—at that time the largest grants in foundation history—in so non-discriminating a fashion speaks powerfully to the lack of any adequate program focus to guide the foundation's work.[92]

Between 1950 and 1956, the Ford Foundation had three presidents—Henry Ford II, who resigned to become board chairman in 1950, Paul Hoffman, and Rowan Gaither. Even geographic stability seemed elusive. In 1951, foundation headquarters were established in Santa Barbara, California, with a financial office in Detroit, and a small office in New York for receiving grant requests. Associate Director Robert M. Hutchins, who lived in Santa Barbara and ran the office there, was evidently regarded as "president" of the foundation, though he lacked the formal title.

The lack of strong, consistent leadership surely played a role in the massive Gaither grants. In an interview conducted on the eve of his departure from the Ford Foundation, Paul Ylvisaker, creator of the foundation's Gray Areas urban-renewal program, attributed those grants to the growing frustration of Donald K. David, chairman of the executive committee of the board, over the Gaither staff's inability to generate exciting program ideas. According to Ylvisaker, those grants were brought about by bypassing Gaither.[93]

With enough money to spend, a foundation sometimes achieves significant impact through sheer chance or trial and error. Ford may have done so with some of its initiatives under president Henry T. Heald (1956–65), including the business school curriculum reform and the foreign area studies initiative, which are described in our cases.[94] But Ford began to hit its stride in 1966 when McGeorge Bundy took over as president. Under Bundy, the foundation established its now-longstanding policy of multi-decade commitment to organizations and causes within its primary fields of concern. Bundy also recruited and empowered a cadre of talented, creative, activist vice presidents, including Mike Sviridoff in National Affairs, David Bell in International Affairs, Harold Howe II in Education, and Fred Friendly in Communications Media, and they collaborated ably with some equally gifted personnel whom Bundy inherited, nurtured, and empowered, especially Paul Ylvisaker and McNeil Lowry. Mike Sviridoff, in turn, recruited, mentored, and empowered Susan Berresford, who became president of Ford in 1996.

Under Susan Berresford, Ford narrowed its focus to three primary areas—Asset Building and Community Development, Peace and Social Justice, and Knowledge, Creativity, and Freedom. In fact, these are the fields in which Ford's earlier highest-impact initiatives had occurred, from LISC, MDRC, and the Grameen Bank, as well as evidence-based knowledge-generation, to Black and Hispanic Voter Registration and Women's Rights, all of which are described in our cases.[95] This narrowing of focus is an excellent example of a foundation's systematically focusing by learning from what it has done best.

As Ford history illustrates, when a founder offers no specific guidance as to areas of focus for his or her foundation, the institution is likely to drift erratically until a later generation of leaders steps up to the challenge of defining the mission clearly and precisely, thereby making high-impact programming possible.

The Ford story also teaches a corollary lesson: When focus is lacking, persistence helps.

When it comes to foundation programming, focus and persistence generally go hand in hand. Without focus, there is usually not enough money for a foundation to persist in supporting the same grantees in the same fields over long periods of time. Without focus, it is virtually impossible for staff to remain active in a field long enough to master it. But if a foundation makes a commitment to persistence in specific program areas over long periods of time, that commitment itself helps to produce a sense of focus.

That is what happened at the Ford Foundation, and it helps to explain that organization's extraordinary track record.

All of Bundy's senior team were richly experienced as activist social entrepreneurs. Mike Sviridoff had been a labor leader, created one of the first city-based redevelopment and community action organizations in the United States, helped shape the Kennedy administration's Office of Economic Opportunity, and served as Mayor John Lindsay's commissioner of human resources. Harold Howe had distinguished himself as a public school principal, as a district superintendent, and as a U.S. Commissioner of Education. David Bell had been director of the Federal Office of Management and Budget and director of the United States Agency for International Development under President Kennedy. Fred Friendly was skilled and highly successful in television production. All understood completely that implementation of ideas often requires a long period of maturation, and they were used to nursing initiatives to sustainability over many years. Bundy and his team jolted the Ford Foundation into focus.

THE CRITICAL ROLE OF LEADERSHIP

It should be obvious that, as in virtually all institutions, resourceful leadership can compensate for almost any flaw, including a lack of donor-imposed focus. There has been no cookie-cut characteristic of "the very model of a modern foundation president," but rather a palette of varying strengths depending on the nature and culture of particular foundations. Of those whom my interviewees identified as exemplary foundation CEOs, some, like David Rogers of RWJF, have brought substantive depth combined with creativity and passion. John Gardner of Carnegie exemplified courage, statesmanship, and unpretentiousness. McGeorge Bundy of Ford was self-confident enough (many would describe him as too much so) to recruit strong vice presidents and delegate authority to them. Roger Heyns of Hewlett had an especially tough mind coupled with great gentleness of spirit. All of them, as well as other great CEOs like them, were wise talent-choosers, had a keen eye for the grantmaking niche, had an instinctive feel for the practical, were strategic in their vision, and, at least most of them, were not impressed by their own importance.

I should add that the last characteristic is of utmost importance in the world of foundations because deploying great sums of money is a heady experience. Yet nonprofits are supposed to treasure a culture of altruism and self-discipline. Talented individuals who otherwise might do well running a foundation can all too easily get into trouble if they crave the trappings that usually go with the exercise of power. Almost all of the foundation CEOs who have run aground recently have had that flaw in common. They may have been brilliant at the job, but their tastes were too rich for a nonprofit culture. And I am inclined to say that the fault lay with the board chairs who selected them and approved the perks to satisfy those tastes.

THE ROLE OF THE BOARD CHAIRMAN

As a general rule, foundation CEOs do a better job when their board chairs are deeply engaged in testing and questioning their decisions, thereby helping to clarify, sharpen, and focus grantmaking in much the same way that donor-imposed boundaries do. History shows that many of the CEOs who've presided over high-performing foundations worked with active, energetic, and strong-willed board chairs. For example, Julius Stratton, formerly chancellor of MIT, was chairman of the Ford Foundation board when Bundy was selected and for five years thereafter. Elihu Root was the Carnegie chair when Frederick Keppel was selected and was succeeded by the wise and capable Russell Leffingwell. William Baker, president of Bell Labs, was a founding trustee of Mellon and served as chair from 1975 well into the 1980s.[96] All of them were exemplary trustee chairs.

I mentioned earlier the division of responsibilities between "church" and "state" at the Robert Wood Johnson Foundation. It is pertinent here to draw special attention to the role of Gus Lienhard, its first chair, as described by Frank Karel, formerly the vice president for communication at RWJF:

> What made RWJF so effective was Dave Rogers's determination to achieve specific objectives through the grantmaking, and the willingness, for the most part, of Gus Lienhard, the board chair, and his fellow business exec trustees, to back Rogers up. Focus and discipline are essential if one is to achieve any objectives. The system set up by General Johnson with business people handling the financial and management side—"state"—and the medical/health pros handling the substance of grantmaking—"church"—worked very well. Rogers and

Lienhard fought with one another daily, but Lienhard, as tough as he was, would always listen. The differences they had were over ideas, not personalities.[97]

DONOR CONSTRAINTS—THE DOWNSIDE

So far, I've emphasized the benefits of strategic constraints established by a founding donor. But there can be negatives as well.

One example are the constraints imposed by founders (or their immediate descendants) who specified that foundation stockholdings must remain invested in the donor's company. This has often had disastrous consequences, as in the case of the Packard Foundation, which did not diversify out of Hewlett-Packard stock soon after the death of David Packard. When HP stock plunged from a high of sixty-eight dollars in 2000 to a low in the mid-teens in 2002, the foundation's assets and spending suffered accordingly. By contrast, William Hewlett wisely encouraged the Hewlett Foundation to diversify its holdings, resulting in a much healthier balance sheet. While HP stock has recently bounced back somewhat under new corporate leadership, the lesson still holds. Overconcentration of investments in a donor's company is a very imprudent course of action.

More significant are the negative effects of founder self-indulgence. Founders with big egos who lack either self-restraint or good taste sometimes create a culture of excessive luxury and permissiveness in their foundations, building headquarters that amount to expensive monuments to themselves and creating extravagant compensation and travel policies for staffers as well. The culture of self-indulgence thus created tends to undermine performance.

No one expects foundation personnel to work in conditions of monastic simplicity and deprivation. But given the fact that foundations are stewards of wealth for the benefit of society—and receive tax advantages on that basis—commonsense policies of moderation in spending would seem to be appropriate.

Finally, a few foundation donors are simply terrible judges of what foundations can or should do, while some are bullies to boot. Such founders tend to inflict themselves on grant-receiving organizations as impossibly demanding, high-maintenance donors whose gifts are better rejected. All who care about America's civic sector must rejoice that such donors are very rare in the foundation world.

ADVICE FOR THE WOULD-BE DONOR: BE PRECISE, CAREFUL, AND PRAYERFUL

No one can tell someone else what he or she should do with their philanthropic dollars. Few decisions are more personal. But for those who have already decided that they want to use their wealth to establish a foundation, and especially if it's to be a perpetual foundation, here is the advice I would offer as to how to make that wealth most effective for the long haul.

First, take great care in crafting your will, trust, or other legal instrument of gift to your foundation to ensure that your intentions are clear and will be carried out as you wish. Specifically describe your motivating intentions, list the objectives to be served, and explicitly proscribe all other objectives. Make clear that you are not trying to tie the hands of your successors but rather providing firm but gentle guidance in focusing what they do with your money. Acknowledge that you recognize that programs must change as times change, but that you are committed to continuity of theme.

Second, tailor your chosen focus to the size of the endowment available. If you try to tackle a huge problem with a modest endowment, you can be almost certain that the income will be frittered away, while dedicating too much money in proportion to the size of a problem can have the same wasteful result. If the problem area is health and health services, the Robert Wood Johnson Foundation's eight billion dollars in assets may not be sufficient, while the Bill and Melinda Gates Foundation's thirty billion dollars—now augmented by Warren Buffett's gradual infusion of thirty-one billion dollars in money to be spent, not placed into endowment, over a period of years—might well be too much. Such judgments are inevitably subjective, but they are important to consider, especially if you are thinking about restricting the use of the income to a particular program field in perpetuity.

Third, in appointing trustees, tailor the selection criteria and personal qualifications as closely as possible to the substantive mission of the foundation. If the asset size of your foundation is large enough, you can likely attract as trustees persons of national and international stature in the substantive fields of your foundation focus. Sift them carefully to identify persons known for good judgment and, if possible, with their ego well under control. If there are respected organizations that embody the same commitments as those you intend for the foundation, consider giving the heads of those institutions a board seat or permitting them to appoint a trustee in perpetuity. If your foundation is small in wealth, confine its giving to the subjects you especially care about, and choose your trustees from among your friends and associates who care passionately about those subjects and whose judgment you trust. Balance the backgrounds of your trustees so that your foundation has the full range of perspectives and skills that you think it will need. Every foundation, whatever its substantive focus, needs some trustees who are generalists, some with business experience, some with a science background.

Fourth, be cautious about naming children or other relatives to the foundation board. Anyone who follows foundations closely knows examples of what can happen when family rivalries or ideological differences surface in grantmaking. It is rarely the case, if ever, that a family pathology can be cured or mitigated by immersion of family members in philanthropy. More often than not, family members who do not get along with one another for whatever reason will simply transfer to charitable giving decisions the same animosities, rivalries, and rancor that color their other relationships with one another. Once the founding donor—usually the father and/or the mother—departs the scene, simmering disputes among descendants frequently force the division of assets among contending trustees or family branches or even the complete reconstitution of the foundation structure, board, or mission.

Of course, some families are blessed by multigenerational harmony. In my personal experience, that has been the case at the Gaylord and Dorothy Donnelley Foundation in Chicago, on whose board I served for several years. Other seemingly harmonious family foundations include the Rockefeller Brothers Fund, the George Gund Foundation, the Nathan Cummings Foundation, the Z. Smith Reynolds Foundation, the Mary Reynolds Babcock Foundation, and the Duke Endowment. But the counterexamples are all too numerous.

My recommendation to would-be founders: Put only one child on the foundation board. If the asset pool is large enough and more than one child is eager for a philanthropic role, create a separate foundation for each child to control, as Warren Buffett did in establishing and endowing three separate foundations for each of his three children, as well as one for his late wife, Susan.

If, however, your philanthropic assets are insufficient to justify separate foundations for each of your children, what might be the alternative if you want to create a foundation rather than distribute your wealth directly to institutions or causes to which you are committed? If you are confident in the harmoniousness of your descendants and if you are determined to create a long-lived family foundation in which they all participate, the lessons we can learn from others' experience still hold. The more you limit the future choices on which disagreement may arise, the easier time your descendants will have in working together constructively. To that end, I encourage you to narrow future giving to benefit a particular geographical region or regions, and/or a specific substantive field or fields, such as religion, education, the arts, or environmental conservation.

Then go ahead and establish your foundation, and put as many of your children on the board as you wish. But also provide in your founding instrument the mechanisms by which, in the case of discord among your descendants, they can consensually narrow the pool of those who will have a role in decisions going forward. In that circumstance, it will help to set up your foundation as a two-tier structure, with those designated as members of the nonprofit membership corporation, initially a small group of the first generation of your descendants, having the power to elect and replace trustees on an annual basis. That can provide an escape valve to restore harmony that is threatened or disrupted.

In any decision about setting up a family foundation, I urge you to consult the National Center for Family Philanthropy (www.ncfp.org), which has the greatest experience and knowledge about how best to set up and run family foundations.

Let me say one more word about family foundations. Where they work well, they are powerful testimony to enduring values in individual families. Where families are deeply rooted in particular communities, whether geographical, religious, or particular cause-related, they have been known to help sustain and improve communities across generations. The family foundation entered the American foundation scene in the same decade—the 1910s—that the first great private foundations were established, with the creation of the Surdna Foundation by John Andrus in 1917. The family foundation category constitutes a significant majority of the private foundations in the United States, so obviously a large number of them are functioning very well. No wonder Surdna describes itself proudly on its letterhead as "A Family Foundation Established by John E. Andrus in 1917." Its existence, its growth, and the wide respect that it has earned proves that, under the right circumstances, a family foundation can indeed prosper and confer great benefits on society. The primary "right circumstances" are probably a family with strong praiseworthy values that are shared by most or all members and successfully transmitted from generation to generation.

In the end, of course, no one can control the future—especially projecting forward into a time when you've departed this world. Hence my final recommendation—be prayerful. Offer your hopes, anxieties, and dreams to whatever God you worship, and have faith that he (or she) will inspire your successor trustees to deploy the wealth you bequeath in conformity with the good intentions you've formed, using them for the ultimate benefit of the world and its people—perhaps in ways you might never even have imagined.

14

SHOULD FOUNDATIONS

BE PERMITTED TO EXIST

IN PERPETUITY?

I am not in sympathy with this policy of perpetuating endowments and believe that more good can be accomplished by expending funds as trustees find opportunities for constructive work than by storing up large sums of money for long periods of time. By adopting a policy of using the Fund within this generation, we may avoid those tendencies toward bureaucracy and a formal or perfunctory attitude toward the work which almost inevitably develop in organizations which prolong their existence indefinitely. Coming generations can be relied upon to provide for their own needs as they arise.

―――――

Julius Rosenwald, founder of the Julius Rosenwald Fund[98]

The vigor of a family foundation is in the first generation, and after the donor dies, the energy dissipates. That is why I believe that foundations in general should not be permitted to exist in perpetuity. But I also believe that some perpetual foundations serve a very good purpose, so for me it is a question of balance and of individual cases.

―――――

David Bergholz, former executive director
of the George Gund Foundation[99]

I don't want to achieve immortality through my work. I
want to achieve it through not dying.

———

Woody Allen

For most of the twentieth century, virtually all large foundation creators
chose to establish their philanthropies in perpetuity. Readers of this book
will have seen their names spread across these pages over and over again—
Rockefeller, Carnegie, Ford, Mellon, Sloan, Robert Wood Johnson,
Hewlett, Packard, and many others. But there have always been some exceptions to foundation perpetuity, most of which, of course, we simply
don't hear about because they have long been deceased along with their
founders. Some of the exceptions, however, are more contemporary and
we do still hear about their activities, such as the Lucille P. Markey Charitable Trust that existed from 1983 to 1987; the Mary Cary Flagler Charitable Trust, whose fifty-year life is due to expire in 2009; the Aaron
Diamond Foundation, whose forty-nine-year life ended in 2004; the John
M. Olin Foundation, which closed its doors in November 2005, after a
fifty-two year run; and the Vincent Astor Foundation, which closed its
doors in 1996 after more than thirty years.

Until recent years, perhaps the best-known foundation that spent itself
out of existence was the Julius Rosenwald Fund created in 1917, whose
founder and namesake not only imposed a life limit on his foundation but
also waged a vigorous campaign against the establishment of perpetual
foundations by others. As the fund's history puts it, "Believing that coming
generations 'will be every bit as humane and enlightened, energetic, and
able, as we are,' he was content to let them care for their own needs, and
he held that the best contribution of a given age was to put the world into
as good shape as possible for those who followed."[100]

Rosenwald was certainly accurate in predicting that later generations
would be just as "humane" in giving generously as the wealthy of his time.
As things have unfolded, our generation is proving to be perhaps even more
generous than his own. Because of the immense amount of wealth that has
been accumulated, especially over the last twenty years, the birthrate of
foundations is higher today than ever before, and the number of foundations of great scale created has been greater than in earlier years.

Moreover, Rosenwald's determined campaign against perpetual foundations seems to have echoed in the pronouncements of many recent foundation creators. Such wealthy, philanthropically inclined individuals as Warren Buffett, Pierre Omidyar, Charles Feeney, Richard Goldman, Sanford Bernstein, Herbert and Marion Sandler, Charles Bronfman, and Bernard Marcus, among others, have publicly stated either that they intend to give away most of their assets during their lifetimes, and not to a perpetual foundation, or have expressly limited the life spans of their already-existing foundations.

Warren Buffett, for example, chose not to create a foundation to bear his own name—either perpetual or time-limited—but rather to donate over a period of years thirty-one billion of the thirty-seven billion dollars in assets he had determined to give away to an already-established perpetual foundation created and administered by others. And it is noteworthy, too, that he required the recipient foundation, the Bill and Melinda Gates Foundation, annually to spend every dollar he is giving them as well as to pay out annually, in addition to his periodic gifts, 5 percent of the Gates Foundation's assets, as required by tax law. The result is that *none* of Warren Buffett's munificence—except for the approximately six billion dollars in gifts he gave to the three foundations administered by his children and the preexisting foundation named for his late wife—will be around in perpetuity.

Charles Feeney, who established and endowed Atlantic Philanthropies in the early 1980s, decided in the late 1990s, almost twenty years later, to spend down his foundation when its assets were more than four billion dollars. At Feeney's prompting, Atlantic Philanthropies has now undertaken a campaign to persuade other wealthy individuals to engage in "giving while living." Other foundation creators, without announcing an explicit spend-down policy, have decided to pay out significantly more than the annual minimum 5 percent of assets required by law and pretty much the standard practice of the perpetual foundations. The Richard and Rhoda Goldman Fund has this policy: "In order to respond to immediate and emerging needs we strive to achieve a 10 percent payout each year with grant payments alone. We encourage others to give more now to address the problems of today."[101] The foundations established by Michael and Lowell Milken are reported to be spending "an average of 15 percent of their assets each year."[102] Unless a foundation is investing very cleverly, it cannot pay out 15 percent a year and survive perpetually!

Not only are such wealthy individuals with philanthropic intentions following Rosenwald's example, but they are giving virtually the same reasons for "sunsetting" their newly established or soon-to-be created foundations that he so passionately preached to the wealthy of his time. They speak of the countless urgent needs—poverty, disease, starvation, refugees, human exploitation, environmental degradation—all across the globe, which electronic and print media hammer home day after day to everyone, needs that resonate in the hearts and minds of everyone's global sensibilities of today. They declare that it is unfair for generations in the far future to benefit from the philanthropic wealth being accumulated by today's entrepreneurs when the cost in lives and health of human beings living today and in the immediate future imposed by neglecting already-existing needs is so great. They express hope, and some even predict, that future generations will generate enough philanthropic dollars themselves to devote to the critical problems of their times, and they assert that it is right and just that those later generations be forced to depend on their own times' self-generated charitable resources.

It is not only the overwhelming problems of today, however, that appear to be pulling philanthropists to focus on present needs rather than those of later generations. Parallel to the focus on today's needs is a growing push away from using the vehicle of perpetual foundations. At or close to the surface of the compelling reasons advanced by some to justify limiting the lives of new foundations, as well as motivating the sunsetting of existing foundations, are frequent hints that an increasing number of today's would-be creators and still-alive founders of foundations are put off by what they observe of the way the perpetual foundations appear to be run. Many of them imply that their decisions to limit the lives of their philanthropies have less to do with a desire to focus only on present needs than with a nagging worry about the trustworthiness and motivation of successor stewards of their philanthropic wealth. As Herbert M. Sandler said, in speaking of his and his wife Marion's decision to give their wealth away now, "If we give it away now, we're going to do a good job with it, instead of leaving it to future generations of foundation folks."[103]

What the Sandlers implied, others make explicit. They confess to having a lack of confidence in how well and how faithfully their children, descendants, or successor foundation managers would steward their philanthropic assets if left to them rather than having been spent during the donors' lifetimes. Some of the foundation sunsetters are determined to put their wealth into the causes and institutions about which they themselves care, and know that that their children don't share their parents' philanthropic priorities. Others, having observed or heard of what they regard as the perpetual foundations' lack of strong direction and purposeful focus after their founders passed away, or the excessive overhead, fancy perks, and high salaries about which the press loves to write, figure that they can assure themselves of their money's being well spent in society's interest only if they spend it while they are around to direct its expenditure themselves. Thus a fear of having their hard-earned wealth squandered or inefficiently spent arises to trump whatever desires for immortality may tempt donors to establish foundations that will be around and giving away money long after their death.

My assessment is that the lack of confidence in the good stewardship of their successor philanthropic administrators is the dominant motivation for establishing time-limited rather than perpetual foundations.

Those fears did not trouble Andrew Carnegie or John D. Rockefeller Sr. because no significant foundations were then in existence to give them pause. They were in the vanguard of the perpetual foundation creators, and their example, as well as their exhortations, especially Carnegie's, led many others to follow in their footsteps. Now the tide seems to be turned slightly away from everlasting foundations to those that are time-limited. That is hardly to predict permanency for such a shift, because the desire for immortality is strong in all human beings, especially those with robust egos.

Carnegie himself did not speak to the issue of perpetuity, although one can infer that he was not moved by the desire to create a perpetual foundation. He strongly urged that the wealthy give away all their money during their lifetimes, which he himself tried, but failed, to accomplish. He simply could not find enough specific objectives about which he cared deeply to which to devote the entirety of his huge fortune to. After making many large gifts to existing organizations and causes, or to found new ones, there remained a great deal of money, which he gave to the Carnegie Corporation of New York and the Carnegie Foundation for Advancement of Teaching, the only perpetual grantmaking foundations he established.

The shift from perpetual to time-limited foundations is not necessarily a bad thing from the point of view of society. Indeed, many believe that that is precisely the right direction for foundation creators to take. There is obviously much greater immediate benefit to those alive in today's society if an entire endowment is itself consumed in solving near-term problems over a limited period of years than can be conferred on society for comparable purposes by a foundation that makes grants each year for all eternity of only the income, usually 5 percent, from an endowment.

Let's consider the arguments for and against the perpetual foundation. I'll start with what I call "the personal calculus"—the considerations most likely to influence the decision of the foundation donor himself or herself. Later, I'll look at the public-interest considerations, asking whether perpetuity tends to increase or diminish the benefits to the general welfare that foundations provide.

THE PERSONAL CALCULUS

How an individual wealthy donor nets out all the conflicting and complementary motivations that weigh on him or her will determine the personal calculus. The desire to make a praiseworthy difference in solving urgent problems today may often be overcome by one's wish to help further a cherished cause or a beloved institution over many years after one dies. It can also be overcome by a less praiseworthy desire simply to live on in history. One can achieve both objectives—sustained support for a cause or institution and historical fame—by either giving wealth directly to operating charities or by establishing a perpetual foundation. Were the wealthy founders or benefactors of great universities that are named for them—John D. Rockefeller Sr., Andrew Carnegie, Leland Stanford, and James Buchanan Duke, among others—moved to make their gifts more by the aim to provide higher education of high quality to deserving students, than by the desire for admiration of later generations? To what extent does it matter, if significant benefits are conferred on society in the process?

The starkest choice facing wealth-holders is between giving away assets outright, along with their control, and placing them in a foundation or some foundation-like vehicle through which the donor or his successors can continue to influence the disposition either for some period of time or in perpetuity.

On the one hand, one can choose to donate accumulated assets directly to operating charities, as many do to universities, museums, human rights organizations, and community foundations, either to spend or to be put into endowments named for the donors. The assets Rockefeller, Stanford, and Carnegie provided to launch the universities named after them were given directly to the universities, which were established as perpetual institutions, although each of them relinquished control over the assets.

On the other hand, one can endow one's own foundation, whether perpetual or life-limited, thereby keeping control of how such wealth is used. Robert W. Woodruff, instead of giving the bulk of his wealth to Emory University, chose to set up a perpetual foundation that has continued to make huge gifts to support that institution. James Buchanan Duke chose a hybrid arrangement—creating a freestanding perpetual charitable trust called the Duke Endowment, with trustees independent of Duke University but with specific designated beneficiaries, including Duke University, which receive prescribed percentages of the Duke Endowment's income, as well as some additional discretionary funding. James B. Duke strongly believed in the checks-and-balances theory of institutional arrangements. By giving to an independent charitable trust what other donors had given directly to the universities they intended to benefit, Duke ensured that there would be greater accountability for the use of his philanthropic assets in perpetuity.

Creating a perpetual foundation and giving assets outright to an operating charity are not the only two options, however. For example, if the donor prefers to benefit a favorite cause or charity over time (while receiving an immediate tax benefit), one doesn't have to create a foundation but can instead donate the full sum to a donor-advised fund, which in turn can, on the later-given advice of the donor, pay the assets, or income on the assets, to the intended cause or charity over a stipulated period of years or in perpetuity. Such donor-advised funds are now widely available among community foundations, United Ways, Jewish federations, and large financial institutions such as Fidelity Investments, which pioneered financial-institution sponsorship of such donor-advised funds.

Another foundation-like form is the supporting organization, which is a close cousin of the donor-advised funds. Many public charities, including universities, will create one for a donor who wishes primarily to benefit that public charity but also to continue playing an influential role in how his or her money is spent in the future.

Would-be philanthropists should start by probing their motives and their personal and family situations to determine whether a perpetual foundation, a time-limited foundation, a donor-advised fund, a supporting organization, or outright contributions to operating charities will best fit their intentions and goals. In the last case, of course, all the money goes to work immediately, unless the assets are used to create a perpetual endowment at the operating charity, in which case only the income will go to work immediately. An outright gift may be preferable, if the donor has clearly in mind a current project of urgent importance or a cause or institution of long-term interest that the donor wants to support.

Some donors are moved to devote their assets to short-run use simply because they believe that the problems facing society are so great as to require massive, immediate help. They prefer to put their dollars to work solving today's problems, leaving tomorrow's problems to future donors. This choice does not necessarily imply any criticism of perpetual foundations, but only a personal preference for solving problems in the here and now while the donor is alive to derive the satisfaction from doing so.

Gifts to be spent in the immediate future, whether by outright gifts to charities or by life-limited foundations, may also be chosen because the donor feels that, if he or she is around to supervise the expenditures, their philanthropic dollars will be devoted to their major interests and will be spent more effectively and economically. Some parents with enough wealth to warrant considering the establishment of a foundation conclude that they don't want to risk leaving the deployment of their philanthropic dollars to their children because their progeny simply don't share their values or their interest in particular charitable causes. They worry that assets they have accumulated may be squandered by their heirs or diverted to purposes the parents would not have approved. If a donor harbors any doubts about the fidelity or competence of his or her successors in administering a charitable trust or foundation, then giving today for current spending may well be the only option.

Concerns like these help to explain the recent increase in involvement by wealthy individuals in administering their philanthropic assets. Whether called venture philanthropy, high-engagement philanthropy, or some other buzzword, many of those who grew staggeringly rich in the 1980s and 1990s have begun to focus on giving their money away personally with the same close attention to effectiveness and efficiency with which they amassed it in the first place. And the very same concerns have also driven the growing popularity of limited life foundations.

The Public Interest Calculus: Arguments Against Perpetuity

The first argument asserted against perpetual foundations is the long-standing presumption in Anglo-American law against perpetual trusts, in particular trusts established for the benefit of particular third parties. Under the Rule Against Perpetuities, which is still the law in both England and in most of the United States, one cannot create a *non*-charitable trust with a life longer than lives already in being plus twenty-one years after those lives end. That rule is motivated by public policy antipathy to perpetuities in general, on the grounds that "the dead hand of the grave" should be able to reach only so far into the future and no further.

While that presumption is still operative with regards to non-charitable trusts, it is not at all operative in the United States with regard to charitable trusts. Many foundations are set up and named as perpetual charitable trusts, and there are many more charitable trusts that are called foundations, not trusts. So, while the law and public policy are very cautious about allowing some things to be established in perpetuity, charitable trusts and foundations are not now among them. Indeed, as a matter of policy the law imposes no limit on the lifetimes of nonprofit organizations, or for-profit corporations for that matter.

As I have noted, perpetuity in foundations does have one major drawback for society. Creating a foundation that pays out only the income on a corpus of assets rather than giving assets outright to nonprofit organizations greatly diminishes the resources available for immediate charitable use. A glance at the figures suggests the extent of the problem. If the full $21.7 billion that Americans are reported to have given to foundations in 2005 had been given instead to operating charities, it would have increased the donations to those charities by about 10 percent, enabling them to spend that much more on their good works that year. By contrast, with that sum going to foundations instead, not even the average five percent income one might expect from such an endowment would likely be available until after a year's investment.

Another argument made by some against perpetuity—one that the evidence doesn't at all support and that frankly most foundation observers and scholars find actually surreal—is that the existence of perpetual foundations helps somehow to perpetuate across generations the power of the upper socioeconomic class to control society. This extreme left position is held only by academic Marxists and conspiracy theorists who cannot bring themselves to imagine that the wealthy might behave in ways not deliberately designed to advance or protect their own interests.

The evidence that puts the lie to this belief is found in the histories of our longest-lasting foundations. Virtually all of them, at one time or another, have been attacked by both the right and the left, which is a pretty good sign of their class neutrality. And although most of their wealthy creators were conservative in their views, any objective analysis of the causes supported by their foundations shows that their actual tendency is either broadly mainstream or slightly left of center—certainly not conservative or reactionary—and hardly the instruments of imagined upper-class hegemony.

Infidelity to donor intent is yet another critique, this one offered mainly by the ideological right. Critics moved by this concern assail foundations for departing in their grantmaking from what their departed donors would have wished or might have been expected to support. In fact, it is the donors themselves who are at fault if anyone is. It is the donors, when they set up their foundations, who failed to take steps at the beginning to guide or bind their successors, who are to blame rather than the successors. Founders who leave no guidance and impose no constraints need to know that, for sure, their successor trustees will do things that the founders would not have done if indeed they could have foreseen them. They could easily do what Alfred P. Sloan, Robert Wood Johnson, and James Buchanan Duke did in confining their successors had they had the wish and wit to do so.

The challenge of the donor intent critics is closely related to the next criticism. One of the seemingly most persuasive charges against perpetual foundations is that the absence of living donors to oversee the spending of the philanthropic dollars they amassed guarantees that those dollars will not be spent with the same attentiveness to efficiency, effectiveness, and economy as the wealth accumulators would have brought to that task. That charge is certainly worrisome, and, as I have noted above, it has been often articulated by many of today's foundation founders who specified life-limited philanthropies. But most of today's perpetual foundations have managed to avoid the appearance, as well as the reality, of wasteful spending, and, as this book documents, have succeeded in making very significant contributions to solving major social problems.

Are there outliers that waste money? Of course there are, but with the increased attention of the public, the press, and governmental regulators to foundations' overhead and spending patterns, the foundations have been put on notice that they must zealously avoid such inappropriate and unstewardly behavior. Moreover, the problems of inefficient, ineffective, and inappropriate spending are hardly limited to perpetual foundations. They arise just as frequently in all other kinds of nonprofit organizations, as well as for-profit corporations, and are more the result of lax oversight than of perpetual existence.

Arguments for Perpetuity

By contrast, a number of strong arguments can be made in support of the perpetual foundation.

First, and perhaps most persuasive, is society's continuing need for well-designed, carefully instructed foundations with perpetual life. In a democratic society in which priorities are established and implementing policies are chosen by transient majorities seeking to rectify intransigent, large, complex problems, perpetual foundations can be countercyclical forces of great value to policy-making and problem-solving. It is only a perpetual foundation with an unlimited lifespan that can take the longer view necessary to understand and deal with the dynamics of significant, persisting social problems through extensive research and/or demonstrations over time.

The clear tendency of donors who limit the lives of their foundations is to allow the urgent to drive out the important. They focus on the problems that press on today, and they do so with the lenses and solutions of today. But most of society's most stubborn problems will require the attention and skills of several generations working across time to solve them. The institutional knowledge and long-term memory that can be created only within perpetual foundations are invaluable assets that are indispensable to producing long-term solutions to complex problems.

Consider the difference in scientific research between basic and applied knowledge. Increasingly, medical scientists have come to recognize that the most likely cures for, and means of preventing, disease will come primarily from the most basic of research, genetic research especially. That lesson applies to social problems, too. While we know that targeting specific social problems for strategic solution is an important key to solving them, we also know that most successful solutions to persistent problems depend not only on our commitment to apply knowledge but also on what we might call basic knowledge about both their causes and solutions.

How does this relate to perpetuity in foundations? It does so directly, because most of the founders of life-limited foundations focus their foundations on applying knowledge rather than generating the basic knowledge that is the indispensable foundation for application of knowledge to problems. Obviously, society needs both basic and applied research at all times, but it is primarily the perpetual foundations with a long enough life and a wide enough scope that support or conduct the basic research that is always essential.

Furthermore, it is almost always the perpetual foundations that have a monopoly on serendipitous discovery. Life-limited foundations are usually so fixated on producing results in the short run that they cannot afford the time or resources to explore the byways of problems where solutions are encountered by chance. Only the perpetual foundations have the luxury to prepare themselves today to solve the problems of tomorrow.

The clear lesson of most of the high-impact cases documented for this book is that significant social benefit can be conferred only by foundations that persist over a long period of time in working on problems and implementing solutions.

Looked at another way, perpetuity is also a means of introducing intergenerational checks and balances into social problem-solving and the filling of social needs. Longstanding foundation endowments allow the values of past generations to provide a counterweight to the values of the present. In a time, for example, when humanistic learning is not in vogue (and indeed it rarely is among donors who are attracted to solving the urgent social problems of any present time), it is essential to the continuing renewal of American society that the Andrew Mellon Foundation is around to do grantmaking in support of the humanities. In periods in which many values important to society cannot be sustained entirely or at all by for-profit market forces, values such as high art and music, it is essential for civilization's future that perpetual institutions, including foundations, be available to preserve and transmit those and similar values to the future.

Consider, too, the important role that perpetual foundations alone can play in preserving the diversity of animal and plant species for future generations, the preservation of dying languages and no-longer-current art and literary forms such as medieval manuscript writing.

At times, the focus on values of the past can be frustrating, especially to the young, who sometimes decry the dead hand of their elders. But fads and fashions are as common in social policy as in clothing or music, and the innovative approach hailed as brilliant today is often revealed as shallow and ineffectual tomorrow. The perpetual foundation, with its institutional history, its slowly changing roster of trustees, and its legal and moral obligation to pursue the goals of its founder when the founder has had the foresight to specify them, represents a force for continuity of civilization in countless ways.

It also represents an influence for stability in social activism, promoting gradual evolution rather than sudden revolution, much as the U.S. Constitution provides a check on those who would too radically alter our system of government under the pressure of immediate problems. We elect congressmen for two years, the president for four years, and senators for six years, but we appoint federal judges for life. Similarly, the civic sector benefits greatly from being continually nourished by the views and values of prior generations.

This, too, is a critical aspect of the polyarchy that I believe the foundation sector helps create for American society. Just as foundations embody the values of conservatives, liberals, centrists, and others of today, it is the perpetual foundations that introduce a multigenerational polyarchy. Without such perpetual foundations, America's civic sector would be greatly impoverished.

The accumulated capital held by perpetual foundations plays a critical balancing role in another, broader sense. Thanks to their power and the slow, steady pressure they exert on behalf of the causes they champion over time, the foundations serve as both a prod and a counterweight to the government. Perpetual foundations are much better able to criticize and stand up to politicians and administrations, if they exercise the courage to do so, than are life-limited foundations. Foundation resources have often been used, discreetly but persistently, to pressure government into social action, to challenge the status quo, and to improve the lot of the disenfranchised, the discriminated-against, and the less-well-off. Without such perpetual foundation counterweights, social, economic, and political opportunities for American minority groups would be much scarcer than they are today.

My conclusion is clear-cut. From the vantage point of social policy, the benefits to the American public from perpetual foundations are significantly greater than the opportunity costs they impose on society. It would be very unwise social policy for the government to enact any legislation that precludes or burdens the establishment of perpetual foundations. Moreover, America's strong commitment to a polyarchical civic sector requires that wealthy individuals who find fulfillment in memorializing themselves by establishing perpetual foundations should be permitted, indeed encouraged, to do so.

That is not to say that individual donors who wish their accumulated assets to be put to immediate use should not follow the lead of their hearts and minds. Obviously they should, because it is primarily their money to benefit society in any way they prefer. If their primary concern in choosing between a life-limited or perpetual foundation, however, is not so much using their assets to solve today's problems today but rather a worry about how well their successors will administer their wealth, they should think hard and creatively about how to constrain their successors' fidelity in carrying out their wishes.

15

ENHANCING FOUNDATION EFFECTIVENESS: SOME NOT-SO-MODEST PROPOSALS

Out of the crooked timber of humanity, no straight thing
was ever made.

———

Immanuel Kant

For all their wealth, power, and remarkable achievements, America's foundations are far more vulnerable than they may seem. They are increasingly regarded by the public, the press, politicians, and regulators as inherently unaccountable and very rich institutions—a troubling problem for a collection of organizations whose very existence depends entirely on their ability to retain public, political, and governmental favor. A recent editorial in *Forbes,* captioned "Term Limits for Foundations?" commented:

Ironically, there is one, largely unaccountable aristocracy in American life today: foundations. These organizations run on in perpetuity. They control hundreds of billions of dollars in assets. They only have to distribute a minimum of 5 percent of their assets each year, and even that mandate can be lessened by various loopholes and legal dodges. They do not answer to the marketplace or an electorate. Most of them are dominated by proactivist-government types vibrating with barely concealed hostility to entrepreneurial capitalism.[104]

Alas, except for the last sentence and the reference to "loopholes and legal dodges," that description of foundations is accurate. But the criticism is unjustified. From the earliest pages of this book, I have stressed that it has been the unfettered freedom of foundations that has enabled them to confer the extraordinary benefits on society that they have over the past century. The independence of foundations from both the marketplace and the voters empowers them to add to the richness and complexity of America's polyarchy, and protects them, in serving the wider public interest, to be effective critics of, as well as counterweights to, both government and for-profits.

If the substance of what foundations do were regulated or if foundations were in any significant way under the thumb of government or corporations, they could not play that role freely, and American polyarchy would be much less dynamic as a result. The issue, therefore, is not whether foundations are free and unfettered; it is whether foundations are abusing the freedom that America has clearly seen fit to give them. As this book suggests throughout, the answer to that question is a vigorous "No!"

Have some foundations violated the trust under which America has endowed them with freedom? Of course they have, but the number of such willful wrongdoers among foundations has been tiny by comparison with the 68,000 U.S. foundations in existence, even if the press invariably blows their malfeasance up out of all proportion. Would more extensive and effective oversight by regulatory authorities help deter and punish misdeeds by foundations? Absolutely, and it is clear that providing additional financial resources to existing state and federal regulators, which is essential, would enable greater oversight to occur. Moreover, if the foundation sector were to mount a serious, ongoing self-regulatory effort, that, too, would likely result in the greater accountability of foundations that most observers of the sector view as desirable.

But it is important to stress that no self-regulatory regime can possibly be effective in deterring willful human beings—"the crooked timber of humanity"—from seeking illegal or inappropriate self-benefit from the foundations in which they hold office. For that, government oversight, press attention, and legal penalties are indispensable.

Why, then, is it essential for the foundation sector to take on self-regulation? Because, while it is clear to anyone who looks objectively at the record that foundations have not abused the freedom they enjoy, it is equally clear that foundations have not been as open with the outside world as their privileges require. All that the overwhelming number of foundations have been guilty of has been the self-imposed secretiveness that has characterized the way they have gone about their work from the beginning of their establishment.

That secretiveness has prevented foundations from benefiting from external criticism and therefore from performing at the highest possible level of which they are capable; it has kept other foundations and the wider nonprofit sector of operating charities from learning how and why foundation initiatives succeeded and failed; and it has contributed to the cocoon-like culture within foundations that allows smugness and arrogance to influence the way foundation officials treat outsiders. Moreover, that same secretiveness creates the suspicion of widespread foundation wrongdoing among the press and the public, and fuels from time to time the political efforts mounted by critics to punish foundations.

These shortcomings of foundations are not illegal and any attempts by government to deal effectively with them are bound to be more heavy-handed than would be either justified by the problems or consonant with the maintenance of foundation independence. But the persistence of such problems is definitely likely to be harmful to the performance of foundations in the future, as well as to the public trust on which foundation independence depends. That is why the problems must be dealt with and also why only the foundation sector itself can do so in a way that doesn't throw out the baby with the bath water.

Of course, any institutions charged with an obligation to reform the status quo and redistribute opportunity and power in society are bound to be caught up in controversy from time to time. It's not surprising, therefore, that foundations have frequently drawn attack from various points on the political spectrum, including that represented above by *Forbes*. For most of the early twentieth century, populist muckrakers and Marxist theorists denounced the "robber barons" who created foundations as acting (so the muckrakers claimed) to cleanse their reputations. Later, politicians from the right got into the act, outraged over what they viewed as the liberal agendas of the great foundations.

The 1969 Tax Reform Act marked the culmination of a decade of populist anti-foundation activity, including a series of hearings presided over by Representative Wright Patman (D-TX), who was especially concerned about foundation control of businesses and inadequate payout appropriate to the size of assets. Southern politicians who opposed the efforts of the Ford Foundation and other foundations to facilitate the registration of black voters in the South joined with political opponents of Robert F. Kennedy (whose staff members had received travel and study grants from the Ford Foundation) in pushing retaliatory legislation through Congress. The new rules imposed the first excise tax ever levied on foundation assets, mandatory minimum annual payout as a percentage of assets, restrictions on foundation voting ownership of for-profit entities, as well as other legal restrictions on foundations, including some that circumscribed the possibility of similar foundation voter registration and travel/study grants in the future.

Today the drumbeat of congressional criticism of nonprofits, including foundations, is being heard once again. From 2002 to 2005, occasional hearings were held on initiatives proposed by the chairs and staff of three powerful committees—the Senate Finance and House Ways and Means committees, as well as the Joint Committee on Taxation. Spurred by these hearings and the accompanying press attention, some state attorneys general and other regulatory officials jumped on the anti-nonprofit bandwagon, and, as of late 2006, a new round of retaliatory federal legislation is under consideration.

But there are differences between today and earlier periods of criticism of foundations. Today's most vociferous critics come from every position on the political spectrum. The right decries what it regards as the deliberate disregard by (liberal) foundation trustees and program staff of the intent of (conservative) donors, while the left opposes the long-term growth of foundation assets as an unhealthy concentration of wealth and power. Warren Buffett's historic gift to the Bill and Melinda Gates Foundation has ratcheted up the concerns about the scale of foundation assets, although, despite the amazingly misleading press reporting of his gift as one to be added to the assets of the Gates Foundation, the Buffett gift is to be entirely spent within a year of the receipt of its installments, and indeed is contingent on the Gates Foundation's also spending a minimum of 5 percent of its own asset value.[105]

And all sides attack what they consider the high-handedness and arrogance of foundations, an impression reinforced by a few high-profile foundation compensation packages and first-class travel policies that have come to public attention in recent years. These complementary impulses have helped spark the recent consideration by Congress to raise the annual minimum payout for foundations from the present 5 percent of assets to 6 percent or more, as well as various proposals to regulate one or another aspect of foundation management.

The foundation community has been fighting back, thanks in part to the energetic leadership of a number of foundation presidents, especially Ford's Susan Berresford, who worked energetically—and successfully—with Congress to head off a threatened payout requirement increase in 2004. In addition, as noted earlier, Independent Sector (IS), the umbrella organization for the nonprofit sector, led by the capable and energetic Diana Aviv, mounted the first really impressive sector-wide mobilization in history to respond to the congressional critics. In fewer than nine months, IS's Panel on the Nonprofit Sector produced three carefully drafted reports with contributions from some two hundred nonprofit leaders, attorneys, regulators, and scholars, which seem to have captured the attention and even the respect of the congressional committees.

Perhaps most impressive, some of the recommendations of the IS panel suggest that, at long last, the civic sector has begun to take seriously its responsibility for establishing and policing standards of professional responsibility for the officers and trustees of civic-sector organizations. The willingness of the panel participants to acknowledge the shortcomings of civic-sector organizations and to propose both legislative and self-enforcement remedies suggests that the knee-jerk defensiveness and sense of victimhood long prevalent among nonprofits, including foundations, is being replaced by a new sense of maturity and self-confidence.

No one knows whether legislative tampering with foundations and other nonprofit organizations is really in the offing. Nevertheless, it seems clear that the root cause of foundations' vulnerability—their obvious lack of accountability—will continue to invite attacks from both left and right and will tend to undermine public trust in foundations.

What can be done to remedy this problem once and for all? In this chapter, I'll offer a few suggestions.

Lack of Accountability and Foundation Underperformance

As I've stressed throughout this book, foundations have an overriding obligation to the public to perform their duties according to the highest standards of effectiveness and stewardship. That obligation arises especially from the tax deductibility of gifts to create foundations and the tax exempt status granted to foundation assets and income once they are established. As a result of these benefits, United States taxpayers annually benefit United States foundations with foregone taxes in excess of twenty billion dollars. For that reason alone, foundations must somehow be made accountable, preferably by means of voluntary action, but, failing that, through legally mandated regulation or through voluntary action.

Many foundations continue to do an excellent job of creating effective programs that benefit the general public and help to improve society. What they have not done is to create a climate of transparency, the lack of which both causes foundations to underperform their potential and creates growing public distrust. It would hardly be surprising if members of the public, whose attention to foundations has now been dramatically drawn by Warren Buffett's thirty-one-billion-dollar gift to the Gates Foundation, find it increasingly incongruous for foundations to operate at that scale while doing so in a secretive manner. So the foundation practices that concern me most include:

- The unwillingness of foundations to provide sufficiently detailed documentation about all their initiatives to permit unbiased outside appraisal.

- The failure of foundations to disclose, analyze, and call attention to their failed initiatives.

- The failure of foundations to communicate openly with grant-seekers and the public about how foundation decisions are made.

- The infrequency of rigorous evaluation by foundations of their own grantmaking initiatives and their unwillingness to make such evaluations available to the public.

- The infrequency of rigorous strategic planning analyses when foundations consider new programs, as well as their unavailability to the public.

- The general "fuzziness" and "mushiness" of many foundation initiatives that result from a failure to analyze them carefully in advance and to assess them during and after implementation.

Imperfections such as these inevitably lead the public to regard foundations as uninterested in what the public thinks about them, as nonresponsive at best, and as willfully arrogant at worst. And whether or not that judgment is fair, such practices are decidedly detrimental to the foundations themselves. Scholars and skilled practitioners of organizational behavior know that organizations that are continuously subject to scrutiny, challenge, criticism, and competition from informed outsiders tend to make wiser, more effective decisions, while organizations that operate in a vacuum frequently commit serious blunders and waste resources unwisely.

The only solution is to introduce a greater degree of transparency and accountability into the foundation world. But how can this be done without unduly limiting the freedom of foundation managers to pursue their objectives as they see fit? Let's consider some alternative possibilities, first with respect to willful wrongdoing and then with respect to facilitating greater transparency.

GOVERNMENT OVERSIGHT REFORM

American foundations are wealthier and more numerous than those in any other country, which makes our foundation sector unique. Nonetheless, it's useful to mention some of the ways in which other nations have sought to assure foundation accountability to the public.

In most other countries, government regulation of the nonprofit sector is significantly stricter than in the United States. In Germany and Japan, for example, government agencies painstakingly review every application to create a foundation, and exercise what Americans would regard as heavy-handed regulatory supervision. Under French law, every foundation is required to have a board member or director appointed by the government. In the United Kingdom, a Charities Commission monitors and supervises all nonprofit organizations, including foundations. And the press has been full of news in 2006 about the Russian government's placing restrictions on the creation and functioning of all nonprofits.

I am not for a moment suggesting that any of those approaches would be appropriate for the United States, and, indeed, I would oppose their consideration. But I must note that, in the United States, by contrast with all of the above countries and many others, the creation of a nonprofit organization, including a foundation, merely requires the filing of incorporation papers with a state's secretary of state or the writing of a charitable trust agreement by a lawyer. Internal Revenue Service approval of the organization's tax exemption as a 501(c)(3) is virtually automatic, valid for five years, and subject to little in-depth substantive review. After creation and preliminary IRS tax exemption approval, foundations are required to file an annual 990-PF form report with the IRS (analogous to the form 990 required to be filed by other charities), but the reports are usually never read. The IRS admits that it lacks the personnel required to review such annual filings, to audit even 1 percent of them on an annual basis, or otherwise provide any serious oversight to civic-sector organizations. In a 2005 paper by Marcus Owens, former director of the IRS Exempt Organization Division, he writes: "In 2003, the most recent year for which the IRS has published statistics, the number of tax-exempt organizations listed on the master file was 1,640,949, of which 909,574 were exempt under section 501(c)(3). The IRS reported that it examined 3,582 returns filed by tax-exempt organizations in that year."[106]

The oversight provided by state charity regulators is no more effective or comprehensive. While some state attorneys general, especially those in New York, Massachusetts, and California, pay close attention to detecting serious legal infractions and ethical misbehavior by foundations and their trustees, most others do not. According to a recent count, there were fewer than one hundred full-time charity supervisory officials among the fifty state governments.

Most observers agree that the present system of nonprofit oversight aimed at willful misbehavior is inadequate. But what kind of reform should be implemented?

Some have suggested that all that is required is making additional financial resources available to the IRS to beef up its Exempt Organization Division, and that certainly should be done. I doubt, however, that such a step alone would make the difference between today's inadequate governmental oversight and what is required for everyone to have confidence in its future effectiveness. From the IRS's point of view, nonprofits are not "where the money is." The fines for willful, illegal misconduct likely to be recoverable from foundations, other nonprofits, or their officers as a result of IRS supervision, will always represent a mere drop in the bucket compared with the financial return from enhanced oversight of individual and corporate taxpayer returns, which amounts to hundreds of millions of dollars annually. The IRS, therefore, has less incentive to focus its attention on the nonprofit sector.

Moreover, aside from that lack of financial incentive for the IRS to focus adequate attention on charities, including foundations, the bureaucracy of the IRS makes it unlikely that it could ever become the means of effective accountability for the nonprofit sector. For example, the decades-long effort to reform the 990 and 990-PF forms so that they are both filer-friendly and comprehensible to members of the public who seek to read them must discourage anyone who is tempted to believe that the IRS could possibly be the right place for nonprofit oversight. And the IRS's culture, heavily oriented toward the privacy of individual and corporate tax information, discourages it from facilitating the transparency obligations of nonprofit organizations and deters it from exchanging information on nonprofit misdeeds with state regulatory authorities.

To create an effective oversight system for all civic-sector organizations, including foundations, one in which the public can be confident that willful misconduct is detected, deterred, and punished, I am persuaded that we must either place some government agency other than the IRS in charge or invent a new arrangement whereby the IRS's role in the oversight process is significantly transformed. In a book chapter published seven years ago, I suggested—as a third-choice possibility, only after two variants of nonprofit self-regulation—the creation of a United States Charities Commission analogous to the one in the United Kingdom. In the interim, I have concluded that such a government bureaucracy is so at odds with the history, culture, and need for independence of America's nonprofit sector that it would be unworkable and, in any event, is unlikely ever to be established.

Of all the oversight possibilities that have been suggested for dealing with willful misconduct by nonprofits, including foundations, the one proposed by Marcus Owens, former director of the IRS Exempt Organization Division, is the only one I know that promises to be effective and also unlikely to infringe on the indispensable freedom of nonprofits. In his very thoughtful and carefully worked out 2005 draft paper, "Charity Oversight: An Alternative Approach," Owens concludes that the IRS is not the best home for charities supervision as currently structured, and calls for the creation of a new congressionally chartered, private, not-for-profit organization that would be related to but independent of the IRS to discharge that function.[107]

Owens's suggested new agency would be modeled on the National Association of Securities Dealers, which regulates brokers and brokerage firms. Like its sister organizations, the Municipal Securities Rulemaking Board and the Public Company Accounting Oversight Board, the NASD assists the Securities and Exchange Commission (SEC) in carrying out its responsibilities. As Owens notes, "All three entities share the common characteristics that they are not structurally part of the federal government, yet all exercise oversight authority by virtue of their relationship with the SEC, including the ability to sanction those who transgress their rules, including the levying of fines."[108]

Owens urges creating an NASD-like agency for tax-exempt organization oversight that would be related to, but independent of, the IRS in much the same way that the NASD is related to, but independent of, the SEC, and would be financed by allowing foundations to obtain a tax credit against their federal foundation tax obligations for payments to support the new agency's operations.

I believe that Owens's analogy to the NASD is exactly right. The financing scheme he proposes is ingenious in that it both essentially costs foundations nothing and also succeeds in refocusing on nonprofit-sector oversight at least some of the revenues yielded by the foundation tax, which was the original rationale given for its imposition in 1969. In fact, that tax has yielded anywhere between three hundred million and seven hundred million dollars depending on the year—only about fifty million of which has ended up in the IRS Exempt Organization budget.

My strong recommendation, therefore, is that the first important action to increase foundation accountability be the establishment by Congress of such an NASD-like private, nonprofit organization related to the IRS in much the same way that the NASD is related to the SEC, with sufficient resources, personnel, and investigative powers to oversee the entire U.S. civic sector, including foundations. The new entity's powers should be carefully circumscribed to prevent it from intruding on substantive foundation and nonprofit decision-making, and to limit it to the enforcement of laws and regulations specifically targeting such matters as nonprofit fidelity to conflict-of-interest, insider self-benefit, transparency, and comparable procedural standards enforced by law.

Reform is also urgently needed at the state level. Greater resources should be made available for the staffs of the agencies responsible for oversight of charities. At the very least, as Harvard's Marion Fremont-Smith has suggested, the Independent Sector's recommendations for substantial exchange of information between the IRS and state enforcement officials should be implemented. In July and August 2006, Congress enacted, and President Bush signed, the Pension Reform Act of 2006, which includes, for the first time, permission for the IRS to share information about particular charities with state regulatory agencies. That permission doesn't guarantee that the IRS will be forthcoming, but it does remove any IRS excuse for failing to do so. Moreover, the IRS should follow the lead of states that have required on their reporting forms more detailed information on nonprofits' finances than is now asked for on the IRS 990 forms. The slowness of the IRS in making the 990 forms more revealing and readable is as distressing as it is incomprehensible. The IRS Advisory Committee on the Form 990 announced in August 2006 that it would soon make specific recommendations for revisions. This is after at least thirty years of talk about doing something.

SELF-POLICING: A VOLUNTARY TRANSPARENCY AND ACCOUNTABILITY CODE

How best can foundations create a climate of transparency? The answer to that question seems obvious—by taking action themselves. That would be a far more satisfactory solution than to have transparency forced upon them by government action. Would they be willing to do? So far, they have not manifested much enthusiasm for any collective, energetic effort to that end, but perhaps the greater public attention to the existence of foundations and the rapid growth in their assets attracted by the 2006 Warren Buffett gift, coupled with the recent increased level of criticism by public officials and the press, will build up some momentum for doing so. I therefore urge foundations themselves to create a transparency-enforcing mechanism that could be implemented in short order by a foundation-sector infrastructure organization.

For example, a group of foundations could develop and promulgate such a "transparency and accountability code" on their own or under the auspices of the Council on Foundations. Some foundations have already broken ranks on transparency—especially the Robert Wood Johnson Foundation, the Wallace Foundation, and the David and Lucile Packard Foundation—and could constitute a core group of initiators. Individual foundations could sign on to the code and agree to be bound by its provisions.

Another scenario would have the Council on Foundations itself promulgate such a code and make it binding on all its members. In past years, the council did take the lead in encouraging its members to publish annual reports, which is a precedent, but the council has not heretofore shown much enthusiasm for controversial initiatives that might tend to diminish the number of dues-paying members. And a policy of thoroughgoing transparency such as I urged above would certainly be resisted by many. The energetic leadership already manifested by the council's new president and CEO, former Congressman Steve Gunderson, gives me hope that he might put his weight behind such an initiative.

Whether or not the Council can muster the courage to make this its own initiative, if the founding group of code members were sufficiently prominent and persistent, it could gradually attract many others to join their number voluntarily. As a marketing device, they could develop a "Seal of Public Accountability," which any self-respecting foundation would want to display on its publications and Web sites.

The next step might be the creation of a foundation-supported transparency-enforcement board to which persons denied information could appeal for redress. This board would work with the signatory foundations in developing standard criteria for disclosure and agreed-upon procedures for appeal.

The third piece in this self-regulatory system would be a requirement that every foundation above a stipulated size employ an ombudsman charged with fairly and independently receiving, evaluating, and acting on complaints about foundation failure to disclose requested documents. If the existence of the ombudsman's office were widely publicized, it could go a long way toward remedying the general perception that foundations are arrogant and indifferent to outsider complaints.

A fourth element would be a foundation sector–initiated and –financed system that would publicly rate foundations on the extent to which they fulfill obligations of transparency. Let's call this the Foundation Transparency Rating Board (FTRB). I am convinced that enough foundations are sufficiently concerned today about the risk of doing nothing that they would provide the financial and moral support for such an effort. They already understand that the tradition of unhampered freedom of foundation decision-making could easily be constrained by future legislation triggered in part by the opaqueness of foundation decision-making. Of all institutions in our democratic society that have no excuses for non-transparency, foundations, because of their quasi-public nature created by the tax benefits that they enjoy, are second only to government itself.

A group of foundation leaders, sparked by Surdna Foundation Executive Director Ed Skloot, tried for a year or so in the late 1990s to develop a plan for an entity that would rate foundations, possibly based on the methodology developed by the Zagat Surveys, but never could reach agreement on the workability and practicality of such an undertaking, or find much enthusiasm among foundations to support it.

Within the past five years, the Center for Effective Philanthropy has created considerable enthusiasm among foundations—as well as among foundation critics—for its pioneering work in rating foundations, but only on process matters. Derived from confidential surveys of grant recipients regarding the grantmaking process that measure qualities such as foundation responsiveness, staff helpfulness, and willingness to support their grantees' fund-raising efforts, the ratings are embodied in Grantee Perception Reports (GPRs), and they have proven very popular among foundations. According to a report done for the center by LaFrance Associates, 97 percent of the foundations that have commissioned GPRs have made changes in the way they operate based on the findings, and many of them have chosen to post on their Web sites the CEP reports on them.[109] The CEP comparative ratings of foundation process performance are the only ones being done by anyone, but individual foundation performance ratings are shared only with the individual foundation and not released publicly.

So far, the center has been hesitant to expand its ratings to more substantive—and subjective—areas such as grant and strategy quality, program effectiveness, and foundation risk tolerance. However, it seems likely that the center intends ultimately to try to include such topics in its reports—a function that some responsible entity certainly needs to perform. If the center shies away from this role, some other organization ought to be created to handle it, preferably launched and financed by foundations themselves.

The Foundation Transparency Rating Board (FTRB) would rate foundations on a transparency scale, including the extent to which they make full use of their Web sites to provide detailed data about, among other things, their grantmaking successes and failures. We need an FTRB because no existing entity is well positioned to focus the pressure of public scrutiny and criticism on what foundations do and how they do it. The normal public give-and-take about scientific findings or public-policy proposals doesn't occur with respect to foundation initiatives. The absence of such potentially self-correcting criticism means that foundations operate without pressure to improve their quality. It is essential that an FTRB limit itself to pressuring foundations to be transparent and not seek to assess the effectiveness of foundations' substantive programs. If foundations provide the information, the free marketplace of ideas will undertake to analyze it.

Another possible solution to the need for some sort of rating system is peer review. As suggested by several people I interviewed for this book, including Neal Graboy of the Carnegie Corporation of New York, such a board might organize a peer-review process for foundations analogous to the periodic reviews for reaccreditation that colleges, universities, and secondary schools undergo from teams of their fellow academics. Knowing that such peer review is in the offing would likely force self-evaluation in advance, which is the main benefit that the colleges and universities obtain from their peer-review processes.

Perhaps this self-regulatory program seems ambitious—some will surely call it cumbersome—especially for a set of institutions that is currently operating with minimal public scrutiny and accountability. But as outside pressure from the media, politicians, and interest groups continues to mount, foundation leaders may find increasingly appealing the idea of self-regulation as a way of fending off more intrusive government control.

Coupled with such self-regulation, the foundation sector must support its own infrastructure. I cannot state the urgency of this issue too strongly. For American foundations to continue to be the important influences on American society that they have been in the past, and to remain free from and unfettered by government, many more foundations must recognize that their own individual interests are increasingly at stake in the battles in behalf of foundations—in the public mind and in the arenas of public policy making—that are being waged by all components of the foundation community infrastructure, and they must back up that responsibility with cash support.

That means support for the strengthening of the Council on Foundations, Independent Sector, and the other organizations actively representing the interests of the foundation sector; support for other organizations that help foundations perform their responsibilities more effectively and efficiently, such as the National Center for Family Philanthropy; support for organizations that assess foundation performance and that provide information to the public about what foundations do and how they do it, such as the Foundation Center and the Center for Effective Philanthropy; support for universities and think tanks that conduct research on the functioning of foundations and for the scholars who do such research; and support for the development of new forms of executive education and development for foundation program officers and trustees, as well as for those contemplating the establishment of foundations.

FEDERAL LEGISLATION TO MANDATE
OR ENCOURAGE FOUNDATION OPENNESS

After nearly a century of complaints about the lack of foundation transparency, anyone would be justified in being skeptical about the likelihood that the problem will be solved by foundation voluntary action alone. If, therefore, foundations do not grasp the nettle themselves within a reasonable period of time, we should consider enacting legal requirements to create a culture of transparency among foundations. It may well be that federal legislation to mandate foundation transparency will prove to be necessary to create the level of openness that the public rightly demands. It may well be, too, that only mandated disclosure can succeed in arming outsiders with sufficient information about foundation decision-making to create the external accountability forces needed to drive foundations to higher levels of effectiveness and efficiency.

If we reach the point that government action is necessary, I suggest considering the enactment of a Foundation Freedom of Information Act, which would require foundations to make public all decision-process documents involving grantmaking initiatives above a specified dollar limit. It could include such documents as I specified above in this chapter.

The freedom-of-information (FOI) paradigm that permits outsider access to internal government documents seems easily applicable to foundation documents. Many government agencies that award grants to individuals and institutions, including the National Institutes of Health, the National Science Foundation, and the Environmental Protection Agency, are required to make available certain decision-chain documents to anyone requesting them, with some statutory and regulatory exceptions. The governmental nexus for such a federal requirement is certainly provided by the tax benefits conferred on foundations by federal tax policy. I see no reason that the same requirement would necessarily hamstring foundation decision-making.

If it becomes clear that only government action will bring about transparency, my recommendation is that any foundation documents used in formulating, implementing, evaluating, and assessing grantmaking strategies, grant clusters, or individual grants in excess of one million dollars should be available to any individual requesting them from the foundation. As with the federal FOI law, specified types of information—including personnel data, protected intellectual property, and national security data—would not be subject to disclosure. If a foundation were to fail to provide the requested documents within a reasonable period of time, the person requesting the information could bring an FOIA disclosure action in the federal courts.

Regulatory changes requiring greater public availability of internal foundation decision documents would help a great deal in informing and activating external critics, as well as provide much more information to scholars and practitioners. While other legislation may well be needed to hold foundations to higher standards with regard to various process issues—such as insider self-benefit, required payout, salary levels, or travel expenses, as discussed above—I can imagine no way for legislation directly to deal in a productive and non-damaging way with the core issue of foundation program decisions, and would oppose any position regulating them.

THE TIME TO ACT

Of course, foundations need not—and should not—wait for government or the civic sector as a whole to act before they tackle their own accountability problems. The trustees of each foundation—today's only real accountability-enforcing mechanisms—can and should act on their own.

A 2005 report by the Center for Effective Philanthropy, *Beyond Compliance: The Trustee Viewpoint on Foundation Governance*, reported that the greatest concern of foundation trustees was the limited extent to which their foundations measured their achievement of strategic goals.[110] Most of the trustees surveyed said they want greater involvement in the assessment of foundation impact and performance. But in truth there are no obstacles that prevent such involvement. What's required is for trustees to assert themselves forcefully and insist upon putting in place the data-generating measures that will facilitate such assessment.

Foundations are far too important to the dynamism of America's civic sector to be allowed to languish in self-protective insulation. Many foundation leaders already know the nature of the fundamental problems facing foundations. Some of them have boldly grasped the nettle and are leading their own institutions into a new era of transparency, along with the greater effectiveness that it is almost certain to produce. Foundation leaders must find the courage and vision to rise above their self-imposed, self-imagined phantoms of insecurity and lead their institutions into a new era of transparency, accountability, and effectiveness. The time to act is now.

A PROPHETIC EPILOGUE:

PHILANTHROPY IN THE

TWENTY-FIRST CENTURY

A LOOK BACK AT FOUNDATIONS IN THE TWENTIETH CENTURY

The twentieth century is the era in which the large private foundation form was born, securely established and robustly replicated across the U.S. landscape. It was perhaps the first time in history that large and unrestricted pools of funds of private wealth had been created to benefit the public interest under independent management. That development signifies a major step, not yet fully recognized, in the evolution of democratic institutions and sociopolitical theory.

Large private foundations first took root in New York, but they are now found in most cities and every region of the country. The philanthropic organizations first created by Carnegie, Rockefeller, Harkness, and Sage in the first two decades of the century grew steadily, and established the grantmaking patterns of the many foundations that gradually emerged in their wake. By the year 2005, there were forty-nine U.S. foundations with assets above one billion dollars.[1]

What catches one's attention at century's end, however, is the significant rate of increase in large foundation founding and the proliferation of permutations of the foundation form as America moved toward and beyond the year 2000. Before speculating about the future, therefore, it is surely worthwhile to look briefly at the momentum of foundation creation at the end of the last century and also at some of those new hybrid philanthropic vehicles. Perhaps we will be able to discern in them the growing seeds from which future philanthropic models and behavior will sprout.

First, notice the momentum increase. During the first eight decades of the twentieth century, the number of large foundations—those with assets above one million dollars or which made grants of one hundred thousand dollars or above—grew each decade at only single digits—2 percent in the period before 1940, 3 percent in the 1940s, 8 percent in the 1950s and 1960s, and 5 percent in the 1970s. Beginning in the 1980s, however, the momentum in foundation creation increased significantly, with 18 percent growth in the 1980s, and 37 percent, or 8,139 new large foundations, created in the 1990s. The first five years, 2000–2004, of the first decade in the twenty-first century saw a further increase of 12 percent.[2] Those decade-by-decade increases seem likely to amount to nearly a doubling of the number of large foundations over the thirty-year period ending in 2009. While the rate of increase will almost certainly slow, the buildup of wealth and the need to dispose of it philanthropically will, as we will see below, likely continue to find an attractive outlet in foundation creation.

EVOLUTION IN FOUNDATION FORM IN THE TWENTIETH CENTURY

Even more noteworthy is the evolution of new forms of philanthropy that essentially embody the foundation function, but which differ from the traditional private foundation model.

In 1914, only seven years after the founding of the Russell Sage Foundation, the foundation form took its first significant evolutionary step. Frederick Harris Goff in Cleveland created America's first community foundation, aggregating assets contributed by many less-wealthy individuals rather than by one very wealthy person or family alone, with the income devoted exclusively to local and regional charitable purposes. While the original community foundation idea was to pool totally unrestricted funds, community foundations soon began accepting gifts restricted to particular fields of grantmaking, such as education or the arts, or even to specified charitable institutions. By the end of the century, there were more than seven hundred such foundations across the United States, holding assets of $38.7 billion and giving away annually about $3 billion, and the community foundation model has now spread to many other countries across the world.

Over the course of the century, community foundations evolved a new kind of open-ended fund whose purpose the donor is not required to specify at the time of creation. Called "donor-advised funds," such funds contribute to particular causes based entirely on subsequent recommendations by the fund's donor, or his or her designee. While the community foundation that creates such a fund is legally required to have the technical final say on gifts made from the fund, in practice, community foundations always follow the "recommendation" of the fund donor or that person's designee, except where specific legal provisions prevent their doing so.

Such donor-advised funds have rapidly gained popularity because they are easier to set up and much less burdensome to administer than freestanding private foundations. Indeed they have proven so attractive that, around the start of the 1990s, the IRS approved the request of commercial financial institutions, first Fidelity and then Vanguard, Charles Schwab, and others, to offer such donor-advised funds themselves. By 2005, seventeen major financial institutions offered such funds, and they held about one-third of the fifteen billion dollars of assets in all donor-advised funds, with the remainder primarily in community foundations. In addition, there are freestanding institutions, such as the American Endowment Foundation, that exist solely to provide home bases for donor-advised funds.[3]

Meanwhile, yet another permutation occurred in the foundation model—the establishment of community foundation-like entities, including unrestricted, restricted, and donor-advised funds by individual religious, ethnic, and racial communities. By the beginning of the new century, most of the Jewish federations, as well as similar organizations for other religious and ethnic groups across the United States, had established replicas of the community foundations to serve their own subcommunities, complete with unrestricted and restricted pools of money alongside a growing number of donor-advised funds. As in the case of the community foundations, gifts large and small for either permanent endowment or near-term spending were solicited to go into such funds.

Soon, individual public charities and educational institutions began establishing what are called by the tax code "supporting organizations," which have a different organizational form but which function very much like donor-advised funds. The major difference is that the donors themselves or their designees cannot be the sole voices advising on the distribution of the donated funds but instead usually constitute a minority of the board members of the supporting organizations created by them, with the majority appointed by the host institutions from whose tax-exempt status as public charities or educational institutions the "supporting organizations" benefit. While the donated funds or the income on them can be granted to charitable organizations other than the host institution, the usual price extracted by the host institution for establishing such organizations is that at least half of the income available must be spent on initiatives internal to the host institution.

Finally, there is the development of charitable foundations established by corporations. Starting in mid-century with the establishment of the General Electric Foundation, the IBM Foundation, and the AT&T Foundation, corporations began to recognize that a private foundation-like vehicle could signal to their stakeholders and the public at large their commitment to a high level of corporate social responsibility. Some corporate foundations have been created by endowment gifts and function very much like private foundations, but most are funded annually by their corporate creators in amounts that usually depend on corporate profits for the preceding year. And of course, the corporate donors determine the distribution of grants from the foundations.

Another new phenomenon of the last decade of the twentieth century and the first decade of this century has been foundation mergers. Usually, the sense of turf among foundation trustees is so powerful that they do not easily entertain the idea of sharing power with trustees of other foundations. Despite that resistance, in July 1999, the Charles E. Culpeper Foundation merged with the Rockefeller Brothers Fund. Seven years later, in July 2006, the Community Foundation of Silicon Valley, in San Jose, CA, and the Peninsula Community Foundation in San Mateo, CA, announced their merger into the Silicon Valley Community Foundation, with combined assets of about $1.5 billion, making it second in size among community foundations only to the New York Community Trust ($1.9 billion in assets).[4] If more foundations can overcome the boundaries of their separate forms as these have done, synergies in the management of their assets and experimentation with entirely new forms—to say nothing of sheer economies of scale—promise significant social benefits.

HYBRIDIZATION OF FOUNDATION FUNCTION IN THE TWENTIETH CENTURY

The last decade of the past century also saw the emergence of venture philanthropy and its first cousin, social entrepreneurship.[5] Venture philanthropy is characterized by an intensive personal engagement of donors—either individually or through their foundations—in the decision-making processes of the recipients of their charitable support, an involvement patterned after and very much like the role of venture capitalists in creating and nurturing new business enterprises. As I have also pointed out at other points in this book, venture philanthropists are conducting themselves much as Andrew Carnegie did and as he urged other wealthy donors to do in his *Gospel of Wealth*.

The practices of social entrepreneurship significantly overlap with those of venture philanthropists. In effect, social enterprise incorporates into the running of grant-receiving organizations the entrepreneurial strategies, the quest for sustainability through income stream diversification, and the benchmarking, evaluation, and measurement techniques that have been developed and refined in many for-profit organizations. Social enterprise can therefore be understood as a hybrid of the nonprofit and for-profit sectors.

One of the most widely known and most successful examples of these trends is Venture Philanthropy Partners, which Mario Morino created by persuading a group of wealthy individuals to join him in establishing a multimillion-dollar fund with which to support a limited number of youth-development organizations in the Washington, DC, and northern Virginia region, providing both money and management-consulting assistance.[6] Other examples include Austin Social Venture Partners; Community Wealth Ventures in Washington, DC; the Entrepreneurs Foundation in San Francisco; the Enterprise Foundation in Portland, OR; Global Partnerships in Seattle; New Profit, Inc. in Boston; New Schools in Palo Alto, CA; Roberts Enterprise Development Fund in San Francisco; Silicon Valley Social Venture Fund in San Jose, CA; Social Venture Network in San Francisco; and Social Venture Partners in Seattle.

A particularly creative venture philanthropy initiative is the Acumen Fund, which was launched by the Rockefeller Foundation to solicit wealthy Americans to invest in for-profit start-ups that manufacture goods and provide services urgently needed in the developing world and sell them for affordable prices. Among its first initiatives are affordable hearing aids, affordable eye glasses, and long-lasting, affordable mosquito nets to reduce the risk of malaria. Acumen, which conducts itself very much like the venture capital fund that it is, has nearly six million dollars under management. The combination of for-profit form with a social mission is characteristic of venture philanthropy and social entrepreneurship.[7] The same is true for the rapid growth of micro-lending funds. Not only have major foundations, such as Ford, Rockefeller, and Bill and Melinda Gates, created grantmaking programs which lend money to finance start-up businesses in developing world countries, but also many other foundations and organizations, including some for-profit mutual funds such as the Calvert Social Investment Foundation, have followed suit.[8]

Venture philanthropy and social entrepreneurship have brought with them a change not only in form but in function as well. Unlike most traditional foundations, the venture philanthropists augment their financial giving with various kinds of consulting advice designed to help recipient organizations achieve their objectives more effectively and efficiently. And some go even further, taking a direct role in solving or ameliorating social problems, often involving existing individual grant-receiving organizations in the effort but augmenting them with newly-created nonprofits and drawing in for-profit organizations when appropriate.

Venture philanthropists and social entrepreneurs have been deliberate and thoroughgoing in their efforts to transform the ways existing nonprofits go about doing their work. They especially insist on the use of formal strategy, the institution of metric-based performance benchmarking, and the attainment of sustainability through the diversification of revenue streams. They have also begun to create new hybrid for-profit/nonprofit organizations for their work and to draw existing for-profit corporations into it as well.

One of the new breed of self-made, wealthy, high-tech philanthropists, eBay founder Pierre Omidyar, was among the first to break the traditional form completely. After establishing a private foundation for his philanthropy, he concluded that that form was too restrictive to serve his purposes. Within a few years, he created the Omidyar Network, which, while including the foundation within it, works extensively with both for-profits and nonprofits in tackling the problems that Omidyar is eager to solve. Omidyar combines tax-deductible contributions with non-tax-deductible expenditures in carrying out his philanthropy, and draws in both nonprofits and for-profits in varying combinations to achieve his objectives. According to reporters, "[a] spokesperson for Mr. Omidyar said that he plans to 'deploy' the 'lion's share' of his net worth—estimated at $10 billion—through Omidyar Network during his lifetime."[9]

Others like Omidyar in spirit and aim, such as Jeff Skoll, share the same goal but have chosen a slightly different form to achieve it. Skoll created both a private foundation, the Skoll Foundation, and a supporting organization, the Skoll Fund, within the local community foundation. Because of its association with the community foundation, the fund is itself a public charity and is free to undertake a variety of initiatives that a private foundation either cannot or cannot as easily undertake. Sergey Brin and Larry Page, founders and controlling stockholders of Google, have been experimenting for some time with other models of social problem-solving. In September 2006, Google announced what may be the first hybrid for-profit/nonprofit fund, to be used for solving social problems, that is held totally within a single corporation.

Called Google.org, the fund has been given about $1 billion of corporate money—that is, stockholders' money—to spend on efforts to solve the problems of poverty, disease, and global warming.[10] Apparently not to be outdone, a week later, Richard Branson, founder and CEO of Virgin Air and affiliated companies, announced still another model of philanthropy, doing so at President Clinton's Global Initiative. He committed to invest 100 percent of all profits from his airline and train companies over the next ten years, expected to amount to roughly $3 billion, in efforts to combat global warming.[11]

Notice that the four preceding models—Omidyar, Skoll, Google, and Branson—are very different structurally. Omidyar's is his personal money plus the foundation he had already established. Skoll's is his foundation in combination with a separate donor-advised fund he established at a community foundation. Google's is a $1 billion fund totally inside a corporation, which includes a pre-existing foundation of about $100 million, and Branson's is the dedication of a profit income stream over a period of ten years. They demonstrate not only how much energy and passion there is today to put large pools of wealth to work solving pressing social problems, but also the seemingly endless hybridization of the means by which they can be put to work. That suggests that the day of private, independent foundations as the exclusive vehicle for philanthropic initiative has ended.

At the end of the twentieth century, the momentum toward venture philanthropy and social entrepreneurship seems to be growing rapidly and significantly reshaping the way more and more foundations, as well as the wealthy individuals who create them, operate. The trend is driven by three factors. The first is the widespread public recognition of the immense problems challenging the entire world, seen by growing numbers to be interdependent—poverty, hunger, disease, ethnic and religious conflict, and environmental degradation, among others. The second is a growing impatience with the inadequacy of governmental and international efforts to solve or ameliorate those problems, along with a recognition that most of them cannot be solved by nonprofits alone but require partnerships of varying kinds with for-profit corporations and government. And the third is the accumulation of vast wealth in the hands of *very impatient* individuals, newly motivated to solve some of these great challenges, individuals who have proved in their wealth-accumulating track records that they know how to solve at least some kinds of problems. Whether their skills transfer effectively to such public problem-solving on a grand scale remains to be seen. Their direct involvement in a big way is heartening, and there are certainly grounds for optimism. The ranks of such individuals appear to be growing rapidly—Bill and Melinda Gates, Warren Buffett, Pierre Omidyar, Jeff Skoll, Sergey Brin, Larry Page, Lawrence Ellison, George Soros, Michael Bloomberg, Alan Parker, Michael Milken, Eli Broad, Ted Forstmann, Doris and Don Fisher, Sanford Weill, Charles Bronfman, Gordon Moore, Richard and Rhoda Goldman, Bernard Marcus, James and Virginia Stowers, Peter Nicholas, John Abele, Donald J. Listwin[12] and Sol Price are but a few of the many who could be named here.

The category of impatient, powerful individuals is hardly limited to persons who have accumulated great wealth, however. Many Americans whose wealth consists primarily in their personal celebrity have recently begun creating foundations and enrolling themselves in national and international efforts to deal with nagging public problems. Popular musicians like Dolly Parton, Wynton and Branford Marsalis, Harry Connick Jr., Alice Cooper, Wyclef Jean, Christopher Brian Bridges (of Ludacris fame), Barbra Streisand, Snoop Dogg, Russell Simmons and his brothers Joseph and Danny, Bette Midler, Queen Latifah, Paul McCartney, and Neil Young, among others, have created foundations or nonprofits to work on particular problems.[13] Many other entertainers have also created foundations or have otherwise personally engaged in a continuing way with major causes both domestic and international. Among them are the late Christopher Reeve, Michael J. Fox, Oprah Winfrey, Robert Redford, and Paul Newman.[14]

What is true of musicians and entertainers is true also of sports stars. They, too, are now routinely establishing their own foundations or otherwise leveraging their celebrity to raise money for nonprofits or causes about which they care deeply. One example will do. Cam Neely, a former Boston Bruins hockey player, announced that his foundation would give two million dollars to support a pediatric bone marrow–transplant facility and five million dollars to improve the neurosurgery program at Tufts-New England Medical Center. Improvements in the neurosurgery center will be named after Neely's father, Michael, who died of brain cancer. Neely's mother also died of cancer. Since its inception in 1997, the Cam Neely Foundation has raised about thirteen million dollars.[15] And Mr. Neely is but one of the many professional athletes to have emerged as a substantial philanthropist.

In the Dawn of the Twenty-First Century

Only six years into the new century, an event occurred in the world of philanthropy that grabbed everyone's notice. Warren Buffett handed over to someone else—Bill and Melinda Gates—to give away most of the wealth he had accumulated during his lifetime. Buffett had taken Julius Rosenwald's example to the extreme. Not only did he not put a finite life on his foundation, but he didn't create a foundation at all. He gave away for use over a period of years the vast wealth that would, in the hands of most others, have constituted the permanent endowment of their own foundations. Someone who could have sealed his reputation in history for all time as one of the world's most generous human beings chose instead to hide his great act of charity from the eyes of those who are to receive its benefits.

As this book goes to press, it is far too soon to say with confidence what the wider ramifications of Buffett's generosity will be. What one can say at this point is that his action riveted the attention of a good part of the world. In the weeks following his June 25, 2006, announcement, leading newspapers and magazines that had only occasionally given coverage to foundations and philanthropic giving were publishing several stories a week on one or another aspect of the subject. In some weeks, the *Wall*

Street Journal published such articles almost every day, often on page one. Two months later, press attention to philanthropy remains much higher than it has been in recent years.

There are signs that suggest that others may be influenced by what Buffett has done. Perhaps it was Buffett's action that triggered the Google and Branson decisions mentioned above.

A hopeful, perhaps even envious, anticipation pervades many private foundations that other wealthy individuals will follow Buffett's example and give *them* assets to deploy. Some are retraining existing staff members or recruiting fund-raisers for the first time to try to draw contributions from others. For several years, both the Ford Foundation and the Pew Charitable Trusts have explored the possibility of persuading wealthy individuals to give them charitable dollars to spend in their behalf. Ford has done little along these lines, but when Pew converted from a private foundation to a public charity in 2004, it began trying to attract funds from others in earnest. Now, in Buffett's wake, it has launched a search for a senior officer in the Donor Services Unit, who will lead a team of five persons dedicated to soliciting funds—which is a first for a private foundation-like institution. If Pew succeeds in that effort, other existing private foundations will surely follow suit. Moreover, if existing foundations succeed in raising money from others, their doing so will leave a happy by-product. It will force them to practice a much higher level of accountability. Those who give other people's foundations their philanthropic dollars to spend will insist on some detailed accounting of what is being accomplished with their dollars. Not only would that be a very good thing in its own right, but it will create spillovers in accountability practices with respect to foundations' own spending.

Of course, not all philanthropists will overcome the desire to control the distribution of their wealth by building their own foundation to memorialize themselves and their families in the eyes of history. Some will do so, but most with the greatest accumulated wealth will not. And, as much as I admire Warren Buffett's action and as great as my regard is for the Bill and Melinda Gates Foundation, I cannot deplore that likely outcome. I believe that the more hands that control the pools of philanthropic dollars, the greater the diversity of the recipients of those dollars. It is the varying values of donors that determine what their foundations decide to do, and the more individual foundations there are, the wider the spread of foundation focuses there will be, to the benefit of our polyarchical civic sector.

It seems likely to me, however, that Buffett's example may indeed increase the flow of charitable dollars to community foundations and donor-advised funds in financial institutions, but that fashion of imitating Buffett does not reduce the vibrancy of our polyarchy. Donor-advised funds *are* deployed according to the values of their creators, and community foundations have done a great deal to empower the diversity of views and interests of society's variety of stakeholders in communities all over the nation.

Whether or not Buffett's example will prompt individuals to give their philanthropic dollars to others' foundations to deploy, there are already signs that it has prompted some foundations to consider engaging more frequently in partnerships with other foundations. In September 2006, the Rockefeller and Gates foundations announced the establishment of the Alliance for a Green Revolution in Africa, which they described as a "strategic partnership" between the two foundations. That is the first time I have seen two foundations describe a joint initiative in that way, and certainly echoes what for-profit corporations have been doing with ever-greater momentum in recent years. The first initiative of that strategic partnership will be a Program for Africa's Seed System, to which Rockefeller and Gates have committed $50 million and $100 million respectively. Such a partnership between Rockefeller and Gates makes great good sense. The Rockefeller Foundation has rich experience and an impressive track record in bringing about the Green Revolution documented in this book, which was all about developing better food grains, and the Gates Foundation needs knowledgeable partners to help it spend the $3.5 billion it will have to spend each year starting in 2009. Perhaps that precedent will help make it easier for existing foundations to leverage one another's strengths and assets than has been the case up to now.

While no one can be confident of how Buffett's example will shape philanthropy in the twenty-first century, I am reasonably certain of the following.

1. America's charitable giving will increase greatly in this century.

There are widely varying estimates of the likely size of the so-called intergenerational wealth transfer, but few deny that a huge wealth transfer will occur over the fifty-five years between 1998 and 2052. It is a matter of common sense that the extraordinary accumulation of wealth toward the end of the last century and the beginning of this one *must* go somewhere when its generators pass on, so the main issue is how much there will be. The estimates of the magnitude of such transfer, which will normally take place by bequest but also by giving during life, range from $136 trillion at the high end down to $10 trillion at the low end, depending on which of the U.S. economy's growth rates one assumes and how one defines the relevant group of present wealth owners. The most frequently cited figure of $41 trillion is that of Boston College's Center on Wealth and Philanthropy and is based on a 2 percent annual growth rate in the economy, and one should note that that figure is the center's *low-end* estimate.[16]

If existing bequest and lifetime-giving patterns hold for the future, and there is little reason to think that they will do anything but go up, the charitable share of such wealth is likely to be in the range of from 10 percent to 15 percent. If the total fifty-five-year transfer proves to be forty-one trillion dollars, the charitable share should end up between four trillion and six trillion dollars. Even if the lowest of the estimates of the overall wealth transfer—ten trillion dollars—proved correct, the charitable share should be between one trillion and one and a half trillion dollars. To put that figure in context, keep in mind that the most recent IRS figures on the total annual expenditures of charities that file the 990 and 990-PF forms show about one trillion dollars being spent. (That does not include expenditures by religious congregations that do not have to report, and in fact don't report.)

So even the lowest-end charitable wealth transfer would equal or exceed the current amount being spent by nonprofits if it were given to be spent. On the other hand, if a sizable amount of the charitable part of the transfer were given to be placed in endowment, which is likely, the addition to assets would be a significant increment over current total assets of nonprofits, including foundations, which, according to the IRS, are about one and one-half trillion dollars at present. If, as I suspect, the higher wealth transfer estimates prove accurate, the infusion of new wealth into foundations and nonprofits could quadruple or sextuple current spending, assets, or both. Even spread over fifty-five years, that would be an enormous increase.

In a single geographical area, the charitable infusion could make an enormous difference. The Boston College Center, using the national $41 trillion estimate calculated the likely wealth transfer for the Washington, DC, area, and concluded that $2.4 trillion would be transferred from one generation to the next in that region, with $460 billion going to area charities.

In short, it does appear that America is in for a golden age of philanthropy. What better launch could it have had than Buffett's bombshell?

2. Philanthropy will continue the evolution and diversification we have seen in form over the past century.

The evolution in forms of charitable giving has been driven by donors' desires to use philanthropic dollars in new and dynamic ways. Just as businesses have radically evolved in the last century in their methods of creating and selling goods and services, as well as in their ways of organizing for-profit endeavor, new forms and strategies for philanthropy have also evolved.

That evolution in form is bound to continue in shapes that we cannot begin to fathom at this point. It has already accelerated markedly just in 2006, as noted above. It will surely result in many related but varying vehicles that will be used for charitable giving. I have no doubt, therefore, that the twenty-first century will be another century of philanthropic diversification.

3. Venture philanthropy and social entrepreneurship will gradually come to dominate philanthropy in this century.

Venture philanthropy and social entrepreneurship will increasingly shape not only the way philanthropy is organized, in the United States as well as in other wealthy countries, but also the ways foundations carry out their grantmaking. It is not only the newly wealthy, recent creators of foundations, who are venture capitalists and new venture creators, who think of themselves as venture philanthropists. Increasingly, long-established foundations will evolve in that direction not only because their boards will increasingly be peopled with today's wealth creators, but also because it is steadily becoming obvious that charitable dollars disbursed by the methods and practices of venture philanthropy and social entrepreneurship significantly overachieve in impact the dollars spent the old-fashioned way.

What is powering that direction of evolution? Two major drives.

First is the widespread emergence of a powerful new social conscience among many of the suddenly fabulously rich young and no-longer-so-young business founders of today, and their determination not to sit on the sidelines. They are determined, while they are still alive and kicking, to make a difference with today's problems.

The second is related to the first. They bring the same focus on results that earned them the wealth on which all foundations, not only the new ones, were created: a focus on measurable results. As Intel's Gordon Moore noted, foundations, especially the recently created ones, are witnessing "a huge push toward measurability."[17] That same focus on measuring results has already made significant inroads among some of the long-standing foundations.

What could possibly be more beneficial for the entire world than a powerful passion to do good for others, a relentless determination to do it well, and a keen sense of responsibility to make oneself continually accountable for achieving one's goals?

I *am* convinced that Warren Buffett has inspired a whole new explosion in the world of philanthropy. As this Epilogue makes clear, he didn't start the change; it was under way for at least two decades before he announced his gift. Nor, I think, will the way he chose to shape his gift significantly influence donors who follow after him. What he has done, however, is to expand the horizons of wealthy individuals in both America and elsewhere by proving that one *can*, if one wills, give away mountains of hard-earned money to benefit others. By planting that seed in the minds of millions, Warren Buffett may well succeed over the long run in benefiting many more human beings than those whose lives will be improved by his own billions. And *that* would indeed be a consummation devoutly to be wished.

APPENDIX I

LIST OF THOSE INTERVIEWED

Name	Title	Affiliation	Interview Date
Adams, John	Founding Director and Former President	Natural Resources Defense Council	10/28/2004
Alberding, Ellen	President	Joyce Foundation	03/11/2004
Altman, Drew	President	Kaiser Family Foundation	01/07/2004, 10/28/2004
Ames, Edward	President	Mary Flagler Cary Charitable Trust	04/28/2004
Armbruster, Timothy	President	Goldseker Foundation	07/29/2004
Bacchetti, Ray	Former Program Officer	Hewlett Foundation	01/08/2004
Bailin, Michael	Former President	Edna McConnell Clark Foundation	10/28/2004
Bergholz, David	Former President	George Gund Foundation	06/11/2004
Berkeley, Seth	President	International AIDS Vaccines Initiative	12/10/2003
Berresford, Susan	President	Ford Foundation	06/14/2004

LIST OF THOSE INTERVIEWED, *cont.*

Name	Title	Affiliation	Interview Date
Blendon, Robert	Former Vice President	Robert Wood Johnson Foundation	07/19/2004
Blumenthal, David	Director of Health Policy	Mass. General Hospital	07/27/2004
Bowen, William	President	Andrew W. Mellon Foundation	12/08/2003
Bradach, Jeff	President and CEO	Bridgespan Group Group	10/27/2003, 11/11/2004, 02/05/2005
—with Samantha Levine			3/04/2004
Brest, Paul	President	Hewlett Foundation	12/07/2004
Carson, Emmett	President	Minneapolis Foundation	06/23/2004
Casper, Gerhard	President Emeritus	Stanford University	01/06/2004
Collins, Dennis	Former President	Irvine Foundation	01/05/2004
Conway, Gordon	President	Rockefeller Foundation	11/11/2003
Covert, Angela	Former Director of Children and Youth Program	Atlantic Philanthropies	09/10/2004
Craig, John	Executive Vice President	Commonwealth Fund	02/23/2004, 05/20/2004
Crane, Robert	President	Jeht Foundation	11/01/2004

LIST OF THOSE INTERVIEWED, *cont.*

Name	*Title*	*Affiliation*	*Interview Date*
Dahl, Michael	Director of Evaluation and Research	Pew Charitable Trusts	10/14/2003
Dale, Harvey	Former CEO	Atlantic Philanthropies	02/02/2004
Damon, William	Professor of Psychology and Education	Stanford University	07/18/2004
Davis, Karen	President	Commonwealth Fund	01/26/2004
DeVita, Christine	President and CEO	Wallace Foundation	11/12/2003, 12/09/2003
Evans, Eli	Former President	Charles Revson Foundation	04/26/2004
Fanton, Jonathan	President and CEO	MacArthur Foundation	03/10/2004
Feldstein, Lewis	President and CEO	New Hampshire Charitable Foundation	06/24/2004
Feldstein, Martin	President and CEO	National Bureau of Economic Research	10/21/2004
Finn, Chester	President	Fordham Foundation	09/29/2004
Fried, Arthur	President	Avi Chai and Keren Keshet Foundations	09/09/2003, 11/10/2003, 09/12/2004, 05/19/2005
Gaberman, Barry	Deputy President	Ford Foundation	02/02/2004

LIST OF THOSE INTERVIEWED, *cont.*

Name	Title	Affiliation	Interview Date
Gardner, Howard	Professor of Education	Harvard University	07/18/2004
Ginsburg, Paul	President	Center for Studying Health System Change	07/30/2004
Goldmark, Peter	Former President	Rockefeller Foundation	12/11/2003
Gomory, Ralph	President and CEO	Ford Foundation	05/28/2004
Graham, Patricia	Former President	Spencer Foundation	10/25/2004
Gray, Hanna	Former President	University of Chicago	05/11/2004
Gregorian, Vartan	President and CEO	Carnegie Corp. of NY	12/10/2003
Grogan, Paul	President	Boston Foundation	10/10/2003
Gueron, Judith	Former President	Manpower Development Research Corp.	12/03/2003, 01/30/2004, 04/26/2004
Harrison, Andrew	Archivist	Robert Wood Johnson Foundation	09/17/2003
Healy, John	President and CEO	Atlantic Philanthropies	05/28/2004
Hennessy, John	President	Stanford University	01/07/2004
Hoxby, Caroline	Professor of Economics	Harvard University	11/04/2004

LIST OF THOSE INTERVIEWED, *cont.*

Name	*Title*	*Affiliation*	*Interview Date*
Joyce, Michael	Former President	Bradley Foundation	07/27/2004
Karel, Frank	Former Vice President	Robert Wood Johnson Foundation	05/19/2004
Katz, Stanley	Professor of Public Policy	Princeton University	09/17/2003
Kennedy, Craig	President	German Marshall Fund of the U.S.	05/20/2004
Knickman, James	Vice President for Research and Evaluation	Robert Wood Johnson Foundation	09/17/2003
Kreamer, Jan	President	Greater Kansas City Community Foundation	07/01/2004
Krupp, Fred	President and CEO	Environmental Defense Fund	02/20/2004
Lagemann, Ellen	Dean	Harvard Graduate School of Education	07/28/2003
Lambeth, Tom	Former Executive Director	Z. Smith Reynolds Foundation	07/13/2004
Larson, Carol	President	David and Lucile Packard Foundation	10/18/2004
Lindblom, Lance	President	Nathan Cummings Foundation	04/05/2004, 06/01/2004

List of Those Interviewed, *cont.*

Name	*Title*	*Affiliation*	*Interview Date*
Locke, Elizabeth	Former President	Duke Endowment	07/14/2004
Lyman, Richard	Former President	Rockefeller Foundation	01/09/2004
Mahoney, Margaret	Former President	Commonwealth Fund	09/22/2003, 12/11/2003, 01/30/2004
Mathews, Jessica	President	Carnegie Endowment for International Peace	06/29/2004
McGee, Vincent	Former President	Aaron Diamond Foundation	05/28/2004
McCormick, Elizabeth	Philanthropic Advisor	Rockefeller Family Office	07/22/2004
McGinnis, Michael	Former Senior Vice President	Robert Wood Johnson Foundation	07/16/2003 —Discussed research plan; September 15–16, 2003 —Interview
McKaughan, Molly	Program Staff	Robert Wood Johnson Foundation	09/17/2003
McPherson, Michael	President	Spencer Foundation	05/10/2004, 06/09/2004
McTier, Charles	President	Robert Woodruff Foundation	06/30/2004
Meyerson, Adam	President	Philanthropy Roundtable	07/30/2004

LIST OF THOSE INTERVIEWED, *cont.*

Name	Title	Affiliation	Interview Date
Miller, Arjay	Former Trustee	William and Flora Hewlett Foundation	01/08/2004
Minter, Steven	Former President	Cleveland Foundation	06/11/2004
Mnookin, Robert	Professor of Law	Harvard University	06/08/2004
Moock, Joyce	Program Officer	Rockefeller Foundation	06/01/2004
Moore, Mark	Professor and Faculty Chair, Hauser Center	Kennedy School of Government, Harvard Univ.	11/19/2003
Morrisett, Lloyd	Former President	Markle Foundation	02/19/2004
Morse, David	Vice President for Communications	Robert Wood Johnson Foundation	09/17/2003
Munitz, Barry	Former President and CEO	Getty Trust	02/26/2004
Neier, Aryeh	President and CEO	Open Society Institute	06/28/2004
Nelson, Douglas	President	Annie E. Casey Foundation	07/29/2004
Pauly, Ed	Vice President for Research and Evaluation	Wallace Foundation	12/09/2003
Piereson, Jim	President	John Olin Foundation	06/28/2004

LIST OF THOSE INTERVIEWED, *cont.*

Name	Title	Affiliation	Interview Date
Posner, Michael	President	Human Rights Watch	02/20/2004
Prewitt, Ken	Former Senior Vice President	Rockefeller Foundation	11/11/2003
Randel, Don	President	University of Chicago	03/11/2004
Reischauer, Robert	President	Urban Institute	05/19/2004
Richardson, William	President	Kellogg Foundation	03/08/2004
Richman, Harold	Director	Chapin Hall Center for Children, University of Chicago	03/10/2004
Rimel, Rebecca	President and CEO	Pew Charitable Trusts	10/14/2003
Robinson, Russell	Board Chair	Duke Endowment	06/18/2004
Romero, Anthony	President	American Civil Liberties Union	05/12/2004
Roth, Kenneth	President	Human Rights Watch	04/02/2004
Schlosberg, Richard	Former President	David and Lucile Packard Foundation	01/07/2004
Schroeder, Steven	Former President	Robert Wood Johnson Foundation	01/09/2004

LIST OF THOSE INTERVIEWED, *cont.*

Name	Title	Affiliation	Interview Date
Semans, Mary D.B.T.	Former Board Chair	Duke Endowment	07/28/2004
Shulman, Lee	President	Carnegie Foundation for the Advancement of Teaching	01/08/2004
Siegel, Bernard	President	Harry and Jeannette Weinberg Foundation	07/29/2004
Simmons, Hildy	Former Managing Director	JP Morgan Philanthropic Office	11/10/2003
Simon, John	Board Chair	Taconic Foundation	06/16/2004
Singer, Arthur L., Jr.	Former Program Officer	Alfred P. Sloan Foundation	02/22/2004
Skloot, Ed	Executive Director	Surdna Foundation	05/24/2004
Slutsky, Lorie	President	New York Community Trust	12/08/2003
Solow, Robert	Professor of Economics	Massachusetts Institute of Technology	02/19/2004
Spero, Joan	President and CEO	Doris Duke Charitable Foundation	12/08/2003
Stewart, Donald	President and CEO	Chicago Community Trust	03/11/2004

LIST OF THOSE INTERVIEWED, *cont.*

Name	Title	Affiliation	Interview Date
Stone, Christopher	Former President	Vera Institute	03/09/2004
Sturz, Herbert	Trustee	Open Society Institute	09/06/2004
Toben, Stephen	President	Flora Fund	01/05/2004
Verrett, Paul	President	St. Paul Foundation	06/23/2004
Wanner, Eric	President	Russell Sage Foundation	03/08/2004
Wood, J. Warren	Sr. Vice President and General Counsel	Robert Wood Johnson Foundation	09/17/2003
Woodruff, Charles	President	Robert Woodruff Foundation	06/30/2004

APPENDIX II

List of Cases

1. Rockefeller University (formerly the Rockefeller Institute for Medical Research), 1901
2. General Education Board Support for Public High Schools, Rockefeller Foundation, 1902
3. The Transformation of American Medical Education: The Flexner Report, Carnegie Foundation for the Advancement of Teaching, 1906
4. Curing and Preventing Disease and Promoting Public Health, Rockefeller Foundation, 1909
5. Carnegie Public Libraries for America's Communities, Andrew Carnegie and the Carnegie Corporation of New York, 1911
6. Learning to Understand the Problems Faced by Cleveland: America's First Community Foundation, Cleveland Foundation, 1915
7. The Development of Insulin to Treat Diabetes, Carnegie Corporation, 1916
8. Providing Scientific Knowledge to Solve Public Problems: National Research Council, Carnegie Corporation, 1917
9. Pensions for America's Educators: TIAA-CREF, One of the Wealthiest Pension Funds in the World, Carnegie Foundation for the Advancement of Teaching, 1918
10. Building Schools for Rural African Americans, Rosenwald Fund, 1920
11. Economic Policy Research of the Highest Quality: National Bureau of Economic Research, Carnegie Corporation, 1921
12. Reforming the Legal Profession through Education and Practice, Carnegie Foundation for the Advancement of Teaching, 1921
13. The Rural Hospitals Program of the Commonwealth Fund, 1927
14. Mount Palomar "Hale" Telescope, Rockefeller Foundation, 1928
15. The Development of Molecular Biology and the Discovery of the Structure of DNA, Rockefeller Foundation, 1933

16. Predecessor to Blue Cross and Blue Shield of North Carolina, Duke Endowment, 1935

17. Transforming America's Perceptions of Relations Among its Races: Gunnar Myrdal's *An American Dilemma*, Carnegie Corporation, 1936

18. Support for the Development of the Pap Smear Test, Commonwealth Fund, 1941

19. Lasker Foundation Support of the National Institutes of Health, Albert and Mary Lasker Foundation, 1942

20. The Green Revolution, Rockefeller Foundation, Ford Foundation, 1943

21. The Rochester Regional Hospital Council, Commonwealth Fund, 1946

22. Institution Building for Evidence-Based Public Policy, Ford Foundation, 1948

23. Preventing Crashes on America's Highways, Dorr Foundation, 1952

24. Curbing Global Population Growth: Rockefeller's Population Council, Rockefeller Foundation, 1952

25. Facilitating Global Knowledge Creation: University Area Studies Programs, Ford Foundation, 1952

26. Howard Hughes Medical Institute, 1953

27. Program to Strengthen Business Education, Ford Foundation, 1954

28. Financing Higher Education for America's Talented Students: National Merit Scholarship Corporation, Ford Foundation, Carnegie Corporation, 1955

29. Vera Institute of Justice: Manhattan Bail Project, Ford Foundation, 1962

30. Measuring American Education Reform: National Assessment of Educational Progress, Carnegie Corporation, 1964

31. The Development of the Nurse Practitioner and Physician Assistant Professions, Commonwealth Fund, Robert Wood Johnson Foundation, Carnegie Corporation, 1965

32. America's System of Public Broadcasting and Public Radio, Carnegie Corporation, 1965

33. Bedford-Stuyvesant and the Rise of the Community Development Corporation, Ford Foundation, 1966

34. Children's Television Workshop and *Sesame Street*, Ford Foundation, Carnegie Corporation, 1966

35. Federal College Scholarships for America's Needy Students, Carnegie Corporation, 1967

36. Social Movements and Civil Rights Litigation, Ford Foundation, 1967

37. The Police Foundation, Ford Foundation, 1969

38. The Robert Wood Johnson Clinical Scholars Program, 1969

39. Environmental Public Interest Law Centers, Ford Foundation, 1970

40. The National Prison Project of the American Civil Liberties Union, Edna McConnell Clark Foundation, 1972

41. Programs to Enhance the Rights and Opportunities of Women, Ford Foundation, 1972
42. The Emergency Medical Services Program of the Robert Wood Johnson Foundation, 1973
43. Hospice Care Movement, Commonwealth Fund, 1974
44. The Tropical Disease Program of the Edna McConnell Clark Foundation, 1974
45. Manpower Demonstration Research Corporation, Ford Foundation, 1974
46. Conservative Legal Advocacy, Olin Foundation, 1975
47. Grameen Bank, Ford Foundation, 1976
48. Monterey Bay Aquarium and Research Institute, David and Lucile Packard Foundation, 1977
49. Human Rights and the International Criminal Court, John D. and Catherine T. MacArthur Foundation, Ford Foundation, Open Society Institute, 1978
50. The Nurse-Family Partnership, Robert Wood Johnson Foundation, 1978
51. Revolutionizing Legal Discourse: Law and Economics, John M. Olin Foundation, 1978
52. Local Initiatives Support Corporation (LISC), Ford Foundation, 1979
53. Support of Democratization and Civil Societies in Central and Eastern Europe, Open Society Institute, Soros Foundation Network, 1980
54. MacArthur Fellows Program, John D. and Catherine T. MacArthur Foundation, 1981
55. The Enterprise Foundation, Surdna Foundation, 1982
56. Self-Help, Ford Foundation, et al., 1984
57. Conflict Resolution Program, Hewlett Foundation, 1984
58. The Health Care for the Homeless Program, Robert Wood Johnson Foundation, Pew Charitable Trusts, 1985
59. Certifying America's Teachers' Competence in the Subjects They Teach, Carnegie Corporation, 1985
60. Cleaning Up Boston's Harbor and Waterfront, Boston Foundation, 1986
61. Biodiversity Protection, John D. and Catherine T. MacArthur Foundation, 1986
62. School Choice: Vouchers in Milwaukee, Bradley Foundation, Joyce Foundation, 1986
63. The Aaron Diamond AIDS Research Center, Aaron Diamond Foundation, 1987
64. Clare Boothe Luce Program, Henry R. Luce Foundation, 1987
65. Balancing the Power in College Sports, Knight Foundation, 1989
66. Goldman Environmental Prize, Richard and Rhoda Goldman Environmental Foundation, 1989

67. Cooperative Security and the Nunn-Lugar Act, John D. and Catherine T. MacArthur Foundation, Carnegie Corporation, 1989
68. Care at the End of Life: Programs of the Robert Wood Johnson Foundation and the Open Society Institute, 1989 and 1994
69. New Standards Project, Pew Charitable Trusts and John D. and Catherine T. MacArthur Foundation, 1990
70. Sustainable Environment Programs, Pew Charitable Trusts, 1990
71. KIDS COUNT, Annie E. Casey Foundation, 1991
72. The Transformation of the Kaiser Family Foundation, Henry J. Kaiser Family Foundation, 1991
73. The Energy Foundation, MacArthur, Pew, Rockefeller, Hewlett, Packard, and McKnight foundations, 1991
74. Central European University, Open Society Institute, 1991
75. Living Cities, National Community Development Initiative, 1991
76. The Tobacco Use Programs of the Robert Wood Johnson Foundation, 1991
77. Charter Schools Funding, Walton Family Foundation, 1991
78. JSTOR, Andrew W. Mellon Foundation, 1992
79. International Science Foundation, Soros Foundations/Open Society Institute, 1992
80. Support for Asian Studies and Cultural Exchange, Freeman Foundation, 1993
81. The Prostate Cancer Foundation, 1993
82. Paul B. Beeson Career Development Awards in Aging Research Program, Commonwealth Fund, Hartford Foundation, Atlantic Philanthropies, and the Starr Foundation, 1994
83. Picker Institute, Commonwealth Fund, 1994
84. College and Beyond Database, Andrew W. Mellon Foundation, 1994
85. National Violent Death Reporting System, Joyce Foundation, 1994
86. National Urban Reconstruction and Housing Agency (NURCHA), Open Society Institute, 1995
87. Pew Research Center for the People and the Press, Pew Charitable Trusts, 1995
88. Sloan Digital Sky Survey, Alfred P. Sloan Foundation, 1995
89. Computational Molecular Biology, Alfred P. Sloan Foundation, 1995
90. Grantmakers for Effective Organizations, David and Lucile Packard Foundation, 1996
91. United Nations Arrears Campaign, United Nations Foundation/Better World Fund, 1997
92. Youth Development Program, Edna McConnell Clark Foundation, 1999
93. The Plan for Transformation of Public Housing in Chicago, John D. and Catherine T. MacArthur Foundation, 1999

94. China Sustainable Energy Program, David and Lucile Packard Foundation and the William and Flora Hewlett Foundation, 1999
95. Smart Growth Initiative, Surdna Foundation, et al., 1999
96. International Fellowships Program, Ford Foundation, 2000
97. Sustainable Development in the Great Bear Rainforest, David and Lucile Packard Foundation, Rockefeller Brothers Fund, et al., 2000
98. Talented Students in the Arts Initiative, Surdna Foundation and Doris Duke Charitable Foundation, 2000
99. A Model for the New Inner-City School: KIPP Academies, Pisces Foundation, 2000
100. Connecting for Health: A Public-Private Collaborative, John and Mary R. Markle Foundation, 2002

NOTES

Preface

1. Carol J. Loomis, "A Conversation with Warren Buffett," *Fortune,* June 25, 2006.
2. I think that, for the reasons given about music, the same is true for drama, poetry, and the novel, but will leave speculation about that to another book.
3. Recent books on foundations that are particularly good are the following: Marion Fremont-Smith, *Governing Nonprofit Organizations: Federal and State Law and Regulation* (Cambridge: Harvard University Press, 2004); Ellen Condliffe Lagemann, *The Politics of Knowledge: The Carnegie Corporation, Philanthropy, and Public Policy* (Middletown, CT: Wesleyan University Press, 1989); Lagemann, *Private Power for the Public Good: A History of the Carniege Foundation for the Advancement of Teaching* (Middletown, CT: Wesleyan University Press, 1983); Stephen C. Wheatley, *The Politics of Philanthropy: Abraham Flexner and Medical Education* (Madison: University of Wisconsin Press, 1988); and Gerald Freund, *Narcissism and Philanthropy: Ideas and Talent Denied* (New York: Viking, 1996. Warren Weaver's *U.S. Philanthropic Foundations; Their History, Structure, Management, and Record* (New York: Viking, 1967) is an older book that has stood the test of time.
4. From 1993–2000, I was president of the Atlantic Philanthropic Service Company, which served as the program staff in the United States for Atlantic Philanthropies, a worldwide foundation whose president was Harvey P. Dale. Atlantic Philanthropic Service Company formulated philanthropic program strategies within the geographical areas for which it was responsible and recommended to Atlantic Philanthropies grants pursuant to those strategies.

Part One

1. Arthur W. Fried, interview with the author, November 10, 2003.

2. See "Certifying America's Teachers' Competence in the Subjects They Teach," case #54.

3. See "Institution Building for Evidence-Based Public Policy," case #22.

4. See "Manpower Demonstration Research Corporation," case #45.

5. Alexis de Tocqueville, *Democracy in America*, J. P. Mayer and M. Lerner, eds., George Lawrence, trans. (New York: Harper and Row, 1966).

6. Figures from 2005. The $260 billion total includes $199 billion in contributions by living individuals and another $60 billion from foundations, corporations, and bequests. *Giving USA 2006*, a publication of Giving USA Foundation, researched and written by the Center on Philanthropy at Indiana University, 11.

7. There seems to be no dispute about calling government at all levels the "public sector." In addition, most people refer to the corporate sector as the "private sector," which is too imperial a misnomer if there ever was one. Calling the "for-profit sector" the "private sector" explicitly claims that it is the one and only "private sector," when nothing could be further from the truth. Whatever we choose to call it, the "non-profit sector" is every bit as private and voluntary in character as the for-profit sector.

8. Tocqueville, *Democracy in America*.

9. *Giving USA 2005*, 58. Note that about one million are the formally registered charitable organizations, and the other half-million the registered non-charitable nonprofits. Note, too, that there are studies that find considerably more nonprofits functioning at the state levels than are registered at the federal level.

10. See Paul Arnsberger, "Charities and Other Tax-Exempt Organizations, 2001," Internal Revenue Service, Statistics of Income, http://www.irs.gov/pub/irs-soi/01eochin.pdf.

11. See "Volunteering in the United States, 2005," Bureau of Labor Statistics, 2005, http://www.bls.gov/rofod/1480.pdf.

12. See "Value of Volunteer Time," Independent Sector, 2005, http://www.independentsector.org/programs/research/volunteer_time.html.

13. *Giving USA 2006*, 14.

14. Figures for 2005. *Giving USA 2006*, 18, 33.

15. John W. Gardner, *Living, Leading, and the American Dream*. Francesca Gardner, ed. (San Francisco: Jossey-Bass, 2003), 206.

16. "Creative Destruction," in Joseph A. Schumpeter, *Capitalism, Socialism and Democracy* (New York: Harper, 1975), 82–85.

17. Brian O'Connell, *America's Voluntary Spirit: A Book of Readings* (New York: Foundation Center, 1983), 1.

18. Max Stackhouse, "Religion and the Social Space for Voluntary Institutions," in *Faith and Philanthropy in America*, Robert Wuthnow and Virginia Ann Hodgkinson (San Francisco: Jossey-Bass, 1990), 25.

19. Cf. Robert Putnam, *Bowling Alone: The Collapse and Revival of the American Community* (New York: Simon & Schuster, 2000). Professor Putnam's seminal work in defining and popularizing "social capital" has been a major contribution to our understanding of the civil sector.

20. David C. Hammack, "Foundations in the American Polity, 1900–1950," in *Philanthropic Foundations: New Scholarship, New Possibilities*, Ellen Condliffe Lagemann, ed. (Bloomington and Indianapolis: Indiana University Press, 1999), 52.

21. Paul C. Light, *Government's Greatest Achievements: From Civil Rights to Homeland Security* (Washington, DC: Brookings Institution Press, 2002); Paul C. Light, *Sustaining Nonprofit Performance: The Case for Capacity Building and the Evidence to Support It* (Washington, DC: Brookings Institution Press, 2004).

22. Ibid., 13.

23. See Shailagh Murray and Paul Farhi, "House Vote Spares Public Broadcasting Funds," *Washington Post*, June 24, 2005, A6.

24. The smaller figure is from *Giving USA 2006*, the larger from the Foundation Center, *Foundation Yearbook: Facts and Figures on Private and Community Foundations* (New York: The Foundation Center, 2006).

25. Peter Frumkin, *Strategic Giving: The Art and Science of Philanthropy* (Chicago: University of Chicago Press, 2006).

26. Case #90, Grantmakers for Effective Organizations. See www.geofunders.org. See also Paul C. Light, *Sustaining Nonprofit Performance: The Case for Capacity Building and the Evidence to Support It* (Washington, DC: Brookings Institution Press, 2004).

27. *Giving USA 2006*. See also Foundation Center, "Highlights of Foundation Yearbook, 2006 Edition," http://www.fdncenter.org/research/trends_analysis/pdf/fyhiltes05.pdf.

28. "Highlights of Foundation Yearbook, 2006 Edition," *Foundation Center*, 2006, http://foundationcenter.org/gainknowledge/research/pdf/fy2006highlights.pdf.

29. Ibid.

30. See Edwin Black, *War Against the Weak: Eugenics and America's Campaign to Create a Master Race* (New York: Four Walls Eight Windows, 2003). Black's book is intemperate and inflammatory but offers a valuable account of the excesses of the eugenics movement.

31. Robert Bremner, *American Philanthropy* (Chicago: University of Chicago Press, 1988), 2.

32. See *Giving USA 2006*, 107.

33. Peter Krass, *Carnegie* (New York: John Wiley & Sons, 2002), 247–48; Ron Chernow, *Titan: The Life of John D. Rockefeller, Sr.* (New York: Random House, 1998), 314.

34. Chernow, *Titan*, 306.

35. The lengthy restraint-of-trade trial against Microsoft commenced on October 19, 1998. Rajiv Chandrasekaran, "Microsoft Trial Set To Open," *Washington Post*, October 19, 1998, A1. The creation of the Bill and Melinda Gates Foundation, the result of a merger of two earlier Gates Foundations and instantly the largest foundation in the United States, occurred in August, 1999. Helen Jung, "Gates Merger Forms Charity Colossus," *Seattle Times*, August 23, 1999, B1.

36. See Chapter 13.

37. Richard I. Kirkland Jr., "Should You Leave It All to the Children?" *Fortune*, September 29, 1986, 18.

38. Krass, *Carnegie*, 471, 501; Chernow, *Titan*, 302.

39. Chernow, *Titan*, 321.

40. F. Emerson Andrews, *Philanthropic Foundations* (New York: Russell Sage Foundation, 1956), 70.

41. Chernow, *Titan*, 563.

42. Chernow, *Titan*, 564.

43. From comments on my manuscript by Professor Harvey P. Dale, Director, National Center for Philanthropy and Law, New York University, January 9, 2006.

44. Krass, *Carnegie*, 277–303; Chernow, *Titan*, 571–90.

45. Clayton M. Christensen, *The Innovator's Dilemma: When New Technologies Cause Great Firms to Fail* (Boston: Harvard Business School Press, 1997).

46. Current dollar estimates of the Carnegie and Rockefeller fortunes vary widely. These figures come from Krass, *Carnegie*, 538.

47. John D. Rockefeller Sr., *Random Reminiscences of Men and Events* (New York: Doubleday, Page & Company, 1909), 140–41.

48. Chernow, *Titan*, 313.

49. Andrew Carnegie, "The Gospel of Wealth," reprinted in *The Responsibilities of Wealth*, Dwight F. Burlingame, ed., (Bloomington: Indiana University Press, 1992); David C. Hammack, *Making the Nonprofit Sector in the United States: A Reader* (Bloomington: Indiana University Press, 1998), 287.

50. Edward H. Berman, *The Ideology of Philanthropy: The Influence of the Carnegie, Ford and Rockefeller Foundations on American Foreign Policy* (Albany: State University of New York Press, 1983); Robert F. Arnove, *Philanthropic and Cultural Imperialism: The Foundations at Home and Abroad* (Boston: G.K. Hill, 1980); Judith Sealander, *Private Wealth and Public Life: Foundation Philanthropy and the Reshaping of American Social Policy from the Progressive Era to the New Deal* (Baltimore: Johns Hopkins University Press, 1997); Teresa Odendahl, *Charity Begins at Home: Generosity and Self-Interest Among the Philanthropic Elite* (New York: Basic Books, 1990).

51. See Danan Brakman Reiser, "Dismembering Civil Society: The Social Cost of Internally Undemocratic Nonprofits," 82, *Oregon Law Review* 829, Fall 2003, arguing that nonprofits are generally "better," meaning more democratic and accountable, if their structure empowers members to control selection of directors, than if the directors/trustees have the power of self-selection in perpetuity.

52. Resolution passed in 1914 by the Normal Department of the National Education Association. Lagemann, *Private Power*, 187.

53. See *New York Times* Staff, "I.R.S. Is Expanding Inquiry Into Charities," *New York Times*, August 11, 2004, A13, referencing an announcement by the IRS that it was ratcheting up the level of its scrutiny of foundation salaries. It announced that it was adding more than seventy new auditors for nonprofit organizations, bringing the total to three hundred. In addition, it announced that more than five hundred organizations would be subject to on-premises IRS agent presence for purposes of examining records.

54. Chernow, *Titan*, 314.

55. See Mordechai Feingold, "Philanthropy, Pomp and Patronage," *Daedalus* 116, No. 1, 1987, 155–77.

56. Kenneth Prewitt, *Social Sciences and Private Philanthropy: The Quest for Social Relevance*, Essays on Philanthropy, No. 15 (Indianapolis: Indiana University Center on Philanthropy, 1995), 13.

57. Babylonian Talmud, Avot 2:21.

58. *Giving USA 2005*, 40. In *Giving USA 2004*, 71, the percentage of bequest dollars for which a charitable deduction going to foundations was claimed was 39.7 percent in 2001, when the total bequest dollars figure was $16.51 billion; and 53.1 percent in 2002, when the total bequest dollars figure was $17.83 billion. In 2003, total giving by bequest was $21.6 billion, and the estimated percentage going to foundations is thought to be about 50 percent, or approximately $10.5 billion. In 2004, total giving by bequest was $19.8 billion. *Giving USA 2005*, 195. In 2005, total bequest giving was $17.44 billion. *Giving USA 2006*, 15.

59. These figures are based on *Giving USA 2004*, 32. In addition to the $21.44 billion reported as given to foundations in 2003, *Giving USA 2004* reports that $21.6 billion were given by bequests in 2003, but does not break out the amount of the total that went to foundations. The Joint Committee on Taxation publishes annually a report on tax expenditures, which includes an estimate of the cost to the U.S. Treasury of all deducted contributions, *not* just those to foundations, and the total cost for 2003 is shown as $36.9 billion. The Internal Revenue Service reports, in its Statistics of Income Series, that total itemized charitable contributions in 2003 amounted to $143.5 billion, and we can safely assume that all gifts to foundations were

deducted. As $21.6 billion is approximately 14 percent of $143.5 billion, we can also assume that 14 percent of the Joint Committee's estimated tax loss of $36.9 billion from all charitable deductions—or approximately $5.1 billion—are attributable to deductible contributions in 2003. See Urban Institute, Center on Nonprofits and Philanthropy, "Profiles on Individual Charitable Contributions by States, 2003," and IRS Statistics of Income, September 2005: http://www.irs.gov/pub/irs-soi/03in54cm.xls.

60. Margaret Mahoney, interview with the author, December 11, 2004.
61. Warren Weaver, *U.S. Philanthropic Foundations*, 131; Frederick Keppel, *The Foundation: Its Place in American Life* (New York: MacMillan, 1930), 56–57.
62. Weaver, *U.S Philanthropic Foundations*, 131.
63. Raymond B. Fosdick, *A Philosophy for a Foundation* (New York: Rockefeller Foundation, 1963), 20–21.
64. Virginia M. Esposito, ed., "Small Can Be Effective," *Conscience and Community: The Legacy of Paul Ylvisaker* (New York: Peter Lang, 1999), 363.
65. Andrew Carnegie, "The Gospel of Wealth," reprinted in *The Responsibilities of Wealth*, Dwight F. Burlingame, ed., (Bloomington: Indiana University Press, 1992), 26.
66. Ralph Gomory, interview with the author, May 28, 2004.
67. Tony Proscio, *In Other Words: A Plea for Plain Speaking in Foundations* (New York: Edna McConnell Clark Foundation, 2000), 20–21.
68. See, for example, Alfred P. Sloan, *My Years With General Motors* (Garden City: Doubleday, 1964).
69. Lagemann, *Politics of Knowledge*, 7–8.
70. Lee Shulman, interview with the author, January 8, 2004.
71. William Damon, interview with the author, July 18, 2004.
72. Arthur Singer, interview with the author, February 22, 2004.
73. "On Restraint in Design," New York *Herald Tribune*, June 28, 1959.
74. See Kenneth Prewitt, *Social Sciences and Private Philanthropy: The Quest for Social Relevance*, Essays on Philanthropy, No. 15 (Indianapolis: Indiana University Center on Philanthropy, 1995), 13. See "Rockefeller University (Formerly the Rockefeller Institute for Medical Research)," case #1.
75. See Andrew Rich, *Think Tanks, Public Policy and the Politics of Expertise* (New York and Cambridge: Cambridge University Press, 2004).
76. Ibid.
77. See Donald G. McNeil Jr., "New Ideas in Global Health Get a $437 Million Assist," *New York Times*, June 28, 2005, F1; Elizabeth Corcoran, "Chutzpah Science," *Forbes*, July 25, 2005, 64–65.
78. William G. Bowen and Derek Bok, *The Shape of the River* (Princeton: Princeton University Press, 2000); James L. Shulman and William G. Bowen, *The Game of Life* (Princeton: Princeton University Press, 2001).

79. Martin Bulmer and Joan Bulmer, "Philanthropy and Social Science in the 1920s," Beardsley Ruml and the Laura Spelman Rockefeller Memorial, 1922–1929. *Minerva* (col. XIX, no. 3, Autumn 1981), 375, quoted in Kenneth Prewitt, *Social Sciences and Private Philanthropy: The Quest for Social Relevance*, Essays on Philanthropy No. 15 (Indianapolis: Indiana University Center on Philanthropy, 1995), 22.

80. "What Is The Morehead?" The John Motley Morehead Foundation, http://www.moreheadfoundation.org/about/whatisit/.

81. "Claire Booth Luce Program: Description," Henry Luce Foundation, http://www.hluce.org/4cbldefm.html.

82. "Ford Foundation International Fellowships Program: Introduction and Guidelines," Ford Foundation, http://www.fordfound.org/news/more/11272000ifp/index.cfm.

83. "Sloan Research Fellowships," Alfred P. Sloan Foundation, http://www.sloan.org/programs/scitech_fellowships.shtml.

84. "About the Prostate Cancer Foundation," Prostate Cancer Foundation, http://www.prostatecancerfoundation.org/site/c.itIWK2OSG/b.46632/k.E3BA/About_PCF.htm; Cora Daniels, "The Man Who Changed Medicine," *Forbes*, November 29, 2004, 91–112.

85. "About the Violence Policy Center," Violence Policy Center, http://www.vpc.org/aboutvpc.htm.

86. "About Us," The Center for Public Integrity, http://www.publicintegrity.org/about/about.aspx.

87. Michael Posner, interview with the author, February 20, 2004.

88. "Lasker Foundation History," Lasker Foundation, http://www.laskerfoundation.org/about/history.html.

89. "United Nations Arrears Campaign," case #91.

90. Warren Wood, interview with the author, September 17, 2003.

91. Arthur Singer, interview with the author, February 22, 2004.

92. "Goldman Environmental Prize," Richard and Rhoda Goldman Fund, http://www.goldmanfund.org/about/envprize.phpx.

93. "Lasker Awards," Lasker Foundation, http://www.laskerfoundation.org/awards/awards.html.

94. "Prizes," The Kavli Foundation, http://www.kavlifoundation.org/prizes.html.

95. X Prize Foundation, "Welcome," at http://www.xprizefoundation.com. See also Michael A. Prospero, "Fuel for Thought," *Fast Company*, January/February 2006, 102.

96. "About CFE," Campaign for Fiscal Equity, http://www.cfequity.org.

97. Elizabeth Locke, interview with the author, July 14, 2004.

98. Lagemann, *The Politics of Knowledge*, 31.

99. Eli Evans, interview with the author, April 26, 2004.

100. "Public Understanding of Science and Technology," Alfred P. Sloan Foundation, http://www.sloan.org/programs/edu_public.shtml.

PART TWO

1. Lloyd Morrisett, interview with the author, February 19, 2004.

2. John Tirman, *Making the Money Sing* (Lanham, MD: Rowman and Littlefield, 2000), 4–9.

3. Judith Gueron, remarks to the Duke Foundation Impact Research Group Seminar, December 3, 2003.

4. See "The Green Revolution," case #20, "Curbing Global Population Growth: Rockefeller's Population Council," case #24, and "Programs to Enhance the Rights and Opportunities of Women," case #41.

5. See "Grantmakers for Effective Organization," case #90.

6. Peter M. Ascoli, *Julius Rosenwald: The Man who Built Sears, Roebuck and Advanced the Cause of Black Education in the American South* (Bloomington and Indianapolis: Indiana University Press, 2006). See "Building Schools for Rural African Americans," case #10, and "Carnegie Public Libraries for America's Communities," case #5.

7. Eric Wanner, interview with the author, March 8, 2004.

8. Cited by Kenneth Prewitt, interview with the author, November 11, 2003.

9. See "The Development of Molecular Biology and the Discovery of the Structure of DNA," case #15.

10. See "Social Movements and Civil Rights Litigation," case #36.

11. See "Conservative Legal Advocacy," case #46; "Revolutionizing Legal Discourse: Law and Economics," case #51; "School Choice: Vouchers in Milwaukee," case #62; and "Charter Schools Funding," case #77.

12. Ford Foundation, *Ford Foundation Grantees and the Pursuit of Justice*, available at http://www.fordfound.org/publications/recent_articles/docs/lawgrantees.pdf, 15.

13. See "Programs to Enhance the Rights and Opportunities of Women," case #41.

14. See "The Transformation of American Medical Education: The Flexner Report," case #3.

15. See "Grameen Bank," case #47.

16. Esposito, *Conscience and Community*, 363.

17. "Carnegie Millions for College Pension Fund," *New York Times*, April 28, 1905, 1.

18. Andrew Carnegie, "The Best Fields for Philanthropy," *North American Review*, 149 (1889), 691.

19. Ibid.

20. Wheatley, *Politics of Philanthropy*, 22.

21. Ibid., 14–15.

22. Ibid., 27–28.

23. Ibid., 27–28.

24. Henry Pritchett, "Introduction," in Abraham Flexner, *Medical Education in the United States and Canada* (New York City: Carnegie Foundation for the Advancement of Teaching, 1910 [Reprint 1972]), vii, available at http://www.carnegiefoundation.org/files/elibrary/flexner_report.pdf.

25. Nicholas Murray Butler, "The Carnegie Foundation as an Educational Factor," *New York Times*, September 18, 1909, 10.

26. Kenneth M. Ludmerer, *Learning to Heal* (New York: Basic Books, 1985), 170.

27. Wheatley, *Politics of Philanthropy*, 47–49.

28. "The Making of Doctors," *New York Times*, June 12, 1910, 12.

29. Flexner, *Medical Education in the United States and Canada*.

30. Wheatley, *Politics of Philanthropy*, 49.

31. Ibid., 50–51.

32. Howard J. Savage, *Fruit of an Impulse: Forty-Five Years of the Carnegie Foundation, 1905–1950.* (New York: Harcourt, Brace, 1953), 104–08.

33. Ibid.

34. Ibid.

35. Raymond B. Fosdick, *The Story of the Rockefeller Foundation* (New York: Harper & Brothers, 1952), 96.

36. Wheatley, *Politics of Philanthropy*, 83.

37. Fosdick, *Story of the Rockefeller Foundation*, 97.

38. Ibid., 99.

39. Ibid., 98.

40. Robert P. Hudson, "Abraham Flexner in Perspective: American Medical Education, 1865–1910," *Bulletin of the History of Medicine 46* (1972), 545–61.

41. Kenneth M. Ludmerer, *Learning to Heal: The Development of American Medical Education* (New York: Basic Books, 1985), 192.

42. Ibid., 180.

43. Ibid., 208.

44. Alicia S. Roberts, "Rosenwald, Julius," Learning to Give, http://www.learningtogive.com/papers/people/julius_rosenwald.html.

45. Ibid.

46. Rosenwald, Julius, "The Burden of Wealth," *Saturday Evening Post*, January 5, 1929, 136.

47. George Brown Tindall, *The Emergence of the New South, 1913–1945* (Baton Rouge: Louisiana State University Press, 1967), 271.

48. "History," The Rosenwald Schools Initiative, http://www.rosenwald-schools.com/history.html#5.

49. S. L. Smith, *Builders of Goodwill: The Story of the State Agents of Negro Education in the South, 1910 to 1950* (Nashville: Tennessee Book Company, 1950), 72–74.

50. Tindall, *The Emergence of the New South*, 271.

51. Lagemann, *The Politics of Knowledge*, 52.

52. Ibid., 53–54.

53. Ibid., 53–54.

54. Ibid., 54.

55. Ibid., 55.

56. Ibid., 56.

57. Ibid., 57.

58. Ibid., 58–59.

59. Ibid., 59.

60. Ibid., 59.

61. Ibid., 60.

62. Ibid., 61.

63. Ibid., 62.

64. Ibid., 62.

65. Ibid., 63–64.

66. Ibid., 65.

67. Ibid., 69.

68. "NBER Information," National Bureau of Economic Research, http://www.nber.org/info.html, accessed on 7/27/2004.

69. Lagemann, *Politics of Knowledge*, 124.

70. Ibid., 123.

71. Ibid., 127–29.

72. Ibid., 132–33.

73. Ibid., 134–35.

74. Ibid., 136.

75. Ibid., 139.

76. Ibid., 140.

77. Ibid., 140.

78. Ibid., 142–45.

79. Ibid., 124.

80. David W. Southern, *Gunnar Myrdal and Black-White Relations: The Use and Abuse of An American Dilemma, 1944–1969* (Baton Rouge: Louisiana State University Press, 1987), 294.

81. Jack Greenberg, *Crusaders in the Court: How a Dedicated Band of Lawyers Fought for the Civil Rights Revolution* (New York: Basic Books, 1994), 197–98.

82. *McClesky v. Kemp*, 481 U.S. 279, 303 (1987); *United Steelworkers of America v. Weber*, 443 U.S. 193, 199 (1979); *Frontiero v. Richardson*, 411 U.S. 677, 685 (1973); *Brown v. Board of Education*, 346 U.S. 483, 495 (1954); *Hughes v. Superior Court of California*, 339 U.S. 460, 463 (1950).

83. Laughlin McDonald, *A Voting Rights Odyssey: Black Enfranchisement in Georgia* (Cambridge: Cambridge University Press, 2003), 58.

84. John H. Stanfield, *Philanthropy and Jim Crow in American Social Science* (Westport: Greenwood Press, 1985), 174.

85. Ibid., 174.

86. Lagemann, *Politics of Knowledge*, 146.

87. Elizabeth Weise, "The Man Who Fed the World," *USA Today*, October 21, 2003, 9D.

88. Norman Borlaug, "Nobel Lecture: The Green Revolution, Peace, and Humanity," December 11, 1970, http://nobelprize.org/nobel_prizes/peace/laureates/1970/borlaug-lecture.html.

89. John C. Culver and John Hyde, *American Dreamer: The Life and Times of Henry A. Wallace* (New York: Norton, 2000).

90. 1962 Annual Report of the Rockefeller Foundation.

91. Gordon Conway, *The Doubly Green Revolution: Food for All in the Twentieth Century* (New York: Comstock, 1997), 47.

92. Borlaug, "Nobel Lecture."

93. Conway, *Doubly Green Revolution*, 47.

94. Borlaug, "Nobel Lecture."

95. Borlaug, "Nobel Lecture."

96. Conway, *Doubly Green Revolution*, 54.

97. Deborah Fitzgerald, "Exporting American Agriculture," in *Missionaries of Science: The Rockefeller Foundation and Latin America*, Marcos Cueto, ed. (Bloomington: Indiana University Press, 1994), 72.

98. Furthermore, Fitzgerald argues, the Americans had not done enough to bring small farmers in at the planning stages of the MAP. Therefore, tactics to promote widespread adoption of new practices were initially geared toward a farming community, like that of the United States, which was based on the land-grant system.

99. It was important to develop crops that could flourish regardless of the length of the days, because such crops would grow in dissimilar regions of the world and could be planted twice a year, thereby doubling the potential yield per hectare.

100. Dwarf wheat has two major advantages over taller varieties. First, wheat evolved to compete for sunlight (that is, to grow very tall) and has a tendency to fall down once it is laden too heavily with kernels. Second, shorter wheat hybrids do not expend as much energy growing inedible stalks, so they are more efficient producers of grain.

101. William Paddock and Paul Paddock, *Famine—1975! America's Decision: Who Will Survive?* (Boston: Little, Brown, 1967).

102. The Paddocks do acknowledge the advances that had theretofore been made by Dr. Borlaug and the Rockefeller Foundation. However, they argue that the spread of new agricultural technologies, like Mexican dwarf wheat, will be limited by the availability of qualified scientific personnel to adapt them to new (especially tropical) environments. Ultimately, they conclude that, "The population-food collision is inevitable: It is foredoomed."

103. Ambassador David C. Mulford, "U.S.-India Partnership: Creating Economic Opportunities in Agriculture," remarks given on April 16, 2004, http://newdelhi.usembassy.gov/ambapr162004a.html.

104. Borlaug, "Nobel Lecture."

105. Conway, *Doubly Green Revolution*, 55.

106. 1968 Annual Report of the Rockefeller Foundation.

107. Pakistan and India had gone to war with one another while the first shipment of dwarf-wheat seed to the region was on its way from Mexico.

108. Gregg Easterbrook, "Forgotten Benefactor of Humanity," *Atlantic Monthly*, Vol. 279, No. 1, January 1997, 74.

109. The Paddocks wrote of the Philippines, "no matter how miraculously the new research programs may improve agriculture the gains will be washed out by [a] tidal wave of new births." This has not proved to be the case.

110. The Nobel Committee awarded Borlaug its Peace Prize, as he explains in his acceptance speech, in recognition of "the actual and potential contributions of agricultural production to prosperity and peace among the nations and peoples of the world."

111. Weise, "The Man Who Fed the World."

112. Ibid.

113. 1968 Annual Report of the Rockefeller Foundation.

114. Norman Borlaug, "The Green Revolution Revisited and The Road Ahead," remarks given on September 8, 2000, http://nobelprize.org/nobel_prizes/peace/articles/borlaug/borlaug-lecture.pdf.

115. Once the centers proved promising, the U.S. government provided funds. Over one million dollars was allocated between 1966 and 1968, for example.

116. Borlaug, "The Green Revolution Revisited and The Road Ahead."

117. In the 1970 annual report of the Rockefeller Foundation, President George Harrar lays out an in-depth assessment of the various critiques leveled at the Green Revolution. Ultimately, he concludes that the problems will be mitigated by further research and that, in any event, they are outweighed by the benefits.

118. Weise, "The Man Who Fed the World."

119. Steven W. Sinding, "The Great Population Debates: How Relevant Are

They for the 21st Century?" *American Journal of Public Health*, Vol. 90, No. 12 (December 2000), 1841.

120. "About the Population Council: History," *Population Council*, http://www.popcouncil.org/about/history.html, February 2005.

121. *The Population Council: A Chronicle of the First Twenty-Five Years, 1952–1977*, New York: Population Council, 1978, 12–13.

122. Michael S. Teitelbaum, "The Population Threat," *Foreign Affairs*, Vol. 71, No. 5 (Winter 1992), 63.

123. *The Population Council: A Chronicle*, 14.

124. Ibid., 23.

125. "Highlights in Council History," *Population Council*, http://www.popcouncil.org/about/timeline.html, May 1, 2006.

126. "About the Population Council: History," *Population Council*, http://www.popcouncil.org/about/history.html, February 2005.

127. *The Population Council: A Chronicle*, 25–26.

128. Ibid., 27.

129. Teitelbaum, "The Population Threat," 63.

130. *The Population Council: A Chronicle*, 28.

131. Ibid., 60–62.

132. Ibid., 62.

133. "Highlights in Council History," *Population Council*, May 1, 2006.

134. Kathleen Teltsch, "U.N. Officials See Birth-Control Project as Important Step Forward," *New York Times*, March 11, 1970, 8.

135. "About the Population Council: History," *Population Council*, http://www.popcouncil.org/about/history.html, February 2005.

136. Sinding, "Great Population Debates," 1841.

137. James Day, *The Vanishing Vision: The Inside Story of Public Television*, (Berkeley: University of California Press, 1995), 146–47.

138. *Ford Foundation Annual Report*, 1969, 3; *Carnegie Corporation Annual Report*, 1968, 20.

139. *Carnegie Corporation Annual Report*, 1968, 20.

140. Day, *Vanishing Vision*, 145–46.

141. Richard M. Polsky, *Getting to Sesame Street: Origins of the Children's Television Workshop* (New York: Praeger Publishers, 1974), 2.

142. Ibid., 9.

143. Lagemann, *Politics of Knowledge*, 232.

144. Polsky, *Getting to Sesame Street*, 25–26.

145. Ibid., 26.

146. Ibid., 64–65.

147. Lagemann, *Politics of Knowledge*, 232.

148. Day, *Vanishing Vision*, 152.

149. Ibid., 152–53.
150. Peter B. Mann, *Sesame Street Research: A 20th Anniversary Symposium*. New York: Children's Television Workshop, 1990, 5.
151. Lagemann, *Politics of Knowledge*, 234.
152. Day, *Vanishing Vision*, 160.
153. Mann, *Sesame Street Research*, 15.
154. Ibid.
155. Lagemann, *Politics of Knowledge*, 235–36.
156. "The World's Longest Street," *Sesame Workshop*, http://www.sesameworkshop.org/aboutus/around_longest.php.
157. "Sesame Street Tops Guinness World Record with Most Emmys of All Time," Press Release, *Sesame Workshop*, http://www.sesameworkshop.org/aboutus/inside_press.php?contentId=14325318.
158. John J. Miller, *Strategic Investment in Ideas: How Two Foundations Reshaped America* (Washington, DC: The Philanthropy Roundtable, 2003), 10.
159. Ibid., 28.
160. Ibid., 28–29.
161. Ibid., 29.
162. Ibid.
163. Ibid., 32.
164. Ibid., 30.
165. Thomas B. Edsall, "Federalist Society Becomes a Force in Washington," *Washington Post*, April 18, 2001, A4.
166. John M. Olin Programs in Higher Education, Books on Public Affairs and Litigation, Internal Foundation Memo, Spring 2002, 8.
167. Ibid., 7.
168. Ibid., 8.
169. Rone Tempest, "Bangladesh: A Bank Just for the Poor Breaks Many Rules," *Los Angeles Times*. November 28, 1987, 1.
170. "Background Note: Bangladesh," U.S. Department of State, http://www.state.gov/r/pa/ei/bgn/3452.htm, August 2005.
171. Alan Jolis, "The Good Banker," *Independent, Sunday Review*, May 5, 1996, 15.
172. *Grameen Bank Annual Report, 2003*, http://www.grameen.com/annualreport/annualreport2003/index.html.
173. Tempest, "Bangladesh: A Bank Just for the Poor."
174. Jolis, "The Good Banker."
175. Grameen borrowers have used their Grameen loans for diverse enterprises, from manufacturing musical conch shells to processing animal entrails and more. Ibid.
176. Today, "Grameen Bank finances 100 per cent of its outstanding loan from its own fund and the savings from its depositors. Over 63 per cent of its de-

posits come from the bank's own borrowers." Muhammad Yunus, "Grameen Bank at a Glance," *Grameen Bank*, http://www.grameen-info. org/bank/GBGlance.htm.

177. M. Kabir Hassan and Luis Renteria-Guerrero, "The Experience of the Grameen Bank of Bangladesh in Community Development," *International Journal of Social Economics*, Vol. 24, Issue 12 (December 1997), 1488.

178. Susan V. Berresford, remarks given at the University of Southern California's Center on Philanthropy and Public Policy, February 13, 2003, http://www.fordfound.org/news/view_speeches_detail.cfm?news_index=125.

179. Yunus, Mohammad, *Banker to the Poor: Micro-Lending and the Battle Against World Poverty.* (New York: PublicAffairs, 1999.)

180. "Key Information of Grameen Bank," Grameen Bank, http://www. grameen-info.org/infoharvus$.htm.

181. Ibid.

182. Grameen borrowers also commit to a set of "16 Decisions" for a healthy and productive life, including such promises as, "We shall educate our children and ensure that they can earn to pay for their education," and, "We shall not take any dowry at our sons' weddings, neither shall we give any dowry at our daughters wedding. We shall keep our centre free from the curse of dowry. We shall not practice child marriage."

183. Anwarul K. Chowdhury, United Nations Under-Secretary-General and High Representative for the Least Developed Countries, Landlocked Developing Countries and Small Island Developing States, "Statement in the Second Committee of the 59th Session of the General Assembly." November 25, 2004.

184. Jolis, "The Good Banker."

185. Bruce Shenitz, "What Poor Bangladesh Can Teach Rich America: A $100 Loan May Not Sound Like Much, but if You're an Ambitious Entrepreneur, It Can be a Ladder to Economic Success," *Los Angeles Times*, May 9, 1993. The foundation has given further support to the spread of microfinance, including a Chinese replica: the Yixian Grameen Bank. See Jasper Becker, "Bank Plants Seeds of Independence," *South China Morning Post*, August 14, 1995.

186. Chowdhury, "Statement."

187. "FC Stats: The Foundation Center's Statistical Information Service," http://www.foundationcenter.org/findfunders/statistics/pdf/11_topfdn_type/ top50_tg_all.pdf, 2003.

188. "About Us: Overview," Open Society Institute, http://www.soros.org/ about/overview.

189. "FC Stats."

190. Michael T. Kaufman, *Soros: The Life and Times of a Messianic Billionaire* (New York: Alfred A. Knopf, 2002), 185.

191. Karen Pallarito, "Soros' New Mission," *Journal of Mental Health Counseling*, Vol. 27, Issue 44 (Nov. 3, 1997), 20.

192. "Giving it Away," *Economist*, October 25, 1997, 77.

193. "Opening Russian Society," editorial, *New York Times*, June 12, 2003, 34.

194. Kaufman, *Soros*, 196–200.

195. Ibid., 199.

196. Ibid., 177.

197. Soros's Ukraine Foundation pursued a similar program, which trained some seventy thousand former soldiers before Soros's feud with Ukraine's president, Leonid Kuchma, brought operations to a halt.

198. Pallarito, "Soros' New Mission."

199. Kaufman, *Soros,* 178.

200. Ibid., 281.

201. Ibid., 262–63.

202. E-mail from Katie Jamieson, director of the office of the president, OSI, to Scott Kohler, April 6, 2005, on file with the author.

203. "Opening Russian Society," *New York Times*.

204. C. Tracy Orleans and Joseph Alper, "Helping Addicted Smokers Quit: The Foundation's Tobacco-Cessation Programs," *The Robert Wood Johnson Foundation Anthology: To Improve Health and Health Care*, Volume VI, Stephen L. Isaacs and James R. Knickman, eds. (San Francisco: Jossey-Bass, 2003), 125–48.

205. Phillip Morris, the nation's largest cigarette manufacturer, proclaims on its Web site that, "Phillip Morris USA (PM USA) agrees with the overwhelming medical and scientific consensus that cigarette smoking causes lung cancer, heart disease, emphysema and other serious diseases in smokers. Smokers are far more likely to develop serious diseases, like lung cancer, than non-smokers. There is no safe cigarette." http://www.phillipmorris-usa.com/.

206. "Nicotine and Cigarettes," Frontline: Inside the Tobacco Deal, http://www.pbs.org/wgbh/pages/frontline/shows/settlement/timelines/april94.html.

207. C. Tracy Orleans and Joseph Alper. "Helping Addicted Smokers Quit."

208. Robert G. Hughes, "Adopting the Substance Abuse Goal: A Story of Philanthropic Decision Making," in *The Robert Wood Johnson Foundation Anthology: To Improve Health and Health Care 1998–1999*, Vol. II, Stephen L. Isaacs and James R. Knickman, eds. (San Francisco: Jossey-Bass, 2000), 3–18.

209. Steven Schroeder, interview with the author, January 9, 2004.

210. John Mintz, "Curb on Tobacco Ads Proposed," *Washington Post*, May 29, 1997, E1.

211. The estimated 435,000 people per year killed by tobacco was more than four times the number estimated to die as a result of alcohol (100,000) and

more than twenty times the number estimated to be killed by illegal drugs (20,000). Robert G. Hughes, "Adopting the Substance Abuse Goal: A Story of Philanthropic Decision Making."

212. These five programs are only a sample of the foundation's many undertakings in tobacco and substance abuse–related areas. I believe they are indicative of the breadth and depth of the foundation's involvement in tobacco issues, and they include the most significant examples of RWJF efforts on several fronts of the effort.

213. C. Tracy Orleans, "Challenges and Opportunities for Tobacco Control: the Robert Wood Johnson Foundation Agenda," *Tobacco Control Online*, 1998, http://tc.bmjjournals.com/cgi/content/full/7/suppl_1/S8.

214. Nancy J. Kaufman and Karyn L. Feiden. "Linking Biomedical and Behavioral Research for Tobacco Use Prevention: Sundance and Beyond," *The Robert Wood Johnson Foundation Anthology: To Improve Health and Health Care 2000*, Vol. III, Stephen L. Isaacs and James R. Knickman, eds. (San Francisco: Jossey-Bass, 1999), 161–85.

215. This story has been extensively chronicled by the news media. Sheryl Gay Stolberg, "Beleaguered Tobacco Foe Holds Key to Talks," *New York Times*, June 4, 1997; Digby Diehl, "The Center for Tobacco-Free Kids and the Tobacco-Settlement Negotiations," *The Robert Wood Johnson Anthology: To Improve Health and Health Care*, Vol. VI, Stephen L. Isaacs and James R. Knickman, eds. (San Francisco: Jossey-Bass, 2003), 101–24; Michael Pertschuk, *Smoke in Their Eyes: Lessons in Movement Leadership from the Tobacco Wars* (Nashville: Vanderbilt University, 2001).

216. Kaufman and Feiden, "Linking Biomedical and Behavioral Research for Tobacco Use Prevention: Sundance and Beyond."

217. Other private foundations now involved in tobacco research, advocacy, and control include the Commonwealth Fund, the Ford Foundation, the Annie E. Casey Foundation, the Joyce Foundation, the Kaiser Family Foundation, and others.

218. Leonard Koppett, "The National Spit Tobacco Education Program," *The Robert Wood Johnson Foundation Anthology: To Improve Health and Health Care 1998–1999*, Vol. II, Stephen L. Isaacs and James R. Knickman, eds. (San Francisco: Jossey-Bass, 1998), 43–56.

219. "Q & A with Risa Lavizzo-Mourey, M.D., M.B.A.: Tobacco Strategy," Robert Wood Johnson Foundation, available from http://www.rwjf.org/news/special/tobaccoStrategy.jhtml.

220. The David and Lucile Packard Foundation, "Program Profiles: China Sustainable Energy Program," available from http://www.packard.org/index.cgi?page=consci-profile&id=0003.

221. Ibid.

222. "China Sustainable Energy Foundation," *EF China*, http://www.efchina. org/home.cfm.

223. The David and Lucile Packard Foundation, "Program Profiles: China Sustainable Energy Program," available from http://www.packard.org/index. cgi?page=consci-profile&id=0003.

224. This was renewed the following year with an additional two million dollar grant. 2003 Annual Report, The William and Flora Hewlett Foundation.

225. Final Report: Evaluation of China Sustainable Energy Program, prepared by Energy Resources International, Inc., July 5, 2003.

226. Ibid.

227. Ibid.

228. The David and Lucile Packard Foundation, "Program Profiles: China Sustainable Energy Program," available from http://www.packard.org/index. cgi?page=consci-profile&id=0003.

229. Final Report: Evaluation of China Sustainable Energy Program, prepared by Energy Resources International, Inc., July 5, 2003. The Hewlett Foundation's projection, in its 2003 annual report, is the considerably lower figure of 1.6 billion barrels (and over one hundred billion dollars in energy import savings). Both estimates, however, project significant savings, even in the context of China's massive economy.

230. The David and Lucile Packard Foundation, "Program Profiles: China Sustainable Energy Program," available from http://www.packard.org/index. cgi?page=consci-profile&id=0003.

231. Final Report: Evaluation of China Sustainable Energy Program, prepared by Energy Resources International, Inc., July 5, 2003.

Part Three

1. Doug Nelson, interview with the author, July 29, 2004.

2. Geri Mannion, "Are You Arrogant?" *Foundation News and Commentary*, July/August 1997, 24.

3. Ibid.

4. Ibid.

5. *Foundation Yearbook: Facts and Figures on Private and Community Foundations* (New York: The Foundation Center, 2006).

6. Lagemann, *Politics of Knowledge*, 185.

7. Matthew Hale, et al., "The Nonprofit Sector and the Press: Coverage of Philanthropy and Nonprofits in Nine Major Newspapers," Center on Philanthropy and Public Policy, USC, Research Paper No. 22, February 2005.

8. Center on Philanthropy and Public Policy, USC, Research and Analysis to Advance Public Problem Solving, Vol. 5, No. 1, July 2005, 2.

9. "About Us," National Committee for Responsive Philanthropy, http://www.ncrp.org/about_us/index.asp. Capital Research Center, http://www.capitalresearch.org.

10. For the other exceptions, see Chapter 12. See also, "The Eye of the Storm: Ten Years on the Front Lines of New Futures," a report of the Annie Casey Foundation's New Futures Program, available at http://www.aecf.org/publications/eyeofstorm/intro.htm.

11. Orville G. Brim Jr., "Do We Know What We Are Doing?" Chapter 8, *The Future of Foundations, The American Assembly*, Columbia University, 1973 (New York: Prentice Hall, 1973), 219, quoting in part from Arnold J. Zurcher and Jane Dustan, *The Foundation Administrator: A Study of Those Who Manage America's Foundations* (New York: Russell Sage Foundation, 1972).

12. Richard Lyman, interview with the author, January 9, 2004.

13. David C. Bloomfield, "Come Clean on Small Schools," *Education Week*, January 5, 2006, Vol. 25, Issue 20, 34–35.

14. Survey by Wirthlin Associates (now Harris International) for the Council on Foundations.

15. Perhaps the growing practice of foundations' "advertising" on NPR can help familiarize some portion of the public with their existence, although the cryptic, one-phrase descriptions that characterize their mention seem unlikely to make much of an impression in the public mind of exactly what foundations do, and how they benefit society in specific ways.

16. Ellen Condliffe Lagemann, *The Politics of Knowledge: The Carnegie Corporation, Philanthropy, and Public Policy* (Middletown, CT: Wesleyan University Press, 1989); Lagemann, *Private Power for the Public Good: A History of the Carnegie Foundation for the Advancement of Teaching* (Middletown, CT: Wesleyan University Press, 1983); Edward R. Embree and Julia Waxman, *Investment in People: The Story of the Julius Rosenwald Fund* (New York: Harper, 1949); Peter Krass, *Carnegie* (New York: John Wiley & Sons, 2002); Ron Chernow, *Titan: The Life of John D. Rockefeller, Sr.* (New York: Random House, 1998); Peter Max Ascoli, *Julius Rosenwald: The Man Who Built Sears, Roebuck and Advanced the Cause of Black Education in the American South* (Bloomington and Indianapolis: Indiana University Press, 2006); Lawrence G. Foster, *Robert Wood Johnson: The Gentleman Rebel*, (State College, PA: Lillian Press, 1999).

17. Steven Wheatley, *The Politics of Philanthropy: Abraham Flexner and Medical Education* (Madison: University of Wisconsin Press, 1988); William H. Schneider, ed., *Rockefeller Philanthropy and Modern Biomedicine: International Initiatives from World War II to the Cold War* (Bloomington: Indiana University Press, 2002).

18. *The Big Foundations* (New York: Columbia University Press, 1972); *The*

Endangered Sector (New York: Columbia University Press, 1979); *Golden Donors: A New Anatomy of the Great Foundations*, (New York: Truman Talley Books, 1985); *Inside American Philanthropy: The Dramas of Donorship* (Norman: University of Oklahoma Press, 1996).

19. *Philanthropic Foundations: New Scholarship, New Possibilities* (Bloomington and Indianapolis: Indiana University Press, 1999).

20. Warren Weaver, *U.S. Philanthropic Foundations; Their History, Structure, Management, and Record* (New York: Viking, 1967).

21. Joan Roelefs, *Foundations and Public Policy: The Mask of Pluralism* (Albany: State University of New York Press, 2003).

22. Kenneth Prewitt, *Social Sciences and Private Philanthropy: The Quest for Social Relevance*, Essays on Philanthropy, No. 15 (Indianapolis: Indiana University Center on Philanthropy, 1995).

23. See http://www.effectivephilanthropy.org. In the interest of full disclosure, I report that I am a member of the Center's Board of Trustees, and was the head of the program staff of one of the foundations—Atlantic Philanthropies—which provided early and continuing support for the center.

24. See "Staff Discussion Draft" at http://www.finance.senate.gov/hearings/testimony/2004test.

25. Marion Fremont-Smith and Andras Kosaras, "Wrongdoing by Officers and Directors of Charities: A Survey of Press Reports, 1995–2002," Hauser Center Working Paper No. 20, Hauser Center for Nonprofit Organizations, September 2003.

26. "The Right to Privacy," 4 *Harvard Law Review* 193 (1890).

27. Herbert Agar, *The Saving Remnant* (New York: The Viking Press, Compass Edition, 1962).

28. Ibid., 147, 150.

29. The Center for Effective Philanthropy, "Higher Impact: Improving Foundation Performance," 2005, http://www.effectivephilanthropy.com/images/pdfs/CEP_Higher_Impact_2005.pdf.

30. James Surowieki, *The Wisdom of Crowds* (New York: Doubleday, 2004).

31. Ellen Condliffe Lagemann, *The Politics of Knowledge*, 7.

32. Ibid., 13.

33. See "The Transformation of American Medical Education: The Flexner Report," case #3.

34. See "Curing and Preventing Disease and Promoting Public Health," case #4.

35. See "Learning to Understand the Problems faced by Cleveland: America's First Community Foundation," case #6.

36. Lagemann, *Private Power*, 68.

37. Wheatley, *The Politics of Philanthropy*.

38. Lagemann, *Private Power*, 72.

39. Ibid., 73.
40. Ibid., 85.
41. Ibid., 75–82.
42. Ibid., 82. See "Reforming the Legal Profession Through Education and Practice," case #12.
43. Ibid., 71.
44. See "The Rural Hospitals Program of the Commonwealth Fund," case #13.
45. See "Pensions for America's Educators: TIAA-CREF," case #9.
46. Howard Berliner, *A System of Science for Medicine* (New York and London: Tavistock, 1985), 31–32.
47. Ibid., 33.
48. See "Providing Scientific Knowledge to Solve Public Problems: National Research Council," case #8; and "Economic Policy Research of the Highest Quality: National Bureau of Economic Research," case #11.
49. See "America's System of Public Broadcasting and Public Radio," case #32.
50. Elizabeth McCormick, interview with author, January 7, 2005.
51. Fred Krupp, interview with the author, February 20, 2004.
52. J. Gregory Dees, "Entrepreneurship in Philanthropy," Center for the Advancement of Social Entrepreneurship, Fuqua School of Business, Duke University, http://www.fuqua.duke.edu/centers/case/articles/0805.
53. David Bergholz, interview with the author on June 11, 2004.
54. Michael E. Porter and Mark R. Kramer, "Philanthropy's New Agenda: Creating Value," *Harvard Business Review*, November-December, 1999, 121–30.
55. See "Youth Development Program," case #92.
56. See "Talented Students in the Arts Initiative," case #98.
57. See "Institution Building for Evidence-Based Public Policy," case #22.
58. Robert Crane, interview with the author, November 1, 2004.
59. Warren Wood, interview with the author, September 17, 2003.
60. Avi Chai Foundation, 2005 Annual Report, 9.
61. See David Ransom, "The Berkeley Mafia and the Indonesian Massacre," *Ramparts*, Vol. 9, No. 4, October 1970, 26–29, 40–49.
62. See "Care at the End of Life," case #68.
63. Ethan Bronner, "The Teaching Nursing Home Program," *The Robert Wood Johnson Foundation Anthology: To Improve Health and Health Care*, Vol. IV, Stephen L. Isaacs and James R. Knickman, eds. (San Francisco: Jossey-Bass, 2004). See also "The Nurse-Family Partnership," case #50.
64. Barry Gaberman, interview with the author, February 2, 2004.
65. See "The Green Revolution," case #20.
66. Richard Lyman, interview with the author, January 9, 2004.
67. "Annenberg Challenge," The Annenberg Foundation, http://www.annenbergfoundation.org/other/other_list.htm?cat_id=260.
68. William Damon, interview with the author, July 18, 2004.

69. Anthony Romero, interview with the author, May 12, 2004.

70. Howard Gardner, interview with the author, July 18, 2004.

71. William Bowen, interview with the author, December 8, 2003.

72. David Morse, interview with the author, September 17, 2003.

73. Thomas Hatch, *What Happens When Multiple Improvement Initiatives Collide*, (Carnegie Foundation for the Advancement of Teaching, 2000). Hatch is now director of the National Center for Research on Schools, Education and Teaching at Columbia Teachers College.

74. Paul Brest, interview with the author, December 7, 2004.

75. Lloyd Morrisett, interview with the author, February 19, 2004.

76. See Richard P. Cunningham, "Why Did One News Council Fail and the Other Succeed?," http://www.newsombudsman.org/cumming3.

77. Lee Shulman, interview with the author, January 8, 2004.

78. Paul Brest, interview with the author, December 7, 2004.

79. James Knickman, interview with the author, September 17, 2003.

80. Lloyd Morrisett, interview with the author, February 19, 2004.

81. Nielsen, *Golden Donors*, 103–15.

82. See "The Emergency Medical Services Program," case #42.

83. Joseph Nye, *Soft Power: The Means to Success in World Politics* (New York: PublicAffairs, 2004).

84. Report of The Andrew W. Mellon Foundation 2004 (New York: 2005), 10.

85. Quoted by Ellen Condliffe Lagemann in her book, *The Politics of Knowledge: The Carnegie Corporation, Philanthropy and Public Policy* (Middletown, CT: Wesleyan University Press, 1989), 22.

86. "Andrew Carnegie's Vision for Carnegie Corporation," Carnegie Corporation of New York, http://www.carnegie.org/sub/philanthropy/carn_vis_carn.html.

87. Foundation Center, "Foundation Giving Trends," 2005.

88. Susan V. Berresford, "Taking a Long View: The Roots and Mission of the Ford Foundation," Ford Foundation Report, Winter 2005, http://www.fordfound.org/publications/ff_report/view_ff_report_detail.cfm?report_index=557.

89. Ibid.

90. Weaver, *U.S. Philanthropic Foundations*, 86.

91. Ibid., 416.

92. See Richard Magat, *The Ford Foundation at Work: Philanthropic Choices, Methods, and Styles* (New York: Plenum Press, 1979), 33, for a more extensive description of these grants. His account varies slightly from the accounts of Weaver and Hechinger. Magat's account is fuller and more precise than the other two.

93. Paul Ylvisaker exit interview, Ford Foundation Archives.

94. See "Program to Strengthen Business Education, case #27, and "Facilitaing Global Knowledge Creation: University Area Studies Program," case #25.

95. See "Local Initiative Support Corporation," case #52; "Manpower Demonstration Research Corporation," case #45; "Grameen Bank," case #47; "Institution Building for Evidence-Based Public Policy," case #22; "Social Movements and Civil Rights Litigation," case #36; and "Programs to Enhance the Rights and Opportunities for Women," case #41.

96. Margaret Mahoney, a president of the Commonwealth Fund, puts great emphasis on the critical role board chairs can, but don't always, play.

97. Frank Karel, interview with the author, May 19, 2004.

98. Edwin R. Embree and Julia Waxman, *Investment in People: The Story of the Julius Rosenwald Fund*, (New York: Harper & Brothers, 1949), 31.

99. David Bergholz, interview with the author, June 11, 2004.

100. Edward R. Embree and Julia Waxman, *Investment in People: The Story of the Julius Rosenwald Fund* (New York: Harper, 1949), 17.

101. "Our Mission," Richard and Rhoda Goldman Fund, http://www.goldman-fund.org/about/mission.

102. John Hechinger and Daniel Golden, "The Great Giveaway," *The Wall Street Journal*, July 8, 2006, 1.

103. Ibid.

104. Steve Forbes, "Term Limits for Foundations," *Forbes*, July 24, 2006, 27.

105. Warren E. Buffett, letter to Mr. and Mrs. William H. Gates III, June 26, 2006, available at http://www.berkshirehathaway.com/donate/bmgfltr.pdf.

106. "Charity Oversight: An Alternative Approach," available either from Marcus S. Owen, Caplin and Drysdale, Washington, DC, mso@capdale.com, or from the National Center on Philanthropy and Law, NYU Law School, http://www.law.nyu.edu/ncpl/.

107. Ibid.

108. Ibid.

109. http://www.effectivephilanthropy.org.

110. Phil Buchanan, et al., Beyond Oversight: The Trustee Viewpoint on Effective Foundation Governance," available at http://effectivephilanthropy.com/images/pdfs/CEP_Beyond_Compliance.pdf.

Epilogue

1. *Foundation Growth and Giving Trends: Current Outlook, 2006 Edition* (New York: The Foundation Center, 2006), 13.

2. Ibid., 11.

3. See Jean Mincer, "Donor-Advised Funds Gain Assets, Popularity," *The Wall*

Street Journal, August 1, 2006, D2; "Philanthropy 101: Donor-Advised Funds," *Journal of Financial Planning*, November 2003, 66–73; also http://www.aefonline.org.

4. See Harvy Lipman, "Two California Foundations Plan to Merge Next Year," *The Chronicle of Philanthropy*, July 20, 2006, 30.

5. See J. Greg Dees and Beth B. Anderson, "Framing a Theory of Social Entrepreneurship: Building on Two Schools of Practice and Thought," in Rachel Mosher Williams, ed., *Research on Social Entrepreneurship: Understanding and Contributing to an Emerging Field* (Indianapolis: Arnova, 2006).

6. See Christopher Conkey, "Strings Attached: Along With Their Big Bucks, Rich Donors Want to Give Charities Their Two Cents," *The Wall Street Journal*, July 3, 2006, 81, and Beth Hunt, "$30 million ventured, so much gained," *Washington Business Journal*, July 21, 2006.

7. See http://www.acumenfund.org.

8. See Knight Kiplinger, "Grass Roots Capitalism," Kiplinger's, http://www.Kiplinger.com/personalfinance/magazine/archives/2005/0f5kak.

9. See John Hechinger and Daniel Golden, "The Great Giveaway," *The Wall Street Journal*, July 8, 2006, A 1.

10. Katie Hafner, *The New York Times*, September 14, 2006, 1.

11. Andrew C. Revkin, *The New York Times*, September 22, 2006, 1.

12. See David P. Hamilton, "Ex-Executive Backs Big Push to Get a Jump on Cancer," *The Wall Street Journal*, July 12, 2006, A1.

13. See Michael Anft, Brennen Jensen, and Ian Wilhelm, "Voicing Support for Charity," *The Chronicle of Philanthropy*, August 3, 2006, and also June 29, 2006, 6–23.

14. See Andrew Pollack, "Fighting Diseases with Checkbooks," *New York Times*, July 7, 2006, C1.

15. Christopher Rowland, "Neely gives double boost to Tufts Medical Center," *The Boston Globe*, April 25, 2006, A1.

16. See John J. Havens and Paul G. Schervish, "Millionaires and the Millennium: New Estimates of the Forthcoming Wealth Transfer and the Prospects for a Golden Age of Philanthropy," (Boston: Boston College Social Welfare Research Institute, October 19, 1999), available at http://www.swri508.bc.edu; and "Transfer of Wealth: Center on Wealth and Philanthropy," Boston: Center on Wealth and Philanthropy, July 26, 2006, available at http://www.bc.edu/research/swri/features/wealthtransfer/.

17. See John Hechinger and Daniel Golden, "The Great Giveaway," *The Wall Street Journal*, July 8, 2006, A1.

SELECTED BIBLIOGRAPHY

Alchon, Guy. The Invisible Hand of Planning: Capitalism, Social Science, and the State in the 1920s. *Princeton: Princeton University Press, 1985.*

Anderson, Eric A., and Alfred A. Moss Jr. The Founding Fortunes: A New Anatomy of the Super-Rich Families in America. *New York: E.P. Dutton, 1987.*

Andrews, F. Emerson. Patman and Foundations: Review and Assessment. *New York: The Foundation Center, 1968.*

———. Philanthropic Foundations. *New York: Russell Sage Foundation, 1956.*

———. Philanthropy in the United States: History and Structure. *New York: Foundation Center, 1974.*

Anheier, Helmut, and Stefan Toepler. Private Funds, Public Purpose: Philanthropic Foundations in International Perspective. *New York: Kluwer Academic-Plenum Publishers, 1999.*

Arnove, Robert F. Philanthropic and Cultural Imperialism: The Foundations at Home and Abroad. *Boston: G.K. Hill, 1980.*

Ascoli, Peter M. Julius Rosenwald: The Man who Built Sears, Roebuck and Advanced the Cause of Black Education in the American South. *Bloomington and Indianapolis: Indiana University Press, 2006.*

Bennett, James T., and Thomas J. DiLorenzo. Unhealthy Charities: Hazardous to Your Health and Wealth. *New York: Basic Books, 1994.*

———. Unfair Competition: The Profits of Nonprofits. *Lanham, MD: Hamilton Press, 1989.*

Berle, Adolf A. Leaning Against the Dawn: An Appreciation of the Twentieth Century Fund and Its Fifty Years of Adventure in Seeking to Influence American Development Toward a More Effectively Just Civilization, 1919–1969. *New York: Twentieth Century Fund, 1969.*

Berliner, Howard S. A System of Scientific Medicine: Philanthropic Foundations in the Flexner Era. *New York: Tavistock Publications, 1985.*

Berman, Edward H. The Ideology of Philanthropy: The Influence of the

Carnegie, Ford, and Rockefeller Foundations on American Foreign Policy. *Albany: State University of New York Press, 1983.*

Berndt, Harry Edward. New Rulers in the Ghetto: The Community Development Corporation and Urban Poverty. *Westport, CT: Greenwood, 1977.*

Black, Edwin. War Against the Weak: Eugenics and America's Campaign to Create a Master Race. *New York: Four Walls Eight Windows, 2003.*

Blumenthal, Sidney. The Rise of the Counter-Establishment: From Conservative Ideology to Political Power. *New York: Times Books, 1986.*

Bobinski, George S. Carnegie Libraries: Their History and Impact on American Public Library Development. *Chicago: American Library Association, 1969.*

Bonner, T. N. Iconoclast: Abraham Flexner and a Life in Learning. *Baltimore: Johns Hopkins University Press, 2002.*

Boris, Elizabeth T., and C. Eugene Steuerle, eds. Nonprofits and Government: Collaboration and Conflict. *Washington, DC: Urban Institute Press, 1999.*

Bornstein, David. How to Change the World: Social Entrepreneurs and the Power of New Ideas. *New York: Oxford University Press, 2004.*

Bowen, William G., and Derek Bok. The Shape of the River: Long-Term Consequences of Considering Race in College and University Admissions. *Princeton: Princeton University Press, 1998.*

Bremner, Robert H. American Philanthropy. *Chicago: University of Chicago Press, 1960; 2nd ed. 1988.*

Brilliant, Eleanor L. Private Charity and Public Inquiry: A History of the Filer and Peterson Commissions. *Bloomington and Indianapolis: Indiana University Press, 2000.*

Brody, Evelyn, ed. Property Tax Exemption for Charities: Mapping the Battlefield. *Washington, DC: Urban Institute Press, 2002.*

Brown, E. Richard. Rockefeller Medicine Men: Medicine and Capitalism in America. *Berkeley: University of California Press, 1979.*

Brown, P., and S. Garg. Foundations and Comprehensive Community Initiatives: The Challenges of Partnership. *Chicago: The Chapin Hall Center for Children, 1997.*

Bruce, Ellen, et al. Foundations and Public Information: Sunshine or Shadow? Preliminary Findings from a Study of the Public Information Accountability of the Country's Largest Foundations. *Washington, DC: National Committee for Responsive Philanthropy, 1980.*

Bullock, Mary Brown. An American Transplant: The Rockefeller Foundation and Peking Union Medical College. *Berkeley: University of California Press, 1980.*

Burlingame, Dwight F., ed. The Responsibilities of Wealth. *Bloomington and Indianapolis: Indiana University Press, 1992.*

Carmichael, Erskine. The Pap Smear: Life of George N. Papanicolaou. *Springfield: Charles C. Thomas, 1973.*

Carnegie, Andrew. The Gospel of Wealth. *London: F.C. Hagen and Co., 1889.*

Carson, Emmett D. A Hand Up: Black Philanthropy and Self-Help in America. *Washington, DC: Joint Center for Political and Economic Studies Press; Lanham, MD: University Press of America, 1993.*

Castle, Alfred L. A Century of Philanthropy: A History of the Samuel N. and Mary Castle Foundation. *Honolulu: Hawaiian Historical Society, 1992.*

Chase, Mary Ellen. Abby Aldrich Rockefeller. *New York: Macmillan, 1950.*

Cheit, Earl F., and Theodore E. Lobman. Foundations and Higher Education: Grant Making From Golden Years Through Steady State. *Berkeley: The Carnegie Council on Policy Studies in Higher Education, 1979.*

Chernow, Ron. Titan: The Life of John D. Rockefeller, Sr. *Random House: New York, 1998.*

Clotfelter, Charles, and Thomas Ehrlich, eds. Philanthropy and the Nonprofit Sector in a Changing America. *Bloomington and Indianapolis: Indiana University Press, 1999.*

Clotfelter, Charles, ed. Who Benefits from the Nonprofit Sector?, *Chicago: University of Chicago Press, 1992.*

Collins, Jim. Good to Great and the Social Sectors: Why Business Thinking Is Not the Answer. *Boulder, CO: Jim Collins, 2005.*

Commission on Foundations and Private Philanthropy. Foundations, Private Giving and Public Policy: Report and Recommendations of the Commission on Foundations and Private Philanthropy. *Chicago: University of Chicago Press, 1970.*

Commission on Foundations and Private Philanthropy (Peterson Commission). Giving in America: Towards a Stronger Voluntary Sector. *Commission on Private Philanthropy and Public Needs, 1975.*

The Commonwealth Fund, The Commonwealth Fund: Historical Sketch, 1918–62. *New York: Harkness House, 1963.*

Conway, Gordon. The Doubly Green Revolution: Food for All in the Twentieth Century. *New York: Comstock, 1997.*

Coon, Horace. Money to Burn: What the Great American Philanthropic Foundations Do With Their Money. *London: Longmans, Green and Co., 1938.*

Council on Foundations. Evaluation for Foundations: Concepts, Cases, Guidelines, and Resources. *San Francisco: Jossey-Bass Publishers, 1993.*

Covington, Sally. Moving a Public Policy Agenda: The Strategic Philanthropy of Conservative Foundations. *Washington, DC: National Committee for Responsive Philanthropy, 1997.*

Covington, Sally, and Larry Parachini. Foundations in the Newt Era. *Washington, DC: The Committee for Responsive Philanthropy, 1995.*

Cueto, Marcos, ed. Missionaries of Science: The Rockefeller Foundation and Latin America. *Bloomington: Indiana University Press, 1994.*

Cullman, Lewis B. Can't Take it With You: The Art of Making and Giving Money. *Hoboken: John Wiley & Sons, 2004.*

Culver, John C., and John Hyde. American Dreamer: The Life and Times of Henry A. Wallace. *New York: Norton, 2000.*

Cuninggim, Merrimon. Private Money and Public Service: The Role of Foundations in American Society. *New York: McGraw-Hill, 1972.*

Curti, Merle. American Philanthropy Abroad. *New Brunswick: Rutgers University Press, 1965.*

Damon, William, and Susan Verducci, eds. Taking Philanthropy Seriously: Beyond Noble Intentions to Responsible Giving. *Bloomington: Indiana University Press, 2006.*

Day, James. The Vanishing Vision: The Inside Story of Public Television. *Berkeley: University of California Press, 1995.*

Dezhina, Irina. The International Science Foundation: The Preservation of Basic Science in the Former Soviet Union. *New York: International Science Foundation, 1997.*

Diamond, Sara. Roads to Dominion: Right-Wing Movements and Political Power in the United States. *New York: Guilford Press, 1995.*

Dickason, John H., and Duncan Neuhauser. Closing a Foundation: The Lucille P. Markey Charitable Trust. *New York: Council on Foundations, 2000.*

Dickinson, Frank G. The Changing Position of Philanthropy in the American Economy. *New York: National Bureau of Economic Research, 1970.*

——, ed. Philanthropy and Public Policy. *New York: National Bureau of Economic Research, 1962.*

Dillingham, George A. The Foundation of the Peabody Tradition. *Lanham, MD: University Press of America, 1989.*

DiLorenzo, Thomas J., Daniel T. Oliver, and Robert E. Winters. Patterns of Corporate Philanthropy: the "Suicidal Impulse." *Washington, DC: Capital Research Center, 1990.*

Dowie, Mark. American Foundations: An Investigative History. *Cambridge: MIT Press, 2001.*

Durden, Robert F. Lasting Legacy to the Carolinas: The Duke Endowment, 1924–1994. *Durham, NC: Duke University Press, 1998.*

Ebrahim, Alnoor. NGOs and Organizational Change: Discourse, Reporting, and Learning. *New York: Cambridge University Press, 2003.*

Embree, Edwin R., and Julia Waxman. Investment in People: The Story of the Julius Rosenwald Fund. *New York: Harper & Brothers Publishers, 1949.*

Ettling, John. The Germ of Laziness: Rockefeller Philanthropy and Public Health in the New South. *Cambridge: Harvard University Press, 1981.*

Farley, John. To Cast Out Disease: A History of the International Health Division of the Rockefeller Foundation, 1913–1951. *Oxford: Oxford University Press, 2004.*

Fisher, Donald. Fundamental Development of the Social Sciences: Rockefeller Philanthropy and the University States Social Science Research Council. *Ann Arbor: University of Michigan Press, 1993.*

Flexner, Abraham. Funds and Foundations: Their Policies Past and Present. *New York: Harper & Brothers, 1952.*

————. Henry S. Pritchett, A Biography. *New York: Columbia University Press, 1943.*

————. I Remember: The Autobiography of Abraham Flexner. *New York: Simon & Schuster, 1940.*

————. Medical Education in the United States and Canada. *New York: Carnegie Foundation for the Advancement of Teaching, 1910 (Reprint 1972).*

Fosdick, Raymond B., with Henry F. Pringle and Katherine Doublas Pringle. Adventure in Giving: The Story of the General Education Board. *New York: Harper & Row, 1962.*

Fosdick, Raymond B. John D. Rockefeller, Jr.: A Portrait. *New York: Harper & Brothers, 1956.*

————. A Philosophy for a Foundation. *New York: Rockefeller Foundation, 1963.*

————. The Story of the Rockefeller Foundation. *New York: Harper & Brothers, 1952.*

Foster, Lawrence G. Robert Wood Johnson: The Gentleman Rebel. *State College, PA: Lillian Press, 1999.*

Fremont-Smith, Marion R. Foundations and Government: State and Federal Law and Supervision. *New York: Russell Sage Foundation, 1965.*

————. Governing Nonprofit Organizations: Federal and State Law and Regulation. *Cambridge: Belknap Press of Harvard University Press, 2004.*

————. Philanthropy and the Business Corporation. *New York: Russell Sage Foundation, 1972.*

Freund, Gerald. Narcissism & Philanthropy: Ideas and Talent Denied. *New York: Viking, 1996.*

Friedman, Lawrence J., and Mark D. McGarvie, eds. Charity, Philanthropy, and Civility in American History. *Cambridge: Cambridge University Press, 2003.*

Frumkin, Peter. Strategic Giving: The Art and Science of Philanthropy. *Chicago: University of Chicago Press, 2006.*

————. On Being Nonprofit: A Conceptual and Policy Primer. *Cambridge: Harvard University Press, 2002.*

Fulk, Austin, and Stuart Nolan. Patterns of Corporate Philanthropy: Giving in the Clinton Era. *Preface by Robert H. Malott. Washington, DC: Capital Research Center, 1996.*

Gardner, John W. Living, Leading, and the American Dream. *Francesca Gardner, ed. San Francisco: Jossey-Bass, 2003.*

Gates, Frederick Taylor. Chapters in My Life. *New York: Free Press, 1977.*

Gaudiani, Claire. The Greater Good: How Philanthropy Drives the American Economy and Can Save Capitalism. *New York: Times Books, 2003.*

Gaul, Gilbert M., and Neill A. Borowski. Free Ride: The Tax-Exempt Economy. *Kansas City: Andrews and McMeel, 1993.*

Geiger, R. L. Research and Relevant Knowledge: The Growth of American Research Universities Since World War II. *New York: Oxford University Press, 1993.*

————. To Advance Knowledge: The Growth of American Research Universities, 1900–1940. *New York: Oxford University Press, 1986.*

Gersick, Kelin E. Generations of Giving: Leadership and Continuity in Family Foundations. *Lanham, MD: Lexington Books, 2004.*

Giving USA, *a publication of the Giving USA Foundation, researched and written by the Center on Philanthropy at Indiana University, 2003–2006.*

Goulden, Joseph C. The Money Givers. *New York: Random House, 1971.*

Grace, Kay Sprinkel, and Alan L. Wendroff. High Impact Philanthropy. *New York: John Wiley and Sons, 2001.*

Graham, Hugh David, and Nancy Diamond. The Rise of American Research Universities: Elites and Challengers in the Postwar Era. *Baltimore: Johns Hopkins University Press, 1997.*

Graham, Mary. Democracy by Disclosure: The Rise of Technopopulism. *Washington, DC: Brookings Institution Press, 2002.*

Gray, George W., ed. Education on an International Scale: A History of the International Education Board, 1923–1938. *New York: Harcourt, Brace, 1941.*

Greenberg, David, Donna Linksz, and Marvin Mandell. Social Experimentation and Public Policymaking. *Washington, DC: Urban Institute Press, 2003.*

Greenberg, Jack. Crusaders in the Court: How a Dedicated Band of Lawyers Fought for the Civil Rights Revolution. *New York: Basic Books, 1994.*

Grimm Jr., Robert T., ed. Notable American Philanthropists: Biographies of Giving and Volunteering. *Westport, CT: Greenwood Press, 2002.*

Grogan, Paul S., and Tony Proscio. Comeback Cities: A Blueprint for Urban Neighborhood Revival. *Boulder, CO: Westview Press, 2000.*

Haar, Charles M. Mastering Boston Harbor. *Cambridge: Harvard University Press, 2005.*

Hall, Peter Dobkin. Investing the Nonprofit Sector and Other Essays on Philanthropy, Voluntarism, and Nonprofit Organizations. *Baltimore: The Johns Hopkins University Press, 1992.*

Hammack, David C., ed. Making the Nonprofit Sector in the United States: A Reader. *Bloomington: Indiana University Press, 1998.*

Hammack, David C., and Stanton Wheeler. Social Science in the Making: Essays on the Russell Sage Foundation, 1907–1972. *New York: Russell Sage Foundation, 1994.*

Harr, John Ensor, and Peter J. Johnson. The Rockefeller Century. *New York: Scribner, 1988.*

———. The Rockefeller Conscience. *New York: Scribner, 1991.*

Harris, Seale. Banting's Miracle: The Story of the Discoverer of Insulin. *Philadelphia: J.B. Lippincott, 1946.*

Harrison, Shelby, and F. Emerson Andrews. American Foundations for Social Welfare. *New York: Russell Sage Foundation, 1946.*

Harvey, A. McGehee, and Susan L. Abrams. "For the Welfare of Mankind": The Commonwealth Fund and American Medicine. *Baltimore: Johns Hopkins University Press, 1986.*

Hayslip Jr., Bert, and Joel Leon. Hospice Care. *Newbury Park, CA: Sage Publications, 1992.*

Heimann, Fritz F., ed. The Future of Foundations. *Englewood Cliffs, NJ: Prentice-Hall, 1973.*

Hodgkinson, Virginia A., and Richard W. Lyman. The Future of the Nonprofit Sector: Challenges, Changes, and Policy Considerations. *San Francisco: Jossey-Bass, 1989.*

Holcombe, Randall G. Writing Off Ideas: Taxation, Foundations and Philanthropy in America. *New Brunswick, NJ: Transaction Publishers, 2000.*

Hollis, Ernest V. Philanthropic Foundations and Higher Education. *New York: Columbia University Press, 1938.*

Isaacs, Stephen L., and James R. Knickman, eds. To Improve Health and Health Care, 1997: The Robert Wood Johnson Foundation Anthology. *San Francisco: Jossey-Bass, 1997.*

———, *eds.* To Improve Health and Health Care: The Robert Wood Johnson Foundation Anthology 1998–1999. *San Francisco: Jossey-Bass, 1998.*

———, *eds.* To Improve Health and Health Care 2000: The Robert Wood Johnson Foundation Anthology. *San Francisco: Jossey-Bass, 1999.*

———, *eds.* To Improve Health and Health Care 2001: The Robert Wood Johnson Foundation Anthology. *San Francisco: Jossey-Bass, 2001.*

———, *eds.* To Improve Health and Health Care, Volume V: The Robert Wood Johnson Foundation Anthology. *San Francisco: Jossey-Bass, 2002.*

———, *eds.* To Improve Health and Health Care, Volume VI: The Robert Wood Johnson Foundation Anthology. *San Francisco: Jossey-Bass, 2003.*

———, *eds.* To Improve Health and Health Care, Volume VII: The Robert Wood Johnson Foundation Anthology. *San Francisco: Jossey-Bass, 2004.*

———, *eds.* To Improve Health and Health Care, Volume VIII: The Robert Wood Johnson Foundation Anthology. *San Francisco: Jossey-Bass, 2005.*

Jonas, G. The Circuit Riders: Rockefeller Money and the Rise of Modern Science. *New York: W.W. Norton & Company, 1989.*

Joseph, James A. The Charitable Impulse: Wealth and Social Conscience in

Communities and Cultures Outside the United States. *New York: The Foundation Center, 1989.*

Karoff, H. Peter, ed. Just Money: A Critique of Contemporary American Philanthropy. *Boston: The Philanthropic Initiative, 2004.*

Kaufman, Michael T. Soros: The Life and Times of a Messianic Billionaire. *New York: Alfred A. Knopf, 2002.*

Kelly, Frank K. Court of Reason: Robert Hutchins and the Fund for the Republic. *New York: Free Press, 1981.*

Keppel, Frederick P. The Foundation: Its Place in American Life. *New York: Macmillan, 1930.*

————. Philanthropy and Learning. *New York: Columbia University Press, 1936.*

Kohler, Robert E. Partners in Science: Foundations and Natural Science, 1900–1945. *Chicago: The University of Chicago Press, 1991.*

Korpivaara, Ari. Building the New South Africa: One House, One Dream at a Time. *Open Society Institute. Connecticut: Herlin Press, 2001.*

Kristol, Irving. Foundations and the Sin of Pride: The Myth of the Third Sector. *New York: Institute for Educational Affairs, 1980.*

Lagemann, Ellen Condliffe. An Elusive Science: The Troubling History of Education Research. *Chicago: University of Chicago Press, 2000.*

————, ed. Philanthropic Foundations: New Scholarship, New Possibilities. *Bloomington and Indianapolis: Indiana University Press, 1999.*

————. Private Power for the Public Good: A History of the Carnegie Foundation for the Advancement of Teaching. *Middletown, CT: Wesleyan University Press, 1983.*

————. The Politics of Philanthropy: The Carnegie Corporation, Philanthropy, and Public Policy. *Middletown, CT: Wesleyan University Press, 1989.*

Layton, Daphne Niobe. Philanthropy and Volunteerism: An Annotated Bibliography. *Washington, DC: The Foundation Center, 1987.*

Lester, Robert M. A Thirty Year Catalog of Grants. *New York: Carnegie Corporation, 1942.*

————. Forty Years of Carnegie Giving: A Summary of the Benefactions of Andrew Carnegie and of the Work of the Philanthropic Trusts Which He Created. *New York: Scribner's Sons, 1941.*

Letts, Christine W., et al. High Performance Nonprofit Organizations: Managing Upstream for Greater Impact. *New York: John Wiley & Sons, 1999.*

Levy, Reynold. Give and Take: A Candid Account of Corporate Philanthropy. *Boston: Harvard Business School Press, 1999.*

Light, Paul C. Government's Greatest Achievements: From Civil Rights to Homeland Defense. *Washington, DC: Brookings Institution Press, 2002.*

————. Sustaining Nonprofit Performance: The Case for Capacity Building and the Evidence to Support It. *Washington, DC: Brookings Institution Press, 2004.*

Lindeman, Eduard C. Wealth and Culture: A Study of One Hundred Foundations and Community Trusts and Their Operations During the Decade 1921–1930. *New Brunswick, NJ: Transaction Books, 1939.*

Lindquist, Jack, ed. Increasing the Impact of Social Innovations Funded by Grantmaking Organizations. *Battle Creek, MI: W. K. Kellogg Foundation, 1979.*

Ludmerer, Kenneth M. Learning to Heal. *New York: Basic Books, 1985.*

MacDonald, Dwight. The Ford Foundation: The Men and the Millions. *New York: Reynal and Company, 1956.*

Magat, Richard, ed. An Agile Servant: Community Leadership by Community Foundations. *New York: Foundation Center, 1989.*

————. The Ford Foundation at Work: Philanthropic Choices, Methods, and Styles. *New York: Plenum Press, 1979.*

————, *ed.* Philanthropic Giving: Studies in Varieties and Goals. *New York: Oxford University Press, 1989.*

————. Unlikely Partners: Philanthropic Foundations and the Labor Movement. *Ithaca: Cornell University Press, 1999.*

Magnet, Myron, ed. What Makes Charity Work: A Century of Public and Private Philanthropy. *Chicago: Ivan R. Dee, 2000.*

Margoluis, Richard, and Nick Salafsky. Measures of Success: Designing, Managing, and Monitoring Conservation and Development Projects. *Washington, DC: Island Press, 1998.*

Marts, Arnaud C. Philanthropy's Role in Civilization: Its Contributions to Human Freedom. *New York: Harper & Bros., 1953.*

McCarthy, Kathleen D. American Creed: Philanthropy and the Rise of Civil Society, 1700–1865. *Chicago: University of Chicago Press, 2003.*

————. Noblesse Oblige: Charity and Cultural Philanthropy in Chicago, 1849–1929. *Chicago: University of Chicago Press, 1982.*

Miller, Howard S. Science and its Patrons in Nineteenth-Century America. *Seattle: University of Washington Press, 1970.*

Miller, John J. Strategic Investment in Ideas: How Two Foundations Reshaped America. *Washington, DC: The Philanthropy Roundtable, 2003.*

Mitchell, Charles, and Susan R. Moody, eds. Foundations of Charity. *Oxford: Hart Publishing, 2000.*

Munnell, Alicia H., and Annika Sunden, eds. Death and Dollars: The Role of Gifts and Bequests in America. *Washington, DC: Brookings Institution Press, 2003.*

Nagai, Althea K., et al. Giving for Social Change: Foundations, Public Policy, and the American Political Agenda. *Westport, CT: Praeger, 1994.*

Nagel, Thomas. The Possibility of Altruism. *Oxford: Clarendon Press, 1970.*

Nason, John W. Foundation Trusteeship: Service in the Public Interest. *New York: Foundation Center, 1989.*

Nielsen, Waldemar A. The Big Foundations. *New York: Columbia University Press, 1972.*

————. The Endangered Sector. *New York: Columbia University Press, 1979.*

————. The Golden Donors: A New Anatomy of the Great Foundations. *New York: Truman Talley Books, 1985.*

————. Inside American Philanthropy: The Dramas of Donorship. *Norman: University of Oklahoma Press, 1996.*

Noble, David F. America By Design: Science, Technology, and the Rise of Corporate Capitalism. *New York: Alfred A. Knopf, 1977.*

O'Connell, Brian, ed. America's Voluntary Spirit: A Book of Readings. *New York: Foundation Center, 1983.*

————. Civil Society: The Underpinnings of American Democracy. *Hanover, NH: University Press of New England, 1999.*

————. Fifty Years in Public Causes: Stories from a Road Less Traveled. *Medford, MA: Tufts University Press, 2005.*

————. Philanthropy in Action. *New York: Foundation Center, 1987.*

O'Connor, Alice. Poverty Knowledge: Social Science, Social Policy, and the Poor in Twentieth-Century U.S. History. *Princeton: Princeton University Press, 2001.*

Odendahl, Teresa, ed. America's Wealthy and the Future of Foundations. *The Foundation Center, 1987.*

————. Charity Begins at Home: Generosity and Self-Interest Among the Philanthropic Elite. *New York: Basic Books, 1990.*

Olasky, Marvin. Patterns of Corporate Philanthropy: Funding False Compassion. *Washington, DC: Capital Research Center, 1991.*

————. Philanthropically Correct: The Story of the Council on Foundations. *Washington, DC: Capital Research Center, 1993.*

Ostrower, Francie. Why the Wealthy Give: The Culture of Elite Philanthropy. *Princeton: Princeton University Press, 1995.*

Owen, David. English Philanthropy, 1660–1960. *Cambridge: Harvard University Press, 1964.*

Paddock, William, and Paul Paddock. Famine—1975! America's Decision: Who Will Survive? *Boston: Little, Brown, 1967.*

Parker, Franklin. George Peabody, a Biography. *Nashville: Vanderbilt University Press, 1995.*

Payton, Robert, et al. Philanthropy: Four Views. *New Brunswick, NJ: Transaction Books, 1988.*

Pennfield, Wilder. The Difficult Art of Giving: The Epic of Alan Gregg. *Boston: Little, Brown, 1967.*

Pertschuck, Michael. Smoke in Their Eyes: Lessons in *Movement Leadership from the Tobacco Wars. Nashville: Vanderbilt University, 2001.*

Polsky, Richard M. Getting to Sesame Street: Origins of the Children's Television Workshop. *New York: Praeger Publishers, 1974.*

Powell, Walter W., and Elisabeth S. Clemens, eds. Private Action and the Public Good. *New Haven: Yale University Press, 1998.*

Prewitt, Kenneth. Social Sciences and Private Philanthropy: The Quest for Social Relevance. *Essays on Philanthropy, No. 15. Indianapolis: Indiana University Center on Philanthropy, 1995.*

Prewitt, Kenneth, et al., eds. The Legitimacy of Philanthropic Foundations: United States and European Perspectives. *New York: Russell Sage Foundation, 2006.*

Proscio, Tony. In Other Words: A Plea for Plain Speaking in Foundations. *New York: Edna McConnell Clark Foundation, 2000.*

Putnam, Robert. Bowling Alone: The Collapse and Revival of the American Community. *New York: Simon & Schuster, 2000.*

Rabinowitz, Alan. Social Change Philanthropy in America. *Westport, CT: Quorum, 1990.*

Rich, Andrew. Think Tanks, Public Policy, and the Politics of Expertise. *Cambridge: Cambridge University Press, 2004.*

Richardson, Theresa, and Donald Fisher, eds. The Development of the Social Sciences in the United States and Canada: The Role of Philanthropy. *Stamford, CT: Ablex Publishing Corp, 1999.*

Rockefeller, David. Memoirs. *New York: Random House, 2002.*

Rockefeller, John D. Random Reminiscences of Men and Events. *New York: Doubleday, Page & Company, 1909.*

Roelofs, Joan. Foundations and Public Policy: The Mask of Pluralism. *Albany: State University of New York Press, 2003.*

Rosenfeld, Leonard S., and Henry B. Makover. The Rochester Regional Hospital Council. *Cambridge: Harvard University Press, 1956.*

Russell, John M. Giving and Taking: Across the Foundation Desk. *New York: Teachers College Press, 1977.*

Russell, Mary Lou, Robert Oksner, and Anne Mackinnon. For the Common Good: The Commonwealth Fund 1918–1993. *New York: The Commonwealth Fund, 1994.*

Sacks, Eleanor W. The Growth of Community Foundations Around the World: An Examination of the Vitality of the Community Foundation Movement. *New York: Council on Foundations, 2002.*

Salamon, Lester M., et al. Global Civil Society: Dimensions of the Nonprofit Sector. *Baltimore: Johns Hopkins Center for Civil Society Studies, 1999.*

———. Global Civil Society: Dimensions of the Nonprofit Sector, Volume Two. *Bloomfield, CT: Kumarian Press, 2004.*

———, *ed.* The International Guide to Nonprofit Law. *New York: John Wiley & Sons, 1997.*

————, ed. The State of Nonprofit America. *Washington, DC: Brookings Institution Press, 2002.*

Samson, Gloria Garrett. The American Fund for Public Service: Charles Garland and Radical Philanthropy, 1922–1941. *Westport, CT: Greenwood Press, 1996.*

Savage, Howard J. Fruit of an Impulse: Forty-Five Years of the Carnegie Foundation, 1905–1950. *New York: Harcourt, Brace, 1953.*

Schlabach, Theron F. Pensions for Professors. *Madison: State Historical Society for Wisconsin, 1963.*

Schneider, William H., ed. Rockefeller Philanthropy and Modern Biomedicine: International Initiatives from World War I to the Cold War. *Bloomington: Indiana University Press, 2002.*

Schonfeld, Roger C. JSTOR: A History. *Princeton: Princeton University Press, 2003.*

Sealander, Judith. Private Wealth and Public Life: Foundation Philanthropy and the Reshaping of American Social Policy from the Progressive Era to the New Deal. *Baltimore: Johns Hopkins University Press, 1997.*

Shulman, James L., and William G. Bowen. The Game of Life. *Princeton: Princeton University Press, 2001.*

Siebold, Cathy. The Hospice Movement: Easing Death's Pains. *New York: Twayne Publishers, 1992.*

Siegel, Daniel, and Jenny Yancey. The Rebirth of Civil Society: The Development of the Nonprofit Sector in East Central Europe and the Role of Western Assistance. *New York: Rockefeller Brothers' Fund, 1992.*

Siegmund-Schultze, Reinhard. Rockefeller and the Internationalization of Mathematics Between the Two World Wars: Documents and Studies for the Social History of Mathematics in the Twentieth Century. *Boston: Birkhäuser Verlag, 2001.*

Simon, William A. A Time for Truth. *New York: Reader's Digest Press, 1978.*

Slemrod, Joel B., ed. Does ATLAS Shrug?: The Economic Consequences of Taxing the Rich. *New York: Russell Sage Foundation, 2000.*

Smith, Bradford. Philanthropy in Communities of Color. *Bloomington: Indiana University Press, 1999.*

Smith, S. L. Builders of Goodwill: The Story of the State Agents of Negro Education in the South, 1910 to 1950. *Nashville: Tennessee Book Company, 1950.*

Smith, Steven, and Michael Lipsky. Nonprofits for Hire: The Welfare State in the Age of Contracting. *Cambridge: Harvard University Press, 1993.*

Soros, George. Soros on Soros. *New York: John Wiley & Sons, 1995.*

————. Underwriting Democracy. *New York: The Free Press, 1991.*

Southern, David W. Gunnar Myrdal and Black-White Relations: The Use and Abuse of An American Dilemma, 1944–1969. *Baton Rouge: Louisiana State University Press, 1987.*

Stanfield, John H. Philanthropy and Jim Crow in American Social Science. *West-port, CT: Greenwood Press, 1985.*

Stapleton, Darwin H., ed. Creating a Tradition of Biomedical Research: Contributions to the History of the Rockefeller University. *New York: Rockefeller University Press, 2004.*

Sviridoff, Mitchell, ed. Inventing Community Renewal: The Trials and Errors that Shaped the Modern Community Development Corporation. *New York: Community Development Research Center. 2004.*

Taylor, Eleanor K. Public Accountability of Foundations and Charitable Trusts. *New York: Russell Sage Foundation, 1953.*

Tindall, George Brown. The Emergence of the New South, 1913–1945. *Baton Rouge: Louisiana State University Press, 1967.*

Tirman, John. Making the Money Sing: Private Wealth and Public Power in the Search for Peace. *Lanham, MD: Rowman & Littlefield, 2000.*

Titmuss, Richard M. The Gift Relationship: From Human Blood to Social Policy. *New York: New Press, 1997.*

Tittle, Diana. Rebuilding Cleveland: The Cleveland Foundation and its Evolving Urban Strategy. *Columbus: Ohio State University Press, 1992.*

Tucker, William H. The Funding of Scientific Racism: Wickliffe Draper and the Pioneer Fund. *Urbana: University of Illinois Press, 2002.*

Von Hoffman, Alexander. House by House, Block by Block: The Rebirth of America's Urban Neighborhoods. *New York: Oxford, 2003.*

Wall, Joseph Frazier. Andrew Carnegie. *New York: Oxford University Press, 1970.*

Weaver, Warren. U.S. Philanthropic Foundations: Their History, Structure, Management, and Record. *New York: Harper & Row, 1967.*

Weisbrod, Burton, ed. To Profit or Not to Profit: The Commercial Transformation of the Nonprofit Sector. *Cambridge: Cambridge University Press, 1998.*

Werner, M. R. Julius Rosenwald: The Life of a Practical Humanitarian. *New York, London: Harper & Brothers, 1939.*

Wheatley, Stephen C. The Politics of Philanthropy: Abraham Flexner and Medical Education. *Madison: University of Wisconsin Press, 1988.*

Whitaker, Ben. The Philanthropoids: Foundations and Society. *New York: William Morrow & Co., 1974.*

Witherspoon, John, and Roselle Kovitz. The History of Public Broadcasting. *Washington, DC: Current, 1989.*

Wolpert, Julian. Patterns of Generosity in America: Who's Holding the Safety Net? *New York: Twentieth Century Fund Press, 1993.*

Wooster, James W. Edward Stephen Harkness, 1874–1940. *New York: The Commonwealth Fund, 1949.*

Wooster, Martin M. The Foundation Builders: Brief Biographies of Twelve Great Philanthropists. *Washington, DC: Philanthropy Roundtable, 2000.*

————. The Great Philanthropists and the Problem of "Donor Intent." *Washington, DC: Capital Research Center, 1994.*

Wuthnow, Robert, and Virginia A. Hodgkinson. Faith and Philanthropy in America: Exploring the Role of Religion in America's Voluntary Sector. *San Francisco: Jossey-Bass Publishers, 1990.*

Young, Clarence H., and William A. Quinn. Foundation for Living: The Story of Charles Stewart Mott and Flint. *New York: McGraw-Hill, 1963.*

Yunus, Mohammad. Micro-Lending and the Battle Against World Poverty. *New York: PublicAffairs, 1999.*

Zurcher, Arnold. The Management of Foundations. *New York: New York University Press, 1972.*

INDEX